# A COMPREHENSIVE TAX HISTORY OF NIGERIA

# A COMPREHENSIVE TAX HISTORY OF NIGERIA

**A publication of the Federal Inland Revenue Service**

*Produced by*
Safari Books Ltd
Ile Ori Detu
1 Shell Close
Onireke Ibadan
*Email: safarinigeria@gmail.com*

© Federal Inland Revenue Service (FIRS)

**A COMPREHENSIVE TAX HISTORY OF NIGERIA**

**Edited by Ifueko Omoigui Okauru**

Published 2012

ISBN: 978-978-48776-4-0

Safari Books Ltd

# CONTENTS

# Foreword

Several volumes have been written on the subject of taxation and even more volumes on the history of Nigeria. However, while some writers may be credited with the occasional treatise on the history of taxation in Nigeria, it is doubtful if a comprehensive treatment of Nigerian taxation has been done from a decidedly historical perspective. Yet, so much that exists in the form or nature of modern Nigerian tax practice is premised substantially on historical antecedents. This publication narrates the historical evolution of taxation in Nigeria, drawing upon linkages from the past that have provided a continuum for the present, with the view that such analysis would provide a useful guiding tool that would enhance policy reforms.

Our country has depended far too long on mineral wealth as a source of government revenue. Persistent fluctuations in global oil prices especially the most recent experience which was occasioned by the global economic meltdown; the exhaustible nature of mineral wealth and in our own case, the insecurity in the Niger Delta have collectively brought to the fore the dangers in our continued dependence on petrodollars. Fortunately, this development has awakened the debate on more sustainable revenue sources to fund government programmes and policies; with the result that taxation now occupies the front burner in our national development debates. This development has also occurred at a time when the Federal Inland Revenue Service, as the government's taxman, has come under the visionary and innovative leadership of Ifueko Omoigui Okauru. The impressive successes recorded in the last eight years in tax administration have had concomitant results on the growth of non-oil revenue. It is hoped that this impressive trend will continue such that non-oil revenue will eventually account for a substantial portion of the country's total revenues.

This book is thoroughly researched and it is my belief that the information and insights offered in it will be useful to a wide range of readers including tax administrators, policy formulators, academics, students, lawyers, historians and tax practitioners. Without a shadow of reservation, I recommend this book to the reading public.

**Ngozi Okonjo-Iweala**
*Coordinating Minister for the Economy and Honourable Minister of Finance*
*Federal Republic of Nigeria*
*Abuja, February 2012*

# Preface

At the Regional Enlarged Management Meeting of the Federal Inland Revenue Service held in Lagos on 17th May 2007, a discussion arose as to what had been happening in the tax system before the advent of comprehensive reforms beginning in 2004. This discussion led to the conception of the museum project as a strategy for preserving developmental milestones in the tax sector for the sake of posterity. As a corollary to the museum project, the idea of documenting a *comprehensive tax history of Nigeria* was also conceived. To this end, the *Tax History and Policy Support Unit* was established in the Office of the Executive Chairman. At the beginning, the terms of reference of the unit was to research and document a comprehensive history of taxation in Nigeria covering pre-colonial, colonial and post-colonial developments. Since then however, the terms of reference of the unit have been expanded to include documentation of the reforms and change processes taking place within the Service and the tax sector. This publication, the unit's first, is the coming to fruition of the initial task bestowed on it.

This book discusses the evolution of taxation in Nigeria within the framework of eight broad themes i.e., *The Origin and Practice of Fiscal Federalism in Nigeria, The Constitutional Context for Taxation, The Three Eras of Taxation in Nigeria, The Structure and Jurisdiction of Nigerian Tax Authorities, Instruments of Tax Policy, Statutory Developments, Beyond Oil Revenue: The Case for Tax Reform* and *Making the Nigerian Tax System Globally Competitive.*

The first chapter looks into the key concepts of fiscal federalism; traces the origin of states' creation; the factors that led to creation of states in Nigeria and the practice of fiscal federalism in Nigeria since 1946. It also analyses the reports and recommendations of the various Revenue Allocation Commissions in Nigeria.

Chapter two analyses the taxing provisions under the various constitutional arrangements Nigeria's has had since the amalgamation of the Northern and Southern Protectorates in 1914. These constitutions, nine in all, include the Lugard, Clifford, Richards, McPherson, Lyttleton, Independence, 1963, 1979 and 1999 Constitutions.

Chapter three is a narrative on the nature and practice of taxation covering the three main eras that define Nigeria's history. These are the pre-colonial, colonial and post-colonial eras. Attempts have been made to juxtapose the evolution of taxation in Nigeria *vis-à-vis* the political formation of pre-colonial empires, bringing out how such political formations, as they were, accounted for varying developmental levels of taxation in those provinces and the impact of colonial policy in redefining not just existing practices but also in creating novel conditions to facilitate colonial rule, conditions which have continued to define or at least, influence the nature and practice of Nigerian taxation.

Chapter four discusses tax administration focusing on tax authorities such as the Federal Inland Revenue Service (FIRS), States Board of Internal Revenue (SBIRs) and Local Governments Revenue Committees (LGRCs). The narrative includes the composition as well as taxes administered by these tax authorities.

Chapter five analyses in detail, the various tax Ordinances, Acts and Decrees (including changes and amendments thereto) since 1903. This analysis is anchored on the fact that legislation is a tool of public policy and a history of taxation would be incomplete without the statutory instruments that give the various taxes their legal status. Chapter six discusses other policy instruments that have influenced the development of Nigerian taxation over time. These include case law, budget speeches, avoidance of double taxation agreements and recently, the National Tax Policy.

Chapter seven of the book highlights the challenges associated with over dependence on mineral wealth; as well as the myriad of developmental challenges that make the case for expanding the revenue base imperative. The eight and last chapter of this work reviews the on-going efforts to place taxation at the pedestal where it would become the pivot of national development. These efforts are essentially reform strategies that beginning with the formation of a Study Group on the Nigerian tax system in 2002, have been implemented towards a more efficient tax administration system.

It is hoped that this book would serve the purpose of providing a historical framework that would benefit the on-going reforms aimed at making the Nigerian tax system globally competitive; provide a useful benchmark for future reforms, and also serve as a veritable reference material for tax academics, practitioners, administrators and students. Although the work is essentially the research work of the Tax History and Policy Support Unit, two external reviewers were briefed to go through the manuscript and ensure structural and narrative harmony as well as content integrity. Needless to say that in spite of everything, the publication, along with any perceived shortcoming, remains that of the Federal Inland Revenue Service.

**Ifueko Omoigui Okauru, MFR**
*Executive Chairman, Federal Inland Revenue Service*
*Abuja, February 2012*

# Acknowledgements

In the course of researching for this publication, the research team met and shared ideas with some scholars and tax experts whose opinions shaped and impacted this work. I would like to especially acknowledge the contributions of Otunba S. A Rabiu, Professor M. T Abdulrazaq, Professor Yakubu A. Ochefu, Dr. Akin Oluwatosin, Dr. Sat Obiyan and Mr. Abiola Sanni. I also wish to acknowledge the library staff of Obafemi Awolowo University Ile-Ife, the Nigerian Institute of Advanced Legal Studies, Nigerian Institute of International Affairs, staff of the National Archives, Ibadan and Kaduna, the Government Printer Lagos, the National Library Lagos and Arewa House Kaduna. These institutions graciously allowed us the use of their libraries and resource materials that substantially account for this book.

I appreciate also, the contributions of Justice Benedict Kanyip and Ms. Belema Obuoforibo. They both read through the manuscript and made useful suggestions that enriched the overall presentation of the book. I must also acknowledge Dr. Teju Somorin, Ms Simplice Olajumoke and Mr Segun Sosimi, for their contributions. Finally, I wish to specially acknowledge the indefatigable research team: Ben Pever, Chinedu Eze, Alhassan Mohammed, Alex Akinyele, Ediketin Iyayi, Ifeanyichukwu Aniyie, Queen Ikwuji and Caroline Boman who worked tirelessly on the manuscripts for the realization of this publication.

Finally, I wish to thank anyone whose name I may have inadvertently omitted but who contributed in whatever way to the publication of this book. Without you, this project would not have seen the light of day.

**Ifueko Omoigui Okauru, MFR**
*Executive Chairman, Federal Inland Revenue Service*
*Abuja, 2012*

# CHAPTER ONE

## THE ORIGIN AND PRACTICE OF FISCAL FEDERALISM IN NIGERIA

### Background

The principles of fiscal federalism are concerned with how taxing, spending and regulatory functions are allocated among the component parts of a federation, and how intergovernmental transfers are structured among these parts.[1] These arrangements are of fundamental importance to the efficiency of the provision of public services. In Nigeria, the practice of fiscal federalism has been riddled with problems, not least of which is the contentious and sometimes acrimonious debate on how best equitable socio-economic development can be achieved within the context of a plural democracy.

This chapter begins by reviewing basic concepts in federalism. It also explains the origin of states' creation in Nigeria, the nature of fiscal relations between and among the federal and regional governments, and an appraisal of the various Fiscal Commissions that were constituted at various times in history and tasked with achieving balance and harmony in inter-governmental fiscal relations. The chapter also provides a comprehensive and systematic analysis of contending principles in revenue allocation and their concomitant political ramifications.

### Conceptual Overview

#### *Meaning of Government*

The Advanced Learner's Dictionary defines government as 'the group of people who are responsible for controlling a country or a state.' It goes further to describe government as

>    a particular system or method of controlling a country e.g. coalition/ communist/totalitarian government, democratic government, Federal Government. Government can as well be expressed as the activities or the manner of controlling a country.[2]

Dare and Oyewole define government as 'the structures and systems by which decisions and rules are determined and enforced for all members of the society.'[3] According to

Appadorai, government can be viewed as 'the agency or machinery through which the will of the state is formulated, expressed and realized'.[4]

The *raison d'etre* for a government is to perform those functions which members of the society cannot, by themselves, perform. There are several ways to classify governments, but for the present purpose, the guiding principle for classification shall be based on the institutional frameworks and structures between and within levels of government; defined to include not only the decision-making units, but also the decision-making processes, practices and interrelationships. Based on the foregoing criteria, government is categorized into unitary, confederal and federal.

## Unitary, Confederal and Federal Systems of Government

Unitary system of government exists in a situation where there is a single level government; or even where there is a multi-tiered system, control of all government functions rests with the central government. This system of government places greater premium on uniformity and equal access to public services than it does on diversity; consequently, the system facilitates centralized decision making to further national unity. The city-states of Singapore and Monaco are single-tiered unitary governments. China, Egypt, France, Indonesia, Italy, Japan, Korea, New Zealand, Norway, the Philippines, Portugal, Sweden, Turkey and the United Kingdom have multi-tiered government based on unitary constitutions.[5]

A confederation is a system where the central government serves as the agent of the member states/units, usually without independent taxing and spending powers. Such a system obtained in the United States between 1781 and 1787. The defunct Union of Soviet Socialist Republics (USSR) also approximated to a confederation.[6] Switzerland is a confederation by law, while in practice it is regarded as a federation.

According to Suberu, 'Federalism involves constitutional and irrevocable division of governmental powers and functions on a territorial basis within a single country'.[7] It entails the division of power between central and constituent authorities, the guarantee that the constituent units have a share in the central power, and that the constituent units cannot be abrogated unilaterally by the central authority. As Tekena puts it:

> Federalism, ... is that form of government where the component units of a
> political organization participate in sharing powers and functions in a

cooperative manner though the combined force of ethnic pluralism and cultural diversity, among others, tend to put their people apart.[8]

According to Friedrich, federalism is:

> the process by which a number of separate political organizations, be they states or any kind of association, enter into agreements for working out solutions, adopting joint policies and making decisions on joint problems or ..., the process through which a hitherto military political community becomes differentiated into a number of organization in which the differentiated communities now separately organized, become capable of working out separately and on their own, those problems they no longer have in common.[9]

Wheare describes the system as the method of dividing powers so that general and regional governments are each, within a sphere, coordinates and independent.[10] It is a principle of organization and practice whose ultimate test is how the federal system operates.

Although the arrangement of functions and responsibilities within a federal state is usually based on some constitutional or legal framework, the constitution may be a poor guide in determining whether a political system is federal or otherwise.[11] To this school of thought, federalism should be understood, not just from the narrow perspective or confines of legal formulation but from the general and systemic interaction of socio-cultural and political factors. Nigeria, Switzerland, the United States, Canada, Germany, Malaysia, Brazil, India and Australia are some of the countries that have adopted federalism as a preferred system of discharging governmental responsibility. A federal form of government promotes decentralized decision making and, therefore, theoretically, engenders greater freedom of choice, diversity of preferences in public services, political participation, innovation, and accountability. It is also better adapted to handle regional conflicts.

Tella identifies two types of federalism on a broad scale, namely, 'dual federalism' and 'cooperative federalism'.[12] The former is a situation where the constitution creates two separate and independent tiers of government with each tier having its own clearly defined areas of responsibility. A major attribute of dual federalism is competition and tension among the constituent parts. Cooperative federalism, on the other hand, refers to making federalism work through cooperation between the various levels of government. It emphasizes the partnership between the different levels of government. The various levels of governments, under this arrangement, are seen as related parts of a single governmental system, and characterized more by cooperation and shared functions than by conflict and competition.[13]

The creation of federal polities has been either *from below*, through the consent of the constituent units such as, for example, the United States and Switzerland, or *top-down*. In the latter case, the system is imposed from the centre, as in the case of India, or by outside forces, as in the case of post World War II Germany.[14] The Nigerian federation falls within the *top-down* model. The creation of federal political system in the United States, following decolonization and the creation of independent states, was motivated by the desire of a majority of the constituent states to enhance the security and economic benefits of limiting the sovereignty of individual states by creating an 'extended republic' with a strong central authority.[15] Security and economic motives as well as the appreciation of cantonal autonomy and cultural diversity were behind the creation of the Swiss federal polity in 1848.[16]

There are three prominent aspects of federalism: political, administrative and fiscal. Political federalism deals with the division of powers among tiers of government such that within certain specified spheres, the powers exercisable by the different tiers are either coordinate or exclusive.[17] To protect the autonomy of each tier within its sphere of authority, there is usually some kind of constitutional or legal provision specifying the nature and extent of powers exercisable by each tier. Administrative federalism involves delegation of functions to lower-level governments, usually according to the guidelines or controls imposed by the higher-level government and, therefore, without the autonomy which is the characteristic of decentralization. Fiscal federalism is not just a derivative of, but also rooted in federalism as a legal and political system. Agiobenebo describes fiscal federalism as 'the scope and structure of the tiers of governmental responsibilities and functions, and the allocation of resources among the tiers of government'.[18] Specifically, fiscal federalism deals with the relations among levels of government pertaining to revenue generation, allocation and utilization in the discharge of defined responsibilities. It is the study of how competent fiscal instruments (revenue side) are allocated across different (vertical) layers of the administration.[19] It also involves the distribution of 'taxing powers' between or among the levels of government for the purpose of generating revenues that are sufficient to discharge jurisdictional functions.

Another important issue relating to fiscal federalism is the system of transfer payments or grants by which a central government shares its revenues with lower levels of government. Federal Governments use this power to enforce national rules and standards. There are two primary types of transfers: conditional and unconditional. A conditional transfer from a federal government to a province, or other territory, involves a certain set of conditions. If the lower level of government is to receive this type of transfer, it must agree to the spending instructions of the federal government. An example of a conditional transfer is the *conditional grant scheme* which the Office of the Senior Special Assistant to the President on Millennium Development Goals, OSSAP-MDGs, allocates to states every year. The funds allocated under the scheme are a portion of the *debt relief gains* granted Nigeria by the Paris Club of creditors and are transferred to pre-qualified states to be used exclusively towards the implementation of the Millennium Development Goals. An unconditional grant on the other hand is usually a cash (or tax point) transfer with no spending instructions. For example, the federal government maintains an *Excess Crude Account* into which revenues accruing above the government's budgeted benchmark from crude oil sales are credited. Occasionally, the federal government shares funds from this account to the states without imposing instructions on how the states may use the disbursements.

The idea of fiscal federalism is relevant for all kinds of government, irrespective of whether they are unitary, federal or confederal systems and *fiscal federalism* is not to be confused with *fiscal decentralization*. While the latter is practiced only in officially declared federations, the former is applicable even to non-federal states (having no formal federal constitutional arrangement) in the sense that it encompasses different levels of government which have *de facto* decision making authority. This however does not mean that all forms of government are *fiscally federal*; all it means is that 'fiscal federalism' is a set of principles that can be applied to all countries attempting 'fiscal decentralization'.[20] Fiscal federalism is a general normative framework for the assignment of functions to the different levels of government, as well as of the appropriate fiscal instruments for the carrying out of those functions. The difference between fiscal federalism and fiscal decentralization is that, while the former constitutes a set of guiding principles that help in *designing* financial relations between the national and sub-national levels of government, the latter refers to the *application* of such principles.

The financial relationship between the central government and the federating units which involves the system of transfers or grants from the centre to the units is generally regarded as *revenue allocation*. The procedure for revenue allocation is hinged on a number of factors which may be within or outside the control of the people in each locality. For example, perhaps by some natural or man-made designs, nations that emerged through the combination of pre-existing sovereign jurisdictions (e.g. states) may retain certain fiscal prerogatives while surrendering others, thereby joining in a compact which determines the fiscal aspects of the federation.

### History of Horizontal Revenue Sharing in Nigeria

Until the hardening of state-based opposition to the financial hegemony of the central government in the 1970s, the most explosive issue in Nigeria's fiscal federalism involved the conflict over the appropriate formula for inter-state sharing of centrally collected revenues. Although now partly eclipsed by vertical revenue sharing conflicts, the debate over horizontal revenue sharing has never been far from the epicentre of Nigeria's federalism. Indeed, the major problem of inter-governmental revenue sharing in Nigeria has always been the formula for sharing revenue among the regions and states, that is, the horizontal revenue sharing scheme. While vertical revenue sharing debates have revolved around the determination of the relative proportions of centrally collected revenues to be allocated to the centre and the sub-national governments, horizontal revenue-sharing conflicts have evolved the issue of the appropriate principles to be used in sharing central revenues standing to the credit of the states or their localities.

Since 1946, several dozens of principles have been developed for the purpose of horizontal revenue sharing, none of which has enjoyed complete acceptance. These principles can be divided into two broad categories:
  a. efficiency principles designed to allocate resources rationally to the most economically efficient units, and
  b. equity principles designed to equalize the fiscal capacities of constituent units by redistributing resources on explicitly political grounds.[21]
Among the efficiency principles of horizontal allocation are derivation, independent revenue sources, absorptive capacity, tax effort and fiscal efficiency. Equity principles include even development, national interest, continuity in government services, minimum responsibility of government, financial comparability (among governments), primary school enrolment or

the social development factor, national minimum standards, equality of access to development opportunities and land mass/terrain.[22] Nigeria's revenue-sharing principles have emphasized equity over efficiency principles. This bias reflects a widely shared official commitment in Nigeria, and elsewhere, to the use of *equalizing fiscal transfers* and other redistributive strategies to maintain national unity and reduce inter-regional economic disparities. Yet, there has been a lack of consensus in Nigeria over the degree of recognition that should be awarded to efficiency principles in the overall revenue-sharing scheme.[23]

Since the reconstitution of the regions into states beginning in 1967, Nigeria's horizontal revenue-sharing practices have been dominated largely by six principles of entitlement namely, equality of states, population, social development factor, land mass and terrain, derivation, and internal revenue generation effort.[24] For instance, in 2004, the Federation Account revenues assigned to the states were shared among the units on the basis of the following five indicators: equality of states (40%), relative population (30%), social development factor (10%), internal revenue generation effort (10%), land mass and terrain (10%).[25]

*Equality of States*

This principle effectively entered into Nigeria's revenue-sharing practice after the creation of twelve states in 1967. Faced with the problem of sharing revenues among the newly created states, the Federal Government simply divided the share of the old North equally among the six successor states to the region. Following the end of the civil war, however, the norm of inter-state equality in revenue sharing was elevated to a general principle of allocation throughout the federation.[26] Throughout the 1970s, one-half of the federal revenues assigned to the states were shared equally among them, while the other half was distributed on the basis of population. Although the weight assigned to the equality principle was reduced to 40 percent in 1981, the principle remains the single most important factor in the horizontal revenue allocation formula.[27]

The norm of units' equality of states has been defended on various grounds. First, the principle gives recognition to the reality that each of the states has to sustain a basic minimum set of public functions and institutions, irrespective of its size or population. It is in this regard that the norm of state equality is often referred to as the principle of minimum responsibility of government. Second, the standard of state equality upholds a fundamental axiom of *"symmetrical federalism"*, according to which each unit in the federation is constitutionally and legally equal to any other unit. Third, compared to other principles of entitlement, the equality principle is virtually unmatched in its simplicity, verifiability, certainty, ease of application and non-reliance on the use of technical and often unavailable socio-economic data. Fourth, given the commitment of successive federal administrations to establishing states of relatively equivalent populations, the principle of inter-unit equality does not necessarily produce *per capita* imbalances in revenues available to the states. Fifth, the equal distribution of revenues among states of relatively equal populations could promote the basic goals of equity, even national development, and national integration. Finally, the application of the equality principle helps to reassure or compensate states that are not populous, large, or rich enough to benefit from other principles of fiscal allocation.[28]

In spite of its seemingly obvious advantages, however, the principle of equality has promoted profound criticisms. One major drawback of the equality principle according to Suberu, is its spurious assumption of comparability or equivalence in the conditions of the states.[29] According to the author, no two states are exactly equal in economic circumstances, geographical conditions, or population. Thus, despite the long-standing official commitment to the creation of states of approximately equal populations, it has not been possible to make all the states exactly or nearly identical. Consequently, under the impact of the equality principle, high population states have essentially remained relatively under-funded on a *per capita* basis in relation to the low population states. Predictably, the more populous states have been the most persistent and strident opponents of the equality principle. The second major limitation of the equality principle is the strong, unremitting pressures it generates for the creation of new states. The application of the equality principle means, in effect, that a greater share of federal revenues can be obtained by the fragmentation of an existing state into two or more units, each of which can then claim its equal share of the portion of the Federation Account that is distributed on the basis of inter-unit equality. The application of the equality principle means, in effect, that a greater share of federal revenues can be obtained by the fragmentation of an existing state into two or more units, each of which can then claim its equal share of the portion of the Federation Account that is distributed on the basis of inter-unit equality.[30] Another weakness of the equality principle, according to Suberu, is that it provides no incentive for the states to mobilize independent revenues of their own and thus encourages the tendency toward fiscal lethargy at the sub-national level. A principle that guarantees each state's substantial revenue by virtue of the simple fact that it constitutes a governmental unit in the federation can only induce a sense of complacency among the states.[31]

*Population and the Social Development Factor*

Population has been a long–standing and contentious principle of revenue allocation in Nigeria. As far back as 1951, for example, the Hicks-Phillipson Commission implicitly recommended the use of the population principle through need, along with derivation and national interest in sharing central revenues among the regions.[32] Subsequent commissions also emphasized the importance of the population factor; if not explicitly then implicitly through the recommendation of such surrogate measures as: needs, primary school enrolment, number of adult male tax payers, or the social development factor.

From 1970 to 1980, half of federal statutory grants to the states were distributed on the basis of population. In 1981, however, the weight attached to the population factor was reduced to 40 percent. In 1990, the principle was further relegated to a weight of 30 percent. Notwithstanding this decline, aggregate population remains the second most important factor of allocation (after inter-unit equality) in Nigeria's horizontal fiscal federalism, and population–related factors (primary school enrolment, ratio of hospital beds to population, and so forth) remain the single most important set of factors shaping the country's revenue sharing practices.[33]

The justification for the relatively strong emphasis on population is not far-fetched. To virtually all of Nigeria's officials, population is the veritable indication of expenditure obligation and all things being equal, the more people there are in a state, the greater the need for the provision of social services and amenities. Moreover, the use of population statistics, which are relatively easy to assemble and verify, helps to obviate the need for more technical and often inaccessible socio-economic data.

The population principle has been extensively and severely criticized. In the view of Suberu, the use of the population principle in revenue allocation has been an important source of the population sensitivity and contentiousness surrounding population statistics in Nigeria.[34] Consequently, the country's census exercises have often degenerated into fierce ethnic and regional contests, and the resulting population figures have usually been severely tarnished by actual or alleged acts of falsification or inflation of figures. Second, the use of unreliable, controversial, or outdated population data distorted the revenue sharing system between

1964 and 1991. Within the mentioned period, the Nigerian Federal Government relied on projections from the 1963 census figures in making population–based grants to the states.[35] Yet, it was widely known that the figures were cynically and extensively inflated and may have been rendered even more dubious by probable changes in the composition and distribution of the nation's population since the organization of the 1963 Census. Third, several critics have argued that raw aggregate population data may say little about the economic circumstances or need of a state. To be meaningful and useful, it is argued, the population principle must incorporate such characteristics of the population as sparsity, density, age composition, rural-urban distribution, and so on. Until the introduction of the social development factor, however, these characteristics were largely neglected in the implementation of population–based allocations in Nigeria. Fourth, many of the smaller Nigerian states complained that they have been unfairly short-changed by the use of the population factor. They contend that while a large population may mean a heavy expenditure obligation, such a population may also imply a higher taxable base.[36] So far, however, the use of the demographic factor in resource allocation in Nigeria has focused exclusively on the expenditure-inducing aspect of the population equation, ignoring its possible revenue generating dimension. Finally, contrary to the expectations of those who advocate population as the ultimate principle of equitable distribution, allocation on population basis is only "moderately equalizing" because it provides no positive assistance in reducing the disparity between wealthy and poor regions but, rather, merely prevents it from increasing. Alternative principles of allocation must, therefore, be implemented if effective equalization is to be achieved.

Since it was introduced under the revenue-sharing scheme of the second republic, the social development factor has mitigated some of the weaknesses associated with the use of raw population data. Under the 1981 Revenue Allocation Scheme, the social development factor was defined to comprise direct and inverse primary school enrolment and was assigned a weight of 15 percent. To assist the states in maintaining those of their population already in school, direct primary school enrolment was assigned a weight of 11.25 percent. And to compensate or encourage those states that had lower primary school enrolment relative to population, inverse enrolment (or the proportion of children of primary school age not yet in school) was assigned a weight of 3.75 percent.[37]

In 1989, however, the Revenue Mobilization Commission reduced the weight attached to the social development factor by five percentage points and introduced fundamental changes in the factor's composition and computation. Simply put, the 10 percent weight now allocated to the social development factor is divided among education, health and water in the ratio of 4:3:3, respectively. The education component of the social development factor was defined to include direct primary school enrolment and direct and inverse secondary school enrolment. The health component gave equal recognition to the direct inverse proportion of hospital beds per state, while the allocation for water supply was divided equally between the 'average annual rainfall' (for state's headquarters for the five most current years) and the territorial spread of water supply in the state.[38]

*Derivation and the Compensation or Protection of Mineral–Producing Areas*
The derivation principle has aroused the most heated arguments in Nigerian revenue–sharing debates. The derivation or origin principle of distribution stipulates that a significant proportion of the revenues collected in the jurisdiction of a sub-national government should be returned to that government. The derivation principle is put to use in the sharing of revenue among the various units making up the federation in the proportion of certain taxes assumed to have been paid by the citizens. Revenue allocation on the basis of derivation penalizes the relatively backward or poor states. Besides, the principle is not easy to apply as the burden of taxes collected within a state is not necessarily borne by the residents of that state alone.[39] The derivation principle dominated revenue-sharing practices and politics during the early stages of federation in Nigeria. In the late 1950s and early 1960s, for instance, all export duties on agricultural commodities and import and excise duties on tobacco and motor fuel were simply returned to the region of production or consumption. But the derivation principle soon came under severe criticism for very obvious reasons. Basically, the principle had a detrimental impact on interregional equity and national unity. It tended to make the rich regions richer and to arouse invidious opposition and resentment from the relatively less endowed regions. The application of the derivation principle to the allocation of growing oil revenues during the 1970s accented the economically inequitable and politically contentious nature of the principle. For instance, the approved estimates of statutory grants for the 1974–1975 fiscal years allocated 241 million naira to the oil-producing states of Rivers and Mid-West, which had a combined population of 4.1 million, whereas the Western, East-Central, North-Western and North-Eastern States, with a total population of 30.2 million received 102.3 million naira under the same scheme.[40] This imbalance was the result

of a policy that returned 45 percent of onshore oil rents and royalties to the states of derivation or production. But such egregious asymmetry in the financial fortunes of the states served to galvanize opposition to the derivation principle and nudge the central government into downgrading the principle in favour of revenue–sharing strategy that increased the amount of resources available for distribution among all the states.

Apart from its economic impact and politically contentious nature, the derivation principle has been criticized for restricting the capacity of national authorities to initiate and implement redistributive or macroeconomic reforms, requiring the use of often unavailable economic data regarding the inter-regional consumption and production of goods, often rewarding units not on the basis of any superior productive effort but by dint of geography, and unleashing political counter pressures against the free mobility of goods and services in the federation. Given these limitations, it is not surprising that the derivation principle has sometimes been condemned as the "devil" of Nigeria's fiscal federalism. Both the Aboyade Technical Committee and the Okigbo Commission recommended the elimination of the principle from Nigeria's revenue-sharing practices as it threatened national integration.[41] Only the intervention of the Shagari' Government, which enjoyed considerable electoral support among the southern ethnic minority oil-producing states, ensured the survival of the derivation principle during the Second Republic, when 2 percent of funds in the Federation Account were assigned to the mineral-producing states on the basis of derivation.

Indeed, over the years, the principle has suffered a systematic decline. Whereas in the late 1960s, excise and import duties on tobacco and petroleum products were transferred wholly to the state of derivation, today these revenue receipts are paid into the Federation Account, which is shared on the basis of a principle that gives only relatively marginal recognition to the derivation criteria. Moreover, as far back as 1971, all offshore mineral revenues were rested in the Federation, thereby depriving the littoral oil-producing states of their previous claim to about half of the rents and royalties from these revenues. The systematic downgrading of the derivation principle has fueled criticisms from ethnic minority elites in the oil-producing states who see the decline of derivation as just another expression of oppression and domination of minorities in the Nigerian federation.[42]

Nevertheless, the decline of the derivation principle has occurred in tandem with a growing recognition of the need to devise a system of special grants (as opposed to shared revenues) to compensate the mineral-producing areas for the ecological and social costs of oil extraction. As extensively documented by the elites of the mineral-producing states and areas, these costs include the loss of agricultural land, the destruction of aquatic life and the pollution of the general environment, all of which have resulted from oil spillage, gas flares, the construction of oil pipelines and related oil producing activities.[43]

In 1977, the Aboyade Technical Committee recommended that 3 percent of the Federation Account be allocated to the mineral-producing areas and to other communities beset by ecological or related problems. Some three years later, the Okigbo Commission proposed devoting 2 percent of the Federation Account to the amelioration of the mineral-producing areas' special problems.[44] Although this amount was increased to 3 percent of the Federation Account in the initial (and eventually nullified) 1981 Revenue Allocation Law, it was eventually reduced to 1.5 percent in the revised 1981 Revenue Allocation Act endorsed by President Shagari in January 1982.[45] Following persistent and increasingly strident demands by the oil producing communities, however, the Babangida Administration in June 1992, increased the special fund for mineral-producing areas to 3 percent of mineral revenues in the Federation Account.[46]

By the revenue sharing arrangement in effect as at the time of return to democratic rule in 1999, only 4 percent of mineral revenues in the Federation Account was exclusively allocated to the mineral-producing areas and states (that is, the 3 percent special fund for the rehabilitation of mineral-producing areas plus the 1 percent of mineral revenue paid to the oil-producing states on the basis of derivation). Disenchanted with this negligible allocation, spokesmen for the oil-producing areas demanded the following:-

a. The return to the affected oil-producing areas of all oil rents and royalties (that is, all federally collected oil revenues except the petroleum profits tax).

b. The payment by the Federal Government and the oil companies of reparations to the oil-producing communities for past and ongoing expropriation, despoilment, or neglect of these communities.

c. The abrogation of all legal instruments, including constitutional provisions, that vest in the Federal Government ownership and control of all the country's onshore and offshore minerals, oil and natural gas.

d. The discontinuation of the distinction between onshore and offshore oil revenues in the application of the derivation principle.

e. The enactment of appropriate legislation that would require the state-backed multinational oil companies to protect the environmental rights and identify with the developmental aspirations of their host communities.

f. The establishment of new states, localities, and other appropriate developmental entities in the oil-producing areas as a means of improving the capacity of government to respond adequately and promptly to the special problems and needs of these areas.

g. As an ultimate solution to the problems of the oil-producing communities greater political and economic autonomy.[47]

The campaign for the rights of Nigeria's oil-producing communities was most effectively prosecuted and popularized (both nationally and internationally) by Ken Saro-Wiwa, a noted writer and leader of the Movement for the Survival of the Ogoni People, MOSOP, which published an *Ogoni Bill of Rights* in 1990. In November 1995, the Nigerian Military Government provoked severe international sanctions when it executed Saro-Wiwa and eight other Ogoni activists following their convictions for the May 1994 mob murders of four pro-government Ogoni leaders.[48] By the time of Saro-Wiwa's execution, however, the oil-producing areas' demands for economic rights had yielded an important concession. In October 1995, General Sani Abacha formally approved but did not implement, a 'consensus resolution' of the 1994-95 National Constitutional Conference that 'the principle of derivation shall be constantly reflected in any approved formula as being not less than 13 percent of the revenue accruing to the Federation Account...' directly from any natural resources.[49] This resolution was eventually codified as section 162(2) in the 1999 Constitution. In April 2000, the Federal Government began implementing the provision with retroactive effect from January of the same year. The payment of the 13 percent derivation revenues to the oil-producing States marked perhaps the first major achievement of the Fourth Republic in the federal management of regional conflict. Yet misgivings persist in the oil-producing areas over many aspects of the derivation revenues.

*Land Mass and Terrain*
Land mass and terrain have usually been advocated as legitimate principles of revenue sharing by two groups of geopolitical interests in the federation–the states of Nigeria's North (which account for some 70 percent of the country's territory) and the states of the swampy, oil-rich Delta region of the country's south. These interests contend that their extensive or difficult geographical terrain imposes additional budgetary obligations, which

should be partly offset by the revenue-sharing scheme.[50] Except for a short-lived appearance in the nullified 1981 Revenue Allocation Law, however, the principle of land mass/terrain did not figure in Nigeria's revenue-sharing scheme until 1990, when it was virtually unilaterally imposed by the Babangida Administration.[51]

Since 1990, land mass and terrain (three main terrain types are recognized: wetlands, plains and highlands) have been assigned a combined weight of 10 percent (5 percent each for land mass and terrain) in the interstate allocation formula.[52] Critics identify two major problems in the utilization of land mass as a factor in horizontal revenue allocation. The first relates to the predictable southern opposition to the very obvious advantage that the factor of land mass confers on the North. As a counterpoise to this northern advantage, southern delegates at the 1994-1995 National Constitutional Conference pushed for the introduction into the horizontal sharing formula of the countervailing factor of population density– a variable that can only further complicate the politicization of population data in Nigeria.[53] The second major problem with land mass and terrain as a principle of revenue sharing in the words of Suberu, 'pertains to the surreptitious manner in which it was introduced'.[54]

*Internal Revenue Generation Effort or Independent Revenues*
There is a growing realization in Nigeria for the need to encourage the states to generate or mobilize independent revenues of their own so they will come to regard federal allocations as a supplement to, rather than as the major source of, their revenues. Such an outcome would have the distinct advantage of reducing the intensity and destructiveness of current intergovernmental and inter-segmental competition for centrally controlled resources. The importance of autonomous revenue generation by the regions/states was emphasized in the reports and recommendations of most of the revenue allocation commissions since the 1950s, especially the 1953 Chick Commission, the 1977 Aboyade Technical Committee, the 1980 Okigbo Commission and the 1989 Danjuma Commission that gave birth to the National Revenue Mobilization, Allocation and Fiscal Commission (NRMAFC).[55] But it was the Second Republic[56] that the principle of independent state revenues was explicitly and formally incorporated into Nigeria's revenue-sharing scheme. Under the interstate sharing formula of the revised 1981 Revenue Allocation Act, the principle of internal revenue generation effort was assigned a weight of 5 percent, in line with the recommendation of the Okigbo Commission.[57] The 1989 NRMAFC report however, recommended that the weight be increased to 20 percent.[58] The Babangida administration reduced NRMAFC's

proposed weight by half and shifted the remaining weight of 10 percent to the new principle of land mass and terrain.

Two main problems have plagued the application of the principle of internal revenue generation effort. First, given the absence of reliable data on the budgets and economies of the states, there has been a great deal of confusion regarding the proper measure for ascertaining the internal revenue generation effort of the States. After a protracted search for an adequate measurement of independent revenues, NRMAFC eventually settled for what it called a practical, incremental indicator of internal revenue effort; the percentage increased in internal revenue generated by a state in a specified period over the preceding period.[59] This measure of independent revenue effort differs significantly from the measure recommended by the Okigbo's Commission (the ratio of total internal revenue to total expenditures) or the measure approved by the Shagari administration (the ratio of internal revenue to recurrent expenditures). NRMAFC did recognize the inconclusiveness of the search, and it proclaimed its receptiveness to any novel idea for measuring and enhancing the autonomous fiscal capacity of the states.[60]

The second fundamental problem involves the intensive opposition to the principle of internal revenue generation by several states, particularly in the relatively economically backward north, that feel they have little room for increasing their internally generated revenues either because they are poor or because they have fully exhausted their revenue sources.[61]

## Decentralisation and the Practice of Fiscal Relations in the Colonial Era

Nigeria was created as one entity in 1914 following the amalgamation of the Southern and Northern Protectorates. The new entity was administered as a unitary state under the colonial administration until 1946. The idea of state creation in Nigeria originated from Sir Bernard Bourdillon, who, in 1939, in order to enhance administrative efficiency, divided the western region into two.[62] In 1946, the Richard Constitution divided the country into three regions, namely, the Northern, Western and Eastern regions. These regions were assigned limited responsibilities and the need arose to formulate financial and administrative procedures for them. To this end, the Phillipson Commission was appointed in 1946 to fashion out financial and administrative procedures for the country. Following the recommendations of the Commission, regional revenues were grouped into 'declared' and 'non-declared'. Declared revenues were exclusive to the regional authorities and included personal income tax, licenses, fees, rent, property tax, while non-declared revenues were exclusive to the central government, which also determined the proportion to be transferred to the regional governments. The indices used to allocate revenue to the regions were derivation, even-progress and population, in that order of importance.[63]

This financial arrangement was used until 1951 when the McPherson Constitution replaced the Richard Constitution. The McPherson Constitution devolved more responsibilities to the regions as a result of which the Hicks - Philipson Commission was appointed the same year to develop a new scheme that would achieve a more equitable distribution of revenue. The Commission recommended more powers to the regions to raise, regulate and appropriate certain tax revenues. It also recommended that revenue be shared on the principle of derivation, need and national interest.[64] These recommendations were adopted and operated till 1953 when the Chick Commission was appointed to review the existing revenue allocation scheme. The commission was mandated to ensure that the total revenue available was allocated in such a way that the principle of derivation was followed to the fullest and compatible with the need of the federal and the regional governments. The commission carried out its mandate and further expanded the revenue allocation scheme to include import and excise duty, mining rent, royalties and personal income tax.

The McPherson Constitution was superseded by the Lyttleton Constitution of 1954, which was the first true federal constitution of Nigeria. As a result of the desire of the Federal Government to grow the internally generated revenue and enlarge the fiscal autonomy of the regions, the Chick Commission's report therefore, became inadequate under the new system. In 1958, the Raisman Commission was appointed to review the tax jurisdiction as well as the revenue allocation scheme from federation taxes such that the regions would have the maximum proportion of the revenue within their jurisdiction. For the first time, the Commission created the Distributable Pool Account (DPA) into which a certain percentage of the federally–collected revenue was paid and shared among the regions. The principles for sharing this revenue were derivation and need. Using these principles, the Commission came out with a revenue allocation formula that allocated the funds in the DPA to the regions as follows: Northern Region: 40 percent; Eastern Region: 31 percent; Western Region: 24 percent; and Southern Cameroon, which was then part of Nigeria, 5 percent. The Federal Government retained 70 percent of all federation revenue for its services and transferred 30 percent to the DPA for distribution among the regions.[65]

## Post Colonial Fiscal Relations among Levels of Governments

### *1960-1966*

By 1963 when Nigeria became a republic, the revenue allocation of the Raisman Commission had become unsatisfactory for two main reasons:

a.      the creation of the Mid-western region out of the Western region, resulting in a change in structure from a three–region arrangement to a four-region arrangement; and

b.      the replacement of the Independence Constitution of 1960 by the Republican Constitution of 1963.

Under the Republican Constitution, the Binns Commission was set up to review and make recommendations on the federation revenue comprising mining, rent and royalty, import and export duties, and other taxes, and on the distribution of funds in the DPA. The Commission recommended that transfer of funds from the federation revenue to the DPA be increased from 30 to 35 percent and that the principle of 'financial comparability' be used in addition to need and even development to share the funds among the regions.[66] The revenue allocation formula that was fashioned out by the Commission allocated 42 percent to the Northern Region, 30 percent to the Eastern Region, and 20 and 8 percent to the Western and Mid-Western Regions respectively.[67]

### *1966-1975*

Following the military coup on 15 January 1966, the Constitution was suspended, and in May of the same year, the new military leader, General J.T.U. Aguyi Ironsi promulgated the Unification Decree No. 34 of 1966. The decree changed the formal designation of the federal government to National Military Government, relegated the regions to groups of provinces and unified the regional and federal public services. Further, under the decree, the constitutional mandate of the central government was absolute. Ironsi's government was short-lived and under General Yakubu Gowon's administration that succeeded it in July 1966, the federal structure of the country was restored. General Gowon further restructured the erstwhile four regions into twelve states. The new States were North-Western, North-Central, North-Eastern, Benue-Plateau, Kano, Kwara, Western, Mid-Western, East-Central, South-Eastern, Rivers and Lagos States.[68]

The Federal Military Government empowered the regional/state military governments to assume the constitutional responsibilities of their civilian predecessors in a modified form. Specifically, military governors were delegated the powers to make and implement laws with respect to residual and concurrent subjects under the old civilian constitution, with the provisions that state actions on concurrent matters should be preceded by consultations with the Federal Government. But because these decrees were non-justiciable, even the modest autonomy envisioned for the states under the military regime remained insecure. In essence, the legal status of Nigerian federalism under military government was profoundly ambivalent as the relevant enactments conferred seemingly absolute powers on the centre, while simultaneously providing for the legal continuity and integrity of constituent governments, albeit in a radically modified form. In order to resolve the difficulty created by the abolition of the regions, Decree No. 15 of 1967 was promulgated which provided for the allocation of a percentage of the DPA to the group of states that were created from a particular region. To this effect, the six States created out of the defunct Northern Region (North-West State, North-Central State, Kano State, Benue–Plateau State, North-Eastern State, and Kwara State) were to share 42 percent of the funds in the DPA.[69] The same condition applied to other regions. Decree No. 13 of 1970 adopted population and equality of states as the bases for revenue sharing among the states while Decree No. 2 of 1971 gave the Federal Military Government absolute right to revenue from offshore rent and royalties. Decree No. 6 of 1975 stipulated that all revenues meant to be shared among the states had to pass through the DPA except 20 percent of onshore mining rent and royalties which would be passed directly to the states of origin on the principle of derivation.[70]

On 29 July 1975, General Murtala Muhammed became the Head of State after toppling Gowon in a bloodless coup. The new military administration appointed a Commission headed by Justice Akinola Aguda to advise on the creation of new states and establish a new federal capital at Abuja, in the central area of the country. The Aguda Commission proposed seven more states and, although General Muhammed was killed in an attempted coup on 13 February 1976, his successor and erstwhile deputy, General Olusegun Obasanjo went ahead with the creation and announced seven more states bringing the total number of states to nineteen. The new states were Bauchi, Benue, Borno, Imo, Niger, Ogun and Ondo. The creation of new states was to assuage the agitations, especially among the less populous ethnic groups in the country.

*1975-1979*

In 1977, the Federal Military Government set up the Aboyade Technical Committee on Revenue Allocation to fashion out a revenue allocation which would:

a.  depoliticize revenue sharing in Nigeria;
b.  guarantee each tier of government enough revenue commensurate with its responsibilities;
c.  discourage the possibility of the Federal Government having so much funds that could enable it completely to take over the normal functions of the lower tiers of government; and
d.  enable local governments to undertake meaningful grassroots developments.[71]

In considering fiscal jurisdiction and revenue assignments among the levels of government, the committee weighted two options and later chose the one they considered to be most appropriate. According to Professor Aboyade:

> In consideration of fiscal jurisdiction and revenue assignment among the various levels of government, two options were opened to us. We could arbitrarily decide on which level of government was responsible for collecting and/or retaining particular sources of revenue, and then assign particular functions that could adequately be catered for, given the resources available at that level of government. Alternatively, we could decide on which functions should be performed by the respective levels of government and then allocate funds enough to carry out such functions efficiently. We considered these two options and elected the second; because we believed it is a neater arrangement, in the sense that it is easier in a given period of time to reallocate resources than to reallocate functions among levels of government. The power and functions of the constituent parts of a federal system are normally entrenched in the supreme law of the land, which is the Constitution. The provisions for amending such entrenched provisions are usually very stringent, and may in any case take the life span of a revenue arrangement before a constitutional amendment could be effected. Having been persuaded by the need to match available resources with expenditure functions at the various levels of government, and the need to take a decision on the latter before

the allocation of fiscal jurisdiction, we then start to look at the possible and feasible allocation of expenditure functions within a federal system and in the Nigerian setting.[72]

In the interest of federalism, the committee recommended that fiscal policy should move in the direction of transferring more constitutional functions and fiscal responsibilities from the Federal Government to the lower tiers of government. With efficiency and economic consideration as a guide, the committee allocated functions such as defence and security, external relations, inter-state and international roads, ports facilities, railways, airport facilities, power, communications, higher education and heavy industries to the Federal Government. The Committee recommended that states should be vested with secondary education, health, urban water supply, housing, lighter infrastructures, agriculture, light industries, town and country planning and rural electrification. Finally, local governments were recommended to be responsible for sewage disposal, maintenance of feeder roads, primary education, market stalls, rural health and cottage industries.

Having settled with the constitutional functions of the various levels of government, the committee then allocated fiscal powers and tax revenues to each level to enable them perform efficiently the broad functions assigned to them. The Federal Government was given jurisdiction over the following sources of revenue: import duties, excise duties, export duties, mining rents and royalties, petroleum profit tax, company income tax, capital gains tax (legal basis only), personal income tax (legal basis only), personal income tax of the armed forces, external affairs officers and federal capital territory (retention), sales or purchase taxes (legal basis only), stamp duties (legal basis only).[73]

States were given jurisdiction over the following: sales or purchase taxes (except on commodities so designated by the Federal Government) (administration and retention), football pools and other betting taxes, estate duties, gift tax, land tax (other than agricultural land), land registration fees (legal basis only), capital gains tax (administration and retention), personal income tax (administration and retention), company tax (administration only), stamp duties (administration and retention).[74] The local governments were conferred with jurisdiction over the following sources: property tax, market and trading license and fees, motor vehicle tax and drivers license fees, land registration fees (administration and retention), license fees on television and wireless radio (administration and retention).[75]

The Committee, among other things, also recommended that all federally collected revenue, except personal income tax collected by the federal or state government, be transferred into the Federation Account and shared as follows: 57 percent to the Federal Government, 30 percent to the states jointly, 10 percent to the local government jointly, and 3 percent to the Special Funds Account to be administered by the Federal Government in meeting national emergencies.[76] The committee recommended the following principles and factors as bases for sharing the funds among states:

a.  equality of access to development;

b.  national minimum standards for national integration;

c.  Absorption capability to be measured by the proportion of actual capital expenditure to the planned capital expenditures;

d.  independent revenue efforts to be measured by internal tax revenue and recurrent expenditure and;

e.  fiscal efficiency to be measured by the proportion of personal emolument to recurrent expenditure.

For the first time, direct provision was made for local governments in the Federation Account. Also, the states were to pass on to their local governments, a certain percentage of their internally generated revenue. In accepting the committee's recommendation on the sharing formula, the Federal Government added the 3 percent allocation to special funds to its own share. The final revenue allocation formula that emerged, therefore, was 60, 30 and 10 percent, for the federal, state and local governments, respectively.[77]

### The Impact of the 1979 Constituent Assembly on Nigerian Fiscal Relations

Under the military administration of Murtala/Obasanjo a Constituent Assembly was inaugurated to fashion a workable constitution for the forthcoming democratic government in 1979. The Constitution Drafting Committee of the Assembly presented to the military government a draft constitution that incorporated the recommendations of the Aboyade Technical Committee. The draft Constitution declared Nigeria as a 'Federal Republic'. The basis for the change from parliamentary to presidential system as evidenced in 1979 Constitution was the desire of the administration to establish a more centralized and integrated polity.[78] The drafters of the new Constitution sought to replace the dual, divided, and weak executive of the first republic with a single, effective symbol of federal executive authority and national unity.[79] Moreover, a presidential system is regarded as more consistent with Nigeria's federal structure and democratic aspirations for three different reasons. First, the separation of powers between the executive and the legislature in presidential systems (unlike the parliamentary system) was considered to be more congruent with the federalist principle of constitutionally dispersed authority. Second, the coordinate status assigned to second legislative chambers in presidential federations (in contrast to the parliamentary tradition of establishing weak second chambers) was expected to give more effective protection to states and minority rights. Third, the presidential system's fixed electoral cycles (unlike the discretionary electoral cycles associated with parliamentary systems) would presumably be more effective in reducing the already enormous advantages of incumbency in the Nigerian setting.[80]

## 1979-1983

The Shagari Administration considered the Aboyade Committee revenue sharing indices as too technical and unworkable. It therefore set up the Okigbo Revenue Allocation Commission in November 1979, about one month into office, to review the recommendations of the Aboyade Technical Committee as well as other related matters and fashion out workable and acceptable revenue allocation arrangements. The committee submitted its reports on 30 June 1980. It recommended that funds in the Federation Account be shared as follows: the Federal Government: 55 percent; state governments: 30.5 percent; local governments: 10 percent, and special funds: 4.5 percent. The 4.5 percent allocation to special funds was to be shared on the basis of 3.5 percent to mineral mining states and 1.0 percent for ecological problems.[81]

Following the adoption of Okigbo Commission report, several changes in revenue allocation formula and arrangements were carried out by successive governments, oftentimes in budget announcements. For example, the Federal Government's share of the Federation Account was reduced from 55 percent to 50 percent in 1990, and again to 48.5 percent in 1993.[82] In addition, with the interlude of civilian rule between 1979 and 1983, the state governments predictably sought to regain some measure of constitutional autonomy and fiscal capability. In order to reassert their rights to generate independent revenues, several state governments revived such previously abolished independent revenue sources such as poll, community and casino taxes.[83]

## 1983-1999

The modest financial gains made by the states during the Second Republic (1979-1983) were reversed after the re-imposition of military rule at the end of 1983. Thus, while over time, the local government's statutory share of the Federation Account increased from 10 percent in 1983 to 15 percent in 1990 and again to 20 percent in 1992, the states' share declined from 35 percent to 24 percent during the same period. Meanwhile, the Federal Government retained 48.5 percent of the Federation Account for its own use, while assuming direct or indirect responsibility for the administration of another 7.5 percent of the Federation Account designated as special funds.[84]

On 23 September 1987, the Babangida administration increased the number of states of the federation to 21 with the creation of Akwa Ibom and Katsina States; one each from Eastern and Northern Regions. The creation of these two new states generated pressures among other sections of the country for the creation of more states out of the former regions. Due to these persistent pressures, the Babangida government created additional nine states on 27 August 1991. The additional states were Abia, Adamawa, Delta, Enugu, Jigawa, Kebbi, Kogi, Osun and Taraba states. This brought the total number of states of the federation to thirty. On 1 October 1996, military Head of State General Sani Abacha created six new states bringing the total number of states to the current thirty six. These were Bayelsa, Ebonyi, Ekiti, Gombe, Nassarawa and Zamfara.

As earlier stated, the period of military rule witnessed a continuous decline in the financial position of the states owing to the reduction of states' share of revenue allocation relative to 1983 levels. This trend was further aggravated by the violation of revenue allocation law by military administrations. Successive central military administrations simply ignored constitutional provisions that required the federal government to pay all federally collected revenues (with the exception of the income taxes of the military, police, diplomatic personnel and residents of Abuja, the Federal Capital Territory) into the Federation Account for redistribution among the three tiers of government.[85]

Several other measures were adopted by the military government between 1984 and 1999 that further contributed to fiscal recentralization such as the replacement of the state administered sales tax with the federally administered Value Added Tax. Another instance was the unilateral revision of personal income tax rates and the regulation of the residual taxing powers of the states through the promulgation of the Taxes and Levies Decrees of 1998.[86] The VAT is centrally collected by Federal Inland Revenue Service as an agent of the Federal Government and paid into the VAT Pool Account. At inception, the Federal Government was to retain 20 percent of the VAT proceeds while the states were to share the remaining 80 percent.[87] The local governments were not expected to benefit from the sales tax which VAT replaced. In January, 1995 however, the revenue generated from VAT was shared on a ratio of 50: 25: 25: for federal, state and local governments before it was revised in 1996 to 35:40:25: percent for Federal, State and Local governments.[88] The formula was further adjusted in the 1999 Budget on the basis of 15:50:35 percent for Federal, State and Local Governments respectively.[89] Because of centrist regulations and manipulations, especially the underpayment of the federal revenue into the Federation Account, the Federal Government's share of public expenditures expanded dramatically from 52 percent in 1983 to 74 percent in 1995, while the state governments' share declined from more than 40 percent to less than 20 percent during the same period. A major consequence of the military's disengagement from the administration of the economy in 1999 was to put an end to the more egregious abuse of revenue allocation that had existed since 1984. However, pressures for the alteration of the entire vertical revenue sharing formula in favor of the sub-federal tier have continued and even intensified.[90] The Political Bureau- a Presidential Panel made up of political scientists- that coordinated the debate on Nigeria's political future during 1986 and 1987 reported general public support for a revenue sharing scheme that would put the federal and state's share of the Federation Account at 40 percent apiece with the localities receiving the remaining 20 percent. The Bureau also referred to:

> A considerable body of opinion advocating the re-allocation of fiscal powers among the three tiers of government to give more powers to the local and state governments in the collection of revenue in their areas of jurisdiction.[91]

The Revenue Allocation Committee of the 1994 - 1995 National Constitutional Conference proposed the allocation of only 33 percent of the Federation Account to the Federal Government and 32.5, 20, and 14.5 percent for states, localities, and special funds respectively.[92]

## *Horizontal Revenue Allocation under the 1999 Constitution*

The 1999 Constitution of the Federal Republic of Nigeria reechoes many of the familiar themes in horizontal revenue allocation formula. The allocation principles recognised by the Constitution are population, equality of States; internal revenue generation, land mass, terrain, population density and derivation. Section 162 (2) of the Constitution provides that:

> The President, upon the receipt of advice from the Revenue Mobilisation Allocation and Fiscal Commission, shall table before the National Assembly proposals for revenue allocation from the Federation Account, and in determining the formula, the National Assembly shall take into account, the allocation principles especially those of population, equality of States; internal revenue generation, land mass, terrain as well as population density:
>
> Provided that the principle of derivation shall be constantly reflected in any approved formula as being not less than thirteen per cent of the revenue accruing to the Federation Account directly from any natural resources.

In August 2001, the Revenue Mobilisation, Allocation and Fiscal Commission submitted a formula to President Obasanjo in compliance to the constitutional requirement. While deliberations were still going on, the Supreme Court delivered judgment in the case of *Attorney General of Abia State & 2 others Vs. Attorney General of the Federation & others (No. 2)* on 5 April 2002[93] in which the court nullified the practice of first line charges on the Federation Account. Prior to the judgment, the Federal Government deducted from the Federation Account funds meant for the Judiciary; servicing of external debts; allocation to the Federal Capital Territory; and Joint Venture Agreements and priority projects of the Nigerian National Petroleum Corporation before the balance from the Federation Account was shared among the three tiers of government. Following the judgment of the Supreme Court abolishing first line charges, the Commission withdrew the formula earlier submitted in August 2001 and re-submitted a new formula reflecting the implications of the Supreme Court judgment to the president in December 2002. However, the Revenue Allocation Formula Bill has not been passed by the National Assembly to date. Save for slight modifications, the formula being used to allocate revenue from the Federation Account among the tiers of government is that introduced by the Federal Military Government since 1992. The 1992 formula was subjected to series of review through Executive Orders between 2002 and 2004. The latest of such Executive Orders was issued in March 2004 and is the basis for allocation of revenue to date. The formula is as follows:

**With 13 % Derivation:**

Federal Government:     46%

State Government:        23%

Local Government:        18%

Derivation:              13%

**Total**:               **100%**

**Net of 13% Derivation:**

Federal Government:     52.68%

State Government:        26.72%

Local Government:        20.60%

**Total**:               **100%**

The Federation Account is just one of several accounts from which the three tiers of the Federation allocate revenues. Another account which is the subject of horizontal revenue sharing is the Value Added Tax Pool Account. Section 40 of the Value Added Tax Act, as amended, provides that proceeds of VAT Account should be allocated on the basis of 50 percent to the States and the Federal Capital Territory; 35 percent to the Local Governments and 15 percent to the Federal Government. The proviso to Section 40 further provides for the principle of derivation of not less than 20 percent to be reflected in the share of States and Local Governments.

## Postscript

The extent of influence exerted by the Federal Government over its constituent units varies from one system to another. In Nigeria, Germany, Australia, India, and South Africa, such influence is enormous. It is relatively weaker in countries like Canada, Switzerland and the United States.

Over the years, the most explosive issue in Nigeria's fiscal federalism involved the conflict over the appropriate formula for the inter-state sharing of centrally collected revenues. Over twenty principles have being employed in allocating revenue to the states since 1946. Among these principles, equality of states seems to be the most acceptable. In most cases, opposition to this principle comes from the most populous states of the federation. Aside from this, the derivation principle has over the years generated a lot of controversies as to what percentage of the resources should go to the state from which a particular resource is explored. While the 1999 Constitution pegs the weight to be attached to derivation at a minmum of 13% of the resource derived from the states, resource rich states continually demand for higher percentage of such revenue.

Another salient factor in the debate over fiscal relations in the Nigerian federation is the manner in which states creation have shaped the content and character of central allocations to the states. After the creation of the twelve states from the four regions in 1967, the problem of how to allocate resources among the states arose. To address this challenge, the Federal Government simply divided the percentage allocated to the old northern region equally among the six states created from it. In any case, creation of new states usually brings about changes not just in the quantum of revenues accruable to the federating units but also the dynamics that influence the factors used in allocation of federally collected revenues.

# References

1   Anwar, S., 'Principle of Fiscal Federalism', in Anwar, S & Kincaid, J. (ed), *The Practice of Fiscal Federalism: Comparative Perspectives* (Montreal: McGill-Queen's University Press, 2007).

2   *Oxford Advanced Learner's Dictionary*, (6th ed) (Oxford: Oxford University Press, 2000).

3   Dare, L. & Oyewole, A., *Government for Secondary Schools* (Ibadan: Onibonoje Press and Book Industries (Nig.) Ltd., 1987) 1.

4   Appadorai, A., *The Substance of Politics* (India: Oxford University Press, 1975) 12.

5   Anwar, S., *op. cit.* , 4.

6   *Ibid* , 7.

7   Suberu, R.T., *Federalism and Ethnic Conflict in Nigeria* (Washington D.C: United States Institute of Peace Press, 2001) 3. Hereafter referred to as 'Suberu, *Conflict* '.

8   Tekena, T., 'Nigerian Federalism in Historical Perspectives ' in Amuwo, K., *et al* (ed) *Federalism and Political Restructuring in Nigeria* (Ibadan: Spectrum Books Ltd, 1998) 13.

9   Friedrich, C., *Federalism: National and International* (New York: Oxford University Press, 1963).

10  Wheare, K. C., *Federal Government* (New York: Oxford University Press, 1963).

11  Oni, M.A., 'Federalism and Power Struggle in Nigeria ' *Nigerian Society for Economics and Research* , Mono. Series No. 17, 1997.

12  Tella, S. A. 'Promoting States' Economic Independence through Financial Market Cooperation' in *Fiscal Development and Nigeria's Economic Development Fiscal Federalism and Nigeria's Economic Development: Selected Papers for the 1999 Annual Conference of the Nigerian Economic Society* (Ibadan: The Nigerian Economic Society, 1999) 173.

13  *Ibid,* 174.

14  See *Federalism,* available at *http://www.answer.com/topic/federalism* , 22 (accessed on 16/05/2009).

15  *Ibid* .

16  *Ibid*.

17  Oates, W.E., *Fiscal Federalism* (New York: Harcourt Brace Jovanovich, 1972).

18  Agiobenebo, T. J., 'Assignment, Criteria and the Fiscal Constitution: An Excursion into a Theory of Rational Fiscal Federalism' in The Nigerian Economic Society, *Fiscal*

*Federalism and Nigeria's Economic Development: Selected Papers for the 1999 Annual Conference of the Nigerian Economic Society* (Ibadan: The Nigerian Economic Society, 1999) 26.

19      See *Fiscal Federalism* , available at http://en.wikipedia.org/wiki/fiscal_federalism (accessed on 25/5/2009).

20      *Ibid.*

21      Agiobenebo *op.cit.*

22      *Ibid* .

23      *Ibid* . p. 58

24      Fajana, O., Three and a Half Decades of Fiscal Federalism in Nigeria' in Eliagwu, I. &      Akindele R. A., (eds.), *Foundations of Nigerian Federalism, 1960*-1995 (Jos: Institute of Governance and Social Research, 2001) 87 – 124, pp. 118 - 119.

25      Suberu, R.T., 'Attractions and Limitations of Multi - Ethnic Federalism: The Nigerian Experience'. Faculty Lecture Series No.12 (2004). Faculty of Social Science, University of Ibadan.

26      See *Suberu Conflict,* 58.

27      *Ibid.*

28      *Ibid*, 60.

29      *Ibid.*

30      *Ibid.*

31      *Ibid*, 61.

32      Rabiu, S.A., *Personal Income Tax in Nigeria: Procedures and Problems*   (Lagos: J West Publication, 1981)   .

33      Suberu, *Conflict, op. cit* ,61.

34      *Ibid*, 62.

35      *Ibid.*

36      *Ibid.*

37      *Ibid*, 63.

38      *Ibid.*

39      Olowononi, G.D., 'Revenue Allocation and Economics of Federalism' in Amuwo, K. *et al*, *Federalism and Political Restructuring in Nigeria* (Ibadan: Spectum Books Ltd., 1998) 247 – 260, 250.

40      Suberu, *Conflict,* 64.

41      *Ibid.*

42      *Ibid*, 65.

43    *Ibid*, 66.

44    *Ibid*.

45    *Ibid*.

46    *Ibid*.

47    *Ibid*.

48    *Ibid*, 67.

49    *Ibid*.

50    *Ibid*.

51    *Ibid*.

52    *Ibid*, 69.

53    *Ibid*.

54    *Ibid*.

55    Rabiu, S.A.,*op. cit*, 3 - 12

56    Second Republic is the period between 1979 and 1983 when civilian government was put in place for the second time in Nigeria.

57    Suberu, *Conflict*, 70.

58    *Ibid*.

59    *Ibid*.

60    *Ibid*, 70.

61    *Ibid*.

62    Ayoade, J.A.A., 'The Changing Structure of Nigerian Federalism' in Elaigwu, J. I. & Akindele R.A. (eds), *Foundations of Nigerian Federalism, 1960-1995* (Jos: Institute of Governance and Social Research, 2001) 49.

63    Ebajemito, J.O. & Abudu, M.I., 'Intergovernmental Fiscal Relations in a Federal System: The Nigerian Experience' in *Fiscal Federalism and Nigeria's Economic Development, Fiscal Development: Selected Papers for the 1999 Annual Conference of the Nigerian Economic Society* (Ibadan: The Nigerian Economic Society, 1999) 223.

64    *Ibid*.

65    *Ibid*.

66    *Ibid*, 224.

67    *Ibid*.

68    See *List of Nigerian States by Date of Statehood*, available at http://en.wikipedia.org/wiki/List_of_Nigerian_states_by_date_of_statehood (accessed on 15/01/2009).

69    Federal Republic of Nigeria, *Report of Technical Committee on Revenue Allocation in the Military Era* (Lagos: Federal Government Press, 1979) 13.

70    Ebajemito, J.O. & Abudu, M.I., 'Intergovernmental Fiscal Relations in a Federal System *op. cit*, 223.

71    *Ibid*, 225.

72    Federal Republic of Nigeria, *Report of Technical Committee on Revenue Allocation in the Military Era*, *op. cit*, 41.

73    *Ibid*, 43.

74    *Ibid*.

75    *Ibid*.

76    *Ibid*, 44.

77    *Ibid*.

78    Suberu, *Conflict, op. cit*, 36.

79    *Ibid*.

80    *Ibid*, 36 – 37.

81    Ebajemito, J.O. & Abudu, M.I., *op. cit*, 226.

82    *Ibid*.

83    Suberu, *Conflict, op. cit*, 53.

84    *Ibid*, 55.

85    Suberu, *Conflict, op. cit*, 55.

86    *Ibid*, 55.

87    Ebajemito, J.O. & Abudu, M.I. *op. cit*, 226.

88    *Ibid*.

89    *Ibid*.

90    Suberu, *op. cit*, 56.

91    *Ibid*, 56.

92    *Ibid*.

93    (2002) 6 NWLR (Part 764) 542.

# CHAPTER TWO

## THE CONSTITUTIONAL CONTEXT FOR TAXATION

### Background

This chapter traces the constitutional development of Nigeria since the 1914 amalgamation. It explains how different constitutional arrangements in Nigeria have provided the enabling framework for taxation and how government taxing powers have evolved through different political and constitutional epochs. This analysis provides further insight on the impact the various constitutional arrangements have had in defining the nature of relations among the different tiers of government especially in the area of fiscal matters.

### Conceptual Issues

It is important to explain what taxation means in order that the term *tax* may not be confused with other forms of exactions such as fees, penalties and fines. Soyode and Kajola define tax as 'a compulsory exaction of money by a public authority for public purpose' and taxation as 'a system of raising money for the purposes of government by means of contributions from individual person or corporate body'.[1] A judicial definition of tax was given in *Mathews v. Chicory Marketing Board (v)*[2] - a High Court of Australia case that considered section 90 of the Australian Constitution, which prohibits States from levying excise (taxes) - as 'a compulsory exaction of money by a public authority for public purposes'. Summing up definitions of tax as offered by various other sources, Ayua concludes that:

> The most important thing is a pecuniary burden laid upon individuals or persons or property to support the government and is *a payment exacted by legislative authority*[3] (emphasis supplied).

The exaction of tax by government is not tied to any particular benefit to the taxpayer. It is this feature, according to Soyode and Kajola, which distinguishes a tax from other forms of exactions such as fees, penalties and fines.[4] A fee is an amount paid in return for a specific and measurable service. An example of a fee paid to government includes payment for a certificate of occupancy. Fines and penalties are exactions by way of punishment for infringement of state laws or regulations. Thus while fees are charged to defray the cost of a service rendered, fines and penalties are punitive measures imposed against a law breaker.

Although payment of tax is not necessarily tied to the conferment of any specific benefit to the taxpayer, it is implicitly recognised by taxpayer and tax collector that the judicious use of tax revenue by the government for the public good is the *quid pro quo* for taxing the citizens. Indeed, it has been observed that transparency, accountability and good governance are critical factors in ensuring voluntary tax compliance.[5]

A tax may be *direct* or *indirect*. It is direct where it is levied on the person who it is intended, should pay the tax. This is usually the case in the taxation of incomes. E.g companies' income tax and personal income tax are direct taxes. It is indirect if the levy is imposed on one person who pays with the expectation to pass the burden unto third parties. Custom duties and value added tax are examples of indirect taxes because the levy imposed by government is factored into the price of the item upon which they are levied and passed unto the consumer. Apart from direct and indirect taxes, Ayua[6] further classifies tax types into proportional, progressive and regressive taxes. A tax is proportional when the proportion paid by each taxpayer bears the same ratio to the amount to be raised as the value of his property bears to the total taxable income. It is based on a constant proportion of income and therefore, neutral. A progressive tax is a graduated system that applies higher rates as income increases. A regressive tax is a structure that applies lesser rates as the value of the property increases.

Historically, the sole objective of taxation was to raise revenue for government. Kings or emperors levied their subjects to generate revenues to provide for the defense of the kingdom and also for the general welfare of the empire. In modern times, generating revenues for government is still an important objective of taxation but it is no longer the sole objective. Taxes are used by modern governments to generate revenue but in addition, to also fund governance, ensure resource redistribution, streamline consumption of certain goods, reduce inflation, generate employment and stimulate growth in the economy.[7] Taxation has therefore, become a veritable tool of fiscal and economic policy.

According to Fashola, the philosophy underpinning taxation is that the expenses of government, being for the general good, ought to be borne by the public generally.[8] The foregoing view finds support in Akanle's treatise; *The Meaning and Nature of Taxation Power*. He opined that:

> The justification of these powers rests on the assumption of the common law that every citizen is entitled to the protection of his life, liberty and property by the state. But for the state (i.e government) to preserve such life, liberty and property it must be enabled so to do, and this is done through the concept of implied powers of taxation, police and eminent domain.[9]

The funds provided by taxes are used by the states to support certain state obligations such as education systems, health care systems, pension for the elderly, unemployment benefits, and public transportation.

Closely tied to the objectives of taxation are the fundamental principles or *canons* of taxation. These canons are equity, certainty, convenience and economy.[10] The canon of equity, also called the ability to pay means that all taxpayers should contribute according to their ability; i.e the poor should be taxed less and the rich should be taxed more. The canon of certainty means that every taxpayer should know the amount to be paid, when to pay, and where to pay. The canon of convenience is to the effect that the method of payment should not be burdensome to the taxpayer. This explains the collection of income tax at source or sales tax at the point of sales. Lastly, the canon of economy means that the cost of collecting revenue must be kept as low as possible. This is because where the cost of collection is higher than the revenue collected, the primary aim of taxation as a revenue generating scheme is defeated.

## Nigeria and Constitutional Taxation

### Background

Taxes were already levied in the various empires that existed before the creation of Nigeria. This was especially true in the cases of centralised empires such as the northern Emirates, and the kingdoms of the western and mid-western regions of the area that eventually became Nigeria. However, the era of colonialism marked a new dimension in taxation for these kingdoms. Not only were these taxes now being paid to a foreign government, the practice was extended into territories where it was hitherto unknown. Furthermore, the era of colonialism witnessed a change in the style and manner of tax administration; one that derived legislative authority from colonial enactments. Thus the first colonial income tax was introduced in Northern Nigeria in 1906 by virtue of the *Native Revenue Proclamation No. 2 1906*.[11] This was later extended to the western and eastern territories through the *Native Revenue Ordinances* in 1918 and 1927 respectively. Several other legislations were subsequently passed by the colonial government to administer and regulate various types and aspects of taxation before Nigeria finally acquired independence in 1960.

*The Foreign Jurisdiction Act 1890* facilitated the exercise by the English Crown of the jurisdiction acquired by it in foreign territories.[12] The legislative authority of the British Parliament to make laws for Nigeria was derived from this enactment as well as from the *Colonial Laws Validity Act 1865*. In furtherance to this jurisdiction, not only did certain laws passed by the British Parliament became applicable to Nigeria, the relevant representatives of the Crown in the colony and protectorates were also empowered in specified cases to exercise this jurisdiction on behalf of the Imperial Government. Although the colonial administration exercised this power in Northern Nigeria in 1906 to impose direct taxation, the first attempt at constitution making for the colony and protectorate was in 1914. By 1960, when Nigeria became independent, at least five constitutional instruments had been enacted at different times for the protectorate of Nigeria.

## Pre-Independent Constitutions

### Lugard Constitution 1914

The instrument sometimes referred to as the Lugard Constitution or the 1914 Constitution was in fact, an Order-in-Council that was passed in 1913. Its most significant impact was that it amalgamated the erstwhile Northern and Southern Protectorates into the Protectorate of Nigeria. It came into force on 1st January 1914. Both the executive and legislative powers of the new protectorate were vested in the Governor and Commander-in-Chief of the protectorate. The preamble to the *Nigeria Protectorate Order in Council 1913* provided, *inter alia,* that:

> And whereas it is expedient that the Protectorates of Northern Nigeria and Southern Nigeria shall be formed into one Protectorate under the name of the Protectorate of Nigeria.

Sections IV and VIII of the Order empowered the governor to exercise both executive and legislative powers including powers to raise revenue. The sections provided thus:

IV.     The Governor and Commander-in-Chief for the time being of the Colony of Nigeria (hereinafter called the Governor) shall be the Governor and Commander-in-Chief of the Protectorate of Nigeria and he is hereby authorized, empowered and commanded to exercise on His Majesty's behalf all such powers and jurisdiction as His Majesty at any time before or after the passing of this Order had or may have within the said territories, and to that end to take or cause to be taken all such measures and to do or cause to be done all such matters and things therein as are lawful and as in the interest of His Majesty's service he may think expedient, subject to such instructions as he may from time to time receive from His Majesty or through a Secretary of State.

VIII.   It shall be lawful for the Governor, from time to time, by Ordinance, to provide for the administration of justice, *the raising of revenue*, and generally for the peace, order, and good government of the Protectorate, and all persons therein, including the prohibition and punishment of acts tending to disturb the public peace. (Emphasis supplied)

The authority of the Governor to pass legislation (including tax legislation) was therefore guaranteed by the specific provisions of paragraph VIII of the amalgamation constitution. Drawing from this constitutional authority, the *Native Revenue Proclamation 1906* was re-enacted in 1917 as the *Native Revenue Ordinance No. 1 1917*. Amendments to the ordinance were made in 1918 and 1927 to extend the taxation of incomes to the western and eastern provinces.[13]

### Clifford Constitution 1922

The constitutional instrument often referred to as the Clifford Constitution established, at least in theory, a separate Legislative Council from the Executive Council. Section IV of the *Nigeria Protectorate Order-in-Council 1922* was in *pari materia* with section IV of the *Nigeria*

*Protectorate Order in Council 1913*. The 1922 Order however, introduced some new provisions that were not contained in the 1913 Order. For example, the legislative powers vested in the Commander-in-Chief to, from time to time, by ordinance 'provide for the administration of justice, *the raising of revenue*, and generally for the peace, order, and good government of the Protectorate' under section VIII of the 1913 Order were limited under section X of the 1922 Order to apply only to the northern provinces of the Protectorate. By virtue of section IX of the 1922 Order, legislative powers for the southern provinces of the Protectorate (as well as the colony of Lagos) were vested in the Legislative Council provided for under section VIII of the 1922 Order. The combined effect of sections VIII and X of the 1922 Order was that while the Legislative Council had legislative competence to make laws for the southern provinces, legislative authority in respect of the northern provinces was vested in the Governor and Commander-in-Chief. Nwabueze submits that:

> It is true the governor could no longer legislate within the area of the jurisdiction of the council without its consent, yet the consent of the council was a mere formality, given always as a matter of course. This was because all the various legislative councils that functioned in the country up to 1922 were composed predominantly of officials appointed by the governor and bound to vote as directed by him.[14]

Further, not only was the governor (who was head of the Executive Council) a member of the Legislative Council, he also possessed the power to veto any ordinance passed by the Legislative Council. Sections VIII and IX provided thus:

VIII.   On and after a date to be fixed by the Governor by Proclamation in the Nigeria Gazette, there shall be a Legislative Council constituted in such manner and consisting of the Governor and such persons as are directed by His Majesty by an Order in His Privy Council bearing even date herewith and known as the Nigeria (Legislative Council) Order in Council, 1922, or by any Order in Council amending or substituted for the same, or by any Instructions under His Sign Manual and Signet or through a Secretary of State.

IX.   The persons who shall from time to time compose the said Legislative Council shall have full power and authority, subject always to any conditions, provisos and limitations prescribed by the said Order in Council, or by any other Order in Council, or by any Instructions under His Majesty's Sign Manual and Signet, to establish such Ordinances, and to constitute such Courts and Officers, and to make provisions and regulations for the proceedings in such Courts, and for the administration of justice, as may be necessary for the peace, order, and good Government of that portion of the Protectorate of Nigeria known as the Southern Provinces.

Provided that it shall be lawful for the Governor by Proclamation issued with His Majesty's approval signified through a Secretary of State to add to or otherwise vary the territories defined as the Southern Provinces for the purposes of this Order.

The Governor shall have a negative voice in the making and passing of all such Ordinances.

In spite of the drawbacks in the make-up and procedure of the Legislative Council, the Council, at least, laid the foundation for the eventual emergence of the legislature as a distinct organ from the executive powers of the governor, in that, at least in theory, the Council was making laws for the southern provinces while the Governor continued to make laws that applied to Northern Nigeria.

### Richard Constitution 1946

The Richard Constitution, as the constitution of 1946 is called was unique in two significant ways. First, under it, the northern provinces were brought within the competence of a legislative council created under Section 4 of the Nigeria (Legislative Council) Order in Council. The section provided:

The Legislative Council as constituted under the existing Orders immediately before the appointed day shall cease to exist and there shall be constituted a Legislative Council in and for Nigeria, in accordance with the provisions of this order.

The 'existing Orders' that were to cease existing were those of 1922 (under the Clifford constitutional instrument), 1928 and 1941. The 1946 arrangement therefore, abrogated the system whereby the Legislative Council made laws for the southern provinces while the governor made laws for Northern Nigeria by vesting all legislative powers in the governor on the *'advice and consent'* of the Legislative Council. The mode of exercising legislative power under the new Constitution was laid down under section 21 of the Order thus:

> Subject to the provisions of this Order, it shall be lawful for the Governor, with advice and consent of the Legislative Council, to make laws for the peace, order and good government of Nigeria.

Under the 1946 constitutional arrangement, therefore, legislative authority for the entire country was vested in the governor but the exercise of that power was subject to the 'advice and consent' of the Legislative Council. Further, the number of the unofficial members of the Council, who were to be appointed from the regional legislatures established under sections 33, 34 and 35, was greater than the official members of Council, suggesting that the new Legislative Council was not intended to be a rubber stamp of the governor *simplicita*. This, again, was a progressive, if slight departure from the 1922 arrangement under which the number of official members was greater than the unofficial members.[15] Nwabueze submits that although the consent of the Legislative Council to the governor's proposals in the past might had been almost always forthcoming, the said consent could no longer be taken for granted because of the unofficial majority in the new council. The learned author however concludes that:

> The existence of an unofficial majority of 11 in the legislative council must not be taken to have seriously weakened the internal control of the British authorities. It had merely created a possibility that the council might refuse to approve a measure initiated by the governor, who remained as before the principal instrument of policy and responsible for practically all bills introduced in the council, with a power to veto legislation initiated otherwise than with his previous approval or to refuse to assent thereto and reserve it for the signification of H.M's pleasure.[16]

Under section 22, no bill that, *inter alia,* imposed, altered or repealed any rate, tax or duty could be introduced in the Legislative Council without the prior consent of the governor first had and obtained. The section provided that:

Subject to the provisions of this Order and of the Standing Rules and Orders of the Legislative Council, any member may introduce any Bill or propose any motion for debate in, or may present any petition to, the Legislative Council, and the same shall be debated and disposed of according to the Standing Rules and Orders;

Provided that, except by the direction or with the sanction or recommendation of the Governor signified thereto, the Council shall not proceed upon any Bill, amendment, motion or petition which, in the opinion of the Governor or in that of the Presiding Member, would dispose of or alter any disposition thereof or charge thereon, or impose, alter or repeal any rate, tax or duty.

Sections 33, 34 and 35 established regional Houses of Assembly for the Northern, Western and Eastern Regions respectively. Under section 33 (1) the Northern House of Assembly consisted of a House of Chiefs and a House of Assembly; but the Western and Eastern Houses of Assembly created under sections 34 and 35 respectively did not consist of separate chambers for chiefs. The functions of the three regional Houses were spelt out under section 51 thus:

Subject to the provisions of sub-section (2) of this section, the functions of each House shall be:

(a)     to appoint Members to the Legislative Council as provided in Part II of this Order; and

(b)     to exercise the powers in relation to the estimates of the region and in relation to Bills conferred upon the House by the provisions of this Part of this Order; and

(c)     to consider and, by resolution, advise on any question or matter referred to the House by the Governor and on any question or matter introduced by a member for the consideration of the House in accordance with the provisions of this Order; and

(d)     to perform such other functions as may be prescribed by or under any law for the time being in force in Nigeria.

Thus, under the 1946 Constitution, regional assemblies did not possess inherent legislative powers. Furthermore, while owing to the majority of unofficial members, the Legislative

Council created a possibility where the governor's legislative power could be curtailed; such a possibility only went so far as non-tax bills were concerned. As far as tax bills were concerned, such a possibility collapsed in the light of the proviso to section 22.

### MacPherson Constitution 1951

The 1951 Constitution, also called the MacPherson Constitution, was an improvement on the 1946 Constitution both in terms of devolution of powers to the regions and in terms of composition of the legislative assemblies. The constitution provided for an elected majority in both the central legislature and the regional assemblies for the first time.[17] Two legislative houses were established for the northern region styled the 'the Northern House of Chiefs and the Northern House of Assembly' under section 15 of the Constitution. Similarly, section 26 established two legislative houses styled 'the Western House of Chiefs and the Western House of Assembly'. The Eastern legislative house was established under section 36 and unlike the northern and western regions, comprised of a single house styled 'the Eastern House of Assembly'.

The central legislature was established under section 67 of the Constitution. The section provided that:

> There shall be, in and for Nigeria, a House of Representatives consisting of:
> (a)   a President;
> (b)   six ex officio Members;
> (c)   one hundred and thirty-six Representatives Members, who shall be elected in accordance with the provisions of this Chapter; and
> (d)   such Special Members as may be appointed under the provisions of Section 70 of this Order.

The power of the House of Representatives to make laws was provided for under section 83. Section 84 however curtailed the powers of the central legislature with regards to bills of monetary nature, including tax bills. The section provided thus:

> Except upon the recommendation of the Governor or with the consent of the Governor signified thereto, the House of Representatives shall not proceed upon any Bill, motion or petition which, in the opinion of the President or other member presiding, would dispose of or charge any public

revenue or public funds or revoke or alter any disposition thereof or charge thereon, or impose, alter or repeal any rate, tax or duty.

The extent of the power of the regional assemblies to make laws was provided under section 92 of the Constitution. The section provided as follows:

(1) Any matter (being a matter not mentioned in the Third Schedule to this Order but with respect to which the Central Legislature may make laws) shall be within the competency of the legislature of a Region if it is declared so to be by any Central law.

(2) Any such matter, which has been declared as aforesaid to be within the competency of the legislature of a Region, shall cease to be within the competency of such legislature if the enactment embodying such declaration is repealed or otherwise ceases to have effect; but any law enacted by such legislature by virtue of that declaration shall remain in force but shall be subject to amendment and repeal as if it were a Central law.

(3) For the avoidance of doubts it is hereby declared that where, by virtue of a declaration made under this section, any matter is within the competency of the legislature of a Region, the power of the Central Legislature to make laws with respect to such matter shall not thereby be abridged, altered or in any way affected.

The Third Schedule referred to in section 92 (1) was the list of items in respect of which a regional legislature could make laws. Item 24 thereto provided that a regional legislature could make laws on 'taxation to such extent as may be prescribed by or under any Order of His Majesty in Council'. There was no Exclusive Legislative List conferring, among other powers, exclusive jurisdiction of certain taxes on the central government under the 1951 Constitution. Such a list was unnecessary in the light of section 92 (1) – (3). The combined effect of the said sub-sections, read alongside item 24 of the Third Schedule was that the power of the regional assemblies to pass legislation was only to such extent as was *delegated* by the central legislature and no more. Residual tax jurisdiction, as it were, therefore, was vested in the central legislature. In subsequent Constitutions, this trend was to be reversed to the extent that the taxes vested in the central legislature would always be spelt out under the Exclusive Legislative List, supposing that residual tax jurisdiction was now transferred to the regions/states.

### Lyttleton Constitution 1954

The 1954 Constitution was the product of several Orders-in-Council passed between 1951 and 1954. It was an improvement on the 1951 Constitution and can be said to be the first truly federalist Constitution because the devolution of powers under it was more comprehensive than any Constitution enacted hitherto. Legislative Houses were established for the federation, the three regions and the Southern Cameroons under section 5 of the 1954 Constitution. The section provided thus:

(1)     There shall be, for the Federation, a Legislative House, which shall be styled the House of Representatives

(2)     There shall be, for the Northern Region, two Legislative Houses, which shall be styled, respectively, the Northern House of Chiefs and the Northern House of Assembly

(3)     There shall be, for the Western Region, two Legislative Houses, which shall be styled, respectively, the Western House of Chiefs and the Western House of Assembly

(4)     There shall be, for the Eastern Region, a Legislative House, which shall be styled, the Eastern House of Assembly

(5)     There shall be, for the Southern Cameroons, a Legislative House, which shall be styled, the House of Assembly of the Southern Cameroons.

The composition of the House of Representatives was contained in section 6 while the composition of the Northern, Western and Eastern Houses was contained in sections 17, 24 and 32 respectively. The composition of the House of Assembly of the Southern Cameroons was contained in Section 34. Under section 61 the consent of the Governor General in the case of the (House of Representatives) or Governor (in the case of a regional

House of Assembly) was required before any of the legislative houses could consider a bill that, *inter alia,* imposed, altered or repealed a tax, rate or duty. Section 61 (1) provided that:

> Except upon the recommendation of the Governor-General or with the consent of the Governor-General, the House of Representatives shall not proceed upon any Bill, motion or petition that, in the opinion of the Speaker or any other officer presiding, would dispose of or charge any public revenue or public funds or revoke or alter any disposition thereof or charge thereon, or impose, alter or repeal any rate, tax or duty.

Subsections (2) and (3) of section 61 placed the same restriction on the regional legislative houses and the House of Assembly of the Southern Cameroons by requiring the consent of the regional governor in the case of the regional assemblies or commissioner in the case of the Southern Cameroons.

Section 162 contained provisions on the allocation of federal income tax. The Section provided that:

> (1)    Where under any law enacted by the Federal Legislature any tax is levied on incomes or profits, there shall be paid by the Federation to each Region in respect of each year of assessment after the thirty-first day of March, 1954, a sum equal to the amount of that part of the proceeds of that tax for that year that is declared by the prescribed authority to be attributable to the incomes and profits of persons, other than bodies corporate, resident in that Region during that year.

> (2)    (a)    For the purpose of this section the proceeds of a tax for a year of assessment shall be the amount that is declared by the prescribed authority to be the amount remaining from the receipts from that tax that are collected in respect of that year after any refunds or other repayments relating to those receipts have been made or allowed for;
>
>         Provided that for the purpose of calculating the receipts from any tax collected in respect of the year beginning on the first day of April, 1954, no account shall be taken of any sums

collected before the commencement of this Order or of any refunds or other repayments relating to any sums so collected.

(b)     In this section "year of assessment" means, in relation to a tax levied under any law, a year of assessment for the purposes of that law.

(3)     The Governor-General may by regulation make provision for determining the residence of any person for the purposes of this section.

Legislative competence regarding taxes on incomes and profits was contained in the Exclusive Legislative List, which was Part I to the First Schedule to the Constitution. Item 36 thereto provided that:

> Taxes on income and profits, except taxes on the incomes or profits accruing in or derived from, any Region or the Southern Cameroons of Africans resident in any Region or the Southern Cameroons and African communities in any Region or the Southern Cameroons.

It follows from the above provision that corporate income taxation and personal income taxation of residents of the Federal Territory of Lagos and expatriates was vested in the federal parliament while taxes from the income and profits of Africans resident in the regions were within the legislative competence of the regional assemblies.

## Post-Independent Constitutions

### *Independence Constitution 1960*

The Independence Constitution came into operation on October 1 1960 as a result of the independent status granted Nigeria within the Commonwealth by virtue of the Nigeria Independence Act 1960. Section 1 (1) and (2) of the Act provided as follows:

(1)     On the first day of October, nineteen hundred and sixty (in this Act referred to as "the appointed day"), the Colony and the Protectorate as respectively defined by the Nigeria (Constitution) Orders in

Council, 1954 to 1960, shall together constitute part of Her Majesty dominions under the name of Nigeria.

(2)     No Act of the Parliament of the United Kingdom passed on or after the appointed day shall extend, or be deemed to extend, to Nigeria or any part thereof as part of the law thereof, and as from that day:

(a)     Her Majesty's Government in the United Kingdom shall have no responsibility for the government of Nigeria or any part thereof; and

(b)     the provisions of the First Schedule to this Act shall have effect with respect to legislative powers in Nigeria.

The First Schedule to the Act referred to in (2) (b) provided, *inter alia,* that:

The Colonial Laws Validity Act, 1865, shall not apply to any law made on or after the appointed day by any legislature established for Nigeria or any part thereof.

In addition, section 10 (1) of the Nigeria (Constitution) Order-in-Council 1960 provided that:

The Parliament of the Federation of Nigeria may make laws for the peace, order and good government of any Region of the Federation with respect to taxes on income and profits, not being taxes on the income or profits accruing in, or derived from, that Region, of Africans resident in that Region and African communities in that Region.

Section 30 of the Constitution guaranteed protection against compulsory acquisition of property without adequate compensation, and also conferred a right to action to determine the compensation on the person so deprived. Subsection (3) (a) however provided that 'nothing in this section shall be construed as affecting any general law for the imposition or enforcement of any tax, rate or duty'.

The federal legislature was established under section 36 of the Constitution which provided that 'there shall be a Parliament of the Federation, which shall consist of Her Majesty, a Senate and a House of Representatives'. Exercise of legislative power was by both chambers of parliament as provided by section 57 while under subsection (2) of section 57, a restriction was placed on the Senate in its exercise of legislative power regarding bills of a monetary nature. The subsection provided that 'A bill other than a money bill may originate in either House of Parliament but a money bill may originate only in the House of Representatives'. Further, section 58 (1) (a) (i) and (2) (a) (i) provided that:

(1) The Senate shall not:

    (a) proceed upon any bill, other than a bill sent from the House of Representatives, that, in the opinion of the person presiding, makes provision for any of the following purposes:

    (i) for the imposition, repeal or alteration of taxation

(2) Except upon the recommendation of the Governor-General signified by a Minister of the Government of the Federation, the House of Representatives shall not:

    (a) proceed upon any bill (including any amendment to a bill) that, in the opinion of the person presiding, makes provision for any of the following purposes:

    (i) for the imposition of taxation or the alteration of taxation otherwise than by reduction.

The effect of section 58 was that the legislature could not initiate a tax bill or an amendment to a tax bill, save for the purpose of reduction. Any other proposal of a tax bill had to come from the Executive arm and could only be introduced at the House of Representatives. Section 64 (1) (a) re-echoed the provisions of section 10 (1) of the Nigeria (Constitution) Order-in-Council to the extent that the Parliament had power to make laws:

for the peace, order and good government of Nigeria (other than the Federal territory) or any part thereof with respect to any matter included in the Legislative Lists; and (b) for the peace, order and good government of the Federal territory with respect to any matter, whether or not it is included in the Legislative Lists.

Under subsection (5) the legislature of a region could also make laws with respect to any matter not included in the Exclusive Legislative Lists, but by subsection (4) where a law enacted by a regional legislature was inconsistent with that of Parliament, the law enacted by Parliament prevailed and to the extent of its inconsistency, the regional law was null and void.

Section 70 expressly defined the taxing powers of the Parliament regarding income and profits. The section provided thus:

(1)      Parliament may make laws for Nigeria or any part thereof with respect to taxes on income and profits other than the income and profits of companies for the purpose of:

    (a)      implementing any treaty, convention or agreement between the Federation and other country or any arrangement with or decision of an international organization of which the Federation is a member with respect to taxes on income and profits;

    (b)      securing uniform principles for the taxation of income and profits accruing to persons in Nigeria from countries other than Nigeria and of income and profits derived from Nigeria by persons outside Nigeria;

    (c)      securing uniform principles for the computation of income and profits of all persons (including members of partnerships) for purposes of assessment of tax and for the treatment of losses, depreciation of assets and contributions to pension or provident funds or schemes;

    (d)      regulating the liability to tax of persons within Nigeria by reference to their places of residence or otherwise for the purpose of ensuring that any income or profit does not bear tax under the laws of more than one territory;

    (e)      providing, in pursuance of any arrangement in that behalf subsisting between the Government of the Federation and the Government of a Region, for the exemption from liability to tax in respect of all or part of the income or profits of any person or class of persons;

(f)     obtaining information with respect to income or profits from any source and providing for the exchange of information between different tax authorities; and

(g)     providing, in pursuance of any arrangement in that behalf subsisting between the Government of the Federation and the Government of a Region, for the establishment and regulation of authorities empowered to promote uniformity of taxation and to discharge such other functions relating to the taxation of income and profits as may be conferred upon them in pursuance of any such agreement.

(2)     Parliament may make laws for Nigeria or any part thereof with respect to taxes on the estates of deceased persons and the succession to their property for the purpose of ensuring that any estate or part thereof does not bear tax under the laws of more than one territory.

(3)     The powers conferred upon Parliament by sub-sections (2) and (3) of this section shall not extend to the imposition of any tax or penalty or the prescribing of rates of tax or personal allowances and reliefs.

(4)     Nothing in subsections (2) and (3) of this section shall preclude the legislature of a Region from making laws with respect to the matters referred to in those sub-sections.

Under subsection (6) companies were defined to exclude:

(a)     A corporation established by or under the Native Authority Law 1954 of Northern Nigeria, the Western Regional Local Government Law, 1952, or the Local Government Law 1957, of Western Nigeria or the Eastern Region Local Government Law 1960 as amended or any law replacing them.

(b)     A purchasing authority established by the legislature of a Region and empowered to acquire any commodity in that Region for export from Nigeria derived from the purchase and sale (whether for purposes of export or otherwise) of that commodity; or

(c) A corporation established by the legislature of a Region for the purpose of fostering the economic development of that Region, provided its income is not derived from profits from a trade or business carried on by it or a share or other interest possessed by it in a trade or business in Nigeria carried on by some other person or authority.

Section 76 empowered Parliament to exempt persons from tax liability with respect to mining or matters connected therewith, matters not included in the Legislative Lists and for the purpose of implementing any agreement between the government of the federation and any person. The proviso to the section however made consultation between the federal government and the regional government a precondition. The section provided:

Parliament may, for the purpose of implementing any agreement between the Government of the Federation and any person relating to mining or matters connected therewith, provide for exempting that person in whole or in part from liability for any tax or rate imposed by or under a law enacted by the legislature of a Region with respect to any matter not included in the Legislative Lists:

Provided that no person shall be granted any exemption in pursuance of this section without prior consultation between the Government of the Federation and the Government of the Region concerned.

Sections 130 to 133 contained provisions on how import, export and excise duties on commodities should be treated by detailing the accounts into which they shall be paid, as well as the manner of their sharing between the federal government and the regions. Section 134 made provisions as to the sharing of mining royalties and rents between the federal government and the regions.

The Legislative Lists were contained in Parts I and II to the Schedule. Part I contained the Exclusive Legislative List while Part II contained the Concurrent Legislative List. Custom duties, including excise and export duties were listed as item 10 on the Exclusive List. Taxes on amounts paid or payable on the sale of commodities (except produce, hides and skins, motor spirit, diesel oil sold or purchased for use in road vehicles, diesel oil sold or purchased for other industrial purposes) were listed as item 38 on the Exclusive Legislative List. Further, any matter incidental or supplementary to anything listed under the Exclusive List was also within the legislative competence of Parliament. Under item 27 of the Concurrent List, the regional legislatures also had legislative competence over matters contained in subsections (2) and (3) of Section 70. This was consistent with Section 70 (5).

### The Regional Constitutions

*Northern Region*

The relevant sections were sections 4, 26, 27 and 30 of the Constitution of Northern Nigeria 1960. Section 4 established the legislature for the region consisting of Her Majesty, a House of Chiefs and a House of Assembly and vested it with powers to make laws for the peace, order and good government of the region. Section 26 (1) provided that the mode of exercising the legislative power of the legislature of the northern region shall be by bills passed by both legislative houses. While a bill could originate in any of the two chambers of the legislature, a money bill could originate only in the House of Assembly but not in the House of Chiefs of the Region. Section 30 (a) defined 'money bill' to mean a bill that in the opinion of the Speaker contains only provisions dealing, *inter alia*, with 'the imposition, repeal, remission, alteration or regulation of taxation'. Furthermore, section 27 (1) (a) (i) and (2) (a) (i) provided that:

(1) The House of Chiefs shall not
   (a) proceed upon any bill, other than a bill sent from the House of Assembly, that, in the opinion of the person presiding, makes provision for any of the following purposes:
   (i) for the imposition, repeal or alteration of taxation;

(2) Except upon the recommendation of the Governor signified by a Minister of the Government of the Region, the House of Assembly shall not
   (a) proceed upon any bill (including any amendment to a bill) that, in the opinion of the person presiding, makes provision for any of the following purposes:

(i) for the imposition of taxation or the alteration of taxation
otherwise than by reduction

These provisions simply reflected at the regional level the nature of legislative relations obtained at the federal level between the Senate and the House of Representatives.

*Western Region*

Section 4 of the Constitution of Western Nigeria 1960 established the legislature of the western region, comprising of a House of Chiefs and a House of Assembly *"to make laws for the peace, order and good government of the Region"*. Section 25 empowered the legislature to exercise its legislative powers through bills passed and assented to it by the governor on behalf of Her Majesty. Under section 25 (2) a money bill could only originate in the House of Assembly, and section 26 (1) (a) (i) prohibited the House of Chiefs from proceeding on any bill which, *inter alia*, imposed, repealed or altered taxation, except if such a bill emanated from the House of Assembly. Subsection (2) (a) (i) of section 26 prohibited the House of Assembly from proceeding on any bill that, inter alia, imposed, repealed or altered taxation other than by way of reduction, except if such a bill was introduced by the governor and so signified by a minister of the regional government. Section 29 defined a money bill to include, *inter alia*, 'the imposition, repeal, remission, alteration or regulation of taxation'.

*Eastern and Mid-Western Regions*

Sections 4, 25, 26 and 29 of the Constitution of Eastern Nigeria 1960, and sections 4, 25, 26 and 29 of the later Constitution of Mid-Western Nigeria 1964 (which was enacted by the federal parliament upon the creation of the mid-western region in 1964) were all *in pari materia* with sections 4, 25, 26 and 29 of the Constitution of Western Nigeria.

### Republican Constitution 1963

The relevant taxing provisions under the 1963 Constitution were contained in sections 62, 63, 76, 136, 137, 138, 139, and 142 as well as items 10 and 38 of Part I to the Schedule and finally, item 28 of Part II to the Schedule. Section 62 provided for the general powers of parliament to make laws. Parliament itself was established by section 41 of the constitution and consisted of 'the President, a Senate and a House of Representatives.' Under section 63 (1) (a) the Senate, among other things, could not consider a bill for the imposition, repeal or alteration of taxation except where such a bill emanated from the House of Representatives. In other words, the Senate did not have jurisdiction to initiate tax bills just like under the

1960 Constitution. Similarly, section 63 (2) restricted the power of the House of Representatives from initiating a bill that imposed or altered taxes except by way of reduction, unless upon the recommendation of the President through a minister. The implication being that the House of Representatives could only initiate tax bills that sought a reduction in tax liability. In any other case of tax legislation, such a bill had to originate from the President.

Section 76 (1) empowered the parliament to make laws for the taxation of income and profits of companies. Subsection (2) of the same section further empowered parliament to tax income and profits other than those of companies for the purposes of:

a.      implementing a multilateral or bilateral agreement

b.      securing uniform principles for the taxation of income and profits accruing to persons in Nigeria from other countries, and income and profits derived from Nigeria by persons outside Nigeria

c.      securing uniform principles for the computation of income and profits of persons for the purposes of tax assessment, treatment of losses, depreciation of assets, and contributions to pension or provident funds and schemes

d.      regulating the liability of persons in Nigeria regarding their places of residence to avoid tax liability under the laws of more than one territory

e.      implementing a subsisting agreement between the federal government and any of the regional governments regarding exemption from liability in respect of all or part of the income or profits of any person or class of persons

f.      obtaining information with respect to income or profits from any source and providing for the exchange of information between different tax authorities

g.      providing for the establishment and regulation of authorities empowered to promote uniformity of taxation and to discharge other functions relating to the taxation of income and profits as may be conferred on them in pursuance of an arrangement between the federal government and regional governments

Section 76 (3) empowered parliament to make laws with respect to taxes on estates of deceased persons and succession to their property to prevent tax liability accruing on them under more than one jurisdiction. Subsection (4) provided that the powers of parliament under subsections (2) and (3) did not extend to the imposition of any tax or penalty or the prescribing of rates of tax or personal allowances and reliefs. Subsection (5) empowered the regional legislatures to make laws on the matters contained in subsections (2) and (3). Finally subsection (6) defined income and profits of companies to exclude the income or profits of corporation sole, corporations established under the native or local government laws of the regions, purchasing authority established pursuant to a law of a regional legislature and empowered to acquire any commodity from that region for export or any corporation established by a regional legislature for the purpose of fostering economic development of that region.

Part 1 of the Schedule to the constitution contained the Exclusive Legislative List and item 10 thereto placed customs, excise and export duties within the exclusive legislative competence of the federal government. Similarly, under item 38 taxes on amounts paid or payable on the sale or purchase of commodities apart from produce, hides and skin, motor spirit, diesel oil sold/purchased for use in road vehicles and diesel oil sold/purchased for other than industrial purposes were within the competence of the federal parliament. By virtue of item 28 of Part II to the Schedule, the matters contained in Section 76 subsections (2) and (3) were on the Concurrent Legislative List.

### The 1979 Constitution

Section 4 of the 1979 Constitution provided that:

(1)   The legislative powers of the Federal Republic of Nigeria shall be vested in a National Assembly for the Federation which shall consist of a Senate and a House of Representatives.

(2)   The National Assembly shall have power to make laws for the peace, order and good government of the Federation or any part thereof with respect to any matter included in the Exclusive Legislative List set out in Part I of the Second Schedule to this Constitution.

Subsection (3) of section 4 vested exclusive jurisdiction in the National Assembly with regards to matters contained on the Exclusive Legislative List which was Part I to the Second Schedule to the Constitution. Section 4 (6) vested legislative powers of a State in the House of Assembly of each State and by subsection (5) any law passed by a State House of Assembly which was inconsistent with an Act of the National Assembly was to be null and void to the extent of its inconsistency. By subsections (4) (a) and (7) (b) both the National Assembly and the States Houses of Assembly could make laws on the matters on the Concurrent Legislative List which was Part II to the Second Schedule to the Constitution. Customs, excise and export duties were listed as items 15 and 22 under the Exclusive Legislative List. Also, stamp duties, taxation of incomes, profits and capital gains were listed on the Exclusive Legislative List under items 57 and 58. Items 7, 8, 9 and 10 of Part II of the Second Schedule (Concurrent List) provided that:

7.  In the exercise of its powers to impose any tax or duty on:
    (a) capital gains, incomes or profits of persons other than companies; and

    (b) documents or transactions by way of stamp duties, the National Assembly may, subject to such conditions as it may prescribe, provide that the collection of any such tax or duty or the administration of the law imposing it shall be carried out by the Government of a State or other authority of a State.

8.  Where an Act of the National Assembly provides for the collection of tax or duty on capital gains, incomes or profit or the administration of any law by an authority of a State in accordance with paragraph 7 hereof, it shall regulate the liability of persons to such tax or duty in such a manner as to ensure that such tax or duty is not levied on the same person by more than one State.

9.  A House of Assembly may, subject to such conditions as it may prescribe, make provisions for the collection of any tax, fee or rate or for the administration of the Law providing for such collection by a local government council.

10. Where a Law of a House of Assembly provides for the collection of tax, fee or rate or for the administration of such Law by a local government council in accordance with the provisions hereof it shall regulate the liability of persons to the tax, fee or rate in such a manner as to ensure that such tax, fee or rate is not levied on the same person in respect of the same liability by more than one local government council.

Section 150 provided for allocation of tax revenue among the tiers of government on the basis of derivation. The section provided that:

> Where under an Act of the National Assembly, tax or duty is imposed in respect of any of the matters specified in item D of Part II of the Second Schedule to this Constitution, the net proceeds of such tax or duty shall be distributed among the States on the basis of derivation; and accordingly:
>
> (a) where such tax or duty is collected by the Government of a State or other authority of the State, the net proceeds shall be treated as part of the Consolidated Revenue Fund of that State.
>
> (b) where such tax or duty is collected by the Government of the Federation or other authority of the Federation, there shall be paid to each State at such times as the National Assembly may prescribe a sum equal to the proportion of the net proceeds of such tax or duty that are derived from that State.

Under section 152, the States were required to pay to the federal government the cost of collecting tax revenue in proportion to the share of the proceeds received by the States in that financial year. The section provided thus:

> Each State shall in respect of each financial year pay to the Federation an amount equal to such part of the expenditure incurred by the Federation during that financial year for the purpose of collection of taxes or duties which are wholly or partly payable to the State pursuant to the provisions of this Chapter or of any Act of the National Assembly as is proportionate to the share of the proceeds of those taxes or duties received by the State in respect of that financial year.

The Fourth Schedule to the constitution listed the functions of local governments in section 1 to include, *inter alia*, collection of rates, radio and television licences, licensing of bicycles, trucks (other than mechanically propelled trucks), canoes, wheel barrows and carts, assessment of privately owned houses or tenements for the purpose of levying such rates as may be prescribed by the House of Assembly of a State. Section 2 (d) also extended the functions of the local government to include 'such other functions as may be conferred on a local government council by the House of Assembly of the State'. This provision was consistent with items 9 and 10 of Part II to the Second Schedule.

### The 1999 Constitution

The relevant provisions under the 1999 Constitution of the Federal Republic of Nigeria[18] are contained in sections 4, 24 (f), 163, 165, 173 (4) and Parts I and II to the Second Schedule. Section 4 (1) vests the legislative powers of the Federal Republic in the National Assembly which shall consist of a Senate and a House of Representatives and under subsections (2) and (3):

(2)  The National Assembly shall have power to make laws for the peace, order and good government of the Federation or any part thereof with respect to any matter included in the Exclusive Legislative List set out in Part I of the Second Schedule to this Constitution.

(3)  The power of the National Assembly to make laws for the peace, order and good government of the Federation with respect to any matter included in the Exclusive Legislative List shall, save as otherwise provided in this Constitution, be to the exclusion of the Houses of Assembly of States.

Similarly, by virtue of subsection (7) the 36 State Houses of Assembly are vested with legislative powers in respect of matters contained on the Concurrent Legislative List as well as those on the Residual Legislative List.[19] Furthermore, by virtue of the provisions of subsection (5), where any law enacted by a State House of Assembly is inconsistent with a law made by the National Assembly, the law made by the National Assembly shall prevail and the law made by the State House of Assembly shall be null and void to the extent of its inconsistency.

Section 24 (f) makes prompt payment of taxes a duty of every citizen of the Federal Republic. The section provides as follows:

It shall be the duty of every citizen to:

(f) declare his income honestly to appropriate and lawful agencies and pay his tax promptly.

Section 163 provides for the treatment of tax revenue where such revenue is collected by the agent of the States pursuant to authority conferred on the agent of the State by the Federal Government; while section 165 requires the States to pay to the Federation the cost of revenue collection where the revenue so shared was collected by an agent of the Federation. The sections provide as follows:

163. Where under an Act of the National Assembly, tax or duty is imposed in respect of any of the matters specified in item D of Part II of the Second Schedule to this Constitution, the next proceeds of such tax or duty shall be distributed among the States on the basis of derivation and accordingly:

(a) where such tax or duty is collected by the Government of a State or authority of a State, the net proceeds shall be treated as part of the Consolidated Revenue Fund of that State;

(b) where such tax or duty is collected by the Government of the federation or other authority of the Federation, there shall be paid to each State at such times as the National Assembly may prescribe a sum equal to the proportion of such tax or duty that are derived from the State.

165. Each State shall, in respect of each financial year, pay to the Federation an amount equal to such part of the expenditure incurred by the Federation during that financial year for the purpose of collection of taxes or duties which are wholly or partly payable to the State pursuant to the provisions of this Part of this Chapter or of any Act of the National Assembly as is proportionate to the proceeds of those taxes or duties received by the State in respect of that financial year.

Section 173 (4) provides that 'pensions in respect of service in the public service of the Federation shall not be taxed'.

Deriving from the provisions of section 4 (1)–(7), Part I of the Second Schedule to the Constitution (i.e. the Exclusive Legislative List) sets out the items in respect of which only the Government of the Federation may exercise legislative jurisdiction. The tax jurisdiction of the federal government under the List include *customs and excise*: item 15, *export duties*: item 25, *stamp duties*: item 58 and *taxation of incomes, profits and capital gains, except as otherwise prescribed by the Constitution*: item 59. There are no items specifically conferred on the States in respect of which they may exercise tax jurisdiction. However, item 7 of Part II to the Second Schedule (i.e. the Concurrent Legislative List) provides:

> In the exercise of its powers to impose any tax or duty on:
> (a) capital gains, incomes or profits of persons other than companies; and
> (b) documents or transactions by way of stamp duties,
> the National Assembly may, subject to such conditions as it may prescribe, provide that the collection of any such tax or duty or the administration of the law imposing it shall be carried out by the Government of a State or authority of a State.

The above provisions are further enhanced by the provisions of items 8, 9 and 10 of Part II to the Second Schedule. The items provide thus:

8.      Where an Act of the National Assembly provides for the collection of tax or duty on capital gains, incomes or profit or the administration of any law by an authority of a State in accordance with paragraph 7 hereof, it shall regulate the liability of persons to such tax or duty in such manner as to ensure that such tax or duty is not levied on the same person by more than one State.

9.      A House of Assembly may, subject to such conditions as it may prescribe, make provisions for the collection of any tax, fee or rate or for the administration of the Law providing for such collection by a local government council.

10.      Where a Law of a House of Assembly provides for the collection of tax, fee or rate or for the administration of such Law by a local government council in accordance with the provisions hereof it shall

regulate the liability of persons to the tax, fee or rate in such a manner as to ensure that such tax, fee or rate is not levied on the same person in respect of the same liability by more than one local government council.

The combined effect of items 58 and 59 of the Exclusive Legislative List; items 7 and 8 of the Concurrent Legislative List; and section 4 (2) to (7), is that although through an Act of the National Assembly, the States may administer stamp duties, personal income tax and capital gains, only the National Assembly can make legislation on the regulation of these taxes. This situation has generated intense public debate on the regulation and administration of stamp duties, taxation of incomes and capital gains. Some commentators argue that in the light of the foregoing constitutional provisions, States administer stamp duties, incomes, and capital gains as agents of the federal government.[20] Other commentators have however, taken the view that in the light of the caution *"except as otherwise prescribed by this Constitution"* contained in item 59 of Part I to the Second Schedule which caution is re-echoed in Section 4 (3) of the constitution, it is obvious that *"the Constitution never intended to give complete and unabridged jurisdiction to the National Assembly over the taxation of incomes and profits, capital gains or stamp duty."*[21]

Be that as it may, while the tax jurisdiction of the federal government is expressly provided for in items 15, 22, 57 and 58 the tax jurisdiction of the States is implied from the provisions of Section 4 (7) and items 7, 8, 9 and 10 of Part II of the Second Schedule. Consequently, in line with item 7 of Part II to the Second Schedule, the States have jurisdiction to administer stamp duties (individuals), capital gains (individuals) and personal income tax having been so enabled by an Act of the federal government. That is not to suggest that the States do not possess tax jurisdiction outside what has been *delegated* to them by the federal government. By the wording of items 9 and 10 of Part II to the Second Schedule, States have *residual* tax jurisdiction in exercise whereof, the States may delegate some of its powers to the local governments. The residual tax jurisdiction of the States was also recognised by Bello, JSC (as he then was) in *Aberuagba v. Attorney General of Ogun State*.[22] Also, commenting on the subject of division of tax powers between the federal government and the States, Akanle submits:

...the enumeration of certain taxes as being within exclusive federal competence cannot be construed as a power over the whole subject of taxation throughout Nigeria. Similarly, the express mention of certain taxes in the Constitution does not mean that the whole field of taxation has been exhausted or that for any tax to be valid, it must be capable of being brought within the scope of the enumerated ones. For as has been rightly pointed out, the federal power of taxation should not be exercised to inhibit the exercise of State taxation power.[23]

The 1999 Constitution also lists the functions of a local government in the Fourth Schedule to the Constitution. The functions are in *pari materia* with the functions of a local government under the 1979 Constitution. The only addition in the 1999 Constitution is the insertion of paragraph (vi) to section 1 of the Schedule which further empowers a local government in the *"licensing, regulation and control of the sale of liquor."*

## Conclusion

From 1914 when Nigeria came into being as a political entity to date, the country has had ten constitutional instruments  enacted in the following years: 1914, 1922, 1946, 1951, 1954, 1960, 1963, 1979, 1989 and 1999. With the exception of the 1989 draft constitution which never came into force, the other nine had had various life spans as dictated by political events in Nigeria's history. Prior to 1954, all taxing powers were vested in the government at the centre. The 1954 Lyttleton Constitution introduced federalism in Nigeria for the first time,[24] and with the devolution of fiscal powers under the Constitution, tax jurisdiction became vested in regional governments, a practice that has endured to date. Since the 1954 Constitution, the constitutional power to tax under our various Constitutions can be summarised as follows:[25]

1954:

|  |  |  |
|---|---|---|
| a. | Federation: | Import duties, export duties, excise, income tax of Africans living in the colony of Lagos, income tax of foreigners, company taxation, mining rents and mineral royalties. |
| b. | Regions: | Produce sales tax, purchase/sales tax on motor vehicle fuel, income tax on Africans living outside Lagos, licences, fees and rents. |

1960:

    a.      Federation:    Import duties, export duties, excise, general sales tax, income tax of Africans resident in Lagos, income tax of foreigners living in Lagos, company tax, mining rents and mineral royalties.

    b.      Regions:    Produce sales tax, purchase/sales tax on motor vehicle fuel, income tax on Africans outside Lagos, income tax on foreigners living outside Lagos, licenses, fees and rents.

1963:

    a.      Federation:    Import duties, export duties, excise, mining rents and royalties, petroleum profits tax, companies income tax, personal income tax and capital gains.

    b.      States:    Personal income tax (administration), sales and purchase tax on produce and other commodities, entertainment tax, cattle tax, pools and betting tax, capital gains (administration), motor vehicle tax and licensing fees.

1979:

    a.      Federation:    Import duties, export duties, excise, mining rents and royalties, petroleum profits tax, companies income tax, capital gains, stamp duties, personal income tax.

    b.      States:    Sales or purchase tax, pools and betting, entertainment tax, estate duties, gift tax, land tax other than agricultural land, land registration fees, capital gains (administration), personal income tax (administration), stamp duties (administration).

    c.      Local Government: Property tax, marketing and trading licences and fees, motor park duties, entertainment tax, licensing fees (of bicycles, non - mechanically propelled trucks, canoes, wheelbarrows, carts) and liquor licences.

1999:

    a.      Federation:    Import duties, export duties, excise, mining rents and royalties, petroleum profits tax, companies income tax, capital gains, stamp duties, personal income tax.

b.    States: Sales or purchase tax, pools and betting, entertainment tax, estate duties, gift tax, land tax other than agricultural land, land registration fees, capital gains (administration), personal income tax (administration), stamp duties (administration).

c.    Local Government: Property tax, marketing and trading licences and fees, motor park duties, entertainment tax, motor vehicle and licensing fees and liquor licences.

It is pertinent to note that the intervention of the military into politics did not derogate substantially from the tax jurisdiction of the various tiers of government as constitutionally guaranteed, the reason being that the constitutional provisions empowering the various tiers of government to administer tax did not form part of the provisions of the Constitutions which successive military regimes traditionally suspended.

# References

1    Soyode, L. & Kajola, S., *Taxation: Principles and Practice in Nigeria.* (Ibadan: Silicon Publishing Co., 2006) 3.

2    (1938) 60 CLR 263, 276.

3    Ayua, I. A., *Nigerian Tax Law* (Ibadan: Spectrum Law Publishing, 1996) 4.

4    Soyode, L. & Kajola, S., *op. cit.*

5    Emmanuel, M., 'Accountability will Raise Tax Compliance Level', *Financial Standard* 22 November 2007, 12.

6    Ayua, I. A., *op. cit*, 11 – 12.

7    See *History of FIRS*. Available at http://www.firs.gov.ng/aboutus/tax_history.aspx (accessed 29/12/2009).

8    Being an address of Babatunde Raji Fashola, SAN, Governor of Lagos State at the Stakeholders Conference on Taxation, 3 December 2007, *Saturday Punch*, 8 December 2007, 56 – 57.

9    Akanle, O., *The Power to Tax and Federalism in Nigeria: Legal and Constitutional Perspective on the Sources of Government Revenue* (Lagos: Centre for Business and Investment Studies, 1988) 1.

10    Smith, A., *An Enquiry into the Nature and Causes of the Wealth of Nations* (1776) 679 – 677. Available at http://www2.hn.psu.edu/faculty/jmanis/adam-smith/Wealth-Nations.pdf (accessed 2/11/2011).

11    *Ibid.*

12    Nwabueze, B. O., *A Constitutional History of Nigeria* (London: C. Hurst & Co., 1982) 16 – 18.

13    These were respectively, the *Native Revenue (Amendment) Ordinance No.29, 1918* and the *Native Revenue (Amendment) Ordinance No.17, 1927.*

14    Nwabueze, *op. cit,* 40.

15    Official members were those appointed by the governor directly.

16    Nwabueze, *op. cit,* 43 - 44.

17    *Ibid*, 46.

18    Hereafter referred to as CFRN 1999.

19    The Residual Legislative List is not a list *per se* in the nature of the Exclusive and Concurrent Legislative Lists. It consists of those functions neither specifically mentioned nor included in the Exclusive or Concurrent List. By virtue of the provisions of section 8 and the Fourth Schedule of CFRN 1999, the power to give effect to this list is vested in the State. See the judgement of the Supreme Court in *Attorney General of Abia State & 35 Ors. v. Attorney General of the Federation* (SC 3/2002); judgement delivered on Thursday, the 28 March 2002.

20    Omoigui, I., 'State Governments, Internally Generated Revenue and Sustainable Development', *Financial Standard,* 8 November, 2007, 41.

21    See *Saturday Punch, op. cit.*

22    [1985]1 NWLR (Pt. 3) 395 at 413.

23    Akanle,O., *Nigerian Income Tax Law and Practice*, 57.

24    Odumosu, O. I., *The Nigerian Constitution: History and Development* (London: Sweet & Maxwell, 1963).

25    *Ibid*, 65 – 72.

# CHAPTER THREE

## THE THREE ERAS OF TAXATION IN NIGERIA

### General Historical Overview of Taxation

Taxes are as old as the history of organised human society. During the reign of the Pharaohs in Egypt tax collectors were called *scribes* and taxes were collected on various items including cooking oil.[1] In the ancient Greek city of Athens, taxes were especially important in times of war. The tax imposed during times of war was known as *eisphora* and no one was exempted from this tax. After the war, when additional resources were gained, the *eisphora* tax was refunded to the taxpayers. Aside this tax, the Athenians imposed a monthly poll tax called *metoikion* on foreigners.[2]

In ancient Rome, the earliest taxes were called *portoria*. These were custom duties on imports and exports. During the reign of Caesar Augustus, several tax reforms were carried out by the Roman government. These included replacing the *publicani* (tax collectors) with city councils as tax collectors, imposing a 5% inheritance tax to provide retirement funds for the military and a 1% sales tax on every item except sale of slaves which attracted a 4% tax rate.[3]

In England the first known tax assessment was during the Roman occupation which began in the year 43 AD with the invasion of Britain by the Roman Emperor, Claudius I and ended about 410 AD.[4] After the collapse of the Roman Empire, the Saxon Kings imposed various types of taxes such as *danegeld* (land tax), *scutage* (a tax paid in lieu of serving in the army) *carucate* (another land tax that replaced *danegeld* and was collected only on plowed land).[5] Most of these taxes were either replaced or modified following the Norman conquest of England in 1066. The first law on income tax was passed by the English Parliament in 1404 and the first deduction of income tax at source was done in 1512.[6]

The point has been made in the preceeding chapter that the various pre-colonial Nigerian empires practiced various forms of taxation. In the northern territories, these included the *zakat* which was charitable tax levied on Muslims for religious and educational purposes, the *kurdin kasa* which was an agricultural tax and the *jangali* which was a cattle tax levied on livestock.[7] In the Yoruba states of southwestern Nigeria, pre-colonial taxes included the *owo-onibode*, a border fee similar to customs duty that was imposed on cross border trade; the tribute tax and capitation tax that were administered by the *Bales* (ward heads) on behalf of the *Obas,* just to mention a few.[8] The Benin Kingdom also had an advance system of taxation which the British found upon their arrival at the close of the 19th century. In 1897, for example, the British Consul-General at Calabar directed the Political Resident in Benin to the effect that in assessing the people for tax purposes, the Resident should take into consideration the basis of assessment which the Edo people were formerly called upon to pay to the *Oba* of Benin, and ensure that the assessment by the Resident was carried out with more fairness.[9]

Following the expansion of the British Empire and the establishment of colonies abroad, Britain either introduced taxation into her colonies or modified the existing systems to suit British imperial interests. In the American colonies for example, colonists were paying taxes under the Molasses Act which was amended as the Sugar Act in 1764 to include import duties on sugar, wine and other commodities. These were subsequently followed by the short-lived Stamp Act 1765 which was the first case of direct taxation of the American colonies. In the case of Nigeria, the British introduced direct taxes first in the north in 1906, in the west in 1918 and the east in 1927.[10] The introduction of taxation in eastern Nigeria sparked off rebellions reminiscent of the Stamp Act rebellion in the American colonies, prompting the colonial government to set up a number of Commissions to look into the revolts.[11]

This chapter discusses the evolution of taxation through the three major stages of Nigeria's history: pre-colonial; colonial and post colonial.

## TAXATION IN THE PRE-COLONIAL ERA

### The Hausa City States

The Hausa people are a powerful cultural and political group in Nigeria. One tradition holds that Hausaland was founded by *Abuyazigu*, sometimes also called *Bayajida* who was said to have fled from Baghdad following a quarrel with his father.[12] Beginning from the eleventh century, seven independent Hausa city states were founded in Northern Nigeria namely, Biram, Daura, Gobir, Kano, Katsina, Zaria and Rano. These seven city states developed as strong trading centres; with economies based on intensive farming, cattle rearing, craft making and later slave trading. Kano and Katsina competed for the lucrative trans-Saharan trade with Kanem Borno, and for a time had to pay tribute to it. The Kano Chronicle relates that the first king of Kano was *Bagauda* (999-1063) and that the city walls for which Kano is so famous were started in the reign of *Bagauda's* son, *Gayamusa*. The walls took a very long time to build and they were not completed until the reign of the fifth king of Kano, Yusa 1136-94.[13] As at 1000 AD, Kano had already developed into a strong and prosperous trading centre, as a result of the trans-Saharan trade. By the 15th century Kano, Zaria, Katsina and Sokoto had grown into great centres of commerce.[14]

Various forms of taxes were developed through this period of rapid economic developments. These included the *gandu,* an agricultural tax levied on one - eighth of every farmers crop which was introduced during the reign of *Naguji* who succeeded *Yusa* as the sixth king of Kano;[15] the *zakkat,* a type of taxation prescribed by the Holy Koran and levied on Moslems for charitable, religious and educational purposes; the *kudin-kasa* or land tax; the *Jangali* or cattle tax. In addition there was a plantation tax called *shukka-shukka* and *kudin sarauta,* an accession duty paid by every chief or holder of an office upon appointment. Finally, there was *gado,* a death duty on a deceased's estate paid to the Emir when there was no recognized or proven heir.

## The Kanem Borno Empire

The Kanem kingdom emerged east of Lake Chad (in present South-western Chad) by around the 9th century AD. Kanem profited from trade ties with North Africa and the Nile Valley, from which it also received Islam. The *Saifawas*, the Kanem's ruling dynasty, periodically enlarge their holdings and territories by conquest and marriage into the ruling families of vassal states. The empire, however, failed to sustain a lasting peace such that between the 12th and 14th centuries, the *Saifawas* were forced to move across Lake Chad into Borno, in present day Northeastern Nigeria.[16] There, the Kanem intermarried with the native peoples, and the new group became known as the Kanuri. The Kanuri State which first centered in Kanem and later moved to Borno, is known by historians as the Kanem-Borno Empire.

The pre-Kanuri inhabitants of Borno were sedentary agriculturalists who supplemented their diet by hunting, fishing and gathering. They practiced agriculture but they contained a considerable nomadic element. Their economic way of life was filled by new pastoral groups-

*fulani* from the west and north-west, *Tubu* from the north and north east and later *Shuwa* Arabs from the east.[17] The camel-owning pastoralists played an important military and economic role in the kingdom providing transport for raid and trade. The fertile soil left by drying lake brought about the immigration of desert dwellers to make their fortune. The desert dwellers were the *Kanuri, Teda*, and the *Zaghawa*. Kanem-Borno was ruled by different rulers who fought and conquered kingdoms to expand their territory. Some of these rulers were *Sayf Dbi Yazan* (1085-97), *Dunama Dibbalemi* 1 and 2, *Ali Ghaji* and *Idris Alooma*. The vast area of Borno over which the empires held its sway is today divided between the Republic of Niger, Chad, Cameroon and Nigeria. Its boundaries coincide to a considerable extent with the boundaries of the Chad basin.

In the 19th century, irrigated farms worked by slaves were farmed along the river banks to provide the courtiers of *Kukawa* (Chadians) with fruits and vegetables. Just as trade must have played a vital role in the growth of the state, so the powerful unified state in turn attracted trade. Agricultural products were generally consumed locally. But trade in grains and dried fish was carried on, supplying the needs of the larger cities and of the people of the desert fringe.[18] Whereas under the *Saifawa dynasty*, succession to fiefs was hereditary, under the *Kanemi* dynasty, the *Chima* (chiefs) held their fiefs simply at the pleasure of the reigning *Shehu*, and such holdings were liable to sequestration (in whole or part) and re-allocation on the slightest pretexts.[19]

By 1830, in addition to trade, an impressive tax system had developed in Kanem Borno, providing a steady source of income to the emirate. Basic to the many taxes and dues in Borno system of taxation was the Islamic *Zakkat*, which in Borno was known as *Sada'a*. The *sada'a*, as an income tax was obligatory on all Muslims. The collection of the *sada'a* was restricted to *Zahir* possessions (i.e. visible articles) and more specifically to farm produce; so much so that it degenerated to nothing more than a grain tax.[20] Every state that was conquered had a resident appointed by the *Mai* (ruler) who made sure they paid their tribute. There was the *Kasasairam* tax, collected from the nomadic group of Borno as grazing fee similar to the *sheede hudo* paid by the Fulani. Another tax was the *hakki binimram*. While the *Sada'a* was recognized as a religious tax, the *Hakki* was recognized distinctively as a secular tax[21] and was collected by the *Chima Kura* (land owners) in kind and in cash. The very word *Hakki* (Kanuri for tax or dues) is derived from the Arabic root word *Haqq* meaning obligation. The payment of *Hakki* normally became due during winter which made it to be called 'winter' tax. The currency used was *wuri* (cowries), *gabaga* (hand woven cloth) or Maria Theresa silver dollars.[22]

Another form of taxation in Borno was *Kaleram* or *Toloram* (both mean the same thing). The *Kaleram* was a fee whereby the peasant farmers obtained an indirect permission of the sovereign (*Shehu*) via the *Chima Kura* to till the land. The fee was however, charged on individual households rather than on the farm. The fee was a fixed one and was paid at a uniform rate irrespective of the number and size of farm belonging to a household. As a rule, the *toloram* was to be paid in hard currency (the Maria Theresa dollar).[23] In some situations, the tax collectors also accepted cowries, cloth or grains as the equivalent of the dollar. *Warata*, another form of tax was paid by deceased subjects to the Shehu. Theoretically, the Shehu had this right over all his subjects, but in practice however, the right was only invoked in cases where the deceased had left behind substantial property-in cash, kind or both.[24] The amount due to the Shehu out of the *warata* was known as *ushr* i.e. a tithe or one–tenth of property. It was normally collected and sent to the Shehu by a village *Alkali* who also acting in judicial capacity, divided the rest of the deceased's estate among his heirs according to the formula laid down by the Sharia.[25] Another form of tax was the *Kafelo* which could be approximated to an obligatory 'gift' by merchants to the ruler. By 1850, another tax called *hadiyya* was being levied. The tax was paid during the Muslim festivals of *Id-el-Kabir*, *Id-el-Fitr* and *Mawlud*, and on each of the three occasions, the amount of tribute (in goods and cash) was specified for each of the provinces according to their respective sizes and wealth.[26]

## The Yoruba States

### *Ife*

It is generally considered among the Yoruba people that Ile–Ife was the centre from which the whole world was created. Ife is also known as the centre of cultural and religious life. It tells of a period when the whole earth was covered with water and god sent his messengers to go and create farmland out of the liquid mass. According to this tradition, the party consisted of the leader, *Obatala* and sixteen *Oye* (mortals). They were given five pieces of iron and a lump of earth tied in a white piece of cloth. Somewhere on the way, *Obatala* got drunk with palm wine and *Oduduwa* seized the paraphernalia of authority from him and eventually led the delegation.[27] The site on which these messengers landed is traditionally identified as the *Oke Oramfe*, in Ife. From this episode the town probably took its name Ile-Ife (the land of spreading).[28]

As the 'father-kingdom' and 'national headquarters' of the Yoruba, Ile-Ife enjoyed a unique constitutional and historical status. It was surrounded by other Yoruba kingdoms that acknowledged its 'fatherhood' and as a result, Ife had no fear of attacks from any quarters. Ife, therefore did not possess an army and the *Orisa* of Ife were not known to be great military leaders. Instead Ile-Ife took its duties as "ritual father" kingdom very seriously. An elaborate chieftaincy system was developed to look after all the known national gods, create and worship more of such gods and bury the remains of the kings brought back from their distant domains. Another notable development in Ife was art. Various objects were made in wood, stone and bronze. The bronze figures were made through the 'melted wax' process which was a technological advancement of the highest kind.[29]

The demand of the Islamic world for forest products and the resultant pull of trade towards the north were especially felt in the geographical belt between the Lower Niger and Dahomey.[30] Ife, situated in the centre of this belt obviously took advantage of the trade and generated revenue through trade tolls and levies.[31] Later there was an important trade route which crossed the Niger River and led northwards to the cities of the Hausa states.[32] In addition to trade tolls, Ife exported its artistic achievements and Benin became the most famous of those who learnt this artistic skill. Furthermore, Ife developed a system of annual levies, special contribution at specific festivals, fees, presents and bribes all collected through the heads of families. These sources provided revenues to the kings and chiefs relied on tributes, tolls and arbitrary levies for their revenues.

## Oyo

Oyo possessed the most organized military and political systems and also acquired the largest territories of all the Yoruba kingdoms, making it the strongest of them all. It emerged as a strong kingdom in the middle of the 16th century. At its height, the empire of Oyo covered a huge area bounded to the north by the Niger, to the east by Benin, to the west by the frontier of modern Togo and to the south by the mangrove swamps and lagoons that form a barrier between the sea and the interior.[33] The rich soil in Oyo allowed the people to grow more crops than they needed. This helped the kingdom of Oyo to easily trade with neighboring groups. The Yoruba kingdom of Oyo started its era of imperial expansion in the early years of the seventeenth century, when *Alafin Obalokun Agani Erin* installed the first *Ajele* (Resident) in *Ijana* of *Ebagdo* district.[34] The previous years witnessed military successes resulting in the expansion of the empire in terms of territory and population. Two advantages aided the economic growth of the empire. Firstly, the empire interacted as a unit of a league of big socio-economic and political systems consisting of the other Yoruba States and the Benin kingdom.[35] Secondly, the whole economic area had a uniform currency in cowry shells. In spite of the opinion held by some scholars that money economy was introduced to West Africa by the colonial rulers in the late nineteenth century, use of the cowry shell as money in Yoruba economic region predated the arrival of the colonialists.[36] To make the maximum use of these two advantages of a common language and a common currency, the Oyo Empire, along with its sister Yoruba States organized a highly complex market system linking up with the markets of their neighbours.[37] Each town or village had one or more markets depending on its size. The towns and various market sites were connected by equally efficient roads. Trade routes led in all directions and were well and regularly maintained. One very important route in Oyo was that leading from Ileto to Dahomey and from thence to Ajase (Porto Novo).[38] There was yet another equally ancient route from Oyo Ile to Badagry. It was established in the early years of the seventeenth century, when *Alafin Obalokun*, installed the first *Ajele* at Ijana.[39] These internal routes linked up with international ones. The routes to the coast also joined the trans-Atlantic sea route from about the beginning of the seventeenth century.[40] There was another route from Oyo to Kano. Yoruba traders who traveled on the various routes and used the different markets organized themselves into trade guilds. In each town, there were at least two guilds of general traders, the *egbe alajada* and the *egba alaroobo*.[41] Members of both guilds engaged in medium and long distance trading going round to other towns and villages to collect their articles for sale in the larger towns or in their own town markets.

In addition to these two guilds, there were the specialized guilds of traders and tradesmen. These were named after the particular items they traded in. There were for example, *egbe alaso* (guild of cloth traders), *egbe alaro* (guild of dyers), *egbe onisona* (guild of carvers).[42] Generally, trade consisted of farm and manufactured products, basic necessities and luxuries. Apart from the food crops, the farmers also grew cotton, silk, shea-nut, palm oil and kola nut. Iron smelting and iron industries were equally widespread and basic to most of the other industries.

From the extensive trade that went on in the kingdom, Oyo was able to generate substantial tax revenues. All traders that went into Oyo paid duties at the gates. *Oyo-Ile* had ten gates, each with a gate- keeper who had a large establishment.[43] Likewise every city in the empire, indeed in the whole of Yoruba land, had gates at which similar tolls were collected on all imports. The number of gates depended on the size of the town or how commercially central the town was. Some of the towns were under the supervision of the chiefs resident in the capital while others were directly responsible to the king. Annually, or at festival times, each town brought either directly or through its supervisory chief, its presents and levies. In addition, conquered provinces paid various forms of tributes. For example, between 1747 and 1820, in addition to other items of goods, Dahomey paid 800,000 cowries annually to Oyo.[44] Moreover, all the towns within the empire paid death duties on all their most important deceased citizens.

### Ibadan

The rise of Ibadan to the status of a great power in south-western Nigeria is one of the most important themes of nineteenth century history of Nigeria. Awe describes Ibadan a 'Republic of warriors' as Ibadan town was founded as a war camp in the 19th century.[45] Akinyele also opined that in Ibadan 'the leading enterprise was warfare; very few people were farmers, and the few were despised. Traders were few'.[46]

Although the political greatness and power of Ibadan in the nineteenth century was achieved mostly with arms, basic to this military strength was an economy which until 1877 was at least, adequate.[47] The most visible index of the rise of Ibadan was in terms of population growth. From a little village in 1827 Ibadan grew to a city of about 60,000 in 1852, and about 150,000 people in 1890. Partly contributing to this growth, and partly as a result of it, was a long series of successful wars which gradually expanded the political influence of Ibadan such that by 1877, she had become the centre of an empire comprising the whole of Ibadan and Ibariba Divisions, Oyo Division, Oshun, Ife and most of Ijesha, Ekiti, Akoko and Igbomina.[48]

Chieftaincy system comprised both a civil and a military segment with the *Bale* and the *Balogun* respectively at the top. In practice, military prowess determined the rise in chieftaincy hierarchy. There was no central army; rather each chief owned, maintained and led its army.[49]

In spite of Akinyele's observation above, Ibadan witnessed impressive growth in Agriculture. Indeed, what the statement means is that there were very few all-time farmers. The land tenure system grew directly from the whole social system, and conducive to full scale exploitation of the land. Every part of the farmland surrounding Ibadan was opened to all citizens, and each had 'a right to such land as he chose to occupy outside the walls, provided only that it be not already appropriated'.[50] In the nineteenth century, Ibadan was an exporter of food, especially to her Ijebu neighbours and through them to Lagos. Even during Ibadan's greatest wars, the town was plentifully supplied with these crops.[51] The demands of the thick population of Ibadan for local manufactures were naturally great, and consequently a large number of people earned living as weavers, dyers, tailors, blacksmiths, carpenters, tanners, leather-dressers, saddlers, potters and soap boilers, while others were employed in extracting palm oil and palm-nut oil.

Ibadan was not only the political, but also the commercial centre of a very large part of the Yoruba country, at least until about the middle of the nineteenth century. All the most important routes from further Yoruba hinterland converged on Ibadan. Of these, the most important were the routes through the Osun district to Ilorin, Igbomina and Ekiti, through Ife and Ijesa to Ekiti, Akoko, Owo and Benin.[52] Along these routes, Ibadan traders enjoyed much protection, as anybody who claimed even the faintest connection with an Ibadan chief was immediately inviolate in any part of the Ibadan Empire. Between Ibadan and the ports along the Atlantic seaboard, the chief routes passed through Egba and Ijebu territories. Of these the most important were the routes through Abeokuta to Lagos, Badagry and Porto Novo, and through Ijebu Remo to Lagos, other routes passed from Ibadan or towns under Ibadan through Oru and Ijebu-Ode to Lagos; from Apomu to Ijebu-Ode; and from Ile-Ife, Isoya, Ijebu-Igbo to Ijebu-Ode.[53]

The administration of these vast territories was made relatively easier because the communities were self-supporting. Each provincial community bore the maintenance of the *Ajele* and his troops of servants, messengers, attendants and hangers-on.[54] Each community paid regular tributes to Ibadan, mostly in cowries, pots of palm oil, and slaves. It is on record that in every town, 'a proportionate tax is levied on every house, which has to be paid every week or at farthest fortnight to the (local) king, who transmits it'.[55]

Colonial personnel recognised three distinct taxes being enforced in Ibadan and the whole of Yoruba land by the traditional institution. They were:

i.      *Ishakole:* which was a kind of universal land rent

ii.     *Owo ode:* a tribute paid by men and women alike, partly in cash and partly in kind. Half of this was sent to the paramount chief and half retained by the local chiefs. The tax was for the support of the chiefs and was in no way a religious impost. Tax defaulters were ordered to leave their land.

iii.    *Owo Asinghu:* consisted of personal service (such as building and repairing of town walls, working on the farm of chiefs, etc.) together with contributions of food.[56]

Each town had one of the chiefs in Ibadan as its *Babakekere* (small father or guardian) through whom the tributes had to be sent to the Ibadan Council. As the *Babakekere* was entitled to retain some portion of the tributes before transmitting them, his guardianship was a substantial source of wealth to him. To Ibadan, such tributes constituted a substantial central fund and in addition, whenever Ibadan went to war, each provincial town was obliged on request, to send contingents of troops and food to Ibadan.

## The Benin Kingdom

The word *Benin* was originally used broadly to cover the kingdom, the capital city, the empire, the language and its people.[57] The empire embraced both the Edo speaking people or the *Bini* proper and a large non-Edo speaking population. In describing the Benin kingdom, however a much smaller area bounded by Asaba and Ishan division on the east, Warri, western Urhobo and Aboh divisions in the South-east, Owo and Okiti-pupa divisions in the north and west respectively comes within this description.[58]

Pre-colonial Benin was a politically centralized kingdom where social status, political role and power depended largely on a well defined hierarchical system that recognized title holding.[59] The highest groups of title holders were the *Uzama* chiefs who were *quasi-Obas* in villages just outside the inner walls of the city.[60] These were followed by the title holders within the three palace societies of *Iwebo, Iweguae* and *Ibiwe.*[61]

The early political history of Benin is traced to the rule of *Igodo*, said to be the founder in about 900 AD.[62] There were several other dynasties such as the *Eweka* dynasty under *Ewedo* (1255-1280 AD), *Ewuare the Great* (1440-1473 AD). *Oba Ewuare* was known as *the Great* because his reign was arguably one of the most remarkable of all the Obas of Benin.[63] During his reign, Benin became a powerful and wealthy metropolis attracting artists, and experts in medicine and religion. Some of Benin's finest carvings, brass and bronze works date back to *Ewuare's* reign. *Ewuare* was able to control his powerful chiefs by creating the two orders of *'Palace Chiefs'* and *'Town Chiefs'* and assigning to them variety of administrative duties. *Ewuare* further embarked on series of military campaigns and conquered large areas of eastern Yoruba land, including the kingdoms of Owo, Akure etc.[64] The rulers of the places and towns conquered by *Ewuare* were forced to pay tribute to Benin. These conquests gave Benin power and prestige and this was also reflected in the development of the city itself with its good road system, skilled craftsmen and imposing buildings.[65] The relevance of this political structure is that it was largely related to the social and economic structure of the state. Benin also got much wealth from the slave trade, as the empire made its port of Ughoton available for the transportation of slaves and in the process shared in the wealth brought by the trade.[66] By the early fifteenth century, a sailing ship using triangular sails had been developed by the Portuguese with which they plied the slave trade in which Benin participated. Despite the wealth the trans-Atlantic slave trade brought to Benin, it also affected them negatively. As the trade became more lucrative, communities within the empire turned on themselves to carry out slave raids. This affected population growth and a decline in production.

The socio-political organization of Benin during the pre-colonial years of its history was dominated by the special position occupied by the Oba who was the pivot around which everything revolved. By the early part of the eighteenth century, the Oba generated substantial revenues from taxes, most of which came in the form of tributes. One 18th century European visitor to Benin documented the Oba of Benin's sources of revenue thus:

> The king has a very good income, for his territories are very large and full of governors and each one knows how many bags of *boesjes* (cowries), the money of this country, he must raise annually for the king, which amount to a very vast sum, which it is impossible for me to estimate. Others of a lower rank

than the former, instead of money deliver cattle, sheep, fowls, yams and cloths; in short, whatever he wants for his house keeping.[67]

The various palace societies described earlier on, formed the hub of the economic organization of the Benin kingdom, and constituted a bureaucracy over which the Oba presided.[68] The Oba controlled the central administration, appointed the territorial rulers for governing outlaying districts and also participated actively in the most important secular and religious ceremonies as well as in several economic activities including the control of internal and external trade, trading associations, levying of tax, founding of work-camps and the establishments of farms and villages. He could create new titles and thus tilt the balance of power within any group of title holders.[69] The granting of titles was another source of revenue for the *Oba*. For most of the titles, the initiation rites involved the payment of fees and the presentation of gifts to the Oba in addition to those meant for the members of the title grade, association or society. All the titles which were non-hereditary were at the Oba's pleasure to confer on anybody whenever a vacancy existed either through death or on promotion of the holder to a higher rank.[70] Where individuals were given accelerated promotion through the grades to the highest titles, they paid all the fees and satisfied all the ceremonial requirements which were associated with the skipped grade.[71] Another source of income for the Oba was in the form of gifts.[72] Many areas, for example Lagos, continued to send gifts to Benin even after Benin ceased to exert its military influence there. In a similar manner, the Urhobo are said to have paid tribute to Benin up to 1850 while the Weppa and Agenebode people on the Niger in the Etsako section of the Edo-speaking peoples paid tribute up to the 1840s. Apart from the regular tax, tributes and gifts, the Oba could impose special levies, through the palace officials, on all villages and the Benin City chiefs in case of need or emergency. This compulsory exaction was known by the Bini as *Ugamwen*.[73]

Collection of tolls at fixed points was another source of revenue in pre-colonial Benin. For this purpose, there were nine entrances into the city[74] corresponding to the nine entrances into the Oba's palace. Each of these was under the charge of a titled chief who collected tolls from all persons entering the city. The amount paid by the traders was proportional to the value of goods carried. The traditional judicial system also constituted a considerable source of revenue for pre-colonial Benin kingdom. At the quarter level, the settlement of disputes took the form of arbitration and conciliation by the quarter elders. Fines imposed were shared by the elders. From the village level onwards, disputes were settled by the village council of elders and a special age-grade, charged with the responsibility collected fines and ensured payment. Fines paid at the Oba's court by offenders found guilty went to swell the state coffers.[75] All deputations from the villages to the Oba were sent through the chiefs as it was not all the Oba's subjects that had access to him.

The payment of *tributes* in pre-colonial Benin generally took two forms. The first was based on land grants while the second was based on custom and not related to land. Because of the Oba's role in making grants of land as well as re-allocations, he collected tributes from the non-Benin people. And this tribute was paid as a token of gratitude for the land received and as an acknowledgement that the occupier was not the owner of the land. This type of payment made when strangers settled on Benin land was called *Akorhore.*[76]

## The Eastern Provinces

### *The Igbo*

The Igbo people are one of Nigeria's dominant ethnic groups whose egalitarian worldview encouraged individual attainment rather than hereditary aristocracy. Consequently, the evolution of Igbo history did not permit the development of monarchies.[77] There is no agreement among the Igbo about where their ancestors came from. Some believe that they had always lived where they now live and that they did not come from anywhere else. Some of them however believe that their forefathers came from Egypt, Israel or some Eastern country.[78] Many of them accept the tradition that they all first lived in the area known as the *Nri-Awka-Orlu* axis. Linguistic features show the Igbo as belonging to the *Kwa* subgroup of the Niger Congo people; a fact which supports the claim of the Igbo to have existed for more than 6000 years.[79]

One significant difference in the political and social organization of the Igbo from the Yoruba, Kanuri, Hausa and Edo ethnic groups is that the Igbo did not develop monarchical forms of government. This means that they did not have kings. The nucleus of their political and social unit was the lineage.[80] Three types of lineages, classified according to size, could be identified among the Igbo. These were the minimal, major and maximal lineages. There was the age grade which was organized on a village basis. The association grew from boyhood and took a common name to commemorate an event associated with the time of their birth.[81] They collected fines from offenders and they could demand new laws. The age-group was thus a society of companionship and protection. It redeemed members who had lost their money, recovered runaway wives, carried out farm work, and collected debts.[82]

There were a variety of titles some of which were hereditary, while others were secured upon payment of fees to the community. Each town had its own traditional titles and compiled regulations for controlling them. Taking a title was a sign of wealth and high social standing.[83] The title holder was relied upon as a man of character, able to build up some following and contribute to projects of the community. Titled men were called *Ndi Nze* and they virtually monopolized authority in their wards or villages.[84] Thus the title system was of immense political significance in Igbo land. Because social advancement was based on personal merit, the Igbo political system has been described as egalitarian and democratic.[85]

The economic history of Igboland can be studied under three major heads agriculture, trade and manufacture. Each of these three main provinces of economic activity played an important part in the survival of the Igbo as a group and in determining the character and quality of the culture, even of their religion and cosmology.[86] By early thirteenth century, agriculture was the most important economic activity. Every Igbo man and woman was a farmer. Most families produced enough of such staples as yam, cocoyam, cassava and vegetables to last them all year round. Agriculture was highly ritualized. The beginning of the farming season, the date of which varied from one part of Igboland to another as a result of ecological reasons, was a formal occasion marked by a festival and ritual.[87] It was the same with the beginning of the harvest season which was marked by the very important New Yam festival. Subsidiary to agriculture, trade was an important aspect of Igbo economic activity. There were two aspects of trade, the development of regional trade within Igboland and the development of long range trade linking the Igbo people with their neighbours.

The northern Igbo plateau was (and is still) rich in iron ore deposits and in smelters and smiths who transformed the ore into iron, tools and ritual objects.[88] The Niger-Anambra valley produced fish while the Northeastern Igbo areas were endowed with salt (at Uburu) and lead (at Abakaliki).[89] Among the famed long range professional trading groups of Igboland were the Aro, Nri, Awka, Abiriba, Umunneoha and Aboh.[90] Much of the commercial transactions in Igboland in the eighteenth century were done with money. Currencies in use included salt, *umumu*, cowries, manilas, brass rods and copper wires.[91] The salt which came in earthen jars from Uburu was ground into fine powder and moulded into cones of different sizes and used in exchange transactions.[92] Iron money, known as *umumu* was minted on the Northern Igbo Plateau.[93] According to Afigbo, the *umumu* consisted of tiny pieces of iron resembling small squashed tin-tacks half an inch in length, with arrow shaped heads, and stem about the thickness of a large pin.[94]

From about the sixteenth century, the Igbo came in contact with the Portuguese. The *Aro* people in Igboland began to supply the Portuguese with slaves. They were able to maintain a monopoly of the trade by the use of the oracle located in their territory. This oracle called *Ibinukpabi* or 'long juju' was consulted by the Igbo people for various reasons. Because of this oracle, the Aro were feared and respected as children of the gods.[95] Profiting from this widespread respect, the Aro established a network of trading activities which provided an efficient trading system for the traffic in slaves. The Aro had a political organization different from the prevailing system in other parts of Igboland. The Aro clan was served by a general council comprising of representatives of its component villages. These representatives called the *Otusi*, were nine in number and were the heads of the nine main sections of the Aro clan.[96] The Aro built up a network of markets, trade routes and agent communities round the greater portion of Igboland.[97] There was a grid of trade routes connecting markets over the whole of central Igbo land on a regional pattern. The twin markets of Bende and Uzuakoli in South-central Igboland illustrated the convergence of traders from various parts of South-eastern Nigeria during the close of the nineteenth century.[98] One major feature of the commercial practice in these two markets was the system of agency or middlemanship. The Umuahia people served as middlemen for traders from Annang, Ibibio and Ngwa areas, while the Uzuakoli people served as middlemen for Awka, Okigwe and Onitsha traders.[99] This market complex was a meeting place for craftsmen, traders and primary producers. The absence of a monarchy or any form of central authority made it impossible for a standard form of taxation to be practiced in pre-colonial Igbo society. The closest approximation to a tax system could be said to be the contributions to or collective execution of projects such as community roads carried out under the auspices of various social groups such as the age-grade associations.

### The Coastal States

In the Delta region of Nigeria, there was a curious mix of states with varying degrees of political organization. The most powerful of these states were the Nembe, Calabar, Bonny and Brass.[100] Most of them could be referred to as 'city states'; that is, political units centered on a town to which outlaying settlements and villages looked for protection and for trade. These states were very well suited to their environment which was dominated by the saltwater swamps of the Niger Delta.[101] The Ijaw, Efik and Itsekiri are also among the inhabitants of the Niger Delta. Others are the Isoko, Ukwuani and the Urhobo. The latter groups live at the mouth of the River Niger and are served also by the rivers Benin, Cross River, Forcados, Bonny and Escravos, among others. The bulk of the area is swampy although the northern part is dry, and all belong to what has been described as *'a maze of islands, intersected by creeks and rivers.'*[102] The four Delta states of Nembe (Brass), Elem Kalabari (New Calabar), Bonny and Okrika are well known because of their participation in the overseas slave trade[103] in the seventeenth century.

By and large, the Delta province could be divided into the lower delta, comprising of the Ijaw, Itsekiri and Aboh, and the upper delta inhabited by the Isoko, Urhobo and Ukwuani.[104] This division of the province into two natural vegetation types has been an important factor in determining the relations among the peoples of the province in so far as their occupational pursuits have been determined by their varying natural habitats.[105] The lower delta dwellers were fishermen, makers of salt and earthenware and canoe. While the dwellers in the hinterland naturally took to agriculture and the exploitation of the oil palm, with some engaged in fishing.[106] The exchange of the products of their various occupations thus constituted an early determinant of inter-group relations; the 'water people' had fish, crayfish and salt to offer the land people, while the land people offered in return yams, plantain, pepper, and cassava plant. From about 1520 AD, slaves also became an important commodity in the commercial transaction between the two groups.[107]

Exclusive societies constituted an important feature of life among the delta groups. The Isoko had the *Odio* society while the Urhobo had the *Ohonwonre, Ade,* and *Okakuro* societies.[108] Membership of these societies involved the payment of fixed fees and the performance of prescribed ceremonies. Consequently membership of the societies was to some extent, an index of wealth and social status.[109] Among the Efik of Calabar, slaves were able to play an active part in *ekine* and *sekiapu* societies especially during festivities. Generally, too, secret societies played an important role in aspects of the community's affairs such as maintaining law and order, and providing useful training for youths and adults.[110] Conditions of membership varied among the states but certain rules were constant such as exclusion of female membership.

Among the coastal Delta states, the clan (*ibe*) was an important feature of life but it lacked the instruments of central control. Indeed, only the high priest representing the cult of the national god exercised authority over the whole clan.[111] Within the clan each village enjoyed a large degree of independence. The main political authority was the village assembly, known as the *amagula* and because of the great respect for age, the *amagula* was presided over by the town elder. [112] In addition, there were a number of specialized officers within the clan who were responsible for communications and administration of justice. Every village had its own priest representing the town deity. The village was further subdivided into wards which were in turn made up of small units known as *Houses*.[113] The *House System* paved way for the emergence of a new group of powerful chiefs. This was made possible by the Atlantic Slave Trade and the role the *Houses* came to play in the trade as military units.[114]

For most of the coastal tribes, the clan was the highest level of political organization. Their early political system was characterized by an absence of central control and by a large number of independent villages in which secret societies played an important role in all aspects of community affairs; and like in the case of the Igbo, this did not support the development of a tax system. Apart from trade, the other ways of raising revenues for the support of communal life was through payment of fee for initiation into societies and fines as penalties for offences.

## TAXATION IN THE COLONIAL ERA (1861-1960)

The treatment of 1861 as the commencement year of colonial rule in Nigeria does not suggest that the entire region came under colonial rule on the same date as the annexation of Lagos. Indeed, the length of colonial rule in Nigeria varied across geo-political zones. In the case of Lagos, the rule lasted for almost one hundred years (1861-1960). In Eastern Nigeria, British rule was introduced after 1885 therefore; it lasted seventy-five years. In some parts of Northern Nigeria, British rule was introduced only as from 1903 and lasted only fifty-seven years.

Long before the British Government acquired Lagos as a colony, they had worked out a system of colonial administration for their tropical dependencies. This was the crown colony system of administration already established in the West Indies and India. Consequently, when Lagos was acquired in 1861, a typical crown colony administration made its appearance only a year later. A Legislative Council made up of a Chief Justice, Colonial Secretary and a Senior Military Officer in command of British forces within the colony was established in October, 1862.[115]

In imposing the crown colony system of administration on Nigeria or on any other non-white dependent territories for that matter, the British did not bother to reflect on whether this was in any way in agreement with the traditional system of government and administration in those territories. Consequently, it became the responsibility of Nigerians to pay for the administration of the British government and at the same time, maintain their indigenous local governments which were under *Obas* and *Emirs* (where they existed) and warrant chiefs (where the British had to create traditional stools in order to give effect to the *indirect rule* policy of colonial administration). Initially, the colonial administration generated much of its revenue from customs duties because the British government was cautious on introducing direct taxation. In 1866, canoe owners in Lagos were required to license their canoes or boats at the cost of ten shillings each per annum.[116] The government saw this as a good tax because inland waterways were one of the few reliable means of communication at that time. Another source of revenue was created in 1869 when traders using government-built market stalls were charged to pay monthly fees. The evolution of direct taxation in Nigeria as a deliberate policy however, is traceable to Lord Lugard's Administration in Northern Nigeria.

**Indirect Rule and Taxation**

Lugard described indirect rule as:

> rule through the Native Chiefs, who are regarded as an integral part of the machinery of Government, with well-defined powers and functions recognised by Government and by law, and not dependent on the caprice of an Executive Officer.[117]

The British administrators were to rule through the chiefs, educate them in their duties as rulers, seek their co-operation in the general administration, and ensure that their (chiefs') prestige was maintained.[118] This meant that where chiefs did not exist hitherto, the British had to create them in order that indirect rule could succeed.

There were at least three reasons for the British Government's adoption of indirect rule. First, the British had very limited number of administrative (or political) officers available to undertake direct rule of the country. Even if they had been available the country's poor public revenue could have proved inadequate for paying the officers. Second, it was considered unwise to drastically reform existing customs and methods until the British officials had acquired better knowledge of native law and custom. Third, the example of the loyalty and progress of the protected states of India where indirect rule had been practiced encouraged its introduction in Nigeria.[119]

Indirect rule was first implemented in Northern Nigeria and although the Moslem emirates had an impressive political structure in place before the arrival of the British, Lugard was of the opinion that independent non-Moslem communities in the north were not to be placed under Moslem emirs without the governor's consent, because in his words 'good government is no equivalent of self-government'.[120] Non Moslem communities were to be allowed to develop their own customs and traditions, and even where the governor consented that non-Moslem area could be included in a neighbouring emirate; the head of the community had to be a native of the area. The chiefs were not to be regarded as independent but delegates of the British governor as represented by the Residents. The central (British) government was to make laws, control the armed forces and impose taxes. All these limitations were set out in the letter of appointment of higher chiefs.

Direct taxation was introduced in Northern Nigeria by virtue of the *Native Revenue Proclamation No. 2 of 1906*. The actual collection of revenues however started in 1907, but in many parts of the north such as the Tiv areas, little or no tax was collected until the 1920s. The emirate councils were converted into native authorities and thus formed the first *nuclei of local government* in Northern Nigeria. Direct tax was imposed by the central government as the sovereign authority, and the native authorities were to collect and pay the whole to the government who would, in turn, return a large proportion of the collection to the native authorities for the administration of their services. The direct tax, as introduced in Northern Nigeria, was to replace the series of taxes, fines and other forms of irregular collections made by the emirs before the British conquest. Some of these included the *Kurdin kasa* (an agricultural tax on non-Moslems), *Khanraj* (a Moslem community tax), *Gausua* (festival present), *Gado* (death duties which amounted to confiscation of the estate), *Haku Binerum* (graduated income tax in Bornu), and *Jangali* (cattle tax). Some taxes such as the *Jangali*,

*Kurdin Sarauta* and the *Haraji* were however not abolished. There was not much opposition to the collection of the new tax because of the highly organised tax systems that were already in place in the Moslem states prior to the arrival of the British. On the contrary, subjects of the emirates were accepted the new tax as a more just and equitable replacement for the former arbitrary and exorbitant taxes administered by the emirs. The emirs were also satisfied with the new tax system because of the certainty of collection which ensured regular remuneration for them.

The new tax was an income tax based on the total wealth of the community of which agricultural products formed the largest part. This wealth however included the products of local crafts and trades. Although it was a capitation tax, it was in fact a roughly assessed income tax on the people. In the developed Moslem townships like Kano and Zaria, attempts were made to introduce individual income tax assessment and tax receipts were issued to the payers for the purpose of identification. The tax was collected by the village or district heads appointed for the purpose of tax collection in addition to other administrative duties. In return for their services, the tax collectors were paid either a commission or salary.

In the western provinces, direct taxation was introduced by virtue of the *Native Revenue Ordinance* of 1918 but the application of the Ordinance did not extend to Asaba Division of Benin Province and the Warri Province. The tax was also an income tax, based on the income from agriculture and other trades, but mainly on agriculture at the time. This tax replaced a number of irregular collections of tributes and presents such as death duties in Egbaland, road tolls in Ijebu, annual levies in Oyo, and the regular tribute in Ondo province. The rates of tax varied from about six shillings to eight shillings *per capita*. Apart from disorders in Egbaland, there was very little problem of collection in these areas because, as in the north, the people appreciated the advantage of replacing the irregular exactions of the past with a new tax system which was regular and definite. Even the disturbances in Egbaland were rooted in factors remote to the introduction of direct tax by the colonial administration. In 1918, after Lugard persuaded the Colonial Office to allow him to introduce taxation in western Nigeria, he was not aware that the Egba people were seething with discontent on other issues prior to the introduction of the new tax regime. First, a newly promulgated forestry law angered hunters who felt that their area of vocational operation was being restricted. Secondly, the people had been told that free labour on road construction projects would continue even in the face of the new tax. Thirdly, the newly introduced sanitary measures empowered officious half-trained inspectors to poke their noses into women's private quarters to the disgust and annoyance of their husbands. With all these grievances on their mind, the introduction of direct taxation proved to be the spark that ignited the powder keg. In June 1918 the Egba therefore decided to 'go to war' with the British. They mobilised as in the old anti-Dahomey days. They uprooted the railway linking Abeokuta with Lagos and cut the telegraph lines. They ransacked European stores and killed a European trader. Lugard reacted swiftly by sending a crack force of 1,000 soldiers to Egbaland to deal with the rebels. No less than 500 Egba people were killed in the encounter. A Commission of Inquiry was later appointed to look into the 'little war' and give an impartial report. It identified the causes of local discontent and blamed the administration on the timing of the new measures and the handling of the trouble. By the time the report was published, however, Lugard had retired from the Colonial Service and it was left to the new governor, Sir Hugh Clifford, to bind the wounds.[121]

By 1927, government felt there was need to impose taxation on the Itsekiri and the Urhobo (of Asaba and Warri respectively) to provide for road construction, hospitals and schools as was done elsewhere in southern Nigeria. Consequently, the *Native Revenue Ordinance* was amended to make it applicable to Asaba Division Warri Province, and arrangements were set in motion to enumerate the taxable population for the purpose of tax collection. The British attempt to extend the direct tax system to these regions was however met with series of protests, particularly in Warri Province.[122] First, because the throne of the Olu of Warri had been vacant since the interregnum of 1848, there was no native administration in place to administer the ordinance. Second, people who were not educated on the justification for the new policy naturally took a strong objection to it. Furthermore, the fact that the tax was being imposed on a *'per head'* basis evoked repugnant memories of the slave trade when a slave's head or life was redeemable with the payment of a tribute to his owner. The people did not only equate the *per head* basis of the tax with the practice of slavery, they actually considered the tax more oppressive and demeaning because while a slave could be redeemed once and for all with a single lump payment *per head*, the proposed *per head* tax was to be an annual affair. The Itsekiri under the leadership of Eda Otuedon, a professional letter writer, and the Urhobo under the leadership of Oshue met in July 1927 and resolved to resist the introduction of the tax. At a secret meeting held at Igbudu village, some three kilometres from Warri town, the people resolved to:

a.      boycott all trade with Europeans;

b.      suspend further production of palm oil;

c.      ensure the closure of all native courts;

d.      resist arrests by court-messengers or the police; and

e.      forcibly set free anyone arrested by the government functionaries.[123]

Between August and October 1927, these resolutions were translated into action. The Isoko people, who were not invited to the Igbudu meeting, voluntarily adopted the Igbudu resolutions and joined the resistance movement. District Officers were mobbed and their cars damaged and prisoners were set free at Oleh, Owe, Agbarho and Ughienwe.[124] The closure of the native courts was effected by either abducting the warrant chiefs who served as judges in these courts or frightening them to go into hiding. In some places the warrant chiefs were made to pay a fine of £30 each as punishment for their collaboration with the British Administration.

In 1928, the system of direct tax was extended to the eastern provinces sparking off series of demonstrations in Calabar and Owerri Provinces, but the most serious resistance to the introduction of direct taxation in the east was the Aba riot of 1929.[125] The background in the eastern region was rather more complicated than that of the north and the west because whereas in the north and the west, the existence of fairly organised states was instrumental in the entrenchment of indirect rule, the absence of powerful chiefs in the east impelled the British to introduce the system of warrant chiefs. Not only was the notion of kingship alien to the political and social formation of easterners, the warrant chiefs appointed by the British were more or less imposed upon the people as a result of which they were not accepted by the people.[126] Further to the above, the prices of export produce were low and the prices of imports high, creating an economic downturn that could only be further aggravated by the introduction of direct taxes. The other main cause of the riot was the wrong impression that women were going to be taxed.

As stated earlier, direct taxation everywhere in Nigeria was an initiative of the colonial government. This was not an accident because the government made it clear that, as the sovereign power, it had unquestionable right to impose tax. The native authorities were to make the collection with the assistance of administrative officers; and in practice, only the government's share was paid into government coffers to form part of the general government revenue; the balance was retained by the native authorities. The remarkable feature of this arrangement was that a direct financial relationship between the central and the local government was introduced in the administration of public finance in Nigeria. The central government also recognised the need for allocating part of the tax proceeds to the local government authorities for the provision of social services. This was in fact the beginning of what one would describe as the history of local government finance in Nigeria.

A very important innovation introduced by the British Government was the establishment of native treasuries since according to Lugard; 'no tax, no treasury; no treasury, no self-government'.[127] Apart from using it for the efficient administration of tax and other revenues, native treasuries were considered factors of unification among the population. They were financial bonds of unity which reduced the temptation to break off from the native authority as a political unit. This axiom applied very much to Warri Province and eastern Nigeria where the clans were very small and a number of them had to be induced to federate in order to own a joint treasury. Once the treasury was kept going and funds were used to develop all parts of the unit or federation of native authorities without discrimination, there was less temptation to secede.

The advanced emirate and native authorities in the northern and western provinces received 50 to 60 per cent of tax proceeds collected by them while the less developed native treasuries received about 25 per cent. The basis for grading a native authority as organised was that it was capable of undertaking large scale social services because of its wealth and staff, and it was therefore argued that a greater share of the tax revenue should be given to it to administer these services. On the other hand, native authorities which were relatively poorer and therefore could not employ qualified staff were graded as unorganised and it was argued that a small proportion of the tax revenue collected from their areas should be given to them as they could not undertake expensive social services.

Other sources of revenue included *Jangali*, which was imposed in northern Nigeria on a *per capita* basis on all adult cattle at a fixed rate per beast; 10 per cent of this revenue was taken by the government and 90 per cent by the native authorities. In addition, there were the following sources of revenue: market fees, court fines and fees, forest royalties, school fees, and in the north fees for estate administration, revenue from prisoners' labour and their crafts, and in the south earnings from electricity, water, corn mills, fishing permits to aliens,

palm produce permits to aliens, rent on communal land, and other miscellaneous revenues
which were exclusively collected by the native authorities.


In the north, the *kurdi sarauta* was also paid as occasion demanded. Throughout the country,
forced or unpaid labour continued to be used to maintain town and village roads with or
without grants-in-aid from native authorities, but forced labour was prohibited for the
construction of town roads and chiefs' houses. The main heads of native authorities'
expenditure were: the salaries of emirs and chiefs and their staff. To avoid disparity in the
salaries of various chiefs and emirs, all increases in the salaries and the creation of new
posts had to receive the Governor's approval when the estimates were being considered.
The salaries and allowances of the personnel of the following departments of the native
authority and other expenditure incidental to their administration were included: Native
treasurer, native authority police and prisons, judicial, education, agriculture, survey and
public works. Other expenditure of the native authority included pension and allowances
to deposed chiefs and expenses on Moslem religious projects and writing off of losses.[128]
The estimates of the authorities had to be carefully vetted by administrative officers before
the Governor's approval, and rules were made for the control of expenditure, in many cases
by tying it to the relevant revenues.

The peasants, who were emancipated from the former irregular tributes, were now free to
use their initiative and industry to the economic advantage of the country. Unlike the absentee
landlords and tax gatherers they had come to replace, district heads or state officials had to
earn their living as such. The number of titular office holders and tax gatherers was reduced,
and this resulted in saving of public funds. Annual estimates of revenue and expenditure
were regularised, ensuring that native authorities who collected the money had to account
fully for it. Subsequent Native Authority Ordinances (No. 43 of 1933 and 17 of 1943 as
amended by Ordinances Nos. 3 and 73 of 1945) mainly restated the principles in the 1916
Ordinance and made the following provisions: native authorities were required to make
declaration of native custom with respect to the various functions and powers delegated to
them, and such declarations were used by administrative officers as the basis for filling
vacancies in native authorities, whenever the need arose. The supervisory powers of
government officers over native authorities departments, e.g. police and prisons, were clearly
defined. Finally, Native Authority (Amendment) Ordinance No. 34 of 1951 conferred on

native authorities the right of perpetual succession to the ownership of property vested in them.

The inequity associated with the allocation of direct tax proceeds on the basis of *organised* and *unorganised* native authorities continued until 1948 when it was abolished and in its place, a new formula was introduced whereby native authorities paid into the revenue of government six pence *per capita* of tax collected from men and three pence *per capita* of tax collected from women. The balance was to be retained by native authorities. This marked the first uniform system of distributing direct tax revenue between the government on the one hand, and all the native authorities on the other. Further to the above, Sir Sidney Phillipson in his report on revenue allocation[129] strongly objected against the discretion the central government exercised over the allocation of proceeds from the *Native Revenue Proclamation No. 2 of 1906*. Although collection of the tax was done by local authorities, their share of the revenue was unpredictable, being subject as it were to the discretion of the central government. Phillipson recommended that local authorities be given maximum incentive to collect tax by making their share of the proceeds certain and predictable He accordingly proposed a statutory apportionment on a *per capita basis*. In his words:

> I propose the retention of a single tax but with a fundamental change in the method of apportionment. I need hardly emphasize that the scheme is conceived in the interests of the native administrations themselves. Under it, their position will be greatly improved; they will know where they stand, and that for certain approved purposes, they will get financial assistance; apart from such regulated assistance, they will be called upon to exercise the vital responsibility of self-dependent finance.[130]

Sir Sidney Phillipson's recommendations were given legal form by the enactment of Ordinance No. 2 of 1948 pursuant to which native authorities were :

> required to pay into such Government treasury as the Resident may direct, a sum representing an amount collected by the taxpayers of the areas calculated at the appropriate rate per head prescribed in the Schedule of this ordinance.[131]

The schedule was from time to time revised and by 1957, the amount was raised to five shillings per capita on each adult male taxpayer. 10 percent of the cattle tax was also, at this time, paid to the central government. Also as a result of Phillipson's recommendations on revenue allocation, the government published a white paper in 1948 providing for the supervision by government officers of native authority departmental activities in order to ensure that the increased amount of grants-in-aid now going into the hands of native authorities was being properly spent.[132]

The community tax *(haraji)* and the cattle tax *(jangali)* were by far the most important sources of revenue accruing to local authorities in northern Nigeria. These two taxes accounted for about 60 to 70 percent of total local revenues. Although collected locally, they were in fact state government taxes and the local authorities collected the taxes on behalf of the government and the revenue was disposed in accordance with the provisions of the personal tax law. However, at least 75 percent of the proceeds therefrom were retained by the local authorities and the balance remitted to the regional government.

Community tax was payable by all adult males who were *'in good health'* and not liable to income tax. The basic rate was fixed for the community and the *per capita* contribution was agreed upon by the local authority and approved by the Ministry for Local Government. The rate of the tax was decided after careful consideration of the rates payable in the neighbouring community areas; the wealth of the community being assessed; the financial needs of the local authority administering the community area; and any special factor affecting the community concerned; for example if there was a bad harvest owing to draught, then less tax could be demanded.

The factors employed in assessing community tax were fraught with problems. First, the tax assessors had no competence to determine with scientific certainty the medical status of taxpayers and no provision was made for the production of a medical certificate as a yardstick for exemption; therefore, no objective way of determining the good health or otherwise of an adult who was ordinarily chargeable to tax existed. Second, the rates payable in a neighbouring community could only be of limited relevance in determining the level of the tax in the community to be assessed. For example, the rates payable by a neighbouring community that was substantially engaged in trading could not be properly applied to a community that was predominantly agricultural. Third, using the wealth of the community to be assessed as a criterion for determining the rate of tax payable turned up the problem of determining, with some reasonable degree of accuracy, the total income or output of the area. The result was that the assessment was no more than a rough guess based on such factors as the number of newly erected buildings; the quality or quantity of the properties; or sometimes mere hearsay. Fourth, community needs could be multifarious and costly; therefore using the financial needs of a local authority as a yardstick for tax assessment engendered a tendency towards over-taxation which, in turn, could breed discontent and rebellion. Like earlier pointed out, the personnel employed for the purposes of tax assessment and collection were not properly trained for the job and majority of local authorities could not afford to employ trained personnel even if they were available. In spite of the foregoing criticisms, community tax remained a veritable source of revenue for the native authorities.

## Local Government and Taxation in Western and Eastern Nigeria

The Native Authority Ordinance No. 43 of 1933 and No. 17 of 1943, as amended by Ordinance Nos. 3 and 73 of 1945 also applied to the native authorities in Eastern and Western Nigeria up to 1950 and the Western Region Local Government Law, 1952, introduced democratically elected local government councils to replace the native authorities in both regions.

### Western Nigeria

In 1952 as a result of the constitutional changes, native authorities became the responsibility of regional governments and in the same year, the Western Region Local Government Law provided for the establishment of democratically elected local authorities to replace existing native authorities. The law also provided for a limited membership of traditional office holders who did not have to stand for popular election. Until 1952, the native authorities, strictly speaking, were not independent units. They were an indirect arm of the central government and had a very limited sphere for any action independent of the British administrative officers. Another important feature of this system was that subordinate native authorities had no funds of their own; they were the spending arms of the larger native authorities and in some cases, assisted the latter in collecting revenue. The *Western Region Local Government Law 1952* however, provided for the establishment of district and local councils to replace the smaller native authorities. These councils, which derived their powers from the law, were not to be subordinate to the divisional councils and were all to be elected, subject to the addition of traditional members. Another important feature of this law was the increase in the powers given to the councils. For example, they were empowered to maintain secondary and primary schools irrespective of whether voluntary agency or government schools already existed in their areas. They could also build and maintain hospitals and establish any large scale projects subject to the availability of funds and qualified staff. They could employ supervisory staff of their own instead of depending entirely on government staff.

The 1952 Law was replaced in 1957 by the *Western Region Local Government Law 1957*.[133] The new law repealed the *Direct Taxation Ordinance, 1940*, in so far as it applied to the western region, and empowered local authorities to levy general, education, and other rates to finance those services hitherto financed from revenue collected under the *Direct Taxation Ordinance 1940* in so far as it applied to the western region. Provision was made for the appointment of rate assessment committees to make rate assessment, and for appeal tribunals to hear rate appeals, and for the commissioner of income tax to review rate assessments made by assessment committees. In 1960, the Western Region Local Government Law was amended to introduce a major change by removing the powers of local authorities to impose and collect general and primary education rates. In lieu of these, the regional government empowered them to collect the regional government tax and development contribution from self-employed persons on incomes not exceeding £300 per annum.[134]

The Western Region Income Tax Law, together with the amendments made thereto,[135] imposed a progressive income tax on all taxable males 16 years of age and above with incomes of £50 per annum or more, and on taxable females of the same age mark whose incomes exceeded £300 per annum. The rate of this tax varied from nine pence per pound for the first £500 of taxable income to nine shillings of every pound in excess of £4,300 of taxable income.

For the assessment of the local authority share of the tax, assessment committees were appointed by the regional Minister of Local Government for a one-year term, to act as advisers to regional Tax Board inspectors, who carried out the actual assessments in Western Nigeria. In Mid-Western Nigeria, however, the assessment committees still carried out the assessments while the councils' tax clerks revised the nominal rolls to bring in names of taxpayers who became eligible by virtue of age. Thereafter, all self-employed taxpayers on the nominal roll were sent forms for declaration of their taxable incomes for the (previous) tax year ending. On receipt of the declaration forms, the various assessment committees or tax inspectors proceeded to assess the taxable incomes of all self-employed taxpayers and other wage earners whose taxes were not collected under the *Pay – As – You - Earn* system

(PAYE), irrespective of whether the income declaration forms were in fact received from some of the taxpayers. In the course of assessment, a taxpayer could be invited to appear in person before the committees to clarify some points in connection with his income and in some cases he could be asked to forward written explanations. Assessment notices were published in the wards of those concerned whose taxable incomes were between £50 and £300. In some cases the publication of the assessment notices was followed by the issue of individual assessment notices to those whose incomes fell between £51 and £300 per annum. These notices were required to state the date on which the tax and rates became due for payment. After this, collection commenced and this was done by council tax clerks and in the case of some rural areas, with the assistance of commissioned tax collectors. Any tax not paid within two months of becoming due made the taxpayer liable to a surcharge of 10 per cent of the tax, which had to be paid along with the tax. At the end of two months, demand notes were sent to defaulting taxpayers in respect of the tax and the surcharge, and if after a further period of 30 days these were not paid, the defaulters were criminally prosecuted in the magistrate's court under section 58 (IA) of the Income Tax Law. A taxpayer who was convicted under the law was liable to a maximum fine of one hundred pounds or six months' imprisonment, in addition to the payment of his tax and surcharge.

Under section 12(1) of the Income Tax Law certain classes of income such as profits of co-operative societies and health gratuities were exempted from tax. The regional Governor-in-Council could also exempt other persons or classes of persons or their incomes from any source from the income tax. On the regional Tax Board's recommendation, an independent local appeal committee with members appointed by the regional Minister of Finance was formed to hear appeals against tax assessments in the area of a council or a group of councils. An aggrieved taxpayer could appeal against his tax assessment within 30 days of the receipt of such assessment, although he could appeal after this period if the local committee was satisfied with his excuse for not appealing earlier. The aggrieved person was required to pay a fee of five shillings and a deposit with the council concerned of the amount of any tax due under the assessment appealed against, or the amount paid by that person as tax for the preceding year of assessment, whichever was less, and to also appear in person before the committee when his appeal was being considered. The committee could alter his assessment depending on the merit of his case and was further empowered to award costs against the appellant if his appeal was frivolous. The council concerned could also appeal to the committee against an assessment and the appeal was determined based on its merit or otherwise. Either party to the appeal proceedings had a further right of appeal to the High Court whose decision was final; but if the assessable income was £1,000 or more, a further appeal to the Supreme Court was allowed.

*Eastern Nigeria*

The demand for local government reforms in the eastern region led to the passage of the *Eastern Region Local Government Ordinance, 1950*.[136] Under this Ordinance the native authorities in Eastern Nigeria were replaced by counties, districts and local councils; patterning local government administration after the British model.[137] The members of the former were almost entirely elected apart from traditional office holders who were members of some councils. By 1954 all new councils had been established. These councils had wide powers including the power to appoint staff and to determine their salaries and conditions of service independent of the regional government, provided the salaries did not exceed four hundred pounds. They were empowered to collect personal income tax under the Direct Taxation Ordinance of 1940 and to collect rates to finance specific local services.

In 1955, the Eastern Nigeria Local Government Law was passed to address the shortcomings identified in the implementation of the 1950 Ordinance. These shortcomings included, among other things, inadequacies associated with the assessment and collection of taxes. The new law essentially enhanced the powers of the Minister responsible for local government affairs as a check on the excesses and inadequacies of the councils. In 1956, the eastern region passed the Eastern Region Finance Law[138] which superseded the *Direct Taxation Ordinance, 1940*, as it applied to the region. The new law handed over the primary responsibility for income tax assessment and collection to the government Department of Inland Revenue. This change was informed by the realisation that income tax was collected more efficiently on a regional rather than on a local level. During the first few years, councils were used as collecting agents until the department built up its own organisation and took over this function completely from the councils. In lieu of tax revenue, government paid block grants to the councils on population basis, ranging from four shillings and six pence per head of population in each rural council area to six shillings per head for the urban counties and municipal councils.[139]

Local councils existed within the areas of authority of all rural county councils but not within either municipalities or urban county council areas. A point of difference between rural county councils on one hand and urban county and municipal councils on the other hand was that the last two were empowered by their instruments to levy and collect property rates. The difference between municipal councils and county councils was that the former had mayors and deputy mayors while the latter had chairmen and in most cases presidents, in addition. With the exception of these differences, all county and municipal councils in Eastern Nigeria had practically the same powers and functions as those performed by local authorities in other parts of the federation.[140]

*Lagos*

The first semblance of local government was introduced in Lagos when, under the *Public Health Ordinance No. 5 of 1899* a Central Board of Health was established, consisting of the principal medical officer (as president), the sanitary engineer (or whosoever was performing his duties), the health officer of Lagos and not more than four other persons appointed by the governor from time to time. Subject to the approval of the Governor-in-Council, the Board was empowered to make, alter or amend such regulations as might be required to implement the health ordinance provisions, which included sanitation of markets, management of cemeteries, control of animals, and prevention of overcrowding. The functions of the board included night soil disposal, licensing of vehicles and wheel tax, refuse disposal, building regulations, town planning and slaughter-house maintenance.

The rapid urbanisation of Lagos colony and the attendant sanitation concerns led to the metamorphosis of the Board into the Lagos Municipal Board of Health.[141] This was achieved pursuant to the *Lagos Municipal Board of Health Incorporation Ordinance 1909*. Pursuant to the Ordinance, the Board was empowered to enter into contracts and gave the right of perpetual succession and the power to sue and to make bye-laws. It also extended its jurisdiction to include sales by auction, spirit and dog licenses, maintenance of licenses under the Township Ordinances, and licensing of vehicles, with all the fines and fees from prosecutions under these and the public health and certain other ordinances, being assigned to the board as revenue. The Township Ordinance[142] was enacted with the main purpose of establishing the broad principles of municipal responsibility, graduated according to the importance of the community. The Lagos Town Council was set up as a first class township council with a president and vice-president and directed, among other things, to put into effect the provisions of various ordinances affecting the township and the rates, fines and fees accruing from such enforcement went to the council revenue. It was also empowered to make bye-laws to be approved by the governor for collection of vehicle licenses and of fees for the council's services.

To be qualified to vote, the *Lagos Township Ordinance No. 9 of 1941* (which replaced the *Lagos Township Ordinance No. 29 of 1917*) required that a male person be at least 21 years of age, or in the case of a firm, business, company, club, mission, or other body of persons, it had to be:

a. responsible for the payment of rates on a tenement of which the capital value, annual or unimproved value was not less than £225, £15 or £60 respectively or

b. an occupier of such a tenement paying an annual rent of £18 or more and who had occupied the tenement during previous three months.

The Council's main source of revenue was tenement rates which were introduced in 1915 under the *Assessment Ordinance 1915* and assessment of property was made by the town engineer who was empowered as the 'appraiser'.[143] Furthermore, the Council was empowered to levy an annual rate and this meant that the annual general rate could not be varied during the year once it was fixed at the beginning of the year. However, this changed pursuant to the 1941 Ordinance which empowered the Council to levy the rate half-yearly, thus also enabling it to vary the rate mid-year.

An independent rate assessment committee was established for the first time in 1948 to deal with objections under the *1915 Assessment Ordinance*. The new committee was placed under the chairmanship of the commissioner of lands and an officer of the lands department was appointed as secretary. All objections were now sent to the committee which notified the town clerk of its decision for departmental action.[144]

In 1952 Lagos township was merged with the western region of Nigeria;[145] only to be detached from the region again in 1954 and conferred with the status of federal territory[146] and series of legislation were enacted in order to effect the practical changes arising from the constitutional change. In 1959 the Lagos Local Government (Amendment) Ordinance was passed. The law empowered the federal government to make regulations for ensuring, among other things, that the council maintained grant-earning services to meet laid down standards. The bases of government grants to the council were clearly set out percentages.

The functions and powers of the Lagos town council were substantially the same as those of the native authorities in the north and the respective councils in the east and west with the important distinction that unlike native authorities in the north and some councils in the west, Lagos town council did not maintain local government police and prisons.[147]

## Method of Assessment

In the colonial era, there were a variety of methods of assessment for tax purposes and they varied across the country. The basis characteristics of the methods of assessment were that they were not scientific. The reason for this cannot be far from the fact that there was a dearth of information on which the assessment could be based. Also, the literacy level militated against proper assessment. With reference to income tax of individuals, it is on record that there were seven major methods of assessment in Northern Nigeria. These included:

(a) *Locally-distributed income tax*: This was the most general method, being applied to about 90 per cent of the population. This involved the imposition of tax on a community as a whole and the apportionment of the tax to the inhabitants according their ability to pay.

(b) *Poll tax*: This was a flat tax imposed on the inhabitants of a community where the difference in their income was negligible.

(c) *Tax on ascertainable incomes*: this was imposed on civil servants and employees of native authorities and commercial firms who had ascertainable incomes.

(d) *Wealthy traders' tax*: this was imposed on traders. It involved the charging to tax of the estimate of the income of the traders by the local assessment committee.

(e) In mining areas where there was a large and, to some extent, shifting labour force, a tax of was payable.

(f) *Strangers' tax*: This tax applied to to non-Nigerians and Nigerians who were not of northern Nigerian origin by birth. It was based on the apparent wealth of the person concerned, and could be paid in areas where the locally – distributed income tax or poll tax applied.

(g) *Land revenue tax*: Based on a detailed assessment of the average productivity per acre in each revenue survey district.[148]

In the old western provinces, the tax system made use of a combination of flat rate with an income tax. The tax system subsequently metamorphosed and the following types of tax were levied: flat rate, income tax rate, trade taxes and a tax on unearned incomes with the last two been levied in the Oyo and Ijebu provinces only.[149] It should however be noted that company income taxation was not as problematic as personal income taxation as the *Income Tax Ordinance of 1943* fixed company tax at 5 shillings in the pound on taxable profit.

## TAXATION IN THE POST-COLONIAL ERA

Nigeria was granted full independence on October 1, 1960, as a federation of three regions (northern, western, and eastern) under a Constitution that provided for a parliamentary form of government. Under the Constitution, each of the three regions retained a substantial measure of self-government. Prior to 1960, the Raisman Commission was set up to review the existing taxing powers and revenue allocation formula as this had become an issue subsequent to Nigeria becoming a federation in 1954.[150] The Commission recommended that the federal government should have exclusive power over corporations' and companies' taxes as well as taxation of non-residents persons, and to enter into double taxation agreements with other countries. The regions (later states) had exclusive power to impose personal income tax on individuals, sole traders, partnerships, clubs, trusts and other unincorporated associations.[151] These recommendations formed section 70 of the Nigeria (Constitution) Order-in-Council 1960. In giving the regions exclusive power to impose personal income tax on individuals, the Commission identified three problems that might arise:[152]

   a.  the danger that regional personal income tax law might conflict with double taxation agreements which the federal government has entered into, or might do so in the future with foreign governments.
   b.  the danger of internal double taxation.

It was recorded in the Commission's report that the eastern region taxed the individual incomes of its residents while the western region not only taxed those residents in the west, but also taxed any income which was derived from the western region irrespective of the resident of the recipient.[153] The result of this was that a resident in eastern Nigeria working in western Nigeria would be taxed twice on the same income by both governments. The Commission felt it was desirable to define carefully what income would be subject to income tax by which tax authority.[154] Consequently, while granting each regional government the exclusive right to fix tax rates and personal allowances and to decide upon its own method of assessment and administration, the Commission went ahead to recommend areas wherein there needed to be uniformity. These included:

  a.  the definition of taxable income and the basis of charge;

  b.  the period of assessment;

  c.  the taxation of income remitted to Nigeria from overseas sources;

  d.  the taxation of income accruing in Nigeria to residents overseas;

  e.  the approval of pensions and provident funds for tax purposes;

  f.  the treatment of dividends;

  g.  the taxation of partnership;

  h.  the type of information to be exchanged between one tax authority and another.[155]

The acceptance of the foregoing is the basis for section 70 (ii) and (iii) of the 1960 Constitution Order – in - Council which conferred concurrent powers upon Parliament to make laws for Nigeria or any part thereof with respect to certain enumerated uniform principles in relation to personal income tax. The consequence of this was the enactment of the *Income Tax Management Act 1961* (ITMA) and it defined taxable income and the basis of charge, the period of assessment, the list of allowable deductions, the treatment of dividends as well as the general administration of personal income tax.[156] Corporate taxation was placed within the purview of the Federal Board of Inland Revenue, established under the *Companies Income Tax Act No. 22 of 1961*. The Act categorized assessments into four types vis: original assessment, additional assessments, amended assessment and revised assessment.[157]

The complexity of the tax system worsened rather than improve when Nigeria became a Republic in 1963 and the provisions of section 70 of the 1960 Constitution were re-enacted under section 76 of the 1963 Republican Constitution. This is because the mid-western region which was created adopted the tax law of the western region. Thus, while the issue of internal double taxation was sought to be eliminated by ITMA 1961, the issue of different rates of tax, reliefs and personal allowances still prevailed because there were four legal regimes regulating personal income taxation in the four regions.[158]

**1966-1979**

In May 1967, pursuant to Decree No. 14, the Federal Military Government divided the country into 12 states.[159] The newly created states applied the income tax laws prevailing in the region from whence they had been carved. This took the complexity in the Nigerian tax system to another level.

Lagos being one of the newly created states assumed a new status and as a consequence, collection of personal income tax in Lagos was divested from Federal Inland Revenue Department and became the responsibility of Lagos State Internal Revenue Department. Several developments occurred in terms of tax and tax related legislations such that between 1967 and 1975 there were at least twenty-one legislations including ammendments. In 1975, the Federal Board of Inland Revenue (FBIR) established an office in every state capital to enhance maximum cooperation from the state tax authorities. This idea originated during the Jos Conference of the Joint Tax Board (JTB) in 1972, and received the blessing of the Federal Military Government as part of its Third National Development Plan (1975-80).[160] The revenue collected by the FBIR at this period constituted over 60 percent of government total annual revenue, and the major sources of its tax revenue were from petroleum profit tax, companies' income tax, capital gains tax, personal income tax (armed forces and other persons), individual tax arrears, etc.[161]

On January 12, 1977 the Federal Board of Inland Revenue was reorganized such that the Federal Inland Revenue Department became the executive arm of the Board. In the course of the year, legislative changes were also made. With respect to pioneer companies, any agro allied projects whose raw materials were produced locally was entitled to pioneer certificate for the statutory period of 5 years whereby profit made was tax-free as provided under the *Industrial Development Income Tax Relief Decree 1971*. In the realm of personal taxation, a taxpayer became entitled to either 600 naira personal allowance or one tenth of his annual earned income whichever was higher while dependent relative allowance became 400 naira per any taxable person who made a claim.

The government also approved with effect from 1977 to 78 certain fiscal incentives to oil companies in order to create favourable investment atmosphere for the companies, strengthen the mutual confidence between the government and the producing companies and to encourage greater exploration and production activities. The incentives covered expensing of exploration drilling cost, petroleum profits tax and royalty rates modification, amortization in five years of all capitalized expenditure, granting of investment tax credit on the basis of area of operation and increase in company margin for light and medium oils.

In 1978, the Federal Military Government set up a Task Force on tax administration under the chairmanship of Alhaji Shehu Musa, permanent secretary of the federal ministry of finance at the time. The Task Force was to:

i.   examine the source of tax revenue and the structure of tax administration in Nigeria;

ii.  assess the effectiveness in the management of the existing taxes both at the federal and state levels; and

iii. suggest ways and means of making the administration of the tax system more effective and efficient.

The Task Force submitted its report in 1979 and the outcome of that report was the promulgation of the *Companies Income Tax Decree No. 28 of 1979* (CITA 1979) which repealed the Companies Income Tax Decree of 1961. Also, as an outcome of the Shehu Musa Task Force, the government introduced the withholding tax regime which imposed a 10 percent levy on excess profits of banks and 21 percent turnover tax on building and construction companies.[162] The CITA 1979 also established the Federal Board of Inland Revenue[163] and vested it with the administration of the Act as well as the *Capital Gains Tax Act 1967, Petroleum Profit Tax Act 1959, Stamp Duties Act, Armed Forces and Other Persons (Special Provisions) Act 1972* and *Industrial Development Income Tax Relief Act 1971.* Also, section 52 of CITA 1979 established the Body of Appeal Commissioners. The members were appointed by the Honourable Minister of Finance from among members of the accountancy or legal profession and business men who appeared to him to be competent. They were to be 12 in number and to be headed by a chairman. Another improvement brought about by the Act in the course of the year was that cases referred to the Revenue Court needed not be heard afresh. Thus, section 55 (3) of the said Act made a significant improvement such that an award of judgment of the Board of Appeal Commissioners was enforceable as a judgment of the Revenue Court, upon registration of a copy of such award with the Chief Register of the Federal Revenue Court by the judgement creditor. Under the Companies Act 1961, cases could be started afresh at the High Court. In consequence therefore, under CITA 1979, the Body of

Appeal Commissioners became the final arbiter on questions of facts and an appeal from them to the Revenue Court was on point of law by way of a case stated.

## Tax Administration since 1979

In the early 1980s, some state governments notable among which were Bendel, Ogun, Lagos, Oyo, Cross River started agitating for increased taxing powers in order to boost revenue from internal sources to prosecute their development programmes. This agitation revolved around the importance of the sales tax to the revenue needs of the states. A sales tax is a tax levied on the purchase or sale of designated commodities (goods or services). Although it may be collected at any stage in the course of the movement of the commodity between the manufacturer/producer and the consumer; and it may be a single or multiple stage tax, the intention is that it be borne by the final the consumer. Thus it is a consumer or expenditure tax. The sales tax initiative taken by state governments presented some problems prominent among which were:

a.  the likely breach of the country's constitution regarding the appropriate authority to impose tax;

b.  the likely confusion resulting from divergent legislations applicable in different states;

c.  possible arguments relating to the appropriate tax jurisdiction with respect to inter-state trade.

In order to eliminate the above challenges, the federal government promulgated the Sales Tax Decree in 1986.[164] The decree abolished all the previous sales tax enactments by state governments.

Furthermore, certain proposals contained in the 1986 and 1987 budget speeches of military president Ibrahim Babangida were codified into law by the enactment of the *Finance (Miscellaneous Taxation Provision) Decree No. 12 of 1987*. Some of the highlights of the decree were:

a.  the reduction in the rates of companies and individual taxes;

b.  the application of the withholding tax on contract, consultancy, professional and technical services and fees of the individual;

c.  the power to levy 10 per cent penalties on outstanding tax liability on an annual basis;

  d. the need for companies under the Petroleum Profit Tax Act, 1959 to pay their outstanding tax liabilities one month after the decision of the high courts; and

  e. tax exemption on gratuities paid in the private sector.

There were also incentives for capital imported for business in Nigeria and for research and development made by companies and individuals.

In 1987, the federal government also issued the National Economic Emergency Power (surcharge on after tax profit, dividend and rent) Order. The Order confirmed that the National Economic Recovery Fund (NERF) deductions were to be limited to the after-tax profits of the accounts and returns ended on any day in the year 1984 and forming the basis period for 1985 assessment year, the dividends payable out of the profits of the accounts of the year ended on any day in the year 1985 and the rent payable for the year 1986.

Another development within this period was the completion of the avoidance of double taxation agreement with Pakistan, Philippines, Sweden, Belgium and Czechoslovakia. A similar agreement between Nigeria and United Kingdom was signed in 1987 by the representatives of the two countries.

Beginning from the 1987 tax year, a company or an individual deriving income from any company was to enjoy tax free dividend for a period of three years if: the company paying the dividend was incorporated in Nigeria and if engaged in agriculture and petrochemical or Liquified Natural Gas (LNG; five years); the recipients equity participation in the company constitutes at least 10 percent of the share capital of the company; and the equity participation is imported into the country between 1$^{st}$ January 1987 and 31$^{st}$ December, 1992.

## The Beginning of Modern Reforms in the Nigerian Tax System

In 1991, the federal government set up a Study Group of eminent Nigerians headed by Prof. Emmanuel Edozien to review the entire tax system and its administration. The outcome of the Study Group led to the promulgation of the *Finance (Miscellaneous Taxation Provisions) (Amendment) Decree No. 3 of 1993*. The decree recognized the continuing existence of the Federal Board of Inland Revenue and reconstituted the Board by expanding the number of members of the Board to fifteen inclusive of the Board Secretary. The Group, which set out to overhaul the entire system of tax administration came up with the following recommendations:

a. The setting up by law at federal, state and local levels, Federal Inland Revenue Service, States' Internal Revenue Service, and Local Government Revenue Committees respectively;

b. Each Service should have a board which would be its governing body;

c. The Federal Inland Revenue Service should be the operational arm of the Federal Board of Inland Revenue.

The Government in its White Paper accepted the recommendations. The composition, functions and scope of the new board were expanded to cope with modern development and ensure uniformity throughout the country. The Study Group further recommended in paragraph 31 of the White Paper that the Board should be responsible for:

a. Ensuring the effectiveness and optimum collection of all taxes and penalties due to the service under the relevant laws;

b. Making recommendations, where appropriate to the minister or commissioner, as the case may be, on tax policy, tax reform, tax legislation, tax treaties and exemption as may be required from time to time.

c. Ensuring that all amounts collected by the Service are accounted for and paid into government coffers;

d. Generally controlling the management of the Service on matters of policy, subject to the provision of the law setting up the service; and

e. Appointing, promoting, and disciplining employees of the Service.

The new Board was inaugurated on Wednesday 7th April, 1993 by the Honourable Secretary of Finance, Prince Oladele Olashore at the Conference Room of the Federal Ministry of Finance, Abuja. The decree provided for the composition of the Board as follows:

i. an Executive Chairman, who shall be a person within the Service experienced in taxation to be appointed by the President;

ii. the Directors and Heads of Departments of the Service;

iii. the officer from time to time holding or acting in the post of Director with responsibility for planning, research and statistics matters in the Federal Ministry of Finance;

iv. A member of the Board of the Revenue Mobilization Allocation and Fiscal Commission;

v.   A member from the Nigeria National Petroleum Corporation not lower in rank than an Executive Director;

vi.  A Director from the National Planning Commission;

vii. A Director from the Nigerian Customs Service;

viii. The Registrar-General of the Corporate Affairs Commission; and

ix.  The Legal Adviser of the Service.

In spite of the reforms introduced by decree No. 3 of 1993, tax administration still remained a function of the civil service and the Chairman of the Federal Inland Revenue Service was one of the Directors of the Federal Ministry of Finance.[165] The first non-career civil servant to assume the office of Chairman of the Board was Mallam Balama Manu, a private sector banker who assumed office on the 3rd of September, 2001.

Between 2002 and 2005, several initiatives and efforts were made to elevate and update the country's tax system and administration and put it at par with global best practices. There were inputs from several stakeholders including the Presidency, the Federal Executive Council, the National Economic Council, the National Assembly, the Ministry of Finance and Economic Planning as well as the Joint Tax Board. Others were the International Monetary Fund (IMF) and the civil society. In August 2002, the Finance Minister Mallam Adamu Ciroma inaugurated another Study Group headed by Professor Dotun Phillips with terms of reference to:

a.   review all aspects of the Nigerian tax system and recommend improvement therein;

b.   review all tax legislation in Nigeria and recommend amendments where necessary;

c.   review all amendments and collection procedures, including payment procedures, objection and appeal procedure and court proceedings and recommend appropriate improvements;

d.   review the entire tax administration and recommend improvements in the structure for the whole country as well as the administrative structures at the federal, states and local government levels, with a view to enhancing performance and efficiency;

e.   consider and recommend the possibility of the grant of operational and financial autonomy to the revenue authorities;

f.   review and recommend the jurisdiction and scope of tax authorities at the federal, state and local government levels;

g.  examine and recommend the mode of financing revenue authorities to reflect constitutional provisions;

h.  assess the extent of implementation and the impact of the recommendations of the 1991 Study Group;

i.  consider international developments in taxation and recommend suitable adaptation to Nigerian circumstances;

j.  evaluate and confirm the desirability or otherwise of the retention of the portfolio of fiscal incentives enshrined in the tax laws; and

k.  consider and recommend new taxes where necessary, with a view to significantly improving the overall tax system.[166]

In order to make the study easy and detailed, the Study Group was divided into eight sub-committees. The sub-committees were on National Tax Policy, Tax Incentives and Disincentives, Local Government, Oil and Gas Taxation, Taxation and Federalism, Indirect Taxation, Direct Taxation and Tax Administration. The Study Group submitted its report to the Federal Government in July 2003. On 12 January 2004, the new Finance Minister Dr. Ngozi Okonjo-Iweala inaugurated a private sector led Working Group headed by Seyi Bickersteth. The Working Group's terms of reference were to:

a.  critically evaluate the recommendations of the Study Group;

b.  prioritise the strategies necessary to give effect to the reform of the Nigerian tax system; and

c.  segment the strategies into short term, medium term and long term.

At a retreat held between 10 and 11 February 2004, the Working Group prepared its final report and submitted it to the Federal Government. At a Federal Executive Council meeting held on October 18, 2004, the new Executive Chairman of the FIRS outlined the reform agenda necessary to reposition the Nigerian tax system. The reform agenda was distilled mainly from the recommendations of both the Study and the Working Groups with inputs from other stakeholders such as the IMF Mission on Tax Administration, the Federal Ministry of Finance, and the Economic Management Team. The unanimous opinion among all stakeholders was that tax reforms should aim at diversifying the Nigerian economy. The highlights of the presentation to the FEC by the Executive Chairman were as follows: [167]

a. Tax incentives should be streamlined and exceptions made only for the oil sector, industries located and operating in the rural areas and export-oriented industries.

b. The tax administration system should be reformed by adopting the following measures:

    i. Making the Federal Inland Revenue Service autonomous with respect to funding, procurement, recruitment and remuneration;

    ii. Reviewing the organizational structure of the FIRS and ensuring the computerisation of its operations;

    iii. Reduction of tax evasion by naming and shaming recalcitrant and defaulting taxpayers;

    iv. The establishment of a tax or revenue division of the Federal High Court to enable specialization by High Court judges as well as quick disposal of disputes;

    v. The discontinuation of the use of tax consultants for revenue collection by governments at all levels; and

    vi. Harmonising tax procedure codes and the creation of a tax friendly environment.

c. The informal sector must be encouraged to pay taxes, especially personal income tax, and adequate mechanisms provided for sanctions against infringement of statutory requirements such as the failure to disclose income or gains of a person by a bank and forgery of Tax Clearance Certificate.

d. The four year limitation relating to the ability of companies to claim past losses from future profits and carry forward all capital allowances should be expunged from the law. Furthermore, investment tax credit should be replaced with investment allowance and penalties for late filing of returns should be increased.

e. The Education Development Fund be renamed the Education Trust Fund which would be funded through yearly votes and several other sources; Value Added Tax should be included in the Exclusive Legislative List of the Nigerian Constitution; and the VAT Act be amended and an administrative appeals procedure for objections to VAT assessments and refunds be instituted.

f.   A five percent cost of collection should be approved for the Service for its operations; another five percent of collection for tax refunds while a 10 percent cost of collection should be approved for the Nigerian Custom Service. (The Study Group and the Working Group had, respectively, recommended three percent and 10 percent cost of collection for the Service.[168]

g.   Additional incentives should no longer be given to operators of marginal fields in the area of oil and gas sector.

h.   The FIRS would work in conjunction with the FCT administration to develop the tax administration structure of the territory.

i.   The incentives proposed in regard to export processing zones (EPZs) were awaiting the approval of the National Assembly, as well as tax incentives relating to payment of tax on profit and the exemption of payment of VAT on machinery and goods imported by companies operating in EPZs.

Of particular importance on the reform agenda was the need to reposition the Service to deliver on its mandate. The repositioning required improving the work environments of FIRS personnel, overhauling unserviceable equipments, machineries and vehicles, providing adequate working materials and building capacities of employees of the Service. Furthermore, the primary objectives of the reform initiative with respect to the FIRS as an organisation include:

a.   Streamlining the mission, values, goals and organisational structure of the FIRS;

b.   Plugging the leakages in the Service attributable especially to corruption in the system;

c.   Securing adequate funding for the Service;

d.   Operational autonomy coupled with capacity building and the building of the FIRS institution though adequate staff selection, training and deployment;

e.   Expansion of the tax net in Nigeria through the introduction of more services;

f.   Strengthening the newly created Investigation and Enforcement Department;

g.   Invigorating the taxpayer education and services arm of the Service;

h.   Automation of the entire collection and general tax administration system; and

i.   The stoppage of exemptions and waivers.

The FEC largely approved the proposals and objectives of the reforms, particularly the funding of the FIRS through a percentage of revenue collected. It also approved administrative and financial autonomy for the FIRS. The FEC meeting concluded with the constitution of a Presidential Technical Committee to fashion the statutory enactments necessary to implement the proposed tax reforms. The committee comprised of the Attorney General of the Federation and Minister of Justice as the chairman. The Ministers of Finance and Aviation, the Federal Capital Territory, the Chairman of the FIRS, the Economic Adviser to the President, the Accountant-General of the Federation, the Group Managing Director of the Nigerian National Petroleum Corporation, the Director-General of the Budget Office, State House Counsel and former Chairman of the FIRS, Ballama Manu were appointed members of the committee. The Committee further divided itself into subcommittees to address sub-themes. The sub-committees included the National Tax Policy and Legal Sub-Committees. While the former worked on the background to the National Tax Policy document, the latter drafted the bills necessary to give effect to the reforms. The efforts of Presidential Technical Committee resulted in the formulation of the National Tax Policy and the nine tax bills sent by President Obasanjo to the National Assembly in November 2005, seven of which have been passed into law between 2007 and 2011. These were:

a.  the Federal Inland Revenue Service (Establishment) Bill;

b.  the Companies Income Tax (Amendment) Bill;

c.  the Petroleum Profits Tax (Amendment) Bill;

d.  the Personal Income Tax (Amendment) Bill;

e.  the Value Added Tax (Amendment) Bill;

f.  the Tertiary Education Trust Fund (Establishment; etc.) Bill;

g.  the National Automotive Council Tax (Amendment) Bill;

h.  the Customs and Excise Tariff Consolidation (Amendment) Bill; and

i.  the National Sugar Development Council Act

The laws, especially the Federal Inland Revenue Service (Establishment) Law set the stage for the institutional reforms that are ongoing within the Federal Inland Revenue Service.[169] On April 16, 2007, four of the proposed bills were signed into law by President Olusegun Obasanjo. These were: the Federal Inland Revenue Service (Establishment) Act, 2007, Companies Income Tax (Amendment) Act 2007, National Automotive Tax Act Council (Amendment) Act, 2007 and the Value Added Tax (Amendment) Act (VATA) 2007.

In 2007, the Federal Inland Revenue Service recommended an increased rate of 7.5 for VAT. The reason given for the recommendation was to shore up non-oil revenue and, in the light of regional economic integration, ensure that Nigeria's tax policy is consistent with other countries in the region whose VAT rate is far higher than the current 5 percent. The Service also recommended a downward review of corporate and personal income taxes as a demonstration of government's appreciation of the economic conditions of Nigerians.[170] The VAT rate was increased by a ministerial directive to 10% effective from 23rd May 2007.[171] The increase generated controversy as to whether the Minister's power under Section 38 to amend the rate of VAT being a delegated power, could be exercised to override the provisions of a principal legislation, namely Section 4 of the VAT Act which put the rate of VAT at 5%. Pressure from members of the public and the organized private sector compelled the government to reverse the purported increase.

# References

1  See *A History of Taxation*. Available at http://www.taxworld.org/History/ TaxHistory.htm (accessed 14/1/2009).

2  *Ibid*, 1.

3  *Ibid*.

4  *Ibid*, 2. See also *England,* Microsoft Encarta 2008 (accessed 5/1/2009).

5  A History of Taxation, *op. cit.*, 7, 8 and 10.

6  See *Saturday Punch*, 8 December 2007, 56 – 57.

7  Ayua, I. A., *op. cit*, 22.

8  Akanle, O., *Nigerian Income Tax Law and Practice* (Lagos: Centre for Business and Investment Studies Ltd, 1991) 19.

9  *Ibid*, 17 – 18.

10  *The Native Revenue (Amendment) Ordinance1927*
    which extended taxation of incomes to Eastern Nigeria actually came into force in 1928.

11  Akanle, O., *Nigerian Income Tax Law and Practice,* 21 – 22.

12  Omolewa, M., *Certificate History of Nigeria* (Lagos, Longman Group, 1986) 41.

13  *Ibid,* 48.

14  Crowther M., *The Story of Nigeria* (London: Faber & Faber, 1962) 38 *est. seq.*

15  Omolewa, *op. cit*, 48.

16  See *Kanem Bornu Empire*. Available at http://knowledgerush.com/kr/encyclopaedia/ kanem-Bornu_empire (accessed 11/08/09).

17  Lavers, J. E., 'Kanem and Borno to 1808' in Ikime O. (ed.), *op. cit,* 204.

18  *Ibid*.

19  Whitely, G. C., *Magumeri District: Special Report* (Kaduna: NNA, Maiprof, 1919) 264.

20  Benisheikh, A. K., 'A Preliminary Investigation into the Revenue System of the Borno Government in the Nineteenth Century' in Akinjogbin, I. A. & Osoba, S., (eds.), *Topics on Nigerian Economic and Social History* (Ile-Ife: University of Ife Press Ltd, 1980) 66.

21  *Ibid*, 71.

22  The Maria Theresa silver dollar was first used as a currency of the Austrian Empire beginning from 1740. It was used by the empire in its trade with Arab and Mid-east countries who probably introduced it into North Africa via the trans-Saharan trade.

See *Maria Theresa Silver Dollar.* Available at http://www.forafricanart.com/Maria-Theresa-Thaler_ep_58-1.html (accessed 11/08/09).

23    Benisheikh, A. K. *Op. cit,* 73.

24    *Ibid,* 74.

25    *Ibid,* 75.

26    *Ibid,* 76.

27    Akinjogbin, I. A. & Ayandele, E., 'Yorubaland up to 1800' in Ikime, O. (ed.), *op. cit,* 122.

28    *Ibid,* 124.

29    Willet, F., *Ife in the History of West African Sculpture* (London: Thames & Hudson,1967) 126.

30    Shaw, T., *Pre-History of Ife in* Ikime, O., (ed.), *op. cit,* 47.

31    *Ibid.*

32    *Ibid.*

33    Crowther, M., *op. cit,* 49.

34    Akinjogbin, I. A., 'The Economic Foundations of the Oyo Empire in the Eighteenth Century' in Akinjogbin, I. A. & Osoba, S., (eds.), *Topics on Nigerian Economic and Social History, op. cit,* 35.

35    Akinjogbin, I. A., *Dahomey and its Neighbours 1708 – 1818* (London: CUP, 1967) 9.

36    Akinjogbin, I. A., 'The Economic Foundations of the Oyo Empire in the Eighteenth Century', *op. cit.* 38.

37    *Ibid,* 39.

38    *Ibid,* 42.

39    Johnson, S., *The History of Yoruba: From the Earliest Times to the Beginning of the British Protectorate* (Lagos: CMS Nig. 1951) 93.

40    Akinjogbin, I. A., 'The Economic Foundations of the Oyo Empire in the Eighteenth Century', *op. cit,* 49.

41    *Ibid,* 49.

42    *Ibid.*

43    *Ibid,* 53.

44    Akinjogbin, I. A., *Dahomey and its Neighbours, op. cit.*

45    Awe, B.A., *The Rise of Ibadan as a Yoruba Power in the 19th Century* being a PhD Thesis submitted to Oxford University, July 1964, 76 – 120.

46    Akinyele, I. B., *Outline of Ibadan History* (Lagos: Alebiosu Printing Press, 1946) 72.

47 Akintoye, S. A., 'The Economic Foundations of Ibadan's Power in the 19th Century' in
Akinjogbin, I. A. & Osoba, S., (eds.), *Topics on Nigerian Economic and Social History, op. cit*, 55.

48 *Ibid.*

49 *Ibid*, 56.

50 Hinderer, A. M., *Seventeen Years in the Yoruba Country* (London: Seeley, Jackson & Halliday, 1873) 59 – 62.

51 Akintoye, S. A., *op. cit*, 58.

52 Hinderer, A. M., *op. cit.*

53 Akintoye, S. A., *op. cit*, 61.

54 *Ibid*, 63.

55 *Ibid.*

56 Lugard, F., *Political Memoranda: Revision of Instructions to Political Officers on Subjects chiefly Political and Administrative (1913 - 1918) (3rd ed.)* (London: Frank Cass & Co. 1970) 178.

57 Omolewa, M., *op. cit*, 62.

58 Igbafe, A. A., 'The Pre-Colonial Economic Foundations of Benin kingdom' in
Akinjogbin, I. A. & Osoba, S., (eds.), *Topics on Nigerian Economic and Social History, op. cit*, 19.

59 *Ibid*, 20.

60 *Ibid.*

61 *Ibid.* See also, Omolewa, M., *op. cit*, 65 – 66.

62 Omolewa, M., *op. cit*, 64.

63 *Ibid,* 65.

64 *Ibid,* 66.

65 *Ibid,* 67.

66 *Ibid.*

67 Igbafe, P. A., *op. cit*, 22.

68 *Ibid*, 20.

69 *Ibid*, 22.

70 *Ibid*, 21.

71 Egharevba, J. U., *Benin Law and Custom* (Port Harcourt: CMS, 1949) 78.

72 Igbafe, P. A., *op. cit.*

73	*Ibid*, 23.

74	*Ibid*.

75	*Ibid*.

76	Elias T.O., *Nigerian Land, Law and Custom* (London: Routledge & Kegan Paul, 1962) 107.

77	Omolewa M., *op. cit* 81.

78	*Ibid*.

79	*Ibid*.

80	*Ibid*

81	*Ibid*, 84.

82	*Ibid*.

83	*Ibid*.

84	*Ibid*.

85	*Ibid*, 85.

86	Afigbo A. E., 'Economic Foundations of Pre-colonial Igbo Society' in Akinjogbin, I. A. & Osoba, S., (eds.), *Topics on Nigerian Economic and Social History, op. cit*, 2.

87	*Ibid*, 4.

88	*Ibid*, 8.

89	*Ibid*.

90	*Ibid*, 11.

91	*Ibid*, 14.

92	*Ibid*.

93	*Ibid*.

94	*Ibid*.

95	*Ibid*, 88.

96	*Ibid*, 87.

97	Ukwu, U.J., 'The Development of Trade and Markets in Igboland' III (4) (1967) *Journal of the Historical Society of Nigeria* 647.

98	Alagoa, E.J., 'The Eastern Niger Delta and the Hinterland in the 19th Century' in Ikime, O., (ed.), *op. cit*, 260.

99	*Ibid*.

100	Omolewa, M., *op. cit*, 74.

101	*Ibid*.

102	*Ibid*.

103 Alagoa, E. J., 'Peoples of the Cross River Valley and the Eastern Niger Delta' in Ikime, O. (ed.), *op. cit*, 68.

104 *Ibid*, 77.

105 Ikime, O., 'The Peoples and Kingdoms of the Delta Province' in Ikime, O., (ed.), *op. cit*, 89.

106 *Ibid*.

107 *Ibid*.

108 *Ibid*, 97.

109 Omolewa, M.,*op. cit,* 77.

110 *Ibid*.

111 *Ibid*.

112 *Ibid*.

113 *Ibid*.

114 Ikime, O., *op. cit*, 97.

115 Olusanya, G.O., 'Constitutional Developments in Nigeria 1861 -1960' in Ikime, O. (ed.), *op. cit*. 518.

116 Ordinance No.3 of 3rd February, 1866, CO 151/4.

117 Lugard, F., *Political Memoranda, op. cit*, 296.

118 *Ibid*, 297.

119 *Ibid*, 298.

120 *Ibid,* 302.

121 Onabamiro, S., *Glimpses into Nigerian History: Historical Essays* (Lagos: Macmillan Publishers, 1983) 90.

122 *Ibid*, 93.

123 *Ibid*.

124 *Ibid*.

125 *Ibid,*97.

126 *Ibid*

127 Lugard, F., *The Dual Mandate in British Tropical Africa* (Edinburg & London: W. Blackwood & Sons, 1922) 219.

128 See Lugard, F., *Political Memorandum, op. cit*, 25 – 30.

129 Phillipson, S., *Administrative and Financial Procedure under the New Constitution* (Lagos Government Printer, 1946).

130 *Ibid*.

131   Section 17A Direct Taxation (Amendment) Ordinance No. 2 1948.

132   Philipson, S., *op. cit,* paragraph 72.

133   No. 12 of 1957.

134   Section 65B (3), Western Nigeria Income Tax Law No. 30 of 1960.

135   1958, 1959 and 1960.

136   Local government administration was first introduced into Eastern Nigeria by the Native Authority Ordinance, No. 43 of 1933.

137   Mwalimu, C., *The Nigerian Legal System: Public Law*(NY: Peter Lang, 2007) 292.

138   No. 1 of 1956.

139   Orewa, G. O., Taxation in Western Nigeria: The Problems of an Emergent State (Oxford: NISER, 1962) 26 – 27. Hereafter referred to as Orewa, G. O.

140   *Ibid*, 27.

141   Tijani, H., 'The "New" Lagos Town Council and Urban Development: 1950 – 1953' in Falola, T. & Salm, S. (eds.), *Nigerian Cities* (NJ: Africa World Press, 2004) 255.

142   No. 29 of 1917.

143   Orewa, G. O. & Adewumi, J. B., *Local Government in Nigeria: The Changing Scene* (Benin City: Ethiope Pub. Co., 1983) 66.

144   Orewa, G. O., *op. cit,* 31.

145   Orewa, G. O. & Adewumi, J. B., *op. cit,* 65.

146   Orewa, G. O., *op. cit,* 33.

147   *Ibid.* 35

148   Ekundare, R. O., *An Economic History of Nigeria: 1860 – 1960* (London: Methuen Co. 1973) 236.

149   *Ibid*, 237.

150   Dudley, B. J., *Parties and Politics in Northern Nigeria* (London: Routledge, 1968) 268.

151   Ayua, I.A., *Nigerian Tax Law* (Ibadan: Spectrum, 1996) 26.

152   *Ibid*, 27.

153   *Ibid.*

154   *Ibid.*

155   *Ibid.*

156   *Ibid*, 28.

157   See sections 49, 50 (1), 53 (3) and the proviso to 53 (3) respectively.

158   Ayua, I. A., *op. cit.*

159   For more on state creation, see chapter one.

160  *Ibid.* p.10

161  *Ibid.* p. 13

162  Okoh, S., 'Political and Economic Imperatives of the New Tax Reform', *Leadership*, 5 March 2006, 39.

163  See section 1 thereof.

164  No. 7 of 1986.

165  Fiakpa, L., 'Tax Yoke', *Thisday Newspaper,* 5 March 2006, 39.

166  *Nigerian Tax Reforms: 2003 and Beyond,* being the Main Report of the Study Group on the Nigerian Tax System, July 2003, 1.

167  Minutes of the Extra-Ordinary Meeting of the Federal Executive Council held at the Aso Rock Council Chamber, Presidential Villa, Abuja on Monday, 18th October, 2004

168  Four percent of non oil collection had already been approved for the Service and seven percent had already been approved for the Nigerian Customs Service.

169  See Okauru, Ifueko Omoigui(Ed): "Federal Inland Revenue Service and Taxation Reforms in Democratic Nigeria"

170  Oluba, M., "FIRS and this VAT again", *Businessday,* 18 December 2008, 1.

171  Okereaafor, L.: "Are Residential Leases Subject to Value Added Tax in Nigeria?" *Businessday,* 22-24 February, 2008, 21.

# CHAPTER FOUR

## THE STRUCTURE AND JURISDICTION OF NIGERIAN TAX AUTHORITIES

### THE FEDERAL INLAND REVENUE SERVICE

The nucleus of the Federal Inland Revenue Service was formed with the appointment, in 1935, of Frank G. Lloyd as the Commissioner of Income Tax for the Colony and Protectorate of Nigeria. Like his counterparts in Gold Coast (Ghana), Sierra Leone, and Gambia, Lloyd was overseen by Walter B. Dare who was the Commissioner of Income Tax for Anglophone West Africa comprising of Nigeria and the aforementioned colonies. Lloyd was assisted by Fraser G. Selby as the first Assistant Commissioner of Income Tax. In 1943, the Nigerian Inland Revenue Department was carved out of the Anglo-Phone Inland Revenue Department and established as an autonomous body, and W.A.B. Carter of the United Kingdom Inland Revenue was appointed as the first Commissioner of Income Tax of the new agency, a position he held until 1951 when he was succeeded by Fraser G. Selby. The Inland Revenue Department was made up of the following:

a. The Resident appointed by the Governor;

b. Chief and elders in each district;

c. Any native authority, which by native law and custom was recognized as the tax collection authority;

d. Any native council or group of persons appointed by the Governor.

F.G. Reynolds was appointed Commissioner of Income Tax upon the retirement of F.G. Selby in 1960 and was the helmsman for only one year.[1] F. G Reynolds was succeeded by the first Nigerian Chairman of the Federal Board of Inland Revenue, Chief Ephraim A. Osindero.[2] Chief Osindero was chairman from 1961 to 1971. Other chairmen that followed, in chronological order are: Chief Vincent O. A. Ogunba (1971-1978), Chief David A. Olorunleke (1978 - 1992), Mr. James K. Naiyeju (1992-1999), Alhaji Ibrahim Zukogi (1999 - 2001), Mr. Ballama Manu (2001 - 2004), Ifueko Omoigui Okauru (2004 to date). In 1993, the nomenclature of the chief executive of the Service was again changed from 'Chairman' to 'Executive Chairman.'[3]

Although section 3 of the *Income Tax Administration Ordinance No. 39 1958*, which was a fallout from the Raisman Commission Report, statutorily provided for the establishment of the 'Federal Board of Inland Revenue',[4] full effect was only given to that provision under the *Companies Income Tax Act (CITA) 1961*. The Federal Board of Inland Revenue consisted of a Chairman, a Deputy Chairman, and Senior Assistant Secretary with responsibility for revenue matters in the Federal Ministry of Finance; Legal Adviser in the Federal Revenue Department; two other members being Chief Inspector of Taxes or Officers of equivalent rank; and one further member appointed by notice in the Gazette by the Minister.[5] In line with this structure, Ephraim Osindero was appointed on 29th April 1961, a position he held until 1971 when he was succeeded by O. A Ogunba.

The process of re-organization of the Board and its executive arm, the Federal Inland Revenue Department was formally approved by the federal government on the 12th of January, 1977. The purpose of the re-organization was to revitalize the Board and the Department to make them serve as potent weapons for combating the twin problem of tax evasion and avoidance and to cope effectively with the geographical and functional expansion within the Department. The highlights of the reorganization were the changes in the designation of the post of Chairman and Deputy Chairman to Director and Deputy Director of the Department respectively and the increase in the number of Deputy Directors from three to four with specific functions assigned to each Deputy Director. The re-organization also included the increase in the membership of the Board from seven to ten, appointment to the Board, representatives of ministries and other organizations whose mandate had bearing with functions performed by the Board, increase in the number of posts of Chief Inspectors and other established senior posts, upgrading of the post of the Board Secretary, creation of Intelligence Section and so on. The official opening of the inaugural meeting of the Board was performed by the Honourable Federal Commissioner for Finance on the 8th of September, 1977.[6]

The next land mark re-organisation of the Board was the promulgation of the *Finance (Miscellaneous Taxation Provisions) (Amendment) Decree No. 3 of 1993* which reconstituted and expanded the Board's membership. Further transformations came sequel to the recommendations of the Study Group and the Working Group (as earlier analysed), the most fundamental of which was the passage of the *Federal Inland Revenue Service (Establishment) Act in 2007*.

## Composition of the Federal Inland Revenue Service[7]

*Composition of the Board*

The Board comprises of:

a. The Executive Chairman of the FIRS, who shall be a person experienced in taxation to be appointed by the President as Chairman;

b. Six members with relevant qualifications and expertise appointed by the President to represent each of the six geo-political zones.

c. Chairman of the National Revenue Mobilisation, Allocation and Fiscal Commission or his representative;

d. Representative of the Minister of Finance not below the rank of Director

e. Group Managing Director of the Nigeria National Petroleum Corporation or his representative not below the rank of Group Executive Director or its equivalent;

f. The Chief Executive Officer of the National Planning Commission or his representative not below the rank of Director;

g. Comptroller-General of the Nigerian Customs Service or his representative not below the rank of Deputy Comptroller-General;

h. The Registrar General of the Corporate Affairs Commission or his representative not below the rank of Director;

i. A representative of the Attorney-General of the Federation;

j. The Governor of the Central Bank of Nigeria or his representative

*Powers and Duties of the Board*

a. Provision of general policy guidelines relating to the functions of the Service;

b. Management and superintendence of policies of the Service on matters of administration of revenue assessment, collection and accounting under the Act or any enactment;

c. Review and approval of strategic plans for the Service;

d. Employment and determination of terms and conditions of service, including disciplinary measures for the Service;

e. Determination of remuneration, allowances, benefits and pensions of staff of the Service in consultation with the National Salaries, Income and Wages Commission;

f. Such other things which in its opinion are necessary to ensure the efficient performance of the functions of the Service.

There is also a Technical Committee of the Board comprising of the Executive Chairman of the Service as Chairman; all the Directors and Head of Departments of the Service; the Legal Adviser of the Service; the Secretary to the Board; and any person co-opted from the Service by the Committee. The functions of the Committee are:

a. Consideration of all tax matters requiring professional and technical expertise and making recommendations to the Board;

b. Advising the Board on any aspect of the functions and powers of the Service; and

c. Such other matters as may from time to time be referred to it by the Board.

## Taxes administered by the Federal Government

The Taxes and Levies (Approved List for Collection) Act 1998 defines the jurisdiction of the three tiers of government in terms of who administers what taxes. The decree originally passed as Decree No. 21 of 1998 but deemed by the saving and transitional provisions of the 1999 Constitution to be an Act of the National Assembly is now Cap T2 Laws of the Federation of Nigeria 2004. The Act vests the collection of the following taxes in the Federal Inland Revenue Service:

a. Petroleum Profits Tax

b. Companies Income Tax

c. Personal Income Tax (FCT residents, non-residents, members of the Nigerian Police and the Armed Forces, employees of the Federal Ministry of Foreign Affairs)

d. Withholding tax on companies, residents of the FCT and non-residents

e. Capital Gains Tax (corporations, FCT residents and non-residents)

f. Stamp Duties (corporations and FCT residents)

g. Education Tax

h. Value Added Tax

In addition to the eight taxes above, the National Information Technology Development Act 2007 empowers the FIRS to administer the National Information Technology Development Levy imposed by section 12 of the Act. Lastly, the Federal Inland Revenue Service (Establishment) Act 2007 empowers the Service to administer all fees, levies and taxes relating to Oil Exploration License, Oil Mining License, Oil Production License, royalties and rents.

## STATE BOARDS OF INTERNAL REVENUE

The history of State Boards of Internal Revenue is traceable to the history of state creation in Nigeria. In 1967, the Federal Military Government promulgated the *States (Creation and Transitional Provisions) Decree No. 14 1967* under which the country's three regions were divided into twelve states. Lagos, which until then enjoyed the status of federal capital territory, became recognised by the decree as one of the new states. This new status came with certain implications for the state, one of which was the need to generate revenue to support the provision of services for residents of the state. In response to this challenge, collection of personal income tax in Lagos was divested from Federal Inland Revenue Department and was vested in the Lagos State Internal Revenue Department. At the time there was no uniformity in the composition of the State Boards of Internal Revenue. Indeed, some states did not even have Boards of Internal Revenue and the closest thing to a tax authority was the office of a director of tax revenue.[8] The absence of institutional structures led some states to initiate the practice of engaging the services of tax consultants to administer taxes on behalf of the state authorities. This was the position in several states until the report of the 1991 Study Group. One major result of the Group's report was the *Personal Income Tax Decree No. 104 of 1993*. State Boards of Internal Revenue were established for every state by virtue of section 85(1) of the decree. The decree is deemed an Act of the National Assembly and retained as Cap P8, Laws of the Federation of Nigeria 2004. Under the 2004 Act, the relevant provision is section 87. The section provides that:

> There is hereby established for each State, a Board to be known as the State Board of Internal Revenue (in this Act referred to as "the State Board") whose operational arm shall be known as the State Internal Revenue Service (in this Act referred to as "the State Service").

The state board shall comprise of the executive head of the State Service as chairman, who shall be a person experienced in taxation and be appointed by the governor from within the State Service; the director and heads of departments within the State Service; a director from the state ministry of finance; the legal adviser to the State Service; three other persons nominated by the commissioner for finance on their personal merit; and the secretary of the State Service who shall be an ex-officio member appointed by the Board from within the State Service.

*Functions of the State Board of Internal Revenue*

The State Board of Internal Revenue plays the following role in the administration of taxes:

a. ensuring the effectiveness and optimum collection of all taxes and penalties due to the government under the relevant laws;

b. doing all such things as may be deemed necessary and expedient for the assessment and collection of the tax and accounting for all amounts so collected in a manner to be prescribed by the commissioner;

c. making recommendations, where appropriate, to the Joint Tax Board on tax policy, tax reform, tax registration, tax treaties and exemptions as may be required from time to time;

d. generally controlling the management of the State Service on matters of policy, subject to the provisions of the law setting up the State Service; and

e. appointing, promoting, transferring and imposing discipline on employees of the State Service.

The State Board is autonomous in the day-to-day running of the technical, professional and administrative affairs of the State Service. The State Board may, by notice in the gazette or in writing, authorize any person to perform or exercise on behalf of the state board, any function, duty or power conferred on the state board; and receive any notice or other document to be given or delivered to or in consequence of the decree or any subsidiary legislation made under it.

*The Technical Committee of the State Board*

The Act also establishes a technical committee for the state board which comprises of the chairman of the state board as chairman; the directors within the State Service; the legal adviser to the State Service; and the secretary of the State Service. The functions of the technical committee include co-opting additional staff from within the State Service in the discharge of duties; considering all matters that require professional and technical expertise and making appropriate recommendations to the board; advising the board on all its powers and duties as specifically mentioned in section 85B of the Act; and attending to such other matters as may, from time to time, be referred to it by the board.

## Taxes Administered by the State Government

Under the Taxes and Levies (Approved List for Collection) Act, the administration of the following taxes is vested in the States Boards of Internal Revenue:

    a.    Personal income tax in respect of *Pay-As-You-Earn* (PAYE) and direct taxation (self assessment);

    b.    Withholding tax (individuals only);

    c.    Capital gains tax (individuals only);

    d.    Stamp duties on instruments executed by individuals;

    e.    Pools betting and lotteries, gaming and casino taxes;

    f.    Road taxes;

    g.    Business premises registration and renewal of registration fees in respect of urban and rural areas as defined by each state;

    h.    Development levy (individuals only) not more than N100 per annum on all taxable individuals;

    i.    Naming of street registration fees in the state capitals;

    j.    Right of occupancy fees on lands owned by the state government in urban areas of the state;

    k.    Market taxes and levies where state finance is involved.[9]

## LOCAL GOVERNMENT REVENUE COMMITTEES

Decree No. 104 of 1993 also established Local Government Revenue Committees for every local government in all the states. The relevant provision under the 2004 Act is section 85D. The section provides that:

> There shall be established for each local government area of a State a Committee to be known as the Local Government Revenue Committee (in this Act referred to as "the Revenue Committee").

The Revenue Committee comprises of the supervisor for finance as chairman; three local government councillors as members; and two other persons experienced in revenue matters to be nominated by the chairman of the local government on their personal merits. The functions of the Revenue Committee include the assessment and collection of all taxes, fines and rates under the jurisdiction of the local government and accounting for all amounts so collected in a manner to be prescribed by the chairman of the local government.

## Taxes Administered by the Local Governments

By virtue of the Taxes and Levies (Approved List for Collection) Act, the following taxes and levies can be collected at the local government level:

a. Shops and kiosks rates

b. Tenement rates

c. On and off liquor license fees

d. Slaughter slab fees

e. Marriage, birth and death registration fees

f. Naming of street registration fee, excluding any street in the state capital

g. Right of occupancy fees on lands in rural areas, excluding those collectable by the federal and state governments

h. Market taxes and levies excluding any market where state finance is involved

i. Motor park levies

j. Domestic animal license fees

k. Bicycle, truck, canoe, wheelbarrow and cart fees, other than a mechanically propelled truck

l. Cattle tax payable by cattle farmers only

m. Merriment and road closure levy

n. Radio and television license fees (other than radio and television transmitter)

o. Vehicle radio license fees (to be imposed by the local government of the State in which the car is registered)

p. Wrong parking charges

q. Public convenience, sewage and refuse disposal fees

r. Customary burial ground permit fees

s. Religious places establishment permit fees

t. Signboard and advertisement permit fees.[10]

# References

1   "Past Chairmen and Heads of Federal Inland Revenue Service", *Gauge,* October–December, 2008, 14.

2   The nomenclature of Commissioner of Income Tax was changed with the establishment of the Federal Board of Inland Revenue first, in 1958 and then in 1961.

3   Section 15 Finance (Miscellaneous Taxation Provisions) (Amendment) Decree No. 3 of 1993.

4   Hereafter referred to as 'Board'.

5   *Ibid.*

6   FBIR, *Seventh Annual Senior Officers' Conference of the Federal Inland Revenue Department 1977* (Lagos: Federal Ministry of Information Printing Division, 1978) 10.

7   All references are based on the FIRS (Establishment) Act 2007, except otherwise stated.

8   Ndekwu, E. C., *Tax Structure and Administration* (Ibadan: NISER, 1988).

9   See Part II, Schedule 1, Taxes and Levies (Approved List for Collection) Act.

10  See Part III, Schedule 1, *ibid.*

# CHAPTER FIVE

## STATUTORY DEVELOPMENTS

### Background

With the fall of Sokoto in 1903, the entire area of present day Nigeria had come under British domination. As pointed out in the preceding chapters, even prior to the appointment of Sir Frederick Dealtry Lugard as British High Commissioner for the Northern Protectorate in 1900, various forms of taxation had already been in place in Northern Nigeria. As a result, Sir Frederick did not have to introduce taxation to the north as a novel idea. His challenge in this area was to harmonize the various forms of taxes that were already in place. Lugard achieved this through the introduction of statutory enactments in the regulation of taxation. Consequently, the *Stamp Duties Proclamation 1903* was promulgated. This was followed in 1906 by the *Native Revenue Proclamation No. 2 1906*, which, for all intents and purposes, laid the foundation for the regulation of income tax in Nigeria. In the years to follow, political imperatives led to the expansion of income taxation based on this new model into first, the western territories and eventually into the eastern provinces. At the time, there was no clear cut distinction between personal taxation and business taxation in terms of statutory frameworks; rather, the income tax ordinances passed up to 1939 applied equally to both personal and business taxation. This chapter focuses on the statutory instruments that, at different times, shaped the development of the various tax types.

### Introduction of Income Tax Laws in Nigeria

The first income tax law in Nigeria was the *Native Revenue Proclamation No. 2 1906* issued by then Governor of Northern Nigeria, Sir Frederick. As the title suggests, the document was not legislation in the strict modern sense. However, to the extent that the Proclamation was a legal instrument that imposed and levied tax, it qualified as a law for all intents and purposes. The preamble to the Proclamation described it as 'relating to the levying and collection of revenue from native sources' and went on to state that prior to the issuance of the Proclamation 'tributes, rents, taxes and other dues have been levied and collected according to Native Custom by certain chiefs' and that it was:

considered advisable to legalise and regulate the levying and collection of
such taxes and dues aforesaid, and to promote such uniformity of taxation
as may be possible in the Protectorate.[1]

Consequently, and subject to the approval of the Governor, the Resident of each province was empowered to fix and assess tributes on any community or unsettled district[2] within his province and to impose tax on natives residing within his province who were previously subject to *kurdin sarauta, gaisua* and *jangali*.[3] Assessment was based on the estimate of annual value of lands and produce in each community or the annual value of the produce or goods of any trade, goods or implements of the taxpayer or on the value of livestock of herdsmen or such other incomes as were liable to tax under native custom.[4] Every community or unsettled district was required to be notified of the amount assessed against it as well as the time the assessed amount was to be collected.[5]

The Resident was empowered to appoint chiefs or other suitable persons as district headmen and village headmen (in the case of settled districts) and elders or chiefs (in the case of unsettled districts) to assist in the supervision and collection of taxes and tributes.[6] The duties of a district headman included the supervision and collection of tribute in his district; the receipt of all sums collected by village headmen and delivery of same to a recognised chief[7] as directed by the Resident; the collection of taxes from persons in his district, where so directed by the Resident; and the rendering of accounts of all tributes and taxes collected to the Resident.[8] A district headman was entitled to remuneration at an amount not exceeding one fourth of the tribute or taxes received by him.

The duties of village headmen included the collection from each member of the community to which he was appointed, such proportion of the amount at which the community was assessed for tax or tribute; remittance of tribute or tax proceeds to the appropriate district headman or such other person as directed by the Resident; and communication to the district headman the names of persons who either refused or persistently neglected to pay their proportion of tax or tribute.[9] A village headman was also entitled to remuneration from the proceeds of tax or tribute collected by him at an amount not exceeding one fifth of the total sum collected.

A right of appeal existed in favour of a person who felt aggrieved concerning the proportion of tax imposed on him by the village headman (or in the case of an unsettled district, the elders or chiefs). Such an aggrieved person could appeal to the district headman from whom a further right of appeal lied to the Resident whose decision was final.[10]

Revenue due to a recognised chief from tribute and taxes was divided twofold. One moiety (i.e. half) of the proceeds realised from tribute, *kurdin sarauta* and *jangali* were remitted to the Resident to form the general revenue of the protectorate, while the remaining moiety formed part of the revenue of the native authority. A certain proportion of *gaisua* (i.e suzerainty tax) as determined by the Governor was set aside and remitted to the Sultan of Sokoto for the furtherance of religious or other similar purpose, while the balance was remitted to the Resident as revenue for the protectorate.[11] The Governor had a right to exempt a particular property, income or profit from tax or to assign any tribute or tax or a portion thereof to the benefit of any person designated by him or for the furtherance of charitable, educational or religious objectives.[12] It was equally lawful for the Governor to exempt any province or district from the scope of the proclamation.[13]

Five categories of offences were created by the Proclamation. First, it was an offence punishable with a fine not exceeding 50 pounds or imprisonment not exceeding three years or both for any district headman or village headman to:

a.   demand from any community, unsettled district or person an amount in excess of the authorised assessment of tribute or tax;
b.   withhold for his own use or otherwise any portion of the amount collected;
c.   render false returns of the amount collected by him;
d.   willfully misrepresent the taxable capacity of the community, unsettled district or person from which or from whom he was authorised to collect tax or tribute; and
e.   defraud, embezzle or otherwise use his position to deal wrongfully with the government, individual or community.[14]

Secondly, it was an offence punishable with a fine not exceeding 500 pounds or imprisonment not exceeding five years or both for a chief to refuse to give information when so required, to a Resident regarding the taxable capacity of a community paying tax or tribute hitherto, under native custom or to willfully mislead the Resident with reference to the same matter.[15] Thirdly, it was an offence punishable with a fine not exceeding 500 pounds or imprisonment not exceeding five years for a recognised chief to refuse or persistently neglect to remit tax or tribute to a Resident as required by section 15 of the Proclamation.[16] Fourthly, it was unlawful for a person, who not being authorised to collect tax or tribute to attempt to do so; or being authorised, for such person to collect tax or tribute not approved under the Proclamation or any other instrument. In either case, the penalty was a fine not exceeding 500 pounds or imprisonment not exceeding five years.[17] Lastly, it was an offence for any person to refuse or persistently neglect to pay his portion of tax or tribute or incite another person to refuse to pay. The penalty for this offence was a fine not exceeding 50 pounds or imprisonment not exceeding two years.[18] Proceedings to enforce payment of tax, tribute or penalties were vested in provincial courts[19] while the Governor was empowered to make regulations to give better effect to the provisions of the Proclamation.[20]

In 1917, the first income tax ordinance, strictly so called, was passed. This was the *Native Revenue Ordinance No. 1 1917* and it was more or less a re-codification of the 1906 Native Revenue Proclamation and just like the Proclamation, the area of application of the ordinance was the northern provinces.[21] The differences between the two instruments were not substantial. For example, under the 1917 Ordinance, the Resident was to fix and assess tribute to be paid by a community within the province and taxes to be paid by natives residing in the province.[22] This was a deviation from the position under the 1906 Proclamation where taxable persons were specifically listed as those who had been liable to the various Islamic taxes. Second, the 1917 Ordinance extended the meaning of *village headman* to include the head of nomadic herdsmen.[23] Third, the upper limit of the remuneration of a village headman was raised to a maximum amount of one tenth of tribute or taxes collected by him.[24] Furthermore, while the proportion of revenue sharing between the government of the protectorate and the native authority remained the same, the allocation of a portion of *gaisua* tax to the Sultan of Sokoto was removed from the 1917 Ordinance. So was the discretion conferred on the Governor to allocate a portion of the revenue collected to the sole use of a certain chief or person. However, the Governor still retained the power to assign a proportion of tribute or tax to charitable, educational or religious purposes.[25] Finally, section 23 of the 1917 Ordinance conferred jurisdiction on the Supreme Court, High Court, magistrate court or native tribunal to enforce payment of tribute or taxes.

The proviso to section 1 of the 1917 Ordinance empowered the Governor to extend the application of the provisions of the Ordinance to the whole or any part of the southern provinces. As a result, the *Native Revenue (Amendment) Ordinance No. 29 1918* was passed and the provisions of the principal Ordinance was extended to south-western provinces.[26]

Through various Orders-in-Council, the divisions of *Egba, Ijebu Ode* and *Ilaro* in Abeokuta Province, *Ibadan, Oyo* and *Ife* in Oyo Province, *Benin, Kukuruku* and *Ubiaja* in Benin Province and *Ekiti, Owo* and *Ondo* in Ondo Province were brought within the statutory framework of the Native Revenue Ordinance.

By 1927, the colonial government decided that the southeast was ready to be brought within the income tax net. Consequently, the *Native Revenue (Amendment) Ordinance No. 17 1927* was passed to extend the application of the Native Revenue Ordinance to the remaining part of the southern provinces, namely, the southeast including the British Cameroons but excluding the colony of Lagos and this was reflected in the amendment accordingly.[27] The effective date for the commencement of the amendment was 1st April 1928.

In 1931, a landmark legislation was passed in the nature of the *Non-Natives Taxation (Protectorates) Ordinance No. 21 1931*. The Ordinance imposed income tax on non-natives living outside the colony for the first time. The provisions of the Ordinance were similar to those of the *Income Tax (Colony) Ordinance No. 23 1927*[28] in all material respects. Section 1 - which was the citation and application section - made the Ordinance applicable to the protectorate[29] 'including the Cameroons under British Mandate.' Assessment and collection of the tax under the Ordinance was vested in the district officers in the various divisions across the protectorate and they were to pay same to the treasurer to form part of the public revenue of Nigeria by virtue of section 3 (1). Section 4 (1) provided, *inter alia,* for the types of income subject to tax under the Ordinance. It provided thus:

> (1) There shall be levied and collected in a manner hereinafter mentioned an income tax (hereinafter called the tax) in accordance with the rates set out in the Schedule for the year of assessment commencing on the 1st April, 1931, and for each subsequent year, assessed on the chargeable income of any male non-native being in Nigeria, who in respect of the year of assessment has not paid income tax under the Income Tax (Colony) Ordinance, 1927, accruing in or derived from Nigeria in respect of:
>
> > (a)　gains or profits from any trade, business, profession or vocation for whatever period of time such trade, business, profession or vocation may have been carried on or exercised;

(b)    gains or profits from any employment;

(c)    dividends, interests or discounts;

(d)    any pension, charge or annuity;

(e)    rents, royalties, premiums and any other profits arising from property.

Chargeable income was defined as:

> the aggregate amount of the income of any non-native from the sources specified in sub-section (1) after the deduction of all the out-goings and expenses (which, if not actually ascertainable, shall be estimated) wholly and exclusively incurred during the year of assessment or the year immediately preceding the year of assessment, as the case may be, by such person in the production of the income.[30]

Section 4 (4) defined year of assessment as a 'period of twelve months commencing on the 1st April 1931, and each subsequent period of twelve months'. However, where the commissioner was satisfied that a non-native usually made up the accounts of his business on some day other than that immediately preceding any year of assessment, subsection (5) empowered him to permit the gains or profits of such business to be computed upon the income of the year terminating on that day in the year immediately preceding the year of assessment on which the accounts of the said trade or business were usually made. When a trade was business, profession or vocation carried on jointly, the ordinance deemed the income of any partner to be the share to which he was entitled in the income of the partnership and was to be included in the return to be made by such partner.[31] Section 5 exempted the official emoluments of the officer administering the government from tax under the Ordinance, while section 6 exempted temporary residents from income tax under the Ordinance, provided they had not resided in Nigeria at one or more times for a period equal to six months in the year preceding the year of assessment.

Where the gains or profits earned by a non-native were, by the nature of the business or trade in which they were engaged not readily ascertainable, section 7 (1) empowered the commissioner to make such investigations as he deemed fit into the average incomes earned by other non-natives engaged in similar trade or business and in accordance with the findings of his investigations, fix the average income earned by the non-native. By virtue of subsection (2), the commissioner was to compile a list of all such professions, trades, businesses or vocations together with the average incomes as determined by him under subsection (1) and publish same in the gazette. After publication, the average incomes so determined were deemed to be the chargeable incomes upon which non-natives engaged in those businesses were taxed for that particular year.[32]

Section 8 (1) placed a duty on every non-native chargeable with tax under the Ordinance to give notice of his chargeability to the commissioner:

a. on or before 1st of November 1931 or within three months of his arrival in the protectorate whichever was later; and

b. within three months after the commencement of any year of assessment or within three months of his arrival in the protectorate, which ever was later.

The commissioner was also empowered under section 8 (2) to require any non-native to furnish him with a return of income and such other particulars as he required, within a reasonable time for the purposes of determining the income with which such a non-native was chargeable. Failure to comply with the provisions of section 8 (1) and (2) was made an offence by subsection (3).

Section 9 (1) mandated every employer to deliver to the commissioner, vide a return in the prescribed form, the name and residence of every non-native employed by him together with all payments made to such non-native, on or before 1st October 1931 and on or before 1st April in every succeeding year. The proviso to the section however exempted non-natives whose annual remuneration did not exceed thirty pounds. Under section 10, every employer, head of family or householder was duty-bound, where so required by the commissioner or any of his assistants, to give any information that was necessary for the collection of tax under the Ordinance, and failure to give the information where required, or mislead the commissioner was an offence. Upon receiving the return of income, the commissioner could accept the return and make assessment accordingly or refuse the return and use his judgment, subject to the provisions of section 7, to determine the chargeable income of the person and assess him accordingly. Similarly, where a person failed to deliver a return and the commissioner was of the opinion that such a person was liable to pay tax, he could assess the person in line with the provisions of section 7. Such assessment did not however, affect the liability of the person for failing or neglecting to make a return. Further, where the commissioner considered the presence of any person necessary for the purpose of assessment, he could call upon the person to attend at his office irrespective of whether such a person made a return of income and failure to attend when called upon was an offence.[33]

Where it appeared to the commissioner that any person liable to tax under the ordinance had not been assessed or had been assessed at a less amount than he ought to have been assessed, the commissioner could, within the year of assessment or within two years of the expiration thereof, assess the person at such amount or additional amount as according to his judgment he ought to have been assessed.[34]

The commissioner was required to prepare lists of persons assessed to tax to be called *assessment lists*. These were to contain the names, addresses, amount of chargeable incomes, amount of tax payable and such other particulars as were required of all persons liable to tax under the ordinance. He was further obliged to notify each person whose name appeared on the assessment lists, the amount of his chargeable income and amount of tax payable by him.[35]

Section 14 (1) conferred on a non-native the right to apply to court to either cancel or reduce the amount in respect of which he was assessed, if he denied that he was chargeable or objected to the amount of assessment. The petition had to be presented within twenty one days of the notice of assessment being served on the non-native; but where the court was satisfied as to the sufficiency of reason for the delay in petitioning, it could allow a non-native time after the expiration of twenty one days to present the petition. The petitioner bore the onus of proof and where he successfully discharged it, the court could reduce the amount by which he was overcharged. Conversely, where the court was satisfied that the petitioner was undercharged, it could increase the amount of the assessment accordingly. The decision of the court regarding the assessment was final. The right conferred on a non-native in section 14 (1) did not extend to an assessment arrived at by the commissioner acting pursuant to the powers conferred on him under section 7. Petitions arising from the exercise of the commissioners' powers under section 7 were to be considered by a board of three persons, being non-officials, appointed by the Governor on such terms as were described.[36]

Section 15 specified conducts by tax collectors that amounted to offences. Pursuant to this section, any person who being employed in connection to tax by a commissioner demanded from any person an amount in excess of the authorised tax, or withheld for his own use or otherwise any portion of the amount collected, or rendered a false return of the amount collected or received by him or defrauded, embezzled or otherwise used his position to deal wrongfully with the commissioner was guilty of an offence. Similarly, any person who not being authorised under the Ordinance to collect tax but who went ahead to collect or attempted to collect tax was guilty of an offence. In either situation, the culprit was liable to a fine of 300 pounds or three years imprisonment or both.[37] Also, any person who forged, or fraudulently altered or lent or allowed another person to use receipt or token evidencing payment of tax under the Ordinance was guilty of an offence by virtue of section 16. Furthermore, any person who aided or induced another person to refuse to pay tax or made any false statement or representation for the purpose of obtaining a deduction, rebate, repayment or reduction for himself or another, aided or induced another person to deliver a false statement or false accounts or particulars concerning any income on which tax was payable under the Ordinance was guilty of an offence pursuant to section 17 (1) - (3). Section 18 provided a penalty of one hundred pounds as fine or one year imprisonment or both for any offence under the Ordinance in respect of which no specific penalty was prescribed. Section 19 empowered the commissioner to sue in his official name to enforce and recover payment of tax.

A non-native who proved to the satisfaction of the commissioner by way of deduction or otherwise, that he paid tax in excess of the amount with which he was properly chargeable was entitled to a refund of the excess so claimed, but the claim had to be made within two years from the end of the year of assessment to which it related.[38] However, by the provisions of section 20 (2), a person who failed to deliver a return after being served with notice of his assessment was not entitled to refund except if such sums as were repayable on a successful petition or where he proved to the satisfaction of the commissioner that such failure did not proceed from fraud or willful act or omission. Finally, section 21 empowered the Governor-in-Council to make regulations generally for carrying out the purposes and provisions of the ordinance.

The *Non-Natives Income Tax (Protectorate) Ordinance No. 21 1931* underwent series of amendments between 1931 when it was passed and 1940 when it was repealed.[39] The amendments were done in 1936, 1937 and 1939. In 1936, the principal Ordinance was amended twice. Some of the major changes were done by inserting subsections (1) - (6) to section 17A thus:

(1)     Any person who without lawful justification or excuse, the proof whereof shall lie on the person charged, fails, within three months after he shall have been informed by a Commissioner of the amount of the tax at which he has been assessed, to pay such tax, shall be guilty of an offence against this section.

(2)     Where a letter, notice or other document containing a statement of the amount at which a person has been assessed has been sent by post by a registered letter addressed to that person by name at his last known place of abode or business and that letter is not returned through the post office undelivered to the sender at the time at which the registered letter would in the ordinary course be delivered.

(3)     Where the person to whom a registered letter containing a statement of the amount at which he has been assessed for tax is informed of the fact that there is a registered letter awaiting him at a post office and such person refuses or neglects to take delivery of such registered letter he shall be deemed to have had notice of the amount of the tax at which he has been assessed on the date on which he was informed that there was a registered letter awaiting him at a post office.

(4)     Where a person has petitioned the Court against an assessment the period of three months mentioned in subsection (1) shall commence to run from the date on which the petitioner shall be informed by the Commissioner of the amount payable under the assessment as determined by the Court.

(5)     The provisions of this section shall be in addition to and not in derogation of any other provisions of this Ordinance.

(6)     Every person who commits an offence against this section shall be liable to a fine of twenty pounds or to imprisonment for two months or to both.[40]

The 1937 amendment was passed in the form of the *Non-Natives Income Tax (Protectorate) (Amendment) Ordinance No. 5 1937*. This amendment Ordinance repealed the Schedule to the principal Ordinance and substituted a new Schedule thereto. Under the new Schedule, new rates were fixed at a minimum of six shillings on chargeable incomes exceeding thirty pounds but not exceeding fifty pounds and a graduation of ten pounds on incomes exceeding one thousand pounds but not exceeding one thousand one hundred pounds and thereafter, one pound on every additional one hundred pounds or part thereof of chargeable income. In 1939, three amendments were passed to the principal Ordinance. The first was the *Non-Natives Income Tax (Protectorate) (Amendment) Ordinance No. 3 1939* which amended the principal Ordinance in two material respects. First, where ever the term *'non-native'* appeared in the law, it was substituted with the phrase *'male non-native'* thereby excluding non-native females from the operation of the Ordinance. Second, the Schedule to the principal Ordinance was repealed and a new Schedule was provided under section 6 of the amendment. The Schedule increased the chargeable rates from a bench mark of 30 pounds to 50 pounds and minimum tax burden of 15 shillings. Thus by virtue of the new Schedule, a person whose income exceeded 50 pounds but did not exceed 100 pounds was liable to a tax of 15 shillings. This increase in the bottom rates was reflected at all levels, such that under the new Schedule, a person whose income exceeded 1000 pounds but was less than 1100 pounds was liable to a tax of 15 pounds as opposed to 10 pounds under the principal Ordinance. Lastly, every additional 100 pound in excess of the topmost rate attracted a tax of one pound 10 shillings as opposed to one pound under the principal Ordinance.[41] The second 1939 amendment was the *Non-Natives Income Tax (Protectorate) (Amendment No. 2) Ordinance No.18 1939* which amended the principal Ordinance twofold. First, it did by the inclusion of section 19A immediately after section 19 of the principal Ordinance. The new section read:

> Any tax which a company has deducted or is entitled to deduct under section 15 of the Companies Income Tax Ordinance, 1939, from a dividend paid to a shareholder shall, when such dividend is included in the income chargeable of such shareholder chargeable under this Ordinance, be set off for the purposes of collection against the tax charged on that chargeable income.[42]

Secondly, section 20 was amended by repealing the original subsection (1) thereto and in its place, providing a new subsection (1) which read thus:

(1)     If it is proved to the satisfaction of the Financial Secretary that any
        person for any year of assessment has paid tax, by deduction at source
        or otherwise, either under this ordinance or under the Companies
        Income Tax Ordinance, 1939, or under both ordinances, in excess
        of the amount with which he is properly chargeable under this
        Ordinance, such person shall be entitled to have the amount so paid
        in excess refunded. Every claim for repayment under this section
        shall be made within two years from the end of the year of assessment
        to which the claim relates.[43]

Finally, the *Non-Natives Income Tax (Protectorate) (Amendment No. 3) Ordinance No. 29 1939*
amended the principal ordinance by removing districts officers as automatic tax collectors
as envisaged under section 3 of the principal Ordinance. In their place, the Governor could
appoint such other persons as he deemed fit by notice in the gazette.[44]

In 1940, a law was passed that limited the application of the *Native Revenue Ordinance No.
1917*. This was the *Direct Taxation Ordinance No. 4 1940*. The law applied to natives throughout
Nigeria except the township of Lagos[45] and regarding the eastern provinces and natives
resident in the colony, the law specifically repealed the *Native Revenue (Amendment) Ordinance
1927 and the Native Direct Taxation (Colony) Ordinance 1937*.[46] The power to administer tax
under the ordinance was vested in the Resident by section 3. *Resident* was defined in section
2 to mean:

        the officer appointed by the Governor to be in administrative charge of the
        particular province in question and includes any other administrative officer
        authorised by the Resident to perform any duties imposed upon the Resident
        by this Ordinance.

By section 2 (2), references to a province were deemed in respect of the colony to be
references to the colony (apart from the municipal area of Lagos) and the duties imposed on
the Resident in respect of a province under the Ordinance were, in the case of the colony
exercisable by the commissioner of the colony. The Resident was required by section 4 (1)
to act in cooperation with the chiefs or elders or other persons of influence in each district
and to take into cognisance native custom and tradition as far as circumstances permitted,

in determining the estimates of annual profits for assessment purposes. The gains or profits taxable under the Ordinance were listed in section 4(1) (a) to (b) and they included:

a.  annual profits or gains derived from lands by way of rentals or produce by any individual or native community;

b.  annual gains or profits from any trade, manufacture, office or employment engaged by an individual or native community;

c.  annual gains or profits derived from any pension, annuity, dividend or interest by an individual or native community;

d.  the value of all livestock owned by each individual or community.

Community was defined by section 2 to mean 'any group of individuals residing, carrying on business or being within any town, village or settlement or in any locality therein and includes a band of nomad herdsmen'. Section 4 (2) empowered the Resident to appoint a committee for the purpose of enquiring into the annual profits, gains or value in order to arrive at an estimate as required by subsection (1) and to accept, alter or amend the committee's estimate or computation and also fix the amount to be paid as tax. The annual profits, gains or value referred to in section 4 were deemed to be those which could be annually obtained from such lands by a native cultivating and using the same in the manner and up to the average standard of cultivation and use prevailing in the neighbourhood.[47] Subject to the Governor's approval, section 6 (1) empowered the Resident to determine the amount payable as tax based on the computation arrived at pursuant to section 4. However, where no estimate or computation was made pursuant to section 4 in any particular year of assessment, the proviso to section 6 required that the most recent estimate or computation of that community under section 4 made in any previous year of assessment be used, taking into cognisance any decrease or increase of population in the community to justify either an increase or decrease in the amount of assessment. Section 6 (2) empowered the Governor to amend or alter such assessment as appeared just or expedient to him. In lieu of assessment, the Resident, with the Governor's approval, could assess the tax payable by a specific class of persons, or community at such sums as were specified by the Resident notwithstanding the provisions of sections 4 - 6.[48] Section 8 empowered the Resident to cause to be counted all cattle in possession of a person or community and based on the count the Resident could demand tax on the head of such cattle as prescribed by the Governor. Cattle tax was payable in addition to or in lieu of assessments in sections 4 - 7.

After the assessment of persons and communities were approved by the Governor, the Resident was required to make public, in a manner he deemed fit, the amount each person and each community was assessed and the date the tax was payable.[49] Section 10 empowered the native authority by itself or through a tax collector, to fix and apportion among members of a community such amount of the total tax payable as was just and equitable having regard to each members wealth. Section 11 (1) - (3) prescribed the procedure for appeal where a person objected to the amount of tax with which he was charged. The aggrieved party, except otherwise directed by the Resident, had to appeal first to the district headman or his subordinate to cancel or vary the amount. Further appeal was to the native authority and from there to the Resident whose decision was final.

The Governor was empowered by section 12 to exempt any person or class of persons from the operations of the Ordinance or the profits, gains or value of any property from assessment under section 4, for a specified or unspecified period. The Governor could recognise a native authority as tax collection authority based on tradition or custom of the community. Where no native authority was recognised as such the Resident could appoint any native authority, district headman, village council or other suitable person as the tax collection authority in respect of the specified area. The recognised or appointed tax collection authority could in turn appoint other suitable persons as tax collectors and where he failed to do so, the Resident could appoint such tax collectors.[50]

The duties of a tax collection authority were spelt out by section 14 (1) and (2) to include giving information to the Resident – as required by the latter - as to the numbers and names of taxpayers at the time being within the area under him; supervising the collection of tax in his area; receiving from the tax collectors in his area amounts of tax assessed on, and collected from communities and natives, rendering returns to the Resident of the amounts received by him at such times and in such forms as the Resident directed. Similarly, the duties of tax collectors were defined to include furnishing the native authority with the nominal roll of all taxpayers under his mandate; collecting the amount payable from every taxpayer under him; remitting the amount of tax collected to the appropriate collection authority; and reporting to the appropriate tax collection authority the name of any person who failed to pay tax.[51] By virtue of section 16 of the ordinance, natives residing on lands alienated to or occupied by non-natives were nevertheless liable to tax. Tax collection authorities were required by section 17 (1) to deposit tax revenues received by them into the native treasury of the area for which the tax was collected. Subsection (2) required the native authority to pay such proportion of the tax revenue as determined by the Governor into the general revenue of Nigeria while the remaining proportion was transferred to, and formed part of the revenue of the native authority.

Sections 18 - 20 created various offences under the ordinance. By section 20, any tax collector, tax collection authority or any person authorised by any of them who failed to deposit tax money collected or received was guilty of an offence and was liable upon conviction to a fine of 200 pounds or imprisonment for two years or both. Under section 19, a tax collector or tax collection authority who demanded from a community or person an amount in excess of the duly assessed tax; withheld for his own use any portion of tax collected; rendered false returns of the amount collected or received by him; wilfully misrepresented the taxable capacity of a taxpayer; defrauded any person or stole or used his position in any way to the prejudice of the government, tax authority or taxpayer; or failed to carry out his duty (other than the duty prescribed in section 18 failure of which penalty was provided therein) was guilty of an offence and was liable upon conviction to a fine of 50 pounds or imprisonment for one year or both. Where a group of persons was appointed collectively as tax collector or tax collection authority, proceedings under section 19 could be instituted against the members either jointly or severally and upon proof of the commission of the offence being established, every member thereof was deemed individually liable to the prescribed penalties unless he could show to the satisfaction of the court that he was in no way responsible for the commission of the offence.[52] Section 20 made it an offence punishable with a fine of 200 pounds or two years imprisonment or both for any person who collected tax or attempted to do so, not being authorised by the ordinance or any other law.

An employer, head of family, householder or any person whose authority was recognised by a section of the community was obliged, when required by the Resident, tax collection authority or tax collector, to give all such information as was required for the assessment or collection of tax.[53] Failure to supply the required information or wilful misinformation to the aforesaid officials was an offence punishable with a fine of 100 pounds or one year imprisonment or both.[54] By section 24, any person who refused to pay tax at the due date; concealed his taxable property; misrepresented his taxable capacity; or incited any other person to do any of the above was guilty of an offence and was liable upon conviction to a fine of 100 pounds or one year imprisonment or both. Section 25 provided a similar penalty against any person who forged or fraudulently altered; or lent or allowed to be used by another person, a receipt or token indicating payment of tax. Section 26 prescribed a general penalty of 100 pounds or six months imprisonment for any offence for which no specific penalty was defined; while section 27 empowered a tax collection authority or tax collector to enforce the provisions of the ordinance by proceedings instituted in his name as the case warranted, before a magistrate or native court, to the extent of its jurisdiction. The Resident had discretion under section 28 (1) to remit or refund either wholly or partially, the tax payable by any person on the ground of poverty. Section 28 (2) vested the Governor-in-Council with a similar discretion, to be exercised on equitable ground. Finally, section 29 conferred powers on the Governor-in-Council to make regulations for the effective operation of the ordinance.

Another piece of legislation that was passed in 1940 was the *Direct Taxation Ordinance*.[55] Apart from a few alterations, the provisions of this Ordinance were substantially similar to the *Direct Taxation Ordinance No. 4 of 1940*. The alterations were found in sections 7 and 20 of the new Ordinance. Section 7 introduced the phrase 'ascertained annual income' which was defined to mean the amount of annual gains or profits:

i.      ascertained by the Resident;

ii.     accepted by the resident as correct or fair; or

iii.    varied or amended by the Resident and finally considered by the Resident as correct or fair.

Section 20 provided an alternative to the procedure of sharing tax amounts in the native treasury between the native authorities and the central government as contained under section 19.[56] The section provided that:

(1) In lieu of the Governor determining that a proportion of the amounts collected and deposited as tax in the native treasury shall be paid to the credit of the general revenue of Nigeria in accordance with Section 19, the Governor may by order annually require each or any specified native authority to pay, out of the amounts collected as tax under this Ordinance for any area, a specified amount to the credit of the general revenue of Nigeria and all the balance remaining thereafter out of the total amounts collected as tax from any particular area for

the year in respect of which the order is made shall be paid into the native treasury and form part of the revenue of the native authority for the area for which it was collected.

(2) Where a specific amount is required by the Governor by order in accordance with the provisions of sub-section (1) the Governor, in any case in which he considers it advisable so to do, may state that such amount shall not include any amounts paid as tax in respect of-

(a)any particular profit or gain;

(b)any livestock; or

(c)any cattle in respect of which a tax is paid under section 10, and where the Governor has stated that the proceeds of any such tax is not included in the amount specified in the order the proceeds of such tax shall be dealt with in accordance with the provisions of section 19.

It should be noted that the provisions of the aforementioned section 10 is *in pari materia* with section 8, *Direct Taxation Ordinance No. 4 of 1940*. Under the alternative procedure introduced by section 20 (1), the determination of the proportion of amounts to be paid into the general revenue of Nigeria from the native treasury was to be done annually. This was different from the arrangement under section 19 - or section 17 (2) of Ordinance No. 4 of 1940 - where the determination of the amount could be done 'from time to time'. Secondly, section 20 (2) exempted tax proceeds of personal income from forming part of the proportion of the revenue that accrued to the central government, thereby ensuring it was retained by the native authority where it was derived. This provision was not contained anywhere in the *Direct Taxation Ordinance No. 4 of 1940*.

### Introduction of Income Tax Laws in the Colony of Lagos

Before 1927, customs duties, excise and tariffs were the major taxes collected in the colony of Lagos. In 1927 the *Income Tax (Colony) Ordinance No. 23 1927* introduced direct taxation in the colony of Lagos for the first time. Section 1 of the Ordinance limited the application of the law to the colony of Lagos. It provided that: 'This Ordinance may be cited as the Income Tax (Colony) Ordinance, 1927, and shall apply to the Colony only'.

Under section 2 thereof, the power to assess and collect taxes in the colony was vested in the administrator of the colony. The administrator was also mandated after collecting the taxes, to 'pay same to the Treasurer to form part of the public revenue of Nigeria.' Section 3 (1) listed the incomes that were taxable under the Ordinance thus:

> There shall be levied and collected, in manner hereinafter mentioned an income tax (hereinafter called the Tax) in accordance with the rates set out in the Schedule hereto for the year of assessment commencing on the 1st day of April, 1928, and for each subsequent year, assessed as far as circumstances will permit on the chargeable income of any male person resident in the Colony accruing in or derived from Nigeria in respect of:
>
> (a) gains or profits from any trade, business, profession, vocation or employment for whatever period of time such trade, business, profession, vocation or employment may have been carried on or exercise;
>
> (b) dividends, interests or discounts;
>
> (c) any pension, charge, or annuity;
>
> (d) rents, royalties, premiums and any other profit arising from property.

Section 3 (2) provided that the tax under the ordinance was to be charged, levied and collected for each year of assessment upon the estimated chargeable income of any person for the year immediately preceding the year of assessment. 'chargeable income' was defined in subsection (5) to mean:

> the aggregate amount of the income of any person from the sources specified in subsection (1) after the deduction of all the estimated outgoings and expenses wholly and exclusively incurred during the year immediately preceding the year of assessment by such person in the production of the income.

A person was deemed to be resident in the colony for the purposes of tax under the Ordinance if his ordinary place of residence was in the colony or if he was actually present within the colony for any period of the year totalling more than three months in all and the onus was on the person found within the colony at any time to prove he was not resident in the colony within the meaning of the Ordinance.[57] Year of assessment was defined in subsection (6) to mean 'the period of twelve months commencing on the first day of April, 1928, and each subsequent period of twelve months'.

Section 4 exempted the official emoluments of the officer administering the government from tax under the ordinance. Under section 5 (1), the administrator was empowered to make investigations as he deemed fit and determine the average incomes of persons engaged in trades, businesses, professions, vocations or employments in which gains or profits are not by their nature readily ascertainable. Subsection (2) obliged the administrator to publish the list of such trades, businesses, professions or employments in the gazette and under subsection (3), the average incomes as determined and published would become the basis upon which people within the listed sectors would be charged.

Section 6 (1) of the Ordinance made it mandatory for every chargeable person to give notice to the administrator within three months after the commencement of each year of assessment that he was chargeable. Subsection (2) empowered the administrator to make a written request, on a person chargeable, to furnish him with a return of income and such particulars as may be required with respect to the income for which such person was chargeable, within a reasonable time for the purpose of assessment; and subsection (3) made it an offence for a person to fail or neglect to furnish notice of chargeability to the administrator. Section 7 placed a duty on employers to, on or before 1st of April of every year beginning from 1928; deliver to the administrator a return in the prescribed form containing:

a.  the names and places of residence of every person resident in the colony who at the date of the return was employed by him;
b.  the payments made to those persons in respect of that employment during the preceding year

The proviso to section 7 provided however, that it was not necessary to include in the return, a person, living within the municipal area of Lagos whose remuneration did not exceed 30 pounds. Section 8 made it a duty of every employer, head of family, householder and every person so required to give all such information that may assist the administrator or his assistants in the collection of tax and failure to comply constituted an offence.

Under section 9(1), the administrator was required to assess every person chargeable soon after the time allowed such person for the delivery of his return. Subsection (2) empowered the administrator to either accept the return and make an assessment based on it or refuse the return and use his judgment, subject to the provisions of section 5, to determine the amount of the chargeable income of the person and assess him accordingly. Similarly, subsection (3) provided that where a person did not deliver a return, the administrator could, subject to the provisions of section 5, determine his chargeable income and assess him accordingly. Subsection (4) empowered the commissioner to invite any person to attend at his office, whether or not such a person had made a return, if he considered the person's presence necessary for the purpose of assessment and failure to comply with the invitation was an offence.

Section 10 obliged the administrator to compile and publish a list of persons assessed to be taxed. The section contained the following provisions:

(1)   The Administrator shall as soon as possible prepare lists of persons assessed to tax

(2)   Such lists (hereinafter called assessment lists) shall contain the names and addresses of the persons assessed to the tax, the amount of the chargeable income of each person, the amount of tax payable by him and such other particulars as may be required.

(3)    The Administrator shall notify, in such manner as he deems fit, each person whose name appears on the assessment lists of the amount of his chargeable income and the amount of tax payable by him.

Section 11 contained elaborate provisions empowering a person who objected either that he was chargeable or to the amount assessed on him to challenge such chargeability or assessment by way of judicial review. However, by virtue of subsection (8), appeals arising from the exercise of the powers conferred on the administrator under section 5 could only lie to a *board of commissioners* - three in number - appointed by the Governor on such terms as were prescribed.

Section 12 (1) empowered the administrator to delegate his powers to headmen or council of headmen or other responsible persons for the purpose of supervising and collecting taxes in the areas of the colony outside the municipal area of Lagos. Under subsection (2), such headmen were to receive such fees as the administrator, with the approval of the Governor directed. Any person who being a headman, member of council or assistant employed in connection with the collection of tax, demanded from any person an amount in excess of the authorised assessment of tax, withheld for his own use or otherwise any portion of the amount collected, rendered a false return of the amount collected by him, defrauded, embezzled, or used his position to deal wrongfully with the administrator, an individual or community; or not being authorised under the ordinance to do so collected or attempted to collect tax was guilty of an offence which was punishable with a fine of 300 pounds or three years imprisonment or both.[58] It was also an offence under section 14 for any person to forge or fraudulently alter or lend or allow to be used by another person any receipt or token evidencing payment of tax under the Ordinance. Finally, any person who aided or induced another person to refuse to pay tax, made a false statement or representation for the purpose of obtaining any deduction, reduction, rebate or repayment for himself or another, aided or induced another person to make or deliver a false return or statement or prepare any false accounts or particulars concerning any income on which tax was payable under the ordinance was guilty of an offence.[59] Section 16 provided a penalty of 100 pounds as fine or one year imprisonment or both for any offence for which no specific penalty was prescribed under the Ordinance.

Section 17 empowered the administrator to enforce and recover payment of tax in his official name before a court of competent jurisdiction. Section 18 provided for refunds in proved cases of excess charges but not where the claimant neglected or failed to make a return after being served with notice of assessment except he could prove that his failure was not actuated by fraud, or wilful act or omission. Section 19 vested the Governor with powers to make regulations, including, among other things, the classes of persons to be exempted. The Schedule to the Ordinance contained chargeable rates ranging from six shillings to 10 pounds between graduated incomes of 30 pounds to 1100 pounds respectively and thereafter a rate of one pound on every additional 100 pound of chargeable income.

The *Income Tax (Colony) Ordinance No. 23 1927* was amended in 1933 by the *Income Tax (Colony) (Amendment) Ordinance No. 31 1933*. The amendment affected the principal Ordinance in three major ways. First, the amended sections provided more detailed and comprehensive provisions than was contained in the principal Ordinance. Second, the Commissioner of Income Tax replaced the administrator in the administration of the tax under the Ordinance and lastly, the commencement of the year for the purposes of assessment was made more flexible by doing away with the 1st April as the commencement date. The 1933 enactment specifically amended sections 3, 4, 6, 7, 9, 11, 14 and 15 of the principal Ordinance. The duty placed on a person chargeable to income tax under section 6 of the principal Ordinance was expanded by requiring him to give notice of his chargeability to the Commissioner of Income Tax within three months of his arrival in the colony *if* he was absent from the colony at the commencement of the assessment year.[60] Section 7 of the principal Ordinance was amended substituting subsection (1) thereof as follows:

(1) Every employer shall within three months after the commencement of any year of assessment deliver to the Commissioner of Income Tax a return in the prescribed form showing:

(a) the name of every male person resident in the Colony who during the year preceding the year of assessment was receiving from him any remuneration or pension;

(b) the last known address of each such person;

(c) the amount of such remuneration or pension paid to such person during the year preceding the year of assessment.

Provided always that the returns made under this section need not include any person whose remuneration or pension for the year preceding the year of assessment did not if resident in the municipal area of Lagos exceed £30.[61]

The requirement in paragraph (b) was not contained in the principal ordinance; neither was the qualification *'male person'* in paragraph (a) of the amended Ordinance.

Section 9 of the principal Ordinance was amended by repealing subsections (2) and (3) thereto and replacing them with new subsections. Under the new subsection (2), where the Commissioner refused to accept a return, he could assess a person based on the list mentioned in section 5 only *if* the person was engaged in any trade, business, profession, vocation or employment contained in the list mentioned in section 5. If the person was not so engaged in any of the listed vocations, the Commissioner could use his judgment to determine the person's chargeable income and assess him accordingly. A person who did not deliver his return was to be similarly treated under the amendment.[62] Sections 7 and 9 made minor amendments to sections 11 and 15 respectively of the principal ordinance. The words 'on a case being stated' were added to section 11 (7) while subsection (4) was added to section 15 of the principal Ordinance. Some minor amendments were made to the principal ordinance in 1936 but by the following year, the *Colony Taxation Ordinance No. 4 1937* repealed the *Income Tax (Colony) Ordinance No. 23 1927* together with all amendments thereto.[63]

The *Colony Taxation Ordinance No. 4 1937* established a threshold in terms of age on chargeable persons by imposing tax on all 'adult males' under section 3. 'Adult males' was defined in section 2 as 'any male of or above the age of sixteen'. The authority to assess and collect tax under the new Ordinance was vested in the 'tax authority' and the tax collected was to be paid into the 'Treasury to the credit of the general revenue of Nigeria'.[64] Tax authority was defined in section 2 as the treasurer, in the case of the municipal area of Lagos and the Commissioner of the colony, in the case of the reminder of the colony.

Tax was imposed by virtue of section 3 and payable on a preceding year basis by virtue of section 4. Section 4 recognised the 1st of April in each assessment year as the due date for payment but the proviso to the section permitted the tax authority to allow a taxpayer to use some other date as due date where he was satisfied that such taxpayer usually made up accounts of his trade or business on a day other than that immediately preceding the assessment year. Where such permission was given, such a date was to be used in subsequent years as the 'relevant' due date for assessment and collection, subject to such adjustments as the tax authority considered just and reasonable.

The First Schedule to the Ordinance increased the threshold for chargeability of male adults to persons whose income exceeded 50 pounds per annum, up by 20 pounds under the 1927 Ordinance. By virtue of section 6 however, any male adult being in Nigeria, i.e outside the colony, whose income did not exceed 50 pounds and who was unable to prove to the satisfaction of the tax authority that he had paid tax or tribute under the *Native Revenue Ordinance* was liable to pay five shillings under the *Direct Taxation (Colony) Ordinance*, and in the case of an adult male resident outside the municipal area of Lagos, an amount not exceeding five shillings, as the tax authority, with the approval of the Governor specified from time to time. By section 7, where the tax authority was satisfied that the chargeable income, if any, of a person liable to tax under the Ordinance did not exceed 50 pounds, the person could be assessed accordingly without being called upon to disclose particulars of his chargeable income. The distinction between section 6 and section 7 was that the former applied to male adults resident outside the colony, to whom this Ordinance ordinarily did not apply, while the latter section applied to adults resident within the colony whose incomes did not exceed 50 pounds which was the threshold of chargeability. Section 8 contained exemptions to sections 6 and 7. Those exempted included:

a.   Students in regular attendance in classes III, IV, V or VI at a middle school approved by the director of education or at any approved training center, college or institution receiving higher education or training as teachers, priests, pastors or evangelists.

b.   Any person who in the opinion of the tax officer, could not reasonably, on account of age, infirmity or other cause whatsoever, be called upon to pay.

c.   Any person who before 1st April 1937 was awarded the Victoria Cross, the Medal of the Order of the British Empire, the Distinguished Conduct Medal, the Military Medal, the Distinguished Service Medal or the Meritorious Service Medal for services rendered during and in connexion with any war.

d.   Any person who in the opinion of the tax authority, had been permanently disabled in government service, incapacitating him from earning adequate livelihood, or who had been wholly or partially disabled by wounds or injury received in active service or by disease due to active service.

Any person assessed under sections 6 or 7 who felt he qualified for the exemptions listed in section 8 could appeal to the tax authority.[65]

Section 10 brought non-natives whose income exceeded 50 pounds within the ambit of liability under the Ordinance by making them chargeable to the rates contained in the First Schedule to the Ordinance if they were found not to have paid tax under the *Non-Natives Income Tax (Protectorate) Ordinance 1931* in the year of assessment. The rates chargeable on the incomes of such persons resident outside the municipal area of Lagos was to be determined by the tax authority with the approval of the Governor, but in any case could not exceed the rates contained in the First Schedule.[66] The exceptions to section 10 were contained in section 11 of the Ordinance. They included:

a. The official emoluments of the officer administering the government.

b. Such income of a Consul in Nigeria in the service of a foreign government that was derived in his office as Consul.

c. Such income of an official agent, not being a British subject, in the employment of a foreign government in Nigeria, provided such employment was not exercised in connection with any trade, business or other undertaking for the purposes of making profit.

d. Any income derived from the interest payable on any loan charged on the public revenue of Nigeria.

Where any person charged under section 10 objects to his chargeability or the amount charged, he could petition in the prescribed form to either the appeal board of commissioners established under section 12 or a Judge of the Supreme Court to cancel or reduce the assessment as the case warranted.[67]

Section 14 contained the list of chargeable income. The section provided thus:

Income shall be chargeable income if it shall have been derived from one or more of the following sources:

(a) salary;

(b) gains, or profits from any trade, business, profession or vocation for whatever period of time such trade, business, profession or vocation may have been carried on or exercised;

(c) gains or profits from any employment;

(d) dividends, interests or discounts;

(e) any pension, charge or annuity;

(f) rents, royalties, premiums, and any other profits arising from property.

The income of a person in a partnership was deemed to be the share to which he was entitled during the year preceding the year of assessment in the income of the partnership and was to be included in the return to be made by such partner.[68]

Section 16 placed a duty on every chargeable person to give notice of his chargeable income to the tax authority within three months after the commencement of the year of assessment or if he was absent from the colony at the commencement of the year of assessment, within three months after the date of his arrival. Under section 17 (1), the tax authority was empowered to request from any person a return of income and such particulars, including such books as may be required, for the purposes of ascertaining the chargeable income of such person. By subsection (2), failure to comply with subsection (1) amounted to an offence. Section 18 placed a similar duty on employers regarding their employees. Under the said section, every employer was required within three months after the commencement of any year of assessment to deliver to the tax authority a return in the prescribed form showing the name of every adult male person resident in the colony who was receiving a remuneration or pension from him, his last known address and the amount of such remuneration or pension paid such person during the year preceding the year of assessment. Section 19 made it an offence for any employer, head of family, householder or other person to neglect or refuse to give all such information as may be required by the tax authority or his assistants with a view towards assessment and collection of tax. Any person whose stay in Nigeria was temporary, and whose actual residency in Nigeria at one or more times did not equal a period of six months in the whole in the preceding year of assessment, was exempted from tax under the ordinance.[69]

Upon delivery of a return by a person chargeable, the tax authority was empowered to either accept the return and proceed to make an assessment accordingly or refuse the return and use his judgment to determine the amount of the chargeable income of the person and assess based on his judgment.[70] Where a person failed to make a return and the tax authority was of the opinion that the person was liable to pay tax, the tax authority could treat the person as if his return had been refused under section 21 (2) (b).[71] By virtue of section 22, where the tax authority was of the opinion that a person liable to pay tax had not been assessed or had been assessed at an amount less than he ought to have been assessed, the tax authority could within the year of assessment or within two years of the expiration thereof assess such a person at such amount or additional amount as according to his judgment he ought to have been assessed.

The tax authority was obliged to prepare assessment list containing names, addresses, amount of chargeable income, amount of tax paid and such other particulars of every chargeable person and notify every person on the list the amount of his chargeable income, the amount of tax payable and the place where payment should be made.[72] The tax authority was empowered to appoint headmen or council of headmen or other responsible persons for the purposes of supervising and collecting tax in the area of the colony outside the municipal area of Lagos. Where so appointed, the tax authority was to determine such fees for the headmen as approved by the Governor.[73] Pursuant to section 25, claims for excess payments could be honoured by the treasurer provided the claim for refund was made within two years from the year of assessment to which it related. However, no refund could be made to a person in respect of any year in which he failed to deliver a return, unless he showed that such failure was not a result of fraud or wilful omission. Furthermore, the treasurer could, under section 26, remit partly or wholly the tax payable by any person on the ground of poverty or for other good cause(s) and could also for like reason refund the tax or any part thereof.

Legal proceedings to enforce and recover payment of tax could be summarily brought by the Tax Authority suing in his official name under section 27. Sections 28, 29 and 30 contained offences and penalties under the Ordinance. The first category dealt with offences relating to headmen or any person employed by the tax authority to assist in the collection of tax. The offences included where such employees:

a.  demanded from any taxpayer an amount in excess of the authorised assessment or;
b.  withheld for their own use any portion collected;
c.  rendered a false return, written or verbal, of the amounts collected by him;
d.  defrauded any person, embezzled money or otherwise used his position to deal wrongly with either the tax authority or members of a community;
e.  not being authorised under the ordinance collected or attempted to collect tax under the Ordinance.

In any case the offence was punishable with a fine of 300 pounds or three years imprisonment or both.[74] The second category of offences related to third parties who were not necessarily involved in tax administration. Any person who:

a.  aided or induced another person to refuse to pay tax;
b.  made any false representations with a view of obtaining any deduction, rebate, repayment or reduction for himself or for any other person;
c.  aided or induced another person to make or deliver any false return or statement or aided or induced any person to keep or prepare false accounts or particulars concerning any income on which tax was payable under the ordinance;

d.    forged or fraudulently altered or lent or allowed to be used by another person any receipt or token evidencing payment under the ordinance was guilty of an offence.[75]

The third category of offence was created under section 30. The section made it an offence for any person, who without lawful justification, failed to pay tax within three months after been assessed and informed of his liability. By section 31, where a person was guilty of an offence in respect of which no punishment was prescribed under the Ordinance, such a person was liable to a fine of 100 pounds or imprisonment for one year or both. The Governor-in-Council was empowered by section 32 to make regulations generally for the carrying out of the provisions of the Ordinance. The First Schedule to the Ordinance contained rates of chargeable income ranging from 10 shillings (persons whose income exceeded 50 pounds but did not exceed 100 pounds) to 10 pounds (persons whose income exceeded 1000 pounds but did not exceed 1100 pounds and thereafter one pound on every 100 pounds of chargeable income).

Within the same year that the *Colony Taxation Ordinance No. 4 1937* was passed, the colonial government also passed the *Native Direct Taxation (Colony) Ordinance No. 41* 1937. Ordinance No. 41 removed from the jurisdiction of the *Colony Taxation Ordinance No. 4 1937* all natives in the colony, except those in the municipal area of Lagos. Section 1 of the ordinance provided that:

> This Ordinance may be cited as the Native Direct Taxation (Colony) Ordinance, 1937, it shall apply to the Colony, with the exception of the Township of Lagos, and shall come into force on a date to be fixed by the Governor by notice in the Gazette.

Section 3 which imposed the tax to be collected pursuant to the Ordinance provided:

> There shall be levied and collected, in manner hereinafter provided, such sums as, in accordance with the provisions of this Ordinance, the Commissioner with the approval of the Governor, shall fix and assess as tax payable by any native community or any native residing or being within the Colony, but not within the Township of Lagos.

'Commissioner' was defined under section 2 as the officer appointed by the Governor to be in administrative charge of the colony or any person authorised by the said officer, while community was defined by the same section as a *town, village* or *settlement*. By section 4, the sources of income chargeable to tax under the ordinance were:

a.  annual profits or gain derived from lands and rentals thereof and the amount of annual profits of the produce thereof used, occupied or enjoyed by any native community or any native residing or being within the colony;

b.  annual profits or gains from any trade, manufacture, office or employment in which any native community or any native residing or being within the colony may be engaged.

The annual profits contemplated by section 4 were deemed to be those that could be obtained from lands cultivated by a native and using the same in the manner and average standard of cultivation and use prevailing in the neighbourhood.[76] The assessment of tax was based on the estimate of the annual profits or gains referred to in section 4 and the amount of tax payable by any native or community was to be fixed by the Commissioner, on the approval of the Governor, taking into account native custom and tradition. The last requirement did not affect the powers of the Governor to alter or amend the rates of assessment in such manner as he deemed expedient or just.[77]

Where a native community was assessed for tax, section 7 of the Ordinance required the native authority in collaboration with the village councils or such other persons as the native authority saw fit, to fix such proportion of the total tax payable by the community on each member of the community as was considered just and equitable having regard to the individual wealth of each member. After the assessment of the tax was approved by the Governor, the Commissioner was required to publicly make known to each community or person assessed for tax the amount and times such tax was to be collected.[78] Section 9 empowered the Commissioner to appoint native authorities, village councils or other suitable persons, individually or collectively, as tax authorities for the purpose of supervision and collection of tax. Where such tax authorities were appointed, it was their duty to:

a.  give information at such times as the Commissioner required regarding the numbers and names of taxable persons at the time being within its area;

b.  supervise the collection of taxes in its area;

c.  render to the Commissioner returns of such taxes received by it at such times and in such form as the Commissioner directed.

In addition, a native authority appointed to be a tax authority had a further duty to receive from other tax authorities within its area of jurisdiction all sums collected by them.[79] Section 11 (1) required every tax authority in receipt of taxes to deposit same in the native treasury, unless where the Commissioner directed otherwise. Subsection (2) required the native authority, on the direction of the Commissioner, to pay such portion of the tax revenue deposited in the native treasury into the government treasury to form part of the general revenue of Nigeria. The remainder of the deposit formed part of the revenue of the native authority. Pursuant to section 12, failure by a tax authority to deposit tax proceeds collected by him into the native treasury as required by section 11 (1) was to be punished with a fine of 200 pounds or two years imprisonment or both.

Section 13 conferred a right of appeal on any person who either denied his chargeability or objected to the amount of his assessment. The appeal went to the Commissioner who had the powers to either cancel or reduce the amount assessed as the justice of the case demanded. Section 14 further empowered the Commissioner to remit or refund, either wholly or in part, the tax payable by any person on ground of poverty or other good cause. Section 15 empowered the Governor to exempt any class of persons or community from the operation of the Ordinance for a time specified or unspecified, as he thought fit. Section 16 contained a list of offences regarding certain conduct by tax authorities or persons employed by them. Under the section it was an offence punishable with a fine of 50 pounds or one year imprisonment or both for any tax authority, or a person employed by him to:

a.  demand from any community or person an amount in excess of the authorised assessment.

b.  withhold for his own use or otherwise any portion of the amount collected.

c.  render false returns, orally or written, of the amounts collected or received by him.

d.  wilfully misrepresent the taxable capacity of a community or person from whom he was authorised to collect tax.

e.  defraud, steal or otherwise use his position to deal wrongly with the government, tax authority, individual or community.

f.  fail to carry out any duty imposed upon him, either individually or as a member of a tax authority.

Where an offence, as defined under the preceding section, was proved against a tax authority, the liability of every member of the tax authority was joint and several, except where any member could satisfy the court that he was in no way responsible for or party to the commission of the offence.[80] Under section 17, any person who collected or attempted to collect tax without authorization from the Ordinance or any other law was guilty of an offence punishable with a fine of 100 pounds or imprisonment for one year or both.

It was the duty of an employer, head of a family, householder or any person whose authority was recognised by a section of a native authority to give all such information as was required of him by the commissioner to enable the assessment or collection of tax. Failure to cooperate was an offence punishable with a fine of one hundred pounds or one year imprisonment or both.[81] Any person who without lawful justification, refused or persistently neglected to pay tax for which he was assessed, or concealed or failed to produce or notify any taxable property or misrepresented his taxable capacity or incited or assisted any other person to do any of the above was guilty of an offence punishable under section 21 with a fine of 100 pounds or one year imprisonment or both. The same punishment was prescribed for any person who forged, altered or fraudulently lent or allowed another person to use a receipt or token indicating payment of tax under the Ordinance.[82] Finally, section 23 subjected natives who were resident on lands alienated or occupied by non-natives to tax under the Ordinance. The Governor was empowered under section 25 to make rules generally for giving effect to the purposes of the provisions of the ordinance.

The *Colony Taxation Ordinance No. 4 1937* was amended in 1939 by the *Colony Taxation (Amendment) Ordinance No. 2 1939*. The amendments contained in this Ordinance related to sections 2, 3, 6, 10, 16, 18, 20 and the Schedule to the principal Ordinance. Section 2 of the principal Ordinance contained definitions of terms. Pursuant to this amendment, tax authority was redefined as 'the Financial Secretary and includes any other person authorised in writing by the Financial Secretary to perform any duties imposed upon the Tax Authority by this Ordinance'.[83] The phrase 'adult male' contained in section 2 of the principal Ordinance was replaced with 'adult' *simplicita,* and defined as 'any person of or above the age of sixteen years'.[84] The definition of chargeable income was amended by substituting the phrase 'derived from or received in' together with the preceding comma thereto, with the phrase 'or derived from' in the second and third lines of the definition of chargeable income.[85] Section 3 of the principal ordinance was repealed and in its place a new section was introduced to read:

> There shall be levied and collected in the manner hereafter specified a tax
> upon:
>
> (a) each adult non-native and
>
> (b) each adult male native
>
> (each of whom is hereinafter referred to as taxpayer) in accordance with the
> provisions of this Ordinance.[86]

By implication therefore, non-native adult females were no longer exempted from income tax in the colony but native adult females were still exempted. Further, the nomenclature *taxpayer* was introduced to replace *adult male* used in the principal Ordinance.[87] Section 16 of the principal Ordinance was repealed and in its stead the following section was introduced:

> It shall be the duty of every person chargeable with tax to give notice to the
> Tax Authority within three months after the commencement of any year of
> assessment that he is so chargeable.[88]

The requirement that if such a person was not in the colony at the commencement of the year of assessment he could give the required notice within three months of his arrival in the colony was made away with. Section 20 of the principal Ordinance was repealed and a new section 20 introduced. The new section read:

> Tax shall not be payable in respect of any income arising out of Nigeria and
> received therein by any person who is in Nigeria for some temporary purpose
> only and not with any intent to establish his residence therein and who has
> not actually resided in Nigeria at one or more times for a period equal in the
> whole to six months in the year preceding the year of assessment.

Under the principal Ordinance the phrase 'in respect of any income arising out of Nigeria and received therein' was not included. In effect therefore, the amendment expanded the scope of the exemption granted temporary residents. Finally, the Schedule to the principal Ordinance (which contained rates of chargeable income) was repealed and new rates introduced by the Schedule to the amendment. Under the new Schedule, persons with incomes exceeding 50 pounds but not exceeding 100 pounds were taxable at 15 shillings up to a graduation of 15 pounds for persons with incomes exceeding 1000 pounds but not exceeding 1100 pounds and thereafter, one pound 10 shillings on every additional 100 pounds of chargeable income or part thereof. The new Schedule, therefore, brought the tax rates on chargeable income of residents of the colony at par with taxpayers in the protectorate.

In 1939, a major legislation was passed in the form of the *Income Tax (Supplementary) Ordinance No. 28 1939*. This Ordinance was enacted to regulate the income tax regime for the 1939 to 1940 financial year.[89] Its sphere of application was both the colony and protectorate and as such was the first income tax law ever in Nigeria with nationwide applicability.[90] Pursuant to this Ordinance, references to *'principal ordinances'* meant references to the *Non-Natives Income Tax (Protectorate) Ordinance 1931* and/or the *Colony Taxation Ordinance 1937*.[91] *Tax* was defined to mean the supplementary income tax imposed by the instant Ordinance but *tax authority* had the same meaning ascribed to it under section 2 of the *Colony Taxation Ordinance (supra)*. *Taxpayer* meant each adult non-native and each adult male native.[92] 'This Ordinance', where used in the Ordinance, unless otherwise specified, referred to the *Colony Taxation Ordinance (supra)* as set out and modified in the Second Schedule of the instant Ordinance. Year of assessment meant the year commencing on 1st April 1939 and ending on 31st March 1940.

Tax was imposed under the ordinance by virtue of section 3. The section provided that:

> There shall be levied and collected a tax in accordance with the rates set out in the First Schedule for the year of assessment assessed on the chargeable income for the year preceding the year of assessment of any tax-payer whether such tax-payer is in or outside Nigeria:

> Provided that there shall be deducted from the chargeable income of any person chargeable under this section any part of such income respect of which it is proved to the satisfaction of the Commissioner that such person has paid tribute or tax under the Native **Revenue Ordinance or the Native Direct Taxation (Colony) Ordinance, 1937**.

Section 4 incorporated certain provisions of the *Colony Taxation Ordinance 1937* [93] while modifying[94] the unincorporated provisions so as to bring their application in tandem with the application of the instant ordinance. The section provided thus:

For the purposes of the levying and collection of the tax imposed by this Ordinance there shall be incorporated with this Ordinance such provisions of the Colony Taxation Ordinance, 1937 as are set out in the first column of the Second Schedule with such verbal alterations and other modifications not affecting the substance as may be necessary to render them applicable and in particular the said provisions as incorporated in this Ordinance shall be modified in the manner set forth in the second column of the said Schedule.

The officers appointed under section 3 of the *Non-Natives Income Tax (Protectorate) Ordinance 1931* to be Commissioners of Income Tax and the tax authority were deemed Commissioners for the purposes of the instant Ordinance.[95]

A major novelty introduced by the Supplementary Ordinance was the introduction of percentages as the basis for charging tax. By virtue of the First Schedule to the Ordinance, chargeable incomes not exceeding 200 pounds were not taxable. Chargeable incomes exceeding 200 pounds but not exceeding 400 pounds were taxable at one percent, chargeable incomes exceeding 400 pounds but not exceeding 700 pounds were taxable at two percent, chargeable incomes exceeding 700 pounds but not exceeding 1000 pounds were taxable at three percent, chargeable incomes exceeding 1000 pounds but not exceeding 3000 pounds were taxable at four percent, chargeable incomes exceeding 3000 pounds but not exceeding 4000 pounds were taxable at 11 percent and chargeable incomes exceeding 4000 pounds were taxable at 12 ½ percent.

One year after its enactment the *Income Tax (Supplementary) Ordinance No. 28 1939* was superseded by the *Income Tax Ordinance No. 3 1940* which repealed the:

a.  Non-Natives Income Tax (Protectorate) Ordinance No. 21 1931 together with all the amendments thereto (1933, 1936, and Nos. 1, 2 and 3 of 1939);
b.  Colony Taxation Ordinance No. 4 1937 together with the all the amendments thereto (Nos. 1 and 2 of 1938, and Nos. 1 and 2 of 1939);
c.  Companies Income Tax Ordinance No. 14 1939;
d.  Income Tax (Supplementary) Ordinance, 1939.[96]

In consequence, not only did the Ordinance revert back to the erstwhile practice of regulating personal and corporate income tax under a single legal instrument, it further brought the taxation of incomes of all non-natives in Nigeria, as well as residents of the colony of Lagos (natives and non-natives) within one and the same legal regime. Tax under the ordinance was imposed by section 5 on:

a.  gains or profits from any trade, business, profession or vocation, for whatever period of time such trade, business, profession, or vocation may have been carried on or exercised;

b.  gains or profits from any employment;

c.  dividends, interest or discounts;

d.  any pension, charge or annuity; and

e.  rents, royalties, premiums and any other profits arising from property.

The powers of assessment and collection were vested in a Commissioner who was to be appointed by the Governor by notice in the gazette.[97] By the combined provisions of section 3 (2) and (3), the Commissioner could by notice in the gazette or in writing, authorise any person to assist or perform any duty imposed on him by the Ordinance including the receipt of information, returns or documents required to be supplied. Section 4 placed a duty of official secrecy on the Commissioner or his assistants regarding documents in their custody relating to taxation; a breach of which duty amounted to an offence.

The tax imposed by the Ordinance was to be charged, levied and collected for each year of assessment upon the chargeable income of any person for the year immediately preceding the year of assessment.[98] Section 2 defined chargeable income as 'the aggregate amount of income of any person from the sources specified in section 5 remaining after allowing the appropriate deductions and exemptions under the ordinance' and year of assessment as 'the period of twelve months commencing on the 1st day of April, 1940, and each subsequent period of twelve months'.

Where the Commissioner was satisfied that a person usually made up the accounts of his business or trade on some day other than that immediately preceding any year of assessment, section 7 empowered the Commissioner to permit the gains or profits of such trade or business to be computed upon the income of the year terminating on that day in the year immediately preceding the year of assessment on which the accounts of the said trade or business was usually made up. Section 8 contained incomes that were exempted from tax under the Ordinance. The exemptions included:

a.  official emoluments of the officer administering the government;

b.  emoluments payable to members of consular services of foreign countries or in respect of official services rendered by them or income derived by them from sources outside Nigeria;

c.  emoluments payable from the Imperial Funds to His Majesty's Forces in the permanent service of the Imperial government in Nigeria in respect of their offices under the Imperial government;

d.  income of any person who was subject to tax under the *Direct Taxation Ordinance, 1940* in so far as such income was not derived in the municipal area of Lagos;

e.  income of a non-resident whose chargeable income did not exceed 50 pounds;

f.  subject to section 20 of the Ordinance, the income of a woman whose chargeable income did not exceed 50 pounds;

g.  income of a local or native authority or government institution;

h.  income of a statutory or registered building or friendly society in so far as it was not derived from a trade or business;

i.  income of a cooperative society registered under the *Cooperative Societies Ordinance*;

j.  income of an ecclesiastical, charitable or educational institution of a public character in so far as it was not derived from a trade or business;

k.  income of any body of persons formed for the purpose of promoting social or sporting amenities not involving the acquisition of gain by the group or its individuals, subject to such conditions as the Commissioner imposed;

l.  capital sums received by way of retirement or death gratuities or consolidated compensation for death or injury;

m.  capital sums withdrawn by individuals on retirement from any provident society or fund approved by the Commissioner under section 10 (1) (g) of the Ordinance;

n.  disability pensions granted to members of His Majesty's Forces;

o.  annual value of any place of worship and its premises;

p.  interest paid or credited to any individual by the Nigeria Post Office Savings Bank.

The Governor was further empowered by section 9 to exempt from tax, where he deemed fit, any interest payable on any loan charged on the public revenue of Nigeria, either generally or in respect of interest payable to persons not resident in Nigeria or companies other than as defined in section 2. Section 2 defined a company as:

any company incorporated or registered under any law in force in Nigeria and any company which, though incorporated or registered outside Nigeria, carries on business, or has an office or place of business therein.

Section 10 contained the list of deductions allowed under the Ordinance for the purposes of determining chargeable income. The rules providing for the method of calculating or estimating the deductions were to be made by the Governor-in-Council by virtue of subsection (2). The deductions allowed under subsection (1) were all outgoings and expenses wholly and exclusively incurred by a person in the production of income in the preceding year including:

a. sums payable by way of interest upon money borrowed, where the Commissioner was satisfied that the interest was payable on capital employed in acquiring the income;

b. rent paid in respect of land or building occupied for the purpose of acquiring the income;

c. sums expended in replacing any plant or machinery which was used or employed in such trade, business or profession, deducting the total depreciation which had occurred by reason of exhaustion, wear or tear since the date of purchase of such plant or machinery and any sum realised by the sale thereof;

d. sums expended in repairing premises, plant or machinery employed in acquiring the income or for the renewal, repair or alteration of any implement, utensil or article so employed;

e. bad or doubtful debts incurred and proved to the satisfaction of the Commissioner to have become bad during the year immediately preceding the year of assessment. However, sums recovered during the said year previously written off as bad or doubtful debts were to be treated as receipts of the business for that year;

f. contribution or abatement deducted from the salary or pension of a public officer under the *Widows' and Orphans' Pensions Ordinance* or under any approved scheme within the meaning of that ordinance;

g. contributions to pensions, provident or other society fund as approved by the Commissioner;

h. such other deductions as were prescribed by any rule made pursuant to the Ordinance.

In addition, section 11 allowed deduction of 'a reasonable amount' for the exhaustion, wear and tear of property, including plant and machinery, arising out of the use or employment of such property in the business during the year immediately preceding the year of assessment, provided that where such property was leased out subject to the condition that the lessee replaced the property in the event of wear and tear, the lessee was deemed the owner of the property leased. Section 12 outlined a list of expenses for which no deductions were to be allowed under the Ordinance. They included:

a.    domestic or private expenses;

b.    disbursements or expenses not being money wholly and exclusively laid out or expended for the purpose of acquiring the income;

c.    capital withdrawn or sum employed as capital;

d.    capital employed in improvements;

e.    sums recoverable under an insurance or contract of indemnity;

f.    rents or cost of repairs incurred in respect of premises not used in production of the income;

g.    amounts payable in respect of the United Kingdom income tax, super tax or Empire income tax as defined in section 49.[99]

h.    payments to any provident, savings, widows' and orphans' or other society or fund, except as allowed under section 10 (1) (f) and (g).

Section 13 allowed trade losses where the amount of loss incurred by a person or partner in the year preceding the year of assessment was such that it could not be wholly set off against his income from other sources for the same year. The amount of such loss not allowed against his income from other sources for the same year was, to the extent to which it was not allowed, carried forward and set off against his chargeable income for five years in succession; provided the amount of any such loss allowed to be set off in computing the chargeable income of any year could not be set off in computing the chargeable income of any other year and no such set off was allowed to an extent where it reduced the tax payable for any year of assessment to less than half of the amount which was payable had the set off not been allowed. Section 14 contained special provisions on certain companies and businesses. Under subsection (1) thereof, the tax payable by insurance companies other than life insurance companies where the gains or profits accrued in part outside Nigeria was ascertainable by taking the gross premiums, interest and other income received in Nigeria. The tax payable was the net arrived at after deductions for:

a.  premiums returned to the insured or paid on re-insurances;

b.  unexpired risks at the percentage adopted by the company in relation to its operations as a whole for such risks at the end of the year preceding the year of assessment;

c.  unexpired risks outstanding at the commencement of the year preceding the year of assessment;

d.  actual losses, agency expenses in Nigeria and 'a fair proportion of the expenses of the head office of the company'.

In the case of life insurance companies, whether proprietary or mutual, the gains or profits on which tax was payable was the investment income less the management expenses. Where the company received premiums outside Nigeria, the gains or profits were considered to be the same proportion of the total investment income of the company's premiums received in Nigeria bore to the total premiums received, less agency expenses in Nigeria and a fair proportion of the expenses of the head office of the company.[100] Subsection (3) related to the business of a ship-owner. Subsection (3) (b) (i) and (ii) required a ship-owner to produce a certificate to the Commissioner issued by the tax authority where the principal place of business of the company was situated stating that:

i.  the company had furnished the tax authority an account of the whole of its business; and

ii. the ratio of the gains or profits for the relevant accounting year was computed according to the income tax law of that place to the gross earnings of the company's fleet or vessel for that period; less the interest on any money borrowed used in acquiring the gains and profits.

Where the certificate was produced, the gains and profits of the company was deemed by virtue of subsection (3) (a) to be the sum bearing the same ratio to the sums payable in respect of fares or freight for passengers, goods or mails shipped in Nigeria as the company's total profits for the relevant accounting period bore to the gross earnings for that period as shown by the certificate. By paragraph (c) of subsection (3), where the gains or profits of a ship-owning company had been computed on any basis other than the ratio of the gains or profits shown by the certificate referred to, the company could within two years from the end of the year of assessment, produce the certificate and be entitled to such adjustments as were necessary including refund, in case of excess tax paid. Paragraph (d) defined ship-owner as 'an owner or charterer of ships whose principal place of business is situated outside

Nigeria, but in a part of His Majesty's Dominions or in territory under His Majesty's protection'. Section 15 empowered the Governor to exempt from tax under the Ordinance, gains and profits arising from the business of shipping carried on by a company not resident in Nigeria if he was satisfied that an equivalent exemption was granted by the country in which the company was resident to persons resident in Nigeria and the United Kingdom, if the country in question was not the United Kingdom. A company was deemed to be resident in a country in which the central management and control of its business was situated.

Section 15 (1) allowed a deduction of 200 pounds in ascertaining the chargeable income of a person who proved to the satisfaction of the Commissioner that he had a wife in the year preceding the year of assessment. Similarly, subsection (2) allowed deductions for sums paid as alimony to a previous wife in the same proportion as the amount of the alimony so paid but by virtue of subsection (3) the total deductions allowed could not exceed 200 pounds. Section 16 (1) allowed a deduction of 25 pounds in respect of each child[101] in ascertaining the chargeable income of a person but the child in question had to be an unmarried child who was less than 16 years at the commencement of that year or who was receiving full time instruction at a university, college, school or other educational establishment. Pursuant to the proviso to the subsection, a deduction equal to the amount expended but not exceeding 100 pounds on the maintenance and education of a child outside Nigeria was allowed. Furthermore, no deduction was allowed in respect of a child whose chargeable income for the year preceding the year of assessment exceeded the amount of the deduction otherwise allowed but no account was taken of any income to which the child was entitled under a scholarship or similar endowment. Deductions were allowed in respect of a maximum of three children.

A person who took insurance on his life or that of his wife was entitled to deductions equivalent to the amount paid as annual premium to the insurance company, in the computation of his chargeable income.[102] The proviso to section 17 limited the maximum deduction allowed under the section to seven percent of the capital sum secured, in the case of any policy securing a capital sum on death. The proviso also limited the deduction allowed under the section to an amount equal to one-sixth of the chargeable income of such a person estimated *before* the deductions allowed under sections 15, 16 and 17. Where an assessment was made in respect of a part only of the year preceding the year of assessment, the amount of deductions allowed under sections 15 to 17 bore the same proportion to the amount of deduction allowable annually as the number of days in the said part of the year bore to one year.[103] However, it should be noted that by virtue of section 19, the deductions under sections 15 - 18 were only allowed to residents and non-resident British subjects.

The income of a wife who lived with her husband was chargeable in the husband's name because the Ordinance deemed her income to be that of the husband's.[104] The proviso to section 20 (1) provided that the amount chargeable upon the husband which bore the same proportion to the amount the income of the wife bore to their joint income could be collected from the wife, where necessary, notwithstanding that she had not been assessed. The income contemplated under the Ordinance was that which accrued, derived or was received from Nigerian sources.[105] The minimum tax rate for adult males whose income did not exceed 50 pounds was fixed by section 21 at five shillings. "Adult male" under the Ordinance meant a male above the age of 16 years. The following classes of persons were exempted from tax under the proviso to section 21:

a. *bona fide* students in full time attendance at any school, college or training centre;

b. any person who in the opinion of the Commissioner could not reasonably be called upon to pay tax on account of age, infirmity or other disablement;

c. any person who had paid tax in respect of the year of assessment under the *Direct Taxation Ordinance 1940*;

d. any person who, before 1 April 1937 was awarded the Victoria Cross, the Medal of the Order of the British Empire, the Distinguished Conduct Medal, the Military Medal, the Distinguished Service Medal or the Meritorious Service Medal.

The proviso also enabled any person who objected to his assessment on the ground that he fell into category ii above to, within forty two days of the service of assessment, appeal to the Commissioner whose decision was final. Section 21 (2) empowered the Commissioner to assess any person without calling such a person to render a return of his chargeable income; if he was satisfied that such a person was liable to pay tax. Subsection (3) made it an offence punishable with a fine of 10 pounds or one month imprisonment or both for failure, without just cause, to pay tax within three months of assessment.

Tax rates in respect of persons whose income exceeded 50 pounds were imposed by section 22 in accordance with the rates contained in the First Schedule. According to the First Schedule, all chargeable incomes exceeding 50 pounds were taxable at three pence of every pound of the first 200 pounds; six pence of every pound of the second 200 pounds; nine pence of every pound of the third 200 pounds; one shilling of every pound of the fourth 200 pounds; one shilling and three pence of every pound of the fifth 200 pounds; one shilling and six pence of every pound of the next 400 pounds; one shilling and nine pence of every pound of the next 600 pounds; two shillings of every pound of the next 1000 pounds; two shillings and six pence of every pound of the next 2000 pounds; five shillings of every pound of the next 5000 pounds and for every pound exceeding 10,000 pounds, 10 shillings thereof. The proviso to section 22 was to the effect that where the tax levied for any year of assessment on a person amounted to less than three pence of every pound of his chargeable income *before* the deductions allowed under sections 15 to 18 were made, that person was liable to a rate of three pence of every pound of his chargeable income *before* the said deductions were made.

Rate of tax payable by companies was two shillings and six pence of every pound of its chargeable income.[106] Subject to the conditions listed in the proviso thereunder, section 24 (1) allowed deductions in like sum in respect of dividends paid to shareholders where such companies were registered in Nigeria. The conditions were that where tax not paid on the whole income out of which the dividend was paid, the deduction was equally limited to the portion of the dividend which was paid out of the income on which tax was paid by the company. Secondly, through a written notice, the Commissioner could require a company registered in Nigeria to deduct tax from dividends payable to a particular shareholder at rate greater than the rate payable by the company and in such a case, the excess tax so deducted became a debt due from the company to the government and was recoverable as such or in the alternative, assessed and charged upon the company in addition to any other tax it was liable to pay.

Upon payment of a dividend as envisaged by section 24 (1), a company was required to furnish each shareholder with a certificate setting forth the amount of dividend paid to the shareholder and the amount deducted or deductible by the company in respect of that dividend.[107] Section 25 provided relief from double taxation to shareholders. Under the section, where any tax deducted by a company by virtue of section 24 from a dividend paid to a shareholder was included in the chargeable income of such person, the said tax was set off on the tax charged against that chargeable income. Section 26 exempted from tax, incomes of persons who were temporary residents, who had no intention of establishing their residence in Nigeria and whose actual residence in Nigeria at one or more times did not equal in the whole to a period of six months in the year preceding the year of assessment.

A trustee, guardian, curator, committee or receiver appointed by court, having management and control of property or concern on behalf of an incapacitated person was chargeable to tax in like manner and in like amount as such person would have been had he not been incapacitated.[108] A non-resident was assessable and chargeable either directly or through his agent, attorney, manager, branch or representative (howsoever described) and where such a non-resident was not a British subject, no deductions were allowed in respect of wife, child or life insurance.[109] A non-resident was also chargeable in his name in respect of income arising either directly or indirectly from agency, attorneyship or management - however described.

Where a non-resident person or firm, not being a British subject, carried on business with a resident and it appeared to the Commissioner that owing to the close ties between the parties, the resident acquired no profits or less profits than was ordinarily expected of such business, the non-resident was assessed and charged as if he was the principal and the resident was his agent.[110] Subsection (3) provided that where the gains or profits of a non-resident chargeable in the name of a resident was not readily ascertainable, the Commissioner or judge sitting over an appeal could assess and charge the person on a fair and reasonable percentage of the turnover of the business. A non-resident was not chargeable under the provisions of subsections (2) and (3) above where the resident in whose name he would have been chargeable was a broker, general commission agent or other agent not authorised to carry on the regular agency of a non-resident.[111] Similarly, by subsection (5) a non-resident was not chargeable in respect of gains or profits earned in transactions with other non-residents. Subsection (6) allowed an agent, manager, branch, attorney or factor in whose name a non-resident manufacturer or producer was chargeable to apply to the Commissioner or in case of appeal, to a judge to have the assessment made or amended on the basis of profits which might reasonably had been earned by a merchant or, where the goods were retailed having been bought directly from the manufacturer, on the basis of profits reasonably expected to have been earned by the retailer and upon proof of the amount of the profits made in either case, the assessment could be made or amended accordingly.

A person in whose name an incapacitated person or non-resident was chargeable was answerable for all matters required by the Ordinance for the assessment of the income of the person for whom he acted.[112] Section 31 placed a similar responsibility on the manager or principal officer in respect of things required to be done by corporate bodies under the Ordinance. Section 30 required a person who was in receipt of money, in whatever capacity, being taxable income accruing to another person who was chargeable, whether resident or non-resident, to prepare and deliver to the Commissioner, on the latter's request, a list in the prescribed form signed by him containing a true and correct statement of all such income and the name and address of the person to whom the income belonged. Section 32 empowered a person answerable for payment of tax on behalf of another person to retain such part of monies coming into his hand on behalf of the other person as was sufficient to pay tax. The section further indemnified such a representative for payments made by him in compliance thereof. Under section 33 the personal representative of a deceased person was liable to tax to the extent the deceased himself would have been and therefore, answerable to all things the deceased would have been where the deceased died either during the year of assessment or two years from the expiration thereof if no assessment had been made on him. Where the deceased had died during the year preceding the year of assessment and the personal representative had distributed the estate before the commencement of the assessment year, the proviso to the section imposed tax on the representative at the rates in force at the date of distribution of the estate, if the rate for the year of assessment had not been varied at that date. A person representing a dissolved company was placed in a similar position by virtue of section 34.

A person who paid a mortgage or debenture interest to a non-resident was entitled, after claiming the deductions allowed under section 10 (1) (a) to deduct tax from the interest at the rate of two shillings and six pence of every pound of such interest or such greater rate as the Commissioner directed and the tax so deducted was recoverable by government as debt owed it by such person.[113] Where the person referred to in section 35 was a company, subsection (2) required the account to be rendered by the manager or other principal officer of the company. Where it was due to be rendered, subsection (3) made failure to render the account envisaged by the section an offence. Where the chargeable income of a person included a sum from which tax was deducted in accordance with subsection (1), subsection (4) entitled him to a set off against the tax paid by him of the amount of tax so deducted.

Section 36 (1) made it a duty for every person chargeable to tax to give notice of his chargeability to the Commissioner within three months after the commencement of any year of assessment. Under subsection (2) the Commissioner could also require any person to furnish him with a return of income and other particulars within reasonable time for the purposes of assessment and chargeability of such person under the Ordinance. A person who failed to either give such notice or furnish such return or particulars was guilty of an offence under subsection (3). The Commissioner could also require any officer in the public service, by virtue of section 37 (1) to supply him with such particulars as was required for the purposes of the Ordinance. Where so required, it was the duty of such officer under subsection (2) to prepare and deliver to the Commissioner a return containing the names and places of residence of all persons employed by him and payments and allowances made to those persons. Subsection (3) deemed the manager or principal officer as the employer, where the employer was a body of persons, and a director or person engaged in the management of a company as an employee. Subsection (4) further empowered the Commissioner to make a request for such information as he required from a head of family or householder and such head of family or householder was obliged to comply.

The income of a person doing business as a partner or jointly with other persons was deemed to be the share to which he was entitled during the year of assessment in the income of the partnership and was to be included in the return of income made by such partner.[114] Under section 38 (2), the precedent partner was responsible for making a return in respect of the income of the partnership, which return had to include the names and addresses of other partners and the income of the partnership to which each of them was entitled. The subsection defined a precedent partner as:

a. the partner among other resident partners first named in the partnership agreement; or

b. the partner named either singly or with precedence to the other partners in the usual name of the firm where there was no partnership agreement; or

c. the precedent acting partner, if the partner named with precedence was not an acting partner.

If none of the partners was resident, subsection (2) (b) required the return to be made and delivered by the attorney, agent, manager or factor of the firm resident in Nigeria.

Every notice required to be given by the Commissioner under the Ordinance had to be signed by him or some other person authorised by him and any signature purporting to be that of the Commissioner or such other person authorised by him was presumed as regular.[115] Section 40 (1) required notices to be served by registered post or any other lawful means to the registered office of a company registered in Nigeria; or in the case of companies registered outside Nigeria, on the person authorised to accept service at the address filed with the Registrar of Companies under the Companies Ordinance and in the case of an individual to his last known business or private address. The notice was deemed to have been received on the day succeeding the day on which it would have been received by post in the ordinary course of things. Evidence that the letter containing the notice was properly addressed and posted was sufficient proof of service. By subsection (2), where a person was informed that a registered letter was waiting for him at the post office and he neglected or refused to take delivery, he was deemed to have had notice of the amount assessed against him on the date he was informed of the letter.

The Commissioner was obliged by section 41 (1) to assess every person chargeable with tax soon after the time allowed for delivery of return in section 36. Under subsection (2) the commissioner could accept a return delivered to him and proceed to make an assessment accordingly or refuse the return and use his judgment to determine the amount of chargeable income of the person and assess him accordingly. The Commissioner was also empowered by subsection (3) to use his judgment to assess the chargeable income of any person who failed to deliver a return but who in the Commissioner's opinion was liable to tax. The Commissioner's discretion provided in the subsection was without prejudice to any liability incurred by such a person for failure to deliver a return. The Commissioner could also make an assessment or additional assessment as the case demanded, where in his opinion a person liable to tax was not assessed or assessed at an amount less than he ought to have been assessed.[116] The Commissioner was required by section 43 to prepare lists of persons assessed to tax. The assessment lists were to contain the name, address, amount of chargeable income and amount of tax payable and such other particulars as were necessary of every person assessed to tax.

In order to facilitate the assessment of incomes of persons residing in the United Kingdom, the Governor was empowered by section 44 to appoint agents in the United Kingdom to make enquiries to ascertain the chargeable income of such persons and forward their report together with the accounts and computations upon which the report was based to the Commissioner. The Commissioner had discretion to send the report back to the agents for further consideration if it appeared to him that an error had occurred in the accounts or computation prepared by the agents.

The Commissioner was obliged by section 45 (1) to serve or cause to be served personally or by post, notice to every person whose name appeared on the assessment list. The notice was required to state the amount of each person's chargeable income, tax payable and his rights under subsection (2). Subsection (2) conferred a right on a person, other than one assessed under section 21, who disputed the amount with which he was assessed to apply to the Commissioner within forty two days from the date of service of assessment notice on him (or such longer period as the Commissioner upon reasonable grounds allowed), stating the grounds for his objection. On receipt of the objection, the Commissioner could request for further particulars in respect of the person assessed including documents in his custody and also summon any person other than a clerk or other person confidentially in the employ of the person assessed, to attend and give information before him.[117] By subsection (4), where the person objecting reaches an agreement with the Commissioner regarding the amount at which he was liable to be assessed, the assessment was to be amended accordingly and notice of the tax payable served on the person. The proviso to the subsection entitled the person objecting to a right of appeal in accordance with the provisions of section 46, in the event that the said person and the Commissioner failed to agree on the amount to which he was liable to be assessed. Such appeal was to be made to the Supreme Court within fifteen days from the day of the refusal of the Commissioner to amend the assessment as desired or such longer period as the court, on just cause, allowed. The appellant was required to attend court personally or if upon just cause shown, through an agent, clerk or servant. The appellant was required to give notice of seven clear days of the hearing of the appeal to the Commissioner. The onus of proving excess assessment was on the appellant and where the court was convinced that the appellant was overcharged or undercharged, he could reduce or increase the amount of assessment accordingly and notice of the assessment as determined by the court was to be served on the appellant by the Commissioner.

The judge could order an appellant to furnish a specified security for payment of tax, upon application made by the Commissioner that tax may not be recovered from the appellant, and if such security was not given within the required time, the tax assessed against the appellant became recoverable forthwith. Except upon the application of the applicant to the contrary, appeals were required to be heard in camera. The Chief Justice was empowered to make rules regulating procedure on appeals.[118] In lieu of an appeal to the court as provided under section 46 (1), a person aggrieved could appeal against his assessment to a board of commissioners consisting of three persons (being non officials) appointed by the Governor for such period and remunerated as he deemed. The Governor was further empowered to make rules to govern the procedure to be adopted by the board. An aggrieved person could appeal against his assessment within 15 days of the refusal of the Commissioner to amend the assessment, or such longer period as the board - upon just cause - granted and the decision of the board regarding the amount of assessment was final.[119]

No assessment, warrant or proceeding made in accordance with the Ordinance was to be voided for want of form or mistake provided it conformed to the intent and purpose of the Ordinance. Precisely, no assessment could be impeached by reason of mistake therein as to name, description of income, or the amount of tax charged or by reason of any variance between the assessment and the notice of assessment provided the notice contained in substance and effect, the particulars upon which the assessment was made and was duly served on the person intended to be charged. [120]

A person who by deduction or otherwise, paid or was liable to pay tax in the United Kingdom on the same part of his income for which he was also liable under the Ordinance for any year of assessment was entitled to relief under section 48. The rate of relief to which such a person was entitled was the amount by which the rate of tax appropriate to him under the Ordinance exceeded half the appropriate rate of United Kingdom income tax. If however, the appropriate rate to his case under the Ordinance exceeded the appropriate rate of the United Kingdom income tax, he was entitled to relief at a rate equal to half the appropriate rate of United Kingdom income tax. Section 49 granted similar relief in respect of Empire income tax. Empire income tax meant income tax charged under any law in force in any part of His Majesty's Dominions other than the United Kingdom or Nigeria.[121] The rate of relief granted in the case of Empire income tax was the amount paid as Empire tax where the Empire rate did not exceed the rate under the Ordinance by half. In any other case, the relief was half the rate appropriate to his case under the Ordinance. A person who in any year of assessment was resident both in Nigeria and another place where Empire income tax was charged was deemed to be resident in the place where during that year he resided for the longer period. According to section 50, a claim for relief under sections 48 and 49 had to be made within two years from the end of the year of assessment to which it related. By the proviso to section 50 however, such a claim could be made within six years from the end of the assessment year to which it related and within six months from the date upon which the relevant amount of United Kingdom income tax or Empire income tax, which ever was applicable, was ascertained. The official secrecy imposed by section 4 of the Ordinance did not operate to prevent the disclosure to an authorised officer, information that was required of him in the discharge of his duties to determine a relief claimed in respect of income tax paid in Nigeria or any part of His Majesty's Dominions.[122]

Collection of tax was to remain in abeyance where there was notice of an objection or appeal until the dispute was determined. The Commissioner could however enforce the payment of that portion of tax, if any, that was not in dispute.[123] Under section 53, companies and persons whose incomes exceeded 50 pounds were entitled to pay tax in two instalments; the first instalment was payable within 42 days after service of notice of assessment and the second instalment within six months after the service of notice of assessment. This was without prejudice to section 65 (1) (b) which provided for at-source deductions of tax in respect of emoluments and pensions paid out of the revenue of Nigeria. Where a person died after payment of the first instalment, the second instalment, by virtue of section 53 (c) was recoverable from the personal representative of the deceased. Notwithstanding the provisions of section 53, if the Commissioner had reason to believe that a person assessed was likely to leave the country, he could serve a notice on such person specifying time within which such person was to pay tax and except where the person furnished sufficient security, the tax became recoverable forthwith at the expiration of the time so specified.[124] Similarly, if the Commissioner had reason to believe either that tax upon any chargeable income or income chargeable to tax may not be recovered, he could by written notice require any person to make a return and furnish particulars of his income within the time specified. The Commissioner could either make an assessment on the basis of the return or in default of or dissatisfaction with a return, make such assessment as he thought reasonable or require that the person furnish security for payment.[125] While a person who paid tax in accordance with the provisions of section 54 had a right of objection and appeal conferred by sections 45 and 46, the right of the commissioner to make additional assessments under section 42 was equally preserved by section 54 (6).

According to section 55, a person who failed to pay tax within the periods prescribed therein was liable to an additional five percent of the tax payable. In addition, the Commissioner was required to serve a demand note on him and if within one month after the service of the demand note he still defaulted, he was guilty of an offence and also liable to a suit for the purpose of enforcing payment at the instance of the Commissioner.[126] Where the tax was outstanding as a result of an appeal or objection, the amount determined upon objection or appeal was payable within one month after notice of the determined amount was served and where there was a default, the provisions of section 55 applied. Section 58 entitled a person who paid tax in excess of what was lawfully chargeable to repayment; provided the claim for repayment was made within two years from the end of the year of assessment to which it related. This right did not extend to a person who having been served with notice in any year of assessment failed or refused to deliver a return except he could show that his failure or neglect did not proceed from fraud, wilful act or omission.

Section 60 made it an offence for any person to make false returns or forgery or aid in the making of same to either gain an advantage for himself or another. Section 59 provided a penalty of 100 pounds as fine or upon default thereto, six months imprisonment for any offence under the Ordinance for which no specific offence was prescribed. Section 61 made it an offence for a person who, being appointed as an assistant in the assessment and collection of tax demanded, from any person an amount in excess of the authorised tax; withheld for his use any portion of tax collected; rendered a false return of amounts collected by him; defrauded any person or otherwise used his position to deal wrongfully with the Commissioner or any individual; or not being authorised under the ordinance, collected or attempted to collect tax. The penalty for any of the offences so listed was a fine of 300 pounds or three years imprisonment or both.

The Commissioner could remit or refund wholly or in part, tax payable by a person on ground of poverty. Similarly, the Governor could also remit the tax payable, as well as the five percent penalty prescribed under section 55 (1) (a) if he was convinced that it was equitable to do so.[127] The power to alter the tax rates contained in the First Schedule to the Ordinance was vested in the Legislative Council in so far as the alteration affected the colony or southern provinces; and the Governor, in so far as the alteration affected the Northern provinces.[128] Section 65 empowered the Governor-in-Council to make rules generally for carrying out the provisions of the Ordinance.

There was one amendment to the *Income Tax Ordinance No. 3 1940*. Section 23 thereof was amended by substituting the words 'four shillings' for the words 'two shillings and six pence'[129] thereby making four shillings the minimum taxable rates under the Ordinance. The minimum taxable rates related to persons whose income did not exceed 50 pound per annum.

In the area of tax administration, a major milestone was recorded with the passage, in 1958, of the *Income Tax Administration Ordinance No. 39 1958*. The ordinance provided for the establishment of the three bodies to be involved in the administration of income tax. These were the Federal Board of Inland Revenue, the Scrutineer Committees and the Body of Appeal Commissioners. Earlier in 1958, all income tax Ordinances and amendments thereto passed between 1943 and 1955 which were still in force were consolidated as the *Income Tax Ordinance Cap 85*.[130] The *Income Tax Administration Ordinance No. 39 1958* further provided some amendments to the *Income Tax Ordinance Cap 85* and both Ordinances were to be construed as one. The Board was established under section 3 to consist of a maximum of six members including the chairman and the deputy chairman to be appointed by the Governor-General. The Governor-General was also required to appoint a secretary for the Board who was not a member of the Board but was responsible for maintaining minutes and records of the Board. The Board was vested with the power to administer the *Income Tax Ordinance* and all the powers and duties previously exercised by the Commissioner of Income Tax were now vested in the Board.[131] Consequently, the Inland Revenue Department and its offices were re-designated the Federal Inland Revenue Department and Federal Inland Revenue Offices respectively.

Scrutineer Committees were provided for under section 11 (1) for the purpose of making recommendations in relation to the assessment of profits and claims for losses incurred in such cases as may be referred to them. The minister was empowered to establish one or more Scrutineer Committees for such areas as he thought fit consisting of not more than six members with experience in the management of substantial trade or business; none of whom could be a public officer. The Board was required to instruct an officer of the Federal Inland Revenue Department to act as secretary to the Committee. The Third Schedule to the ordinance amended the *Income Tax Ordinance* in areas where it was necessary to bring it into conformity with the provisions of the *Income Tax Administration Ordinance*. One of such amendments established the Body of Appeal Commissioners, the constitution of which was to be done by the minister in such areas of the country as he deemed fit. Each Body of

Appeal Commissioners was to have a maximum number of six members and a secretary none of whom could be a public officer.

Although the Ordinance was passed on October 24 1958 its provisions did not come into effect immediately. The minister was empowered to appoint a day on which the provisions of the ordinance would become operational.[132]

## Companies Income Tax

A paradigm shift in the statutory framework for the regulation of companies' income tax regime was introduced in 1939 through the instrumentality of the *Companies Income Tax Ordinance No. 14 1939*. Before this law came into effect, the regulation of both personal and business taxation was vested in one and the same legal regime. The ordinance imposed a tax of two shillings and sixpence on every pound of a company's chargeable income.[133] The administration of the tax was vested in a commissioner to be appointed for that purpose by the Governor and the proceeds from the tax were to be remitted to the government treasury to form part of the general revenue of Nigeria.[134] A person involved in the administration of tax under the Ordinance was obligated to subscribe to an oath of secrecy.[135] The Ordinance imposed tax on a preceding year basis on the following four sources of a company's income:

a.  gains or profits from any trade or business, for whatever period of time such trade or business had been carried on;

b.  dividends, interest or discounts;

c.  any charge or annuity;

d.  rents, royalties, premiums and any other profits arising from property.[136]

The incomes of statutory or registered building or friendly societies; as well as that of ecclesiastical, charitable or educational institutions of public nature were exempted from tax in so far as such incomes were not derived from a trade or business carried on by any such institution. Other incomes exempted from tax under the Ordinance were those of a company formed purely for the purpose of promoting social or sporting amenities and income derived from the interest payable on any loan charged on the public revenue of Nigeria in respect of interest payable to any company other than a company as defined by section 2 of the ordinance. A company was defined under the said section as:

Any company incorporated or registered under any law in force in Nigeria; any company which, though incorporated or registered outside Nigeria, carries on business, or has an office or place of business therein.[137]

Outgoings and expenses wholly and exclusively incurred by a company in a year of assessment were allowed as deductions in ascertaining the company's chargeable income for that year. Specifically, the following deductions were allowed:

a. sums payable by the company as interest upon money borrowed and employed in the acquisition of income;

b. rent paid by the company in respect of land or buildings occupied for the purpose of acquiring income;

c. expenses incurred by the company in the replacement of plant or machinery less the value of depreciation and the sum realised by the sale of such plant or machinery;

d. sums expended on the repair of premises, plant and machinery or the renewal, repair or alteration of implements employed in the acquisition of income;

e. bad and doubtful debts proved to have become as such during the year immediately preceding the year of assessment; provided that sums recovered during the year on accounts of amounts previously allowed as bad or doubtful debts were considered as income or receipts for that year;

f. such other deductions prescribed by any rule made pursuant to the ordinance.[138]

In addition to the above deductions, section 10 further allowed as deduction a reasonable amount for exhaustion, wear and tear of property (including plant and machinery) arising out of the use of such property in the year immediately preceding the year of assessment in the acquisition of income; provided that where property was leased on the condition that wear and tear be replaced by the lessee, then the lessee company was considered the owner of such leased property and to that extent, entitled to the deduction under section 10. Similarly, trade losses incurred by a company could be carried forward and allowed as deductions against what ought to have been the company's chargeable income for the next five years where the losses were such that they could not be adequately set off against its income for the year of assessment. However, such set off was not allowed to such an extent where it would reduce the tax payable by the company in any assessment year by more than 50 percent of the company's liability.[139] Deductions not allowed in computing companies' income tax under the Ordinance were contained in section 11 and included:

a. disbursements or expenses not wholly and exclusively incurred in the acquisition of income;

b. capital withdrawn or sums employed or intended to be employed as capital;

c. any capital employed in improvements;

d. sums recoverable under a contract of insurance or indemnity;

e. rent or cost of repairs to any premises not used for the purpose of producing income;

f. any amount paid or payable in respect of the United Kingdom income tax or super tax or Empire income tax.

The Ordinance contained special provisions regarding the ascertainment of chargeable income of insurance companies, life insurance companies and ship owners.[140] In the case of an insurance company other than a life insurance company whose gains and profits accrued partly outside Nigeria, its chargeable income was ascertained by:

a. taking the gross premiums, interest and other income receivable in Nigeria, less any premiums paid to the insured or on re-insurances;

b. deducting from the above a reserve for unexpired risks at the percentage adopted by the company for such risks at the year preceding the year of assessment;

c. adding to the above a reserve similarly calculated for unexpired risks outstanding at the commencement of the year preceding the year of assessment;

d. deducting the actual losses (less the amount recovered in respect thereof under re-insurance), agency expenses in Nigeria and a fair proportion of the expenses of the head office of the company.

The gains or profits of life insurance companies chargeable to tax were the investment income less of management expenses and commission. The gains or profits of a ship owning company was the sum bearing the same ratio to the sums payable in respect of fares of freight for passengers, goods or mails shipped in Nigeria as the company's total profits for the relevant period. The company was required to obtain a certificate from the tax authority of the place where the company's principal place of business was located stating that the company had satisfactorily furnished an account of its whole business and also stating the ratio of the gains or profits for the relevant accounting period (less of money borrowed and employed in the acquisition of gain) to the gross earnings of the company's fleet or vessel for that period, computed in accordance with the income tax law of the place of principal business. The profits of a non-resident company engaged in the business of shipping were exempted from tax provided the Governor was satisfied that the company's country of origin extended an equivalent exemption to persons resident in Nigeria and if the country was a country other than the United Kingdom, to persons resident in the United Kingdom.[141]

Every company was obliged to deduct tax from any dividend paid to a share holder at the rate paid or payable by the company as reduced, where applicable, by double taxation or Empire income tax reliefs granted under sections 33 and 34. The company was further obliged to furnish each shareholder with a certificate setting forth the amount paid to the shareholder as and the amount deducted or deductible by the company as tax.[142] Equally, a company that paid a mortgage or debenture interest to a non-resident was obliged to deduct tax at the minimum rate chargeable under the *Colony Taxation Ordinance 1937* and the *Non-Natives Income Tax (Protectorate) Ordinance 1931* and the amount so deducted was a debt owed by the company to the government.[143] The minimum rate under the two Ordinances was five shillings. A company that failed to account for the tax so deducted was guilty of an offence under the Ordinance.

Section 16 contained provisions regarding the chargeability of a non-resident company. A non-resident company was assessable and chargeable to tax in respect of any income arising (directly or indirectly) from any attorneyship, factorship, agency, receivership, branch or management. Such a company was chargeable in the name of the attorney, factor, agent, receiver, branch manager and the person in whose name the company was chargeable was obliged by section 17 to be answerable for all matters required to be done under the ordinance for the assessment of the company. A resident person was deemed to be an agent of a non-resident company and, therefore, chargeable on behalf of the company, where owing to the close connection between the non-resident company and the resident person, the latter pursued the course of business on behalf of the former in such a manner that produced either no profits or less profits to the resident than was ordinarily associated with that business. However, the company was not chargeable in the name of a broker or general commission agent not authorised to carry on the business of the company on a regular agency. Where it appeared to a Commissioner making an assessment or a judge hearing an appeal that the true profits of a non-resident company could not be readily ascertained, the Commissioner or judge could assess the company on a fair and reasonable percentage of the turnover of the company's business done through the resident agent and in such an event, the agent was obliged to comply with the provisions of the Ordinance relating to returns or particulars and the assessment as determined was subject to appeal to the Supreme Court. The Commissioner could require any person in receipt of money in whatever capacity, being income arising from chargeable sources of a company, whether resident or not, to prepare and deliver to him within the period prescribed in the notice a true and correct statement of all such income and the name and address of every person or company to whom the same belonged.[144] All acts, matters and things required to be done by a company to facilitate assessment and payment of tax were to be done by the manager or other principal manager of the company in Nigeria.[145] Section 20 entitled a person answerable on behalf of the company to retain out of money coming into his custody on behalf of the company, so much thereof as was sufficient to pay any tax due and the section further indemnified such a person for any payments made for the foregoing purpose.

A company liable to tax under the Ordinance was obliged to give notice of its chargeability to the Commissioner within three months after the commencement of each assessment year. This obligation was without prejudice to the right of the Commissioner to require the company to furnish him within reasonable time, with a return of income and such further particulars as were necessary with respect to income for which the company was chargeable. A company that failed to give notice of its chargeability or furnish such returns as required by the Commissioner was guilty of an offence under the Act.[146] Notice was to be served by post to the company's registered office in the case of a resident company and to the person authorised to accept service of process in the case of a non-resident company and to the last known address, in the case of a person. Notice was deemed to have been served on the day succeeding the day the notice would ordinarily have been received by post and in proving service, it was sufficient to prove that the notice was properly addressed and posted.[147] As soon as the period allowed for the delivery of return or notice of chargeability elapsed, the Commissioner was required to proceed to assess every company chargeable to tax based either on the return as delivered by the company or the Commissioner's best of judgment. Best of judgment was used where either the return as delivered by the company was rejected by the Commissioner or where the company failed to deliver a return altogether but the Commissioner was of the opinion that the company was chargeable.[148] Also, where the Commissioner was of the opinion that a company was either not assessed or assessed at an amount less than it ought to have been, he could within two years from the expiration of the relevant year of assessment make such assessment or additional assessment as, in his judgment ought to have been made on the company. The Commissioner was further obliged by section 28 to prepare lists of assessment containing the names and addresses in Nigeria of companies assessed to tax; the amount of chargeable income of each company; the amount of tax payable and such other particulars as prescribed.[149]

Provisions relating to objection and appeals were contained in sections 30 and 31. The Commissioner was required to serve a notice of assessment by registered post to every company whose name appeared on the assessment lists. The notice was to contain the amount of the company's chargeable income, its tax liability and its right of objection if it disagreed with the amount of tax liability assessed on it. Within forty two days from service of notice of assessment (or such longer period as the Commissioner, upon good cause allowed) a company disputing the amount of tax assessed on it was required to apply for a review stating the precise grounds of its objection. The Commissioner was allowed to call for such further particulars (including evidence from persons other than those confidentially employed in the affairs of the company to be charged) and where the company and the Commissioner agreed as to the assessable amount, the assessment was amended accordingly and notice thereof served on the company. A company that failed to agree with the Commissioner had a further right of appeal to the Supreme Court within 15 days from the date of the refusal of the Commissioner to amend the assessment. At the hearing of the appeal, the court could either reduce or increase the amount with which the appellant was assessed depending on the merit or otherwise of the case. The Ordinance further empowered the Chief Justice to make rules of procedure relating to appeals.

An assessment, warrant or any other proceedings issued pursuant to the provisions of the Ordinance was not voidable for reason of mere mistake, defect in form or omission provided the same substantially conformed to the intendment of the Ordinance.[150] Section 33 provided relief to companies in cases of double taxation. The reliefs were available to companies that paid tax on the same income within an assessment year either in the United Kingdom or under the Empire income tax.[151] A claim for relief in either case had to be made within two years from the end of the relevant assessment year. The claim could however be made within six years from the end of the relevant assessment year and within six months from the date upon which the relevant amount as United Kingdom income tax or Empire income tax was ascertained.[152]

Under the Ordinance, a company had a timeline of 30 days from the date of service of notice of assessment upon it within which to pay the assessed tax. The foregoing was the position under the Ordinance, even in a situation where the notice followed either a notice of objection or an appeal procedure.[153] Failure to pay tax within the prescribed period attracted a penalty of a sum equal to five percent of the tax liability and the Commissioner was required to serve a demand note upon the company. If within 30 days of service of the demand note, the tax (and penalty) remained unpaid, the Commissioner had the power to sue in his official name to recover the tax with full costs as a debt due to the government.[154] Section 42 allowed tax repayment to be made to a company that paid tax in excess of the amount properly chargeable provided the application was made within two years from the end of the relevant year of assessment. However, no repayment was allowed to a company where either the company neglected to deliver a return or the excess sum was based on the return as delivered by the company, unless the company could show that the failure to deliver a true and correct return was not as a result of fraud or wilful act. A company guilty of an offence under the Ordinance was liable on summary conviction to a fine not exceeding 100 pounds, while a person guilty of an offence was liable on summary conviction to a fine of 100 pounds and in default thereof to imprisonment for a maximum term of six months, with or without labour.[155] These penalties were without prejudice to any criminal proceedings arising against the company or person under any other law.[156] Section 46 empowered the Governor-in-Council to make rules from time to time for the effective administration of the provisions of the ordinance. The *Companies Income Tax Ordinance No. 14 1939* was repealed a year after its passage by the *Income Tax Ordinance No. 3 1940*. The practice of one law regulating both personal and business taxation was re-introduced and carried on for another 21 years when the second separate enactment on companies income tax was again enacted.

The second time a law was passed aimed at the exclusive taxation of companies income was in 1961. This was the *Companies Income Tax Act No. 22 1961* which was a landmark legislation, first, because from the date it came into force, the provisions of the *Income Tax Ordinance Cap 85* and the *Income Tax Administration Ordinance No. 39 1958* together with all rules made thereunder ceased to have effect with respect to companies income tax.[157] Second, the Act established the Federal Board of Inland Revenue as a statutory body and vested it with the power to administer companies' income tax[158] - as well as all federal taxes. Tax on the income of companies was imposed by section 17 in respect of profits accruing in, received from, brought into or received in Nigeria from:

a. any trade or business;

b. rent or any premium arising from a right granted to any other person for the use or occupation of any property;

c. dividends, interest, discounts, charges or annuities;

any other amount not falling within the above categories but qualifying as annual profits or gains or any amount deemed to be income or profits under the Act or arising from a pension or provident fund under the *Income Tax Management Act 1961.*

In the case of Nigerian companies, profits were deemed to accrue in Nigeria irrespective of the fact that such profits where made outside Nigeria's territory or whether or not they were brought into Nigeria. In the case of a non-Nigerian company, only such portion of its profits as were attributable to operations in Nigeria were deemed to be derived from Nigeria.[159]A company was defined as a corporation other than a corporation sole established by law in Nigeria or elsewhere and a Nigerian company referred to a company whose management and control was exercised in Nigeria.[160] Certain profits were exempted from companies income tax under section 26 (1) of the Act. The exempted profits included:

a. the profits of a statutory company or registered society insofar as such profits were not derived from a trade or business carried on by such society;

b. the profits of a co-operative society registered under the *Co-operatives Societies Ordinance*;

c. the profits of any company engaged in ecclesiastical, charitable or educational activities of a public character provided such profits were not derived from a trade or business carried on by such company;

d. the profits of a company formed for the purpose of promoting sporting activities where such profits were wholly expendable for such purposes;

e. the profits of a trade union registered under the *Trade Unions Ordinance* provided such profits were not derived from a trade or business carried on by such union;

f. interest received by a company from the Nigerian Post Office Savings Bank;

g. profits from aircraft or shipping business carried on by a foreign company insofar as in the case of ships, the business was not carried on in inland waters only and provided that an equivalent exemption from tax was granted to Nigerian companies in which the company in question resided;[161]

i. the profits of a company being a body corporate established by a native authority law or local government law;

j.   the profits of a company being a purchasing authority established by the legislature of a region and empowered to acquire any commodity in that region for export;

k.   the profits of a company being a corporation established by the legislature of a region for the purpose of fostering the economic development of that region insofar as they were not derived from any share or other interest possessed by that corporation;

l.   the profits of a foreign company which would have been chargeable to tax solely by reason of their being brought into Nigeria.

In addition, the finance minister was empowered to exempt any company or class of companies or profits earned by any company or class of companies from tax. The powers included the power to amend, add or repeal any exemption as it affected any company. The profit - or loss - of a company for the purpose of ascertaining its tax liability in an accounting period was arrived at after the deductions allowed in section 27. The deductions included:

a.   sums payable as interest on any money borrowed and employed as capital in acquiring the profits;

b.   rents and premiums incurred in respect of land or buildings occupied for the purpose of acquiring the profits;

c.   expenses incurred for the repair of premises, plant, machinery or fixtures employed in acquiring the profits or for the renewal, repair or alteration of any implement, utensil or article so employed;

d.   bad or doubtful debts estimated to have become bad or doubtful within the period were allowed on three conditions. First, deduction for such debts had not already been allowed under the *Income Tax Ordinance*; second, sums recovered within the period in respect of bad or doubtful debts for which allowance had been made were treated as profits; and third, the debts were included as a receipts of the business in the profits of the year within which they were incurred;

e.   contributions made to pension, provident or retirement benefits fund approved by the Joint Tax Board, but excluding penalties paid under the provisions of any Act establishing a provident or retirement benefits scheme;

f.   expenses incurred wholly and exclusively for the purpose of the business during the period but which could not either be referable to any other period; or be referable to the period in question;

g. such other deductions as the minister prescribed under any rules made pursuant to the powers conferred upon him by the Act.

However, the following deductions were not allowed under the Act:

a. expenditure of a capital nature including capital repaid or withdrawn;
b. sums recoverable under an insurance or contract of indemnity;
c. sums paid as taxes on income or profits either in Nigeria or elsewhere, except in the case of taxes levied outside Nigeria on profits which were also chargeable to tax in Nigeria where relief for double taxation of those profits was not given;
d. payments made to savings, widows and orphans, pension, provident or other retirement benefits fund except as permitted under section 27;
e. depreciation of assets;
f. sums reserved out of profits except as permitted by section 27 (d).

The difference between a company's income and the deductions allowed it during an accounting period was its assessable profits which were computed on a preceding year basis.[162] The total profits of a company were calculated on the basis of its assessable profits. A company's total profits were its assessable profits from all sources in any accounting year together with the additions allowed by the Third Schedule, less the deductions allowed by the Act.[163] The deductions allowed included:

a. the amount incurred by the company as loss during the year provided the claim is made within twelve months after the end of the assessment year;
b. the amount incurred by the company as loss during any year preceding the year of assessment which had not been allowed either under the Act or the provisions of the income tax ordinance; provided that the aggregate deduction from the assessable profits or income in respect of such loss did not exceed the amount of such loss and that a deduction made pursuant to the provision above did not exceed the amount, if any, of assessable profits included in the total profits for that year.

Companies were liable to income tax at eight shillings on every pound[164] except small companies which were granted relief by section 33 (1) and (2) for the first six years of operations. Complete exemption from tax was granted small companies for the first two years of assessment while exemption was granted at the rate of two-thirds of the tax liability due for the third and fourth year and one-third of the rate for the fifth and sixth year respectively. Section 33 (3)-(6) contained limitations to the extent to which small companies could be entitled to the reliefs granted in subsections (1) and (2). First, relief at the specified rates could be granted on the total profits assessed for the appropriate years of assessment but not exceeding the first one thousand pounds of such profits. Consequently, where the total profits exceeded one thousand pounds, the amount in excess of one thousand pounds was liable to tax. Further, where the Board was of the opinion that any remuneration charged in the company's accounts as director's fee was excessive in relation to the service rendered or extent of business carried on, it could direct part or the whole of such remuneration to be treated as forming part of the total profits of the company for the purpose of determining the amount by which the profits of the company to be relieved of tax could be reduced. Second, no relief was granted under the foregoing provisions to a company formed to acquire the whole or part of a trade or business previously carried on by another company. Third, the Board could in its discretion, make such assessments to tax on a company to counteract the benefit of relief granted where the company applied any profits in respect of which relief had been given in the payment of dividend (other than a dividend in the form of shares arising from the capitalization of profits); or in the reduction of paid-up share capital or in making any loan to a director of the company. Lastly, such assessments as would counteract the benefit of relief given was to be made upon a liquidator or receiver where the Board was convinced that the benefit of the relief granted was transferred to shareholders of the company in the process of liquidation or winding up.

Section 36 provided relief to a company which had paid or was liable to pay commonwealth income tax. In the case of a Nigerian company, the relief granted was the equivalent of the amount paid or payable as commonwealth tax where the commonwealth tax was only half or less than half of the tax payable under the Act but where the commonwealth tax was more than half of the rate payable under the Act, then the rate of relief was half the amount of tax payable under the Act. In the case of a non-Nigerian company, where the rate of commonwealth tax did not exceed the rate of tax under the Act, the relief granted was the equivalent of fifty percent of the commonwealth tax but where the commonwealth tax exceeded the rate of tax under the Act, the relief granted was the equivalent of the amount by which the rate under the Act was higher than half of the commonwealth rate. Commonwealth income tax was defined to mean tax on income of companies charged under a law in force in any commonwealth country or the Republic of Ireland, which provided relief from tax at home and in Nigeria in a manner corresponding to the foregoing provisions. The power to make double taxation arrangements was vested in the finance minister by section 37.

A company liable to tax could be charged in its own name or the name of any principal, attorney, factor, agent or representative in Nigeria or in the name of a receiver or liquidator.[165] The principal officer or manager of a company in Nigeria was responsible for doing all such things as were required to be done in furtherance to assessment and payment of tax by the company. The Board could also, where it deemed necessary, appoint any person to be the agent of a company for the purpose of giving effect to the provisions of the Act and the agent or any other person answerable for payment of tax under the Act on behalf of the company was empowered and indemnified, to retain out of any money coming into his hands on behalf of the company so much as was sufficient to pay tax for which the company was liable.[166] By section 43, payment of tax took priority over obligations owed to shareholders during winding up to the extent that the liquidator was required not to distribute any assets of the company to the shareholders unless provision had been made for full payment of whatever tax the company owed.

Every company was obliged, whenever so required by the Board, to prepare and deliver to the Board a true and correct statement in writing in such form and containing such particulars as the Board required including the amount of its profits from every source for the period(s) indicated. Whenever so required, a company was obliged to comply whether it was chargeable to tax or not. Furthermore, a company was obliged to give notice of its chargeability to the Board within three months after the commencement of an assessment year where no request to deliver returns had been made by the Board and where a company commenced business during a year of assessment, such notice had to be given within one month from the date of commencement of business.[167] The Board could call for further returns or particulars where it deemed it necessary from a company and could also request any person to attend before an officer of the Federal Inland Revenue Department regarding information contained in the returns. The Board was empowered to direct any company to keep adequate books of account in such form and language as it deemed appropriate, where it was convinced that the books of account of a company were inadequate. Any such direction issued by the Board could be a subject of appeal to the appeal Commissioners who could confirm or modify it as the case warranted.[168]

Upon the expiration of the time allowed for delivery of returns, the Board could proceed to assess every company chargeable to tax. Where a company delivered returns, the Board could either accept the return and base its assessment on such return or reject it and proceed to use its judgment to determine the total profits of the company and assess it accordingly. Similarly, where a company failed to deliver a return, the Board could use its best judgment to determine the amount of total profits of the company and base its assessment on the amount determined. The board's discretion to use its best judgment to assess a company which failed to make a return was without prejudice to whatever liability such company incurred for reason of its default.[169] The Board could also make additional assessment on a company - any time within six years from the expiration of the year in respect to which the assessment relates - if it was convinced that the company was assessed at a lesser amount than it ought to have been assessed.[170] The Board was obliged to prepare assessment lists of all companies assessed. Such lists were to contain the names and addresses of the companies, the names and addresses of the persons in whose names the companies were chargeable, the amount of total profits of each company, the amount paid by each company as tax and such other particulars as the Board deemed appropriate. Notices of assessment and amendments thereto were deemed to constitute assessment lists if they were complete in every detail.[171]

Notice of assessment was required to be served on every company whose name appeared on the assessment lists. The notice was to contain the company's total profits, tax payable, place at which the tax was to be paid and the company's right of objection.[172] A company that disputed the assessment could serve a notice of objection on the Board within forty eight days of receipt of the assessment notice (or such longer period as the Board, upon good cause, allowed) stating the grounds of objection. In considering the notice of objection, the Board could require the company to furnish it with such particulars as it deemed necessary and in addition call for oral evidence from any officer of the company. The Board was obliged to give notice of refusal to amend if no agreement was arrived at; and notice of the amended assessment where the company arrived at an agreement with the Board.[173] No notice of assessment could be impeached on the ground of an error or defect in form provided it was substantially in conformity with the intent and meaning of the Act.[174]

Section 55 (1) provided that the minister could establish, by notice in the gazette, a Body of Appeal Commissioners, to consist of a maximum of six persons none of whom could be a public officer. However, the secretary to the Body of Appeal Commissioners was required to be a public officer. Appeal Commissioners were appointed from among persons with experience and capacity in the management of a substantial trade or the exercise of a profession and held office for duration of three years. A Commissioner could be removed by the minister where (i) he had been absent from two consecutive meetings of the body; (ii) he had become incapacitated by physical or mental illness; (iii) he failed to declare his interest to the Board regarding an appeal pending before the Body of Commissioners as required by section 57 (2) and (iv) he had been convicted of a felony or an offence under any income tax law in Nigeria. The Body of Appeal Commissioners was empowered to consider appeals from a company aggrieved by the notice of refusal to amend assessment. An aggrieved company was required to serve notice of appeal on the Board and the Body of Appeal Commissioners within 30 days (or 60 days, where an extension of time had been granted) from the date of receipt of notice of refusal to amend. The notice of appeal was required to contain:

a.  official number of the assessment and the year of assessment;

b.  the amount of tax assessed;

c.  the amount of total profits upon which the assessment was based;

d.  the date upon which the appellant was served with notice of refusal by the board;

e.  the precise grounds of appeal; and

f.  an address for service.[175]

A pending appeal did not preclude the company and the Board from reaching an agreement on the assessed amount and where this happened, the Board could serve notice of agreement on the Body of Appeal Commissioners and the appeal would be treated as discontinued. The company could also serve notice of discontinuance on the Body of Appeal Commissioners. If no agreement was reached, the Body of Appeal Commissioners was required to fix a date for the hearing of the appeal and give notice of twenty one clear days to the parties. Upon determination of the appeal, the Commissioners could confirm, reduce, increase or annul the assessment as the facts demanded. Notice of the amount as determined by the Commissioners was served on the company which was obliged to pay within one month of receipt of the notice, notwithstanding a further appeal to the court. Failure of the company to pay made it liable to an action for recovery at the instance of the Board.[176] Section 59 provided that a company not satisfied with the decision of the Commissioners had a further right of appeal to the High Court of Lagos. This was because all offences under the Act were deemed to have occurred in Lagos.[177] Where the amount involved did not exceed 200 pounds, the company had to obtain consent of the Board before exercising the further right of appeal.[178]

Where there was no objection or pending appeal as to the assessed amount, the tax assessed was payable within two months from date of receipt of assessment notice but the Board could, in its discretion, extend time within which payment was to be made. Where an objection or appeal was pending, the Board could enforce such portion of the tax, if any, that was not in dispute while the balance remained in abeyance to be paid within one month from the date of determination of the objection or appeal.[179] A company that defaulted in the periods prescribed for payment of tax incurred a liability of 10 percent thereon. The sum due (inclusive of the 10 percent addition) was to be served on the company by way of a demand note and if one month thereafter, the company still defaulted, the Board could bring an action in any court of competent jurisdiction, including a magistrate court, to recover the tax as a debt due to the government of the federation. Such a company was in addition, guilty of an offence under the Act and upon conviction was liable to a fine of 100 pounds.[180] The Governor-General-in-Council could remit wholly or partly the tax payable by any company where he was satisfied as to the equity of the case.[181] A company which paid tax in excess of what it ought to have paid for reason of error in the return or statement of account could within six years from the end of the relevant assessment year apply for relief to the Board and upon being satisfied as to the merit of the application, the Board could give a certificate of the amount to be repaid and the accountant general of the federation upon receipt of the certificate would cause the repayment to be made.[182]

The offences created by the Act could be classified under three categories. Offences against the requirements of the Act, offences by authorised persons and offences by unauthorised persons. Offences against the requirements of the Act included:

a. failure to pay tax within the periods required by sections 61 and 62;
b. failure to comply with the requirements of a notice;
c. failure to attend in answer to a notice or summons or having attended, failure to answer questions lawfully put forward;[183]
d. making an incorrect return by omitting or understating taxable profits or giving incorrect information in relation to any matter affecting tax liability;[184]

e.    aiding or abetting the falsification of a return, account or statement in return for reward. The penalty for this offence was a fine of five hundred pounds or imprisonment for five years or both.[185]

Section 67 (1) prescribed a fine of 100 pounds for any offence in respect of which no specific penalty was provided and if the offence related to failure to keep records or furnish return, statement or information, a further penalty of 20 pounds for each day the failure continued and in default of payment, imprisonment for a period of six months. If the offence related to understating profits, then in addition to the fine of 100 pounds, the company was liable to pay a sum twice the amount understated.[186]

The penalty for a person who not being authorised by the Act, collected or attempted to collect tax was 300 pounds or imprisonment for three years or both. Similar penalties were provided for a person who being authorised to administer the Act:

a.    demanded from a company an amount in excess of the authorised assessment; or
b.    withheld a portion of tax collected for his own use; or
c.    rendered a false return of the amounts of tax collected by him; or
d.    defrauded any person or embezzled any money or otherwise used his position to deal wrongfully with the Board.[187]

The penalties provided by the foregoing sections did not preclude the company's liability to tax due or its culpability for criminal proceedings under any other law.

The *Companies Income Tax Act 1961* was in force until 1979 when it was repealed by the *Companies Income Tax Act No. 28 1979*. During its eighteen year tenure, it underwent series of amendments. For example, in 1967, a new section 30A was introduced which empowered the Federal Board of Inland Revenue to assess and charge a company on a fair and reasonable percentage of the turnover of its business within or outside Nigeria in the case of resident companies, and its turnover of business carried on within Nigeria in the case of a non-Nigerian company, where in the opinion of the Board, the assessable profits of the company were not readily ascertainable.[188] In 1974, the *Companies Income Tax Act 1961* was further amended. First, a new source of chargeable income which included 'fees, dues and allowances (wherever paid) for services rendered' was earmarked by section 17 (f).[189] Second, a company entering into an agreement in respect of any service under paragraph (f) was required to make full written disclosure to the Board of the terms of such agreement.[190] Third, tax relief was granted to every company which had suffered damage in respect of its trade or operations during the civil war but no deduction was allowable to such a company in respect of assets damaged or destroyed during the same period.[191] Fourthly, a company paying another company any sum of money by way of interest, management fee or royalty was required to deduct tax at the rate of one shilling per every pound as prescribed by section 32 of the principal Act and pay the amount so deducted to the Board.[192] Finally, a new expense item was listed as a non-allowable deduction and included as section 28 (g).[193]

The *Companies Income Tax Act 1979* originally promulgated as decree No. 28 of 1979 repealed the *Companies Income Tax Act 1961* and all the amendments thereto[194] and is the current law providing a legal framework for the taxation of companies' income in Nigeria. The administration of the tax was vested in the then Federal Board of Inland Revenue which was established under section 1 of the decree.[195] The duties and powers of the Board included the assessment, collection and accounting for all taxes under the Act, the power to hold and dispose property, the power to delegate some of its powers to another person to exercise on its behalf and the power to sue or be sued in its official name.[196]

In addition to the sources of chargeable profits under the CITA 1961, income accruing or derived from the use in Nigeria of the asset of any foreign company has been added as one more source of income chargeable to tax. For the purposes of taxing dividends, interest, discounts, charges and annuities, interest is deemed to be derived from Nigeria if there is a liability to payment of the interest by a Nigerian company or a company in Nigeria regardless of where or in what form the payment was made; or the interest accrues to a foreign company or person from a Nigerian company or a company in Nigeria regardless of how the interest accrued.[197] As under CITA 1961, the profits of a Nigerian company are deemed to accrue in Nigeria where ever they have arisen irrespective of whether they have been brought into Nigeria or not. The treatment of profits of a non-Nigerian company and companies engaged in shipping, air transport, cable undertakings and insurance under the CITA 1979 are equally similar to that under the CITA 1961.

A point of divergence between CITA 1961 and CITA 1979 is that one of the deductions taken into cognisance in the course of ascertaining total profits under the latter statute which was not provided for in the former is the amount of loss incurred by a company engaged in an agricultural trade or business in the first year of assessment after which the loss is incurred and to the extent to which such deduction cannot be practicably made, then it should be carried forward into the next year of assessment until such a time when the loss has been completely set off against the company's assessable profits.[198]

The rate of tax under the CITA 1979 was originally 50 kobo of each naira for the 1978-1979 assessment year and thereafter 45 kobo of each naira for subsequent years.[199] In the case of companies engaged in building or construction however, tax use to be levied at the rate of two and half percent of the business turn over or 45 kobo of each naira whichever was higher.[200] Further, in the case of banks, there was in addition to the chargeable rate of tax a *special* levy of 10 percent imposed on *excess profits*. Excess profit was defined as the difference between total profits and *normal* profits.[201] For the purpose of this provision, normal profit was determined by adding up the amounts arrived at after applying to the paid up capital, capital (or statutory reserve), general reserve and long term loans percentages of 40, 20, 20, 20 respectively.[202] The excess profit provision has been done away with and in 1996, Decree No. 32 increased the rate of companies' income tax to 30 kobo of every one naira (or 30 percent) of total profit and this is the current rate. The Body of Appeal Commissioners was established under section 50 to consist of a maximum number of 12 members one of whom was to be designated as chairman and none of whom could be a public officer.[203]

The *Companies Income Tax Act 1979* has been amended severally by various *Finance (Miscellaneous Taxation Provisions) Decrees*.[204] In 2007, CITA 1979 was further amended by the *Companies Income Tax (Amendment) Act No. 11 2007* to reflect some of the recommendations of the 2002 Study Group.[205] The following changes were introduced in the 2007 amendment:

a. Sections 1 to 8 of the principal Act relating to the establishment, powers and proceedings of the Federal Board of Inland Revenue have been repealed by Section 2 (1) of the 2007 amendment Act. This repeal is consistent with the establishment of the Federal Inland Revenue Service as the successor to the defunct FBIR.

b. Section 4 of the 2007 amendment Act requires an insurance company that engages the services of an insurance agent, loss adjuster or broker to include a schedule in its annual returns showing details of name, address, duration of employment and payments made to such agent, adjuster or broker.

c.  Section 5 of the amendment Act exempts profits of companies operating in Export Processing Zones (EPZ) or Free Trade Zones from tax under the Act, provided 100 percent of the company's production is for export otherwise proportionate tax is payable on local sales.

d.  The 2007 amendment provides greater incentives for donations to tertiary and research institutions by making such donations tax deductible expenses. The provision of CITA 1979 allowed a limit of 10 percent of total profit for such donations but excluded capital donations. Section 7 of the amendment allows both capital and revenue donations and further increases the allowable ceiling for such donations to either 15 percent of total profits or 25 percent of payable tax, whichever is higher.

e.  Under Section 31 (2) (a) (iii) of the principal Act, a company could not carry forward losses incurred in an assessment year beyond four years from the assessment year the said loss was incurred. The 2007 amendment repealed sub-paragraph (iii) which means there is no limit now as to how long a company may carry losses forward.

f.  Section 38 of the principal Act was also repealed by Section 10 of the amendment Act. Subsection (1) of the repealed section allowed 25 percent investment tax credit on the qualifying capital expenditure of a company engaged wholly in the fabrication of spare parts, tools and equipment for local consumption and export while subsection (2) allowed 15 percent investment tax credit on fixed asset of any company which purchased locally made plant, machinery or equipment for use in its business.

g.  Section 11 of the amendment increased the pre operation levy payable by a new company requiring a Tax Clearance Certificate to 20,000 naira in the first year and 25,000 naira in every subsequent year. Under the old provision, pre operation levy was 500 naira in the first year a company remained out of business and 400 naira for every subsequent year.

h.   Section 14 of the amendment repealed Section 56 of the principal Act which provided for one percent bonus of payable tax to a company that filed its return within the stipulated time.

i.   Sections 71 to 75 of the principal Act which contained provisions relating to the establishment and proceedings of the Body of Appeal Commissioners was repealed by Section 18 (1) of the amendment Act. This is consistent with the establishment of the Tax Appeal Tribunal by the FIRS establishment Act. The TAT takes over the mandate of the BAC as well as the Value Added Tax Tribunal.

j.   Section 21 (a) (i) and (ii) of the amendment increased the penalties contained in Section 92 of the Act. The fine payable as general penalty has been increased from 200 naira to 20,000 naira while the fine payable for failure to furnish statement or keep records has been increased from 40 naira to 2000 naira.

k.   Finally, the power to vary or revoke the rate of companies' income tax earlier vested in the President by Section 100 is now vested in the National Assembly, on the President's proposal.[206]

## Personal Income Tax

The *Income Tax Management Act 1961*[207] was the first enactment that was promulgated with a view to regulate the taxation of personal incomes exclusively and also provide a uniform system of personal income taxation across the federation. The Act had application throughout the federation although the application of its provisions to a particular region could be deferred where the Governor-General (with the consent of the regional government) by an order so determined. The Act did not repeal earlier laws such as the *Direct Taxation Ordinance No. 4 1940* and the *Income Tax Ordinance Cap 85*. Rather, pursuant to an order granted by the Governor-General in line with section 1 of ITMA, upon the application of a region as aforesaid, the provisions of the *Direct Taxation Ordinance No. 4 1940* and the *Income Tax Ordinance Cap 85* continued to apply to the region in question with such modifications as would:

(a)   prevent the taxation of income by more than one tax authority;

(b)   be necessary for the assessment or collection of tax or the continuation of any revenue allocation arrangements previously subsisting in relation to income tax between the government of the federation and the government of that region and such other modifications as the government of that region requested with respect to personal reliefs and rates of tax.[208]

In the absence of a deferment order as provided above, the provisions of the *Income Tax Ordinance,* the *Income Tax Administration Ordinance* and *Direct Taxation Ordinance* together with all rules, regulations and subsidiary legislation passed under them no longer applied in any part of Nigeria in the administration of personal income tax.[209]

The subjects upon whom the Act imposed tax were individuals, itinerant workers, communities, families, trustees and executors whose incomes were taxable under a regional law.[210] As the Act applied throughout the country, the question as to which tax authority could impose tax on any of the subjects listed above was determined in the case of an individual, by his place of residence. Place of residence was determined as provided by the First Schedule to the Act. The relevant determinant was the location of the employee as at 1st April. In the case of an itinerant worker, the basis for determining which tax authority had jurisdiction over his income depended on where he was found during the year. An itinerant worker was entitled to credit to the extent, if any, of tax already paid by him to any other tax authority for the same year. Tax by an indigenous community under the Act was to be imposed by, and payable to the government of the region in which the community was found. Community tax was charged on the estimated total income of community members or the estimated total income of those members whose income was, in the opinion of the relevant tax authority, impracticable to either assess individually or apportion with certainty among community members. In the case of family income where the several interests of the members were indeterminate or uncertain, tax was imposed only by the tax authority in the territory where the member of the family who customarily received that income in the first place ordinarily resided. Finally, the relevant tax authority in respect to income accruing to a trustee or executor was that of the territory where the trust or estate was situated.[211]

Section 4 (1) contained the sources of chargeable income for the purposes of the Act. According to the section, tax was chargeable upon income accruing in, derived from, brought into, or received in Nigeria in respect of:

a.   gains or profits from any trade, business, profession or vocation;

b.   salary, wages, fees, allowances or other gains from an employment paid or payable in money by the employer to the employee other than reimbursements paid to the employee of expenses incurred by him in the performance of his duties; or medical and dental expenses incurred by the employee; or cost of passage to or from Nigeria incurred by the employee; or the cost of child maintenance or education (provided such costs were deductible under the tax law of the region where the tax authority responsible for imposing the tax was located) gains or profits (including premiums) from a right granted to another person for the use or occupation of property;

c.   dividends, interest or discounts;

d.   pension, charge or annuity;

e.   any profits or gains not falling within the above mentioned categories.

The gains or profits of a taxable person whose business was partly carried out in Nigeria and partly outside Nigeria was determined by taking into account the extent of the operations of the business which were carried out in Nigeria and tax was imposed only to the extent to which the gains and profits of the business were derived from Nigeria.[212] The gains and profits of a partner were any remuneration, interest on capital or cost of passage to or from Nigeria mainly undertaken for the purposes of leave or recreation which was charged in the partnership account in respect of that partner and his share in the income of the partnership computed after the deduction of the cost of recreation referred to but before other private or domestic expenditure.[213] The gains of a person deriving income from agricultural land was deemed to be the gains or profits which ordinarily would accrue to him up to the average cultivation or use prevalent in the neighbourhood.[214]

Gains or profits from an employment were deemed to have been derived from Nigeria if they were derived in any of two scenarios. First, if duties of employment were wholly or partly performed in Nigeria then the gains therefrom were deemed to be derived from Nigeria. The exception was where the duties were performed on behalf of an employer who was in a foreign country, and the employee resided in Nigeria during the year of assessment for a period that was less than 183 days in all, and the remuneration of the employee was liable to tax in the country where the employer resided. Second, gains were deemed to be derived from Nigeria if the employer was in Nigeria except where the duties of the employment were wholly performed, and the remuneration paid in a foreign country.[215] Income from a dividend distributed by a Nigerian company was deemed to be derived from Nigeria while income from a dividend distributed by a foreign company was deemed gains derived in Nigeria only to the extent to which the amount of income was brought into or received in Nigeria.[216] Dividends distributed by a Nigerian company were taxable at source but were to be treated as a set off against the individual taxpayer's liability for the relevant assessment year and where the tax deducted upon the dividend exceeded his tax liability as arrived at upon the basis of his assessable income, he was entitled to be refunded the excess.[217] Income from interest on money lent by a person outside Nigeria to another person in Nigeria was deemed to be derived from Nigeria if the interest was payable in Nigeria; or the interest was by deed, will or charged upon the estate, real or personal, of the person paying or as a debt by virtue of a contract entered in Nigeria; or in the case of money lent to a Nigerian company, the loan was evidenced by a mortgage, debenture, loan or other stock issued by the company in recognition of its debt.[218]

A tax authority was empowered to counteract the liability of tax where such liability was reduced by virtue of a fictitious or artificial transaction. The Joint Tax Board was similarly empowered where the interest of more than one taxpayer was involved.[219] The incomes exempted from tax under the Act were as contained in the Third Schedule to the Act.[220] The exempted incomes were similar to those exempted under the *Income Tax Ordinance No. 3 1940* but newer categories of exemption were included under ITMA 1961. The new categories of exempted income included:

a.      Gains or profits from the business of operating ships or aircraft carried on by an individual not resident in Nigeria in so far as in the case of shipping, the business was not carried on in inland waters only and provided that the country of resident of the person accorded a similar exemption to persons resident in Nigeria. A person was deemed resident in the country where the central management and control of the business was exercised.

b.      Interest accruing on any loan charged on the public revenue of the federation and raised in the United Kingdom; or interest on any bond issued by the government of the federation to secure repayment of the loan raised from the International Bank for Reconstruction and Development; or interest on any money borrowed by either the government of the federation or of a region upon such terms which included the exemption of such interest from tax in the hands of a non resident person; or interest on money borrowed outside Nigeria by a corporation established by law in

Nigeria upon terms which included the exemption of such interest from tax in the hands of a non resident, subject to the consent of the finance minister.

c. The income of any national of the United States from employment by the International Co-operation Administration or its agents (including the University of Athens, Ohio in connection with the training of teachers in Nigeria) or an agency formed and directed by the United States Government.

d. Any income in respect of which tax was remitted under the *Consular Conventions Ordinance, Diplomatic Immunities and Privileges (Commonwealth Countries and Republic of Ireland) Ordinance* and the *Diplomatic Privileges Extension Ordinance.*

e. The income of any registered trade union in so far as it was not derived from any trade or business carried on by the union.

f. Gratuities payable to a public officer by either the government of the federation or any region in respect of services rendered by him under a contract of service and specifically described as gratuities by the contract or some other document issued in connection with the contract provided that where the period of service did not amount to five years and the total gratuities exceeded a sum calculated at one hundred and fifty pounds per annum, the excess was not exempt.

g. Gratuities paid to a staff or former staff of the Nigerian College of Arts, Science and Technology, West African Institute for Trypanosomiasis, West African Institute for Oil Palm Research and West African Council for Medical Research in circumstances similar to paragraph f above.

h. Any income of an individual chargeable solely by reason of it being brought into or received in Nigeria if the individual was not in Nigeria in the year of assessment for a total period amounting to at least one hundred and eighty three days.

To ascertain the income or loss of a person for an assessment year, similar deductions as allowed under the *Companies Income Tax Act* were allowed *mutatis mutandis* under ITMA 1961.[221] The following deductions were not allowed:

a. domestic or private expenses;

b. capital withdrawn from a trade, business, profession or vocation and any expenditure of a capital nature;

c. any loss or expense recoverable under an insurance policy or contract of indemnity;

d. rent or cost of repairs to any premises or part thereof not incurred for the purpose of producing income;

e.   taxes on income or profits levied in Nigeria or elsewhere except as provided under the Act;

f.   any payment to a pension, provident, savings or widows' and orphans' society, fund or scheme except as provided under the Act;

g.   depreciation of asset;

h.   any sum reserved out of profits, except as permitted under the Act or estimated by the relevant tax authority.[222]

In addition to the above where a deduction had earlier been allowed in respect of an expense or liability and such liability was subsequently waived or released or the expense refunded, the amount waived, released or refunded was treated as an income on the date it was made.[223] Section 20 provided the basis for computing assessable income. A person's assessable income for each year of assessment was the amount from each source of his income in the year immediately preceding the year of assessment in respect of each such income, even if at the time of assessment, he ceased to possess such income or the source had ceased producing income. Assessable income in respect of a new trade was determined at three levels. In the case of a person in the first year of business, it was the amount of income for that year; in the case of a person in the second year of business it was the amount from the date of commencement of business and in the case of a person in the third year of business the assessable income was computed on a preceding year basis. The assessable income of a person who permanently ceased to carry on trade, business, profession or vocation in Nigeria was as regards the year in which the cessation occurred, the amount of income for that year and as regards the year of assessment preceding that in which the cessation occurred, the amount of the income as computed on the basis of the foregoing provisions or the amount of income for that year, whichever was greater but he was not deemed to have derived any income from the said trade, business, profession or vocation in the assessment year following that in which the cessation occurred. Assessable income with regard to employment or pension was the amount of income from such employment or pension of the year of assessment. Income from an employment was deemed to arise day by day except where it was derived by way of a bonus, commission, allowance or at intervals exceeding one month in any of which case it was deemed to have arisen on the day it was paid. If the income was paid after the cessation of income, it was deemed to have arisen on the last day of employment.

Income respecting settlements, trusts and estates was deemed to be the income of the settlor or person creating the trust if:

a.  the person creating it retained or acquired an immediately exercisable general power of appointment over the capital assets of the settlement or trust or over the income derived from it; or

b.  he made use directly or indirectly of any part of the income arising under the settlement or trust;

c.  the settlement or trust was revocable in circumstances whereby the settlor or the spouse could resume control over any part of the income or assets comprised therein. However a settlement or trust was not considered revocable solely by the reason that the income or assets comprised therein could revert to the settlor or the spouse in the event of the beneficiary pre - deceasing the settlor or by the happening of an uncertain event upon which the settlement or trust was limited.

The income of any settlement or trust other than as described above was so much of that income as was derived whether in Nigeria or elsewhere, provided in the latter case it was brought into or received in Nigeria. The assessable income of an itinerant worker was to be determined either on the basis of the foregoing provisions or on the basis of the year ending 31 December within the year of assessment, if the income tax law of the taxing territory so prescribed.

The procedure for determining a person's total income was defined in section 21. Subsection (1) thereof provided that a person's total income was the amount of his total assessable income from all sources for that year together with additions to be made thereto in accordance with the Fifth Schedule less the deductions allowed in the said Schedule as well as section 21 (2). The deductions allowed under subsection (2) were losses claimed within one year after the end of the assessment year as been incurred in the assessment year and losses which the relevant tax authority was satisfied were incurred in any year preceding the year of assessment which had not been allowed against his assessable income of a preceding year.

The Act granted relief to any person who had paid or was liable to commonwealth income tax, defined as any income tax charged under a law in force within the commonwealth or the

Republic of Ireland.[224] Section 24 empowered the finance minister to make arrangements for the avoidance of double taxation.

Another salient feature of the ITMA was the establishment of the Joint Tax Board.[225] The Board consisted of one member each representing each territory nominated by the regional finance minister and a secretary nominated by the federal Public Service Commission. The Board was mandated to exercise such powers and duties as conferred upon it by the Act, or as agreed by the governments of the respective territories, or as conferred on it by a federal law or finance minister. In addition to the foregoing general powers, the Board was specifically mandated to:

a. advise the government of the federation, on request, in respect of double taxation arrangements concluded or under consideration with other countries, and in respect of rates of capital allowances and other taxation matters having any effect throughout Nigeria and in respect of any amendment to the Act;

b. use its best endeavours to promote uniformity both in the application of the Act and in the incidence of tax on individuals throughout Nigeria.[226]

The ITMA 1961 imposed official secrecy on the Board and its employees regarding taxpayer information in their custody. However, this duty of official secrecy did not apply where legal proceedings required it or where it was in the interest of public revenue to share information between or among tax authorities.[227]

To enhance uniformity and ease of administration, returns, statement or information affecting a person's liability to tax made to one tax authority could be treated by another tax authority where the person was deemed to be resident for all purposes as if the information was made to the second tax authority in the first instance.[228] Further, any matter which had continuing effect in determining the assessable income of a person beyond the relevant year of assessment was given effect by the relevant tax authority in subsequent years notwithstanding any change in the person's place of residence.[229]

In the light of sections 1 and 3 of ITMA 1961, regions of the federation (and the states that were eventually created out of them) passed their respective personal income tax laws. The federal territory of Lagos also passed the *Personal Income Tax (Lagos) Act No. 23 1961* which applied to residents of the federal territory of Lagos alongside the provisions of the ITMA

1961.[230] Between 1961 and 1993, several amendments were made to the ITMA 1961. Some of the major amendments included the *Income Tax (Amendment) Decree No. 58 1968, Income Tax Management (Amendment) Decree No. 35 1968, Income Tax Management (Amendment) Decree No. 24 1971, Income Tax Management (Amendment) Decree No. 41 1973, Income Tax Management (Uniform Taxation Provisions, etc.) Decree No. 7 1975, Income Tax (Armed Forces and Other Persons) (Special Provisions) Decree No. 51 1972.*

The *Income Tax(Amendment) Decree No. 58 1968* amended the ITMA 1961 by taking into cognisance the profit or gains of businesses that were partly carried out in Nigeria by inserting immediately after section 5 a new section 5A which read thus:

(1)     where, in respect of any business carried on by any person it appears to the relevant tax authority that for any year of assessment, the business produces either no assessable income or an assessable income which in the opinion of the relevant tax authority is less than might be expected to arise from that business or, as the case may be, the true amount of the assessable income of that person from the business cannot be readily ascertained, the relevant tax authority may for that year of assessment, in respect of that business, and notwithstanding:

(a) if the whole of the operations of the business are carried on in Nigeria, assess and charge the person carrying on the business on such fair and reasonable percentage of the turnover of the business, as the relevant tax authority may determine;

(b) if only part of the operations of the business are carried on in Nigeria, assess and charge the person carrying on the business on such fair and reasonable percentage of that part of the turnover of the business on such fair and reasonable percentage of that part of the turnover of the business attributable to the operations carried on in Nigeria, as the relevant tax authority may determine;

(2)     as to notices of assessment, appeal and other proceedings shall apply to an assessment or additional assessment made under this section as they apply to assessment or additional assessment made under the Act.

(3)     In this section:

"business" includes any trade, profession or vocation;

"person" in relation to the carrying on of a business has the meaning assigned by section 2 of this Act but does not include a company".

The main purpose of the *Income Tax Management (Amendment) Decree No. 35 1968* was to alter the composition and functions of the Joint Tax Board by substituting section 27 (2) of the ITMA 1961 as follows:

(2)     The Board shall consist of the following members

a.      one member, who shall be a member of the Federal Board of Inland Revenue  as constituted under section 3 of the Companies Income Tax Act 1961 nominated either by name or office from time to time by the Federal Commissioner for Finance; and

b.      one member for each state, being a person experienced in income tax matters nominated either by name or office from time to time by the Commissioner of the State in question charged with responsibilities for matters relating to income tax,

and any nomination made pursuant to the foregoing provisions shall be evidenced by notice thereof in writing delivered to the secretary of the Board.

The *Income Tax Management (Amendment) Decree No. 24 1971* excluded individuals who were employed in the Nigerian armed forces in civilian capacity from the provisions of paragraph 3 (2) of the first schedule to the ITMA 1961.  The paragraph provided as follows:

in the case of an individual other than an itinerant worker, tax for any year of assessment may be imposed only by the territory in which the individual is deemed to be resident for that year under the provisions of the First Schedule to this Act.

The paragraph deemed persons employed in the armed forces to be resident in Lagos. By the amendment however, non-combatant employees of the armed forces became liable to income tax in the state in which they were actually resident as at the 1ˢᵗ day of April.

The *Income Tax Management (Amendment) Decree No. 41 1973* clarified the composition of the Joint Tax Board and appointed the chairman of the Federal Board of Inland Revenue as its permanent chairman. This amendment was achieved by the substitution of section 27 (2) with a new subsection which provided that:

(a)     the Chairman of the Federal Board of Inland Revenue appointed pursuant to section 3 of the Companies Income Tax Act 1961 and was required to be the Chairman of the Board; and

(b)     a representative from each state being a person experienced in income tax matters, and any nomination was required to be evidenced by a notice in writing delivered to the secretary of the Board.

Section 27 (7) was also amended and it provided that the chairman or any authorised representative was required to preside at all meetings of the Board and whenever there was no consensus in arriving at a decision by a majority vote of the members present, the chairman had a casting vote apart from his deliberative vote when there was a deadlock. The legal adviser of the Federal Board of Inland Revenue was required to be in attendance at Board meetings and was to serve as adviser to the Board by virtue of section 7A.

The *Income Tax Management (Uniform Taxation Provisions, etc) Decree No. 7 1975* amended both the ITMA 1961 and the *Income Tax (Armed Forces and Other Persons) (Special Provisions) Decree No. 51 1972* to provide uniformity in the taxation of the income of individuals throughout the country. Uniform income rates were also prescribed but state governments were empowered to retain any existing capitation, community development education, poll or other general tax or levy, and to vary them.

The *Income Tax Management (Uniform Taxation Provisions, etc) Decree No. 7 1975* amended the ITMA 1961 by the insertion of a new section 20A immediately after section 20. The new section provided that where under the income tax law of a territory, income tax was payable on the chargeable income of an individual, the amount of the chargeable income was to be the amount of the total income of that individual as ascertained under the ITMA 1961 after the allowable deductions and exemptions have been taken into cognisance.[231] Section 20A (2) provided that every such individual was allowed a deduction of 600 naira. However, an individual who ordinarily resided in Nigeria or exercised any employment -the whole gain or profits of which were deemed to be derived from Nigeria -or is a person liable to tax under the *Income Tax (Armed Forces and Other Persons) Decree No. 51 1972* not being a person mentioned in section 1(1) (d) was allowed:

a.    a deduction of three hundred naira for a married man who in the preceding year had a wife, or a deduction of any alimony not exceeding three hundred naira paid  to a former spouse under an order of a court of competent jurisdiction where the marriage has been dissolved;

b.    a deduction of two hundred and fifty naira in respect of each unmarried child, who on the first day of the preceding year had not attained sixteen years of age or was receiving full time instruction in a recognised educational establishment or was under articles or indentures in a trade or profession provided a husband or wife which were not formally separated were treated as one individual and the deduction was allowed for only four children. More so, where the maintenance of a child was shared by two or more persons, the relevant tax authority was required to apportion the deduction allowed.

c.    a deduction of cost incurred in maintaining a close relative , spouse or widowed mother who was either incapacitated by old age or infirmity , provided that:

i.    no deduction was allowed in respect of any relative whose income of the year preceding the year of assessment exceeded six hundred naira;

ii.    the aggregate of all deductions to be allowed to two or more individuals in a given year did not exceed four hundred naira in respect of one relative and where the cost incurred exceeded the sum, the amount of deduction allowed was the same proportion of the sum as the cost so incurred bears to the total of the cost incurred;

iii. the aggregate deductions for any one individual was not expected to exceed four hundred naira;

d.  annual premium paid to an insurance company in the year preceding the year of assessment in respect of an insurance for life or spouse or contract for a deferred annuity provided that:

i.  deductions were not allowed to insurance companies save premiums payable on policies securing a capital sum on death which was not to exceed ten per cent of the capital sum exclusive of any additional benefits;

ii.  the aggregate amount of the deductions allowed under the provisions of:

a. this paragraph

b. paragraph (e) of subsection (1) of section 17 of this Act; and

c. in the case of an employee in paragraph (f)of subsection (1) of section 17 of this Act;

did not exceed two thousand naira in the case of an individual for any year of assessment;

iii.  under the provision of this paragraph, the aggregate deductions allowed was not required to exceed an amount equal to one-fifth part of the total income of the individual for that year ; and

iv.  the restrictions provided in sub-paragraphs (ii) and (iii) applied in the case of a husband and his wife or wives not formally separated as though they were one and the same individual whose total income for any one year of assessment was equal to the aggregate total income for that year of such husband and his wife or wives.

Subsection (4) provided that deductions allowed to an individual other than paragraph *(a)* of sub-section *3 (iii)* was allowed an individual or any spouse of the individual not formally separated, but the aggregate of such deductions was not to be allowed such as would exceed the amount if they were treated individually. Where a deduction claimed in respect of a child or dependant for a given year of assessment, by both husband and wife exceeded the deductible amount allowed, the relevant tax authority was required to apportion the amount claimed as it deemed fit for deduction between the spouses in the course of ascertaining their separate chargeable income. Where a deduction was allowed to either a husband or wife and was not claimed, it was required to be apportioned between them as decided by the relevant tax authority. The ITMA 1961 was further amended by the insertion of new sections 21A and 21B. Section 21A imposed tax on every person subject to tax under the law of any territory as provided for in the Seventh Schedule to the ITMA 1961.[232] The proviso to section 21A (1) provided that where the amount of the total income of a person exceeded the minimum amount specified in Table 1 in respect of a particular range of income, such a person was only liable to pay the income rate prescribed in respect of the next lower range of income plus not more than one half of the amount by which his income exceeded the minimum income of that range, subject to the maximum amount of applicable income rate. Subsection (2) provided that a territory was allowed to prescribe a general tax or levy instead of the income tax rates as specified in Table 1 of the Seventh Schedule to the ITMA 1961. The rates under Table 1 of the Seventh Schedule as provided in the amendment were four naira on total income not exceeding 1000 naira; eight naira on total income exceeding 1000 naira but not exceeding 2000 naira; and 20 naira on total income exceeding 2000 naira.

Section 21B provided that where income tax payable under the law of each territory on the chargeable income of an individual were to be ascertained in accordance with the provisions of the ITMA 1961, the rates were to be as specified in Table 2 of the Seventh Schedule. The rates in Table 2 were as follows:

| *Income to be taxed* | | *Rate of Tax* |
|---|---|---|
| For every naira of the first | ₦2,000 | 10k per ₦............10 percent |
| For every naira of the next | ₦2,000 | 15k per ₦.........15 percent |
| For every naira of the next | ₦2,000 | 20k per ₦.........20 percent |
| For every naira of the next | ₦2,000 | 25k per ₦............25 percent |
| For every naira of the next | ₦2,000 | 30k per ₦............30 percent |
| For every naira of the next | ₦5,000 | 35k per ₦............35 percent |
| For every naira of the next | ₦5,000 | 40k per ₦............40 percent |
| For every naira of the next | ₦10,000 | 45k per ₦............45 percent |
| For every naira of the next | ₦30,000 | 50k per ₦............50 percent |

Several other amendments were made to ITMA through the instrumentality of sundry enactments up to 1993[233] when the Personal Income Tax Decree was enacted to replace ITMA.

The *Personal Income Tax Decree No. 104 1993* is the current law regulating the administration of personal income tax in Nigeria and is retained as *Cap P8 Laws of the Federation of Nigeria 2004*.[234] PITA is similar to previous income tax laws in all material respects. But in addition, it contains other provisions that are completely novel in the administration of personal income tax in Nigeria. The provisions on persons and incomes chargeable, deductions allowed, incomes exempted, assessment, returns, offences and double taxation arrangements are similar in substance to that under the ITMA and other erstwhile income tax legislations. The novel provisions under PITA relate to the establishment of tax authorities,[235] the introduction of the Tax Clearance Certificate and the *Pay-As-You-Earn* scheme. A Tax Clearance Certificate (TCC) is required to be issued to a person who, in the last three years preceding the current year of assessment, has paid his tax in full, or is not liable to tax or on whose income no tax is due.[236] Section 85 (2) empowers government ministries, departments or agencies (MDAs) or commercial banks to demand TCC from any person with whom they are involved in transaction(s) that come under the ambit of subsection (4). These transactions include:

a. application for government loan for industry or business;

b. registration of motor vehicle;

c. application for firearms licence;

d. application for foreign exchange or exchange control permission to remit funds outside Nigeria;

e. application for certificate of occupancy;

f. application for award of contracts by government or its agencies and registered companies;

g. application for approval of buildings;

h. application for trade licence;

i. application for transfer of real property;

j. application for import or export licence;

k. application for agent licence;

l. application for pools or gaming licence;

m.  application for registration as a contractor;

n.  application for distributorship;

o.  confirmation of appointment by government as chairman or member of a public board, institution, commission, company or to any other similar position made by government;

p.  stamping of guarantor's form for a Nigerian passport;

q.  application for registration of a limited liability company or of a business name;

r.  application for the allocation of market stalls;

s.  appointment or election into public office.

A Tax Clearance Certificate (TCC) must disclose in respect of the last three years the chargeable income; tax payable; tax paid and outstanding tax or in the alternative, a statement to the effect that no tax is due.[237]

The foundation on which the Pay-As-You-Earn (PAYE) system of tax administration is premised is the provisions of section 81 of the PITA. Under the provision, income tax chargeable on an employee by an assessment, whether or not the assessment has been made, shall, if the relevant tax authority so directs, be recoverable from any emolument paid, or from any payment made on account of the emolument, by the employer to the employee. Rate of tax under the Act is contained in the Sixth Schedule to the Act. The Schedule, which was revised by the *Personal Income Tax (Amendment) Decree No 19 of 1998,* is as follows:

For every naira of the first   N20,000…….. 5 kobo per naira ( 5 percent)

For every naira of the next  N20,000…….. 10 kobo per naira (10 percent)

For every naira of the next  N40,000……....15 kobo per naira (15 percent)

For every naira of the next  N40,000…… 20 kobo  per naira (20 percent)

For every income above     N120,000…… 25 kobo per naira (25 percent)

The *Personal Income Tax Act* was also subject to series of amendments by virtue of various *Finance (Miscellaneous Taxation Provisions) Decrees.*[238] The latest amendments are contained in the Personal Income Tax (Amendment) Act 2011 which was one of the nine tax reform bills submitted to the National Assembly by the President in November 2005. The Personal Income Tax (Amendment) Act 2011 amends/deletes 36 sections of the principal Act and also modifies the First, Second and Third Schedules to the Act. The major amendments introduced in 2011 are as follows:

a. Sections 3 and 33 of the principal Act relating respectively to chargeable income and personal relief have been amended. In respect to chargeable income, pension has been removed as taxable income in line with the provisions of the Pension Reform Act.[239] The amendment further clarifies that temporary employees are also taxable subjects under the Act.[240] Regarding personal reliefs, Section 5 of the amendment replaces the personal relief of 5000 naira plus 20 percent of earned income that was available under Section 33 (1) of the principal Act with the Consolidated Relief Allowance, CRA. The CRA is to be computed at the rate of 200,000 naira or one percent of gross income, whichever is higher, plus 20 percent of gross income.

b. Section 4 of the amendment Act modifies the conditions under which gains or profits derived from employment duties in Nigeria will be exempt from personal income tax as contained in Section 10 (1) (a) (i) to (iii). First, in addition to performing the duties on behalf of a non resident employer, the Act now requires that remuneration of the employee must not be *"borne by a fixed base of the employer in Nigeria."* Second, the number of days spent on annual leave or temporary leave of absence is now to be factored in the computation of days spent by a non resident in determining if the overall period of stay in Nigeria amounts to 183 days. Third, the country in which the employee is liable to tax must now be one that operates an avoidance of double taxation agreement with Nigeria, for such an employee to be exempt from tax under the Act. Furthermore, paragraph (b) of subsection (1) of Section 10 of the principal Act has been replaced with a new paragraph which deems income or gain of employment to be derived from Nigeria if *"the employer is in Nigeria, or has a fixed base in Nigeria."* This new paragraph therefore, expands the definition of an employer to include a non resident with a fixed base in Nigeria.

In the light of the foregoing amendments, subsection (5) of Section 10 of the principal Act became redundant and has been deleted from the statute. The deleted subsection read that *"subject to the foregoing provisions of this section, the gain or profit from any employment, the duties of which are mainly performed outside Nigeria, shall be deemed to be derived from Nigeria to the extent that those duties are performed in Nigeria."*

c. A new subsection (6) has been added to Section 36 of the principal Act empowering the Finance Minister under a "presumptive tax regime" to issue regulations for the purposes of assessing the income of taxpayers who either fail to keep records or whose records are inadequate to enable a proper assessment of income.[241]

d. The rate of minimum tax under Section 37 of the principal Act has been increased from 0.5 percent to one percent of gross income.[242]

e. A new subsection (1) has been introduced by the amendment Act to replace subsection (1) of Section 38 of the principal Act. Under the old subsection, once the Finance Minister issued an order to the effect that "arrangements" were concluded with the government of a named country in relation to offering relief from double taxation, specifying that it was expedient for the said "arrangements" to have effect, the "arrangements" became effective notwithstanding anything contained in any enactment. However, by Section 8 (ii) of the 2011 amendment Act, the power to enter into avoidance of double taxation agreements with foreign countries is now vested in the Government of the Federal Republic of Nigeria and the agreement shall have effect only after ratification of same by the National Assembly. Further, "agreement" now replaces "arrangements" wherever the word appears in the section.

f. Penalties for failure to keep proper books of accounts have been included in the body of Section 52 of the principal Act to apply to taxpayers other than those in salary employment. The penalty is 50,000 naira for individuals and 500,000 naira for corporations.[243]

g. Service of notice of assessment can, in addition to registered post as contained in Section 57 of the principal Act, be made by either courier or electronic mail.[244]

h. Resolution of disputes arising from the operation of the Personal Income Tax Act is now vested in the Tax Appeal Tribunal rather than the erstwhile Body of Appeal Commissioners established under Section 60 of the principal Act.[245] In consequence, Sections 61 to 67 of the principal Act relating to the procedure of the Body of Appeal Commissioners have also been repealed by Section 15 of the amendment Act.

i. Section 74 of the principal Act which relates to penalties for failure to deduct and remit withholding tax has been replaced with a new provision that introduces amendments in three respects. First, a person who fails to deduct withholding tax on a qualifying transaction is still liable to 10 percent of the tax not deducted or remitted but this liability is no longer tied to the prior conviction of the taxpayer. Second, interest for non remittance or late remittance of withholding tax is now based on the prevailing Central Bank of Nigeria monetary policy rate. This is more easily determinable than the "prevailing commercial rate" under the old section. Third, the Accountant General of the Federation is now empowered to recover at source unremitted taxes owed by

Ministries, Departments and Agencies (MDAs) from the budgetary allocation due to such MDAs.[246]

j. Interest for late payment of personal income tax will now be computed on annual basis as opposed to the simple interest basis that previously applied.[247]

k. Section 20 of the amendment Act has introduced three new subsections (2) to (4) to Section 81 of the principal Act, and renumbered the old subsections (2) to (6) as subsections (5) to (9) accordingly. The substance of the three new subsections is that every employer is required to file a return with the relevant tax authority not later than 31st January of every year, all emoluments paid to its employees in the preceding year. Penalty for non compliance is 500,000 naira in cases of corporate employers and 50,000 naira in cases of individual employers.

l. Section 21 of the amendment has introduced new requirements in respect of Tax Clearance Certificate, TCC. First, in addition to the information required by Section 85 (3) taxpayer identification number is now also to be stated on the TCC. Second, in addition to the transactions listed under subsection (4) of Section 85, a TCC is also now required for change of ownership of vehicle by the vendor; application for plot of land; and any other transaction as may be determined from time to time. Third, the penalty for obtaining a TCC through misrepresentation or fraud has been increased from 500 naira to 500,000 naira. Finally, a new subsection (9) has been added to Section 85. The new subsection provides that any MDA or corporation which being obligated by the provisions of Section 85 (2) to demand a TCC in respect of any of the transactions listed in subsection (4) fail to so demand is guilty of an offence and punishable on conviction to a fine of 5000,000 naira or three years imprisonment or both.

m. The appointment of Secretary to the Joint Tax Board, hitherto vested in the Federal Civil Service Commission by Section 86 (3) of the principal Act is now, by virtue of Section 22 (c), vested in the Joint Tax Board itself.

n. Any director outside the State Service can be appointed as a member of a State Board of Internal Revenue established under Section 87 of the Act. Hitherto, only directors within the State Service could be appointed. Also, the "three other persons" to be nominated on personal merit is now the prerogative of the State Governor and no longer the Finance Commissioner; and the three must be selected to represent each senatorial district in the State.[248]

o. Section 24 of the amendment Act introduces a proviso to Section 88 (1) (b) which requires that States Boards of Internal Revenue shall now be funded by cost of collection mechanism of not less than five percent.

p. The threshold for penalties has been increased throughout the Act. The general penalty in Section 94 (1) has been increased from 200 naira to 5000 naira; and in the case of failure to keep records or furnish required returns or information, the penalty has been increased from 40 naira to 100 naira for each day the failure subsists. Second, the penalty for making an incorrect return is now 20,000 naira fine instead of 10 percent of the correct tax as was originally provided under Section 95 of the Act. Third, the penalty for an offender under Section 96 has been increased from 5000 naira to 50,000 naira in the case of an individual or 500,000 naira in the case of a corporation. The Section relates to an offender who for the purpose of obtaining a set-off or relief makes a false representation in a return, statement or account as well as an abettor who aids in the above offence. Finally, the penalty for offences against an official who misuses his position or an unauthorised person who impersonates a tax official under Section 97 of the principal Act has been increased from 1000 naira to 10,000 naira.[249]

q. Section 29 of the amendment Act provides for a new Section 104 to replace the previous section under the principal Act. The section relates to powers conferred on tax authorities to distrain the property of a taxpayer who refuses to pay tax, after the assessment has become final and conclusive and a demand notice has been served but the taxpayer still defaults. The new section introduces three new dimensions to the power to distrain that were not contained under the old provision. First, the power to levy distress is now exercisable only after an *exparte* application has been made and granted by a Judge of the High Court sitting in chambers. Second, the tax authority is now obliged to refund to the taxpayer any excess monies realised from the sale of distressed property after the tax owed and incidental costs are recovered. This refund, where applicable, is to be made 30 days after the sale and where the taxpayer cannot be traced, the excess is to be refunded to the court that granted the order to distrain. Under the old provision, refund of excess money was based on demand made by the taxpayer within one year from the date of sale of the distrained property. Finally, the new provision specifically confers powers on the tax authority to levy the property of a recalcitrant taxpayer wherever it may be found in Nigeria.

r. A new Section 106A has been introduced immediately after Section 106 of the principal Act. The new section empowers the Finance Minister, on the recommendation of the

Joint Tax Board, to make regulations for giving effect to the provisions of the Personal Income Tax Act. Second, it empowers the National Assembly, on the proposal by the President, to impose, increase, reduce, withdraw or cancel any rate of tax, duty or fee chargeable under the Act.[250]

s.  The meaning of "itinerant worker" under Section 108 of the principal Act has been redefined.[251] The old definition referred to "an individual who works at any time during a year of assessment (other than as a member of the armed forces) for a daily wage or customarily earns his livelihood in more than one place in Nigeria and whose total income does not exceed N600." The new provision makes away with the 600 naira threshold but introduces another threshold that the person must have worked in more than one State for a minimum of 20 days in at least three months of every assessment year.

t.  Paragraph 1 of the First Schedule to the Act which has to do with determination of residence has been amended by the addition of a new subparagraph which states that "in the case of an individual who works in the branch office or operational site of a company or other body corporate, the place at which the branch office or operational site is situate: Provided that operational site shall include Oil Terminals, Oil Platforms, Flow Stations, Factories, Quarries, Construction Site with minimum of 50 workers, etc."[252]

u.  Paragraphs 2 and 3 of the Third Schedule to the principal Act which had to do with incomes exempted have been deleted. The implication is that the official emoluments of the President, Vice President, Governors and Deputy Governors which were exempted under those paragraphs are now taxable. Furthermore, Paragraph 7 of the principal Act has been replaced with a new paragraph. The old paragraph exempted interest on loans granted after 1st January 1997 to a person engaged in agricultural trade or business; fabrication of any local plant or machinery; or as working capital for cottage industry established under the Family Economic Advancement Programme; provided the moratorium was not less than 18 months and the rate of interest was not more than base lending rate at the time the loan was granted. The new provision now exempts income earned from bonds issued by any tier of government and corporations as well as interest earned by holders bonds and short term securities.[253]

v.  Finally, the amendment Act has provided for a new income tax table to replace the old table contained in the Sixth Schedule to the principal Act. Under the new table, the first 300,000 naira is taxable at seven percent; the next 300,000 naira at 11 percent; the next

500,000 naira at 15 percent; the next 500,000 naira at 19 percent; the next 1,600,000 naira at 21 percent and above 3,200,000 naira at 24 percent. The new Schedule specifies the National Housing Fund contribution; the National Health Insurance Scheme contribution; Life Assurance Premium; the National Pension Scheme; and gratuities are tax exempt deductions.

The amendment Act was passed by the House of Representatives on 25 May 2011; the Senate on 1 June 2011 and came into force on 14 June 2011 which was the date Presidential Assent was given.

## Petroleum Profits Tax

The discovery of crude oil in commercial quantities at Oloibiri[254] in 1956 and the eventual commencement of operations by Shell Petroleum made it pertinent to impose tax on profits derived from petroleum operations. This led to the enactment of the first petroleum profits tax legislation in Nigeria in 1959 in the form of the *Petroleum Profits Tax Ordinance No. 15 1959*. The long title of the Ordinance is *'An Ordinance to impose a tax upon profits from the winning of petroleum in Nigeria, to provide for the assessment and collection thereof and for purposes connected therewith.'* The ordinance, which is deemed to be an Act of the National Assembly, came into force on the 1st day of January 1958 and its application is throughout the federation. It is now Cap P13 Laws of the Federation of Nigeria 2004.

Section 3 vests the administration of the ordinance and the management of tax collected under it in the *Board*, which is defined by section 2 as the *Federal Board of Inland Revenue*.[255] The section further lists the powers and duties of the Board. By virtue of section 4, an act required to be done by the Board in relation to its powers and duties can be signified under the hand of the chairman of the Board or any officer of the Board authorised by the Board. Section 5 imposes a duty of official secrecy on any person involved in the administration of the Act. The duty of secrecy relates to documents involved in tax administration and can only be waived with authorization by the minister or for the purpose of the Act or other law relating to income in force in Nigeria. Subsection (3) further excludes any such document or information from being tendered or communicated in court in any proceedings other than for the purpose of carrying out the provisions of the Act, or to institute prosecution. The Board can however permit the Auditor - General for the federation (as the successor to the director of federal audit, who had the original power under the principal Ordinance) or an officer authorised by him access to any records or documents as may be necessary in the performance of his duties. The power to make rules generally for the carrying out of the provisions of the Act is vested in the minister while the Board is empowered to specify the form of returns, claims, statements and notices to be used under the Act.[256] Service of notices is to be effected at the registered office of the company to be served in the case of companies registered in Nigeria; and on the individual authorised to accept service in the address filed with the Registrar-General of the Corporate Affairs Commission,[257] or the registered office of the company wherever it may be in the case of a company registered outside Nigeria.

Taxation of petroleum profits is imposed by section 8 of the ordinance in the following terms:

> There shall be levied upon the profits of each accounting period of any company engaged in petroleum operations during that period, a tax to be charged, assessed and payable in accordance with the provisions of this Act.

*Petroleum operations* pursuant to the Act amount to:
> the winning or obtaining and transportation of petroleum or chargeable oil in Nigeria by or on behalf of a company for its own account by any drilling, mining, extracting or any other like operations or process, not including refining at a refinery, in the course of a business carried on by the company engaged in such operations, and all operations incidental thereto and any sale of or disposal of chargeable oil by or on behalf of the company.[258]

In ascertaining the profits of a company involved in petroleum operations, section 9 distinguishes profits, adjusted profits, assessable profits and chargeable profits. By section 9 (1) *profits* of a company within any accounting period shall be taken to be the aggregate of:

a. the proceeds of sale of all chargeable oil sold by the company in that period;[259]
b. the value of all chargeable oil disposed of by the company in that period; and
c. all income of the company of that period incidental to and arising from any one or more of its petroleum operations.

Subsection (2) defines 'the value of all chargeable oil so disposed' to mean the aggregate of:

a. the value of that oil as determined, for the purpose of royalty, in accordance with the provisions of any enactment applicable thereto and any financial agreement or arrangement between the Federal Government of Nigeria and the company;[260]

b. any cost of extraction of that oil deducted in determining its value; and

c. any cost incurred by the company in transportation and storage of that oil between the field of production and the place of its disposal.

The *adjusted profits* of a company in an accounting period are defined as 'the profits of that period after deductions allowed by subsection (1) of section 10 of this Act and any adjustments to be made in accordance with the provisions of section 14 of this Act'.[261] The deductions allowed under section 10 (1) of the original decree were:

a. any rents (other than rents included in the definition of royalties) incurred by the company for that period in respect of land or buildings occupied for its petroleum operations or compensation incurred for disturbance of surface rights or any like disturbance under an oil prospecting licence or oil mining lease;

b. sums incurred by way of interest upon money borrowed by the company where the interest was payable on capital employed in carrying out petroleum operations; (however, such sums would not be allowed as deductions if either company has interest in the other company; or both companies have interests in a third company directly or by proxy; or both companies are subsidiaries of one mother company)

c. any expense incurred for the repair of premises, plant, machinery, or fixtures employed for the purpose of carrying on petroleum operations or for the renewal, repair or alteration of any implement, utensils or articles so employed;

d. debts directly incurred to the company and proved to the satisfaction of the Board to have become bad or doubtful within the accounting period in question notwithstanding that the said debts were due prior to the commencement of the accounting period; provided the deduction allowable as doubtful debt shall neither exceed the portion of debt proved to have become doubtful within that accounting period nor include any amount deducted in determining the adjusted profit of a previous accounting period. Further to the proviso above, all sums recovered by the company within a particular accounting period respecting which deductions were previously allowed shall be treated as income of the company *incidental* to its operations; and finally, the debts for which deductions are claimed must have been included as profits resulting from operations during the accounting period in which such debts were incurred or advances made in the normal course of petroleum operations;

e.  any expenditure directly incurred in connection with drilling an appraisal well but does not include qualifying plant or building expenditure for the purpose of the Second Schedule to the ordinance; or sums deductible under sections 10 and 17;

f.  any contribution to a pension, provident or other society, scheme or fund as the Board may approve; provided that any sum received by or the value of any benefit obtained by the company from any approved pension, provident, scheme or fund in an accounting period shall be treated as income of the company *incidental* to its operations;

g.  such other deductions as may be allowed under any rule made pursuant to the ordinance.

By the combined effect, mostly of the *Finance (Miscellaneous Taxation Provisions) Decrees Nos. 30 1996, 31 1996 and 30 1999* the following deductions also became allowable under section 10:

a.  rents incurred by the company for that period in respect of land or buildings occupied under an oil prospecting licence or an oil mining lease for disturbance of surface rights or for any other like disturbance;

b.  all non-productive rents, the liability for which was incurred by the company during that period;[262]

c.  all royalties, the liability for which was incurred by the company during that period in respect of natural gas sold and actually delivered to the Nigerian National Petroleum Corporation, or sold to any other buyer or customer or disposed of in any commercial manner;

d.  all royalties the liability for which was incurred by the company during that period in respect of crude oil or of casinghead petroleum spirit won in Nigeria;

e.  all sums the liability for which was incurred by the company to the Federal Government of Nigeria during that period by way of customs or excise duty or other like charges levied in respect of machineries, equipment and goods used in the company's petroleum operation

f.  all sums incurred by way of interest on any inter-company loans obtained under terms prevailing in the open market, that is the London Inter-Bank Offer Rate, by companies that engage in crude oil production operations in the Nigerian oil industry;

g.   any other expenditure, including tangible drilling costs directly incurred in connection with drilling and appraisal of a development well, but excluding an expenditure which is a qualifying expenditure for the purpose of the Second Schedule to this Act, and any expense or deduction in respect of a liability incurred which is deductible under any other provision of this section-

    (i) any expenditure (tangible or intangible) directly incurred in connection with the drilling of an exploration well and the next two appraisal wells in the same field whether the wells are productive or not;

    (ii) where a deduction may be given under this section in respect of such expenditure that expenditure shall not be treated as qualifying expenditure for the purpose of the Second Schedule;

h.   all sums, the liability of which was incurred by the company during that period to the federal government, or state government or local government by way of duty, customs and excise duties, stamp duties, education tax or any other tax imposed other than by the PPTA or any rate, fee or charge.[263]

In addition, where a company engaged in petroleum operations is engaged in the transport of chargeable oil by ocean going oil tankers operated by or on behalf of the company from Nigeria to another territory, such adjustments shall be made in computing an adjusted profit or loss as shall effectively exclude therefrom any profit or loss attributable to such transportation.[264]

By section 2, accounting period is defined as:

(a)   a period of one year commencing on 1 January and ending on 31 December of the same year; or

(b)   any shorter period commencing on the day the company first makes a sale or bulk disposal of chargeable oil under a programme of continuous production and sales, domestic, export or both, and ending on 31 December of the same year; or

(c)   any period of less than a year being a period commencing on 1 January of any year and ending on the date in the same year when the company ceases to be engaged in petroleum operations.

The foregoing definition of accounting period was introduced by the *Petroleum Profits Tax (Amendment) Decree No. 15 1973* to replace the original definition of accounting period under the principal ordinance. Under the principal ordinance, accounting period meant:

(a) a period of twelve months commencing on the date of the first sale or bulk disposal of chargeable oil by or on behalf of the company, whichever shall be earlier, or commencing on such date within the calendar month in which such event occurs as may be selected by the company with the approval of the Board; or

(b) such shorter period commencing as aforesaid and ending either on a date selected by the company with the approval of the Board or on the date when the company ceases to be engaged in petroleum operations; or

(c) each subsequent period of twelve months during which the company is engaged in petroleum operations; or

(d) any period of less than twelve months, being a period commencing on the day following the end of any such period of twelve months and ending on the date when the company ceases to be engaged in petroleum operations as the case may be and in the event of any dispute with respect to the date of the first bulk disposal of chargeable oil the Chief Inspector of Mines of the Federation shall determine the same and no appeal shall lie therefrom.[265]

Section 9 (4) defines *assessable profits* of an accounting period as 'the adjusted profit of that period after any deduction allowed by section 20 of this Act'. Section 9 (5) defines *chargeable profits* of an accounting period as 'the assessable profits of that period after the deduction allowed by section 20 of this Act'. Similarly, section 20 (1) defines the *chargeable profits* of an accounting period of a company as 'the amount of assessable profits of that period after the deduction of any amount to be allowed in accordance with the provisions of this section'. The deductions allowed under section 20 are contained in subsections (2) and (4). Under subsection (2) the deductions allowed are the aggregate amount of all allowances due to the company for the accounting year under the provisions of the Second Schedule. The allowances allowed under the provisions of the Second Schedule are:

    *a. Petroleum Investment Allowance:* qualifying expenditures allowed a company in an accounting period in respect of an asset used wholly and exclusively by the company in petroleum operations. The deduction allowable is in respect of the accounting year in which the asset is first used.

    b.  *Annual Allowances:* qualifying expenditure allowed a company in an accounting period in respect of an asset used wholly and exclusively for petroleum operations, whether or not an initial allowance may be due to it. If the accounting period is less than a year, the allowance for the period shall be proportionately reduced.

    c.  *Balancing Allowances:* qualifying expenditure allowed a company in an accounting period in respect of an asset, which immediately prior to its *disposal,* was wholly and exclusively used for petroleum operations. The allowable deduction is the excess of the residue of that expenditure over the value of the asset, at the date of its disposal.

The deduction allowed under subsection (4) is a sum equal to 85 percent of the assessable profits of the accounting period, less 170 percent of the total amount of the deductions allowed under section 17 of the Act for that period. The limitation imposed by subsection (4) shall be applied to ensure that the amount of tax chargeable on the company for the accounting period shall not be less the 15 percent of the tax which would be chargeable on the company for the period, were no deductions allowed under section 20 for that period.[266] Subsection (5) requires that where the total amount of the allowances computed pursuant to subsection (2) cannot be deducted for reasons of insufficiency of assessable profits; or no assessable profits; or the limitation imposed by subsection (4), the total amount or part thereof that has not been deducted shall be added to the aggregate amount of allowances due to the company under the Second Schedule for the subsequent accounting period and shall be deemed to be allowances due to the company for the said subsequent accounting period.

In determining the *adjusted profits* of a company in any accounting period, no deductions shall be allowed in respect of:

    a.  disbursements or expenses not wholly and exclusively incurred in regard to petroleum operations;

    b.  capital withdrawn or any sum employed or intended to be employed as capital;

    c.  capital employed in improvements distinct from repairs;

    d.  sums recoverable under an insurance or contract of indemnity;

e.  rent or cost of repairs to any premises not engaged for the purposes of petroleum operations;

f.  amounts incurred in respect of any income tax, profits tax or other similar tax whether charged within Nigeria or elsewhere;

g.  depreciation of any premises, buildings, structures, works of a permanent nature, plant, machinery or fixtures;

h.  payments to any provident fund, savings, widows' and orphans' society, scheme or fund except as allowed under section 10 (1) (k);

i.  any customs duty on goods (including articles or any other thing) imported by the company either for resale or personal consumption of employees of the company; or where goods of the same quality to those so imported are produced in Nigeria and are available, at the time the imported goods were ordered by the company for sale to the public at prices less or equivalent to the cost to the company of the imported goods;

j.  any expenditure for the purchase of information relating to the existence and extent of petroleum deposits.

Paragraphs (i) and (j) above were inserted respectively by the *Finance (Miscellaneous Taxation Provisions) Decree No. 31 1996* and the *Petroleum Profits Tax (Amendment) Decree No. 15 1973.* The two paragraphs were not in the principal ordinance rather, another deduction that was not allowed under the principal ordinance but which was repealed by the 1996 decree was royalty or other sums deductible in ascertaining chargeable tax payable under section 17 of the said ordinance.

## Assessable Tax and Chargeable Tax

The Act further distinguishes between *assessable tax* and *chargeable tax. Assessable tax* for an accounting period is defined by section 21 (1) as *"an amount equal to 85% of its chargeable profits of that period."* This is a modification of section 16 of the principal Ordinance which originally defined *assessable tax* to be an amount equal to 50 percent of the company's *chargeable profits* for that period. The 85 percent rate was introduced in 1977 by the *Petroleum Profits Tax (Amendment) Decree No. 55 1977.* Similarly, while under section 17 (1) of the original provisions of the principal Ordinance, a company's *chargeable tax* was *"the amount of its assessable tax for that period after the deductions allowed by this section."* The deductions allowed were:

a.  all royalties, the liability for which was incurred by the company during that period in respect of chargeable oil won during that period;

b.  all sums, the liability for which was incurred by the company during that period to any government, provincial or local authority in Nigeria by way of duty, tax (other than the tax imposed under this Ordinance) or any rate, impost, fee or other charge.

The *Finance (Miscellaneous Taxation Provisions) Decree No. 30 1999* however repealed the above provisions and in its place makes the following provisions on *chargeable tax*:

(1)    A crude oil producing company which executed a Production Sharing Contract with the Nigerian National Petroleum Corporation in 1993 shall, throughout the duration of the Production Sharing Contract, be entitled to claim an investment tax credit allowance[267] as an offset against tax in accordance with the provision of the production Sharing Contract.

(2)    The investment tax credit rate applicable to the contract area shall be 50% flat rate of chargeable profit for the duration of the Production Sharing Contract.

(3)    In computing the tax payable, the investment tax credit shall be applicable in full to petroleum operations in the contract area such that the chargeable tax is the amount of the assessable tax less the investment tax credit.

(4)    The chargeable tax computed under subsection (3) of this section shall be split between the Nigerian National Petroleum Corporation and the crude oil producing company in accordance with the proportion of the percentage of profit of oil split.

Only companies are chargeable to tax under the Act because the law does not envisage that individuals or partnerships may engage in petroleum operations. Indeed, it is unlawful for individuals and partnerships to engage in petroleum operations, going by the provisions of section 24 (1). Subsection (2) empowers the minister to make rules governing the tax liabilities of companies engaged in petroleum operations as partners including the ascertainment of their assessable tax but by subsection (6) no such rules may impose a greater tax on a company in partnership than, but for the partnership, it ordinarily would have been liable to pay under the Act. The *Petroleum Profits Tax (Amendment) Decree No.1 1967* introduced certain circumstances under which a company may be liable to additional chargeable tax. The circumstances, now codified as section 23, provide that an additional chargeable tax shall be payable where the amount of chargeable tax payable by a company for an accounting period, calculated in accordance with the provisions of the Act, is less than the amount mentioned in subsection (2) of section 23. The amount referred to is the amount which the chargeable tax of a company within an accounting period would have come to, if in the case of crude oil exported from Nigeria, the reference in section 9 (1) (a) to the proceeds of the sale thereof were a reference to the amount obtained by multiplying the number of barrels of that crude oil by the relevant sum per barrel. The relevant sum per barrel of crude oil exported by a company is the posted price applicable to that crude oil reduced by such allowances, if any, as may from time to time be agreed in writing between the federal government and the company.[268]

A non-resident company carrying on petroleum operations in Nigeria is liable to tax either directly or in the name of its manager or other person employed in the management of the company's operations and such a person is liable to do all matters required for the assessment and payment of tax under the Act.[269] Section 26 imposes a similar obligation on the manager or principal officer of a resident company. Where a company is being wound up or is under a receivership, the company shall be assessed and charged in the name of the liquidator, who shall be answerable for doing all acts required for the assessment of tax under the Act.[270] The tax liability of such a company shall take precedence over claims by creditors and shareholders.[271] Where a company transfers a substantial portion of its assets for the purpose of avoiding tax for an accounting period ending prior to such transfer, section 28 provides that the Board may sue the purchaser for recovery of the tax assessed and charged on the company. Section 29 indemnifies any person who being answerable to tax on behalf of a company retains money in his possession or under his *de facto* control as shall be sufficient to pay tax as assessed and charged on the company.

Section 30 (1) obliges every company engaged in petroleum operations to prepare particulars of profits and loss accounts for each accounting period. The particulars of the accounts shall include:

a. its estimated adjusted profits or loss and its estimated assessable profits of that period;

b.  the residues of its assets for the period, all qualifying petroleum expenditure, the values of disposed assets within the period and allowances due to the company pursuant to the provisions of the Schedule;

c.  its estimated chargeable profits for the period;

d.  a statement of all royalties and other sums deductible under section 22, the liabilities for which were incurred for that period;

e.  a statement of all amounts refunded, repaid, waived or released to it within that period in line with section 20 (5);

f.  its estimated tax for that period

The Board is empowered to call for books, documents or further particulars after a notice of twenty one days on the company, for the purposes of examining such books where the Board requires such examination in order to obtain full information in respect of the company's operations. The Board may further give directions to a company which either keeps no books or keeps inadequate books requiring it to keep such books and accounts in such form and language as the Board may decide.[272] A company is required by section 33 to make a return of its estimated tax within two months after the commencement of an accounting period. Subsection (2) allows a company to submit a further return where after complying with subsection (1), the company becomes aware of a need to revise the return already submitted.[273]

The Board may accept the returns as delivered by the company and proceed to assess the company on the basis of its returns or refuse the returns and proceed to assess the company on its own estimation in line with section 35 (3), as if the company failed to deliver returns. Furthermore, by section 36 where the Board is of the opinion that a company liable to tax under the Act did not pay tax or paid less tax than it ought to have paid, the Board may within six years from the date of the end of that accounting period assess the company at such amount or additional amount as in the opinion of the Board ought to have been charged. An assessment shall be in a form and manner as the Board may authorise but in any event, shall contain the name, address, the relevant accounting period and the amounts of chargeable profits, assessable tax and chargeable tax for the period. An amended assessment shall contain all the above information including the amended or revised amounts and every assessment or amendment thereto shall be filed in a list to be known as an *Assessment List*.[274]

Notices of assessment are required to be served either personally or by post to all companies whose names are contained on the assessment list. The notice of assessment is required to state the relevant accounting period, the amounts of the company's chargeable profits, assessable tax and chargeable tax, the place at which the tax should be paid and the right of the company to object to the amount assessed. A company that disputes the assessed amount shall within twenty one days from receipt from the notice of assessment (or such longer period as the Board may for good reason grant) apply to the Board for review, stating the amount of chargeable profits of the company within the accounting period as well as its assessable tax and the amount which in its opinion should have been stated in the notice. Upon receipt of the objection, the Board may request for further particulars including evidence on oath. Where the company and the Board agree on the amount of tax liable to be assessed, the assessment shall be made amended accordingly and notice of the tax payable served on the company. However, where the parties fail to agree, the Board may revise the amount as it deems and shall serve on the company the revised amendment together with notice of refusal to amend the assessment as desired by the company.[275] An assessment shall not be deemed void or incompetent for reason of a mistake, defect or omission so long as the company assessed is designated therein according to common intent and understanding.[276]

The procedure for appeals under the Act is contained in section 41. A company that receives a notice of refusal to amend may within 30 days (or such longer period not exceeding 60 days, as the Board may for good reason allow) appeal by notice to the Secretary of the Appeal Commissioners. The notice of appeal shall contain:

a.   the official number of the assessment and the relevant accounting period
b.   the amount of tax charged under the assessment
c.   the date on which the appellant was served with notice of refusal to amend
d.   the precise grounds of appeal
e.   an address for service of any notices

All appeals are required by subsection (6) to be conducted *in camera* and subsection (7) empowers the minister to make rules governing the appeal procedure. Further appeal by any aggrieved party from the decision of the Body of Appeal Commissioners lies to the Federal High Court.[277]

Where there is a dispute as to the amount of tax to be paid, collection of tax or the part thereof that is in dispute shall be in abeyance until the determination of the dispute.[278] In the absence of a dispute however, tax for an accounting period of 12 months shall be payable in 12 instalments. The first instalment shall be payable not later than the third month of the accounting period and shall be an amount equal to one-twelfth of the estimated tax as envisaged by section 33 (1). The remainder of the monthly payments shall be payable not later than the last day of the month in question and shall be an amount equal to the amount of tax estimated to be chargeable for such period by reference to the latest returns submitted in accordance with section 33 (2) less so much as has already been paid divided by the number of such monthly payments as are outstanding in the accounting year. The final instalment shall be payable within 21 days after the service of the notice of assessment of tax for such accounting period and shall be the amount assessed for the period less so much as has been paid in the initial instalments.[279] This position differs from the original position under the principal Ordinance where petroleum profits tax was payable in four instalments with the first payment accruing not later than the last day of the ninth month, the second instalment not later than the last day of the accounting period and the third instalment not later than last day of the third month following the expiry of the accounting period. The last instalment was payable within 21 days after the service of the notice of assessment of tax for such accounting period, and the amount payable was such amount as assessed less so much as had been paid in the first three instalments.[280] This change in the mode of payment was made by the *Petroleum Profits Tax (Amendment) Decree No. 15 1973*.

By the provisions of section 46 (1) and (2), failure to pay an instalment of tax at the time it is due makes the company liable to pay in addition to the due amount, a further amount equal to five percent of the instalmental amount due. Under the principal ordinance, this penalty was at the discretion of the Board but the *Petroleum Profits Tax (Amendment) Decree No. 15 1973* introduced the word *shall* in paragraph (a) of subsection (1) to section 46 thereby making it mandatory for the Board to impose the 5 percent penalty in the event of default in payment of tax by a company. The Board shall further serve a demand notice on such a company and if within one month after the service of the notice the company fails to pay, the said company shall be guilty of an offence and the Board shall in addition to the penalty prescribed sue to enforce payment. Section 48 empowers the Board to sue for recovery of tax in its name in a court of competent jurisdiction (including magistrate court, if the amount to be recovered is not in excess of its jurisdiction) and the amount recovered is a debt due to the federal government. Section 49 provides for relief to be given to a company in respect of an excessive assessment owing to an error in the accounts or particulars supplied to the Board. Similarly, section 50 (1) provides for repayment (refund) of tax but in both cases the application must be made within six years from the expiry of the accounting period to which the application relates. Further, while the decision of the Board in respect of an application for relief is final and conclusive, the Board's decision in case of repayment is subject to the appeal procedure prescribed in sections 41 and 42.

Sections 51-55 create different offences under the Act and spell various penalties. The offences include failure to comply with the requirements of a notice, willful making of incorrect accounts, wilful making of false statements and returns, misconduct by tax officials and unauthorised administration of tax. The *Finance (Miscellaneous Taxation Provisions) Decree No. 31 1996* added another category of offence to include failure to deduct withholding tax where same ought to have been deducted under section 56 or where having been deducted, the company fails to make remittance to the Board.[281] Section 56 complements the provisions of section 54 by requiring a company to whom the Act applies to withhold tax (i.e. at-source deduction) when making payment to any company, partnership or person that provides services to it whether or not such company, partnership or person is resident.

Sections 60 - 63 contain miscellaneous provisions. Section 60 precludes the Personal Income Tax Act or any other Act in respect of any income or dividends from taxing income or dividends paid out of profits, which are taken into account under the provisions of the Act.[282] Section 61 vests in the minister the power to make rules for carrying out the provisions of any arrangements on double taxation that may be entered into with another country.[283] Section 62 contains provisions on the method of calculating relief to be allowed under a double taxation arrangement. Section 63 vests the minister with the power to amend the First Schedule to the Act. The First Schedule contains powers and duties to be exercised exclusively by the Board and under the principal Ordinance the power to amend the Schedule was vested in the Governor-General. Finally, the Second Schedule contains capital allowances, including rates of qualifying expenditure, petroleum investment allowance, annual allowances and balancing allowance.

The foregoing analysis of the *Petroleum Profits Tax Act* takes into consideration the amendments passed since the enactment of the principal Ordinance. Most of the amendments currently in force were done by virtue of various Finance (Miscellaneous Taxation Provisions) decrees passed between 1991 and 1999 some of which have already been highlighted. One major amendment which deserves an independent analysis is the *Petroleum Profits Tax (Amendment) (No. 3) Decree No. 95 1979*. This decree is fundamental for the reason that it brought natural gas operations within the purview of petroleum operations and amended the principal ordinance in certain areas to reflect this development. A new provision was inserted requiring 'the value of all chargeable natural gas' to be included as part of the aggregate factors to be taken into account in determining the profits of a company in an accounting period.[284] Decree No. 19 of 1998 even introduced incentives for the utilisation of associated gas which incentives, together with the conditions for their application, are now contained in subsections (1) and (2) respectively of section 11.

In 2005, the *Petroleum Profits Tax (Amendment) Bill* was sent to the National Assembly as an executive bill along with eight other tax related bills. About the same time, the organised private sector was lobbying the National Assembly for the passage of the *Petroleum Industry Bill* which seeks to bring all oil and gas related legislation within the ambit of a single enactment. It was felt that the proposed PPT amendment bill could be aligned with the Petroleum Industry Bill and this was carried out. When passed therefore, the Petroleum Industry Bill will harmonize all oil and gas laws including the PPTA under a single enabling legislation.

### Capital Gains Tax

Taxation of capital gains was first introduced in Nigeria in 1967 by virtue of the *Capital Gains Tax Decree No. 44 1967* which came into force on 1 April 1967. The long title to the decree[285] says the Act is meant to 'provide for the taxation of capital gains accruing on disposal of assets'. Section 2 of the Act fixes the rate of capital gains tax at 10 percent of chargeable gains accruing to a person in an assessment year less of such deductions as may be allowed under section 13 of the Act while section 3 provides that all forms of property shall be assets for the purposes of the Act, whether such property is situated in Nigeria or not and includes:

    a.  options, debts and incorporeal property generally;

    b.  any currency other than Nigerian currency; and

    c.   any form of property created by the person disposing of it, or otherwise coming to be owned without being acquired and includes assets in respect of which qualifying expenditure had been incurred under the *Personal Income Tax Act, Companies Income Tax Act* or *Petroleum Profits Tax Act.*

Under the principal decree, the rate was 20 percent of chargeable gains. The current rate of 10 percent was introduced by the provisions of section 22 (1) *Finance (Miscellaneous Taxation Provisions) Decree No. 18 1998.*

An asset disposed outside Nigeria is chargeable if, in the case of a non-resident individual, the total number of days he resided in Nigeria in the year of assessment exceeds 182 and the amount or part thereof of the disposed asset is received by him in Nigeria; and in the case of a non-resident company, the amount or part thereof of the disposed asset received in Nigeria shall be chargeable.[286] The gains chargeable under the Act are contained in section 6 (1). They include any capital sum received upon the disposal of an asset by way of sale, lease, transfer, assignment or compulsory acquisition and in particular, capital sums received by way of:

    a.   compensation for loss of office or employment;
    b.   insurance policy and risk of any kind of damage or injury to, or loss or depreciation of assets;
    c.   forfeiture or surrender of rights;
    d.   consideration for use or exploitation of any asset

Without prejudice to paragraph (a) above, capital sums received in connection with, or arising by virtue of a trade, vocation, business or profession are also liable to tax under the Act. *Capital sum* means money or money's worth and *disposal of assets* include part disposal of the asset.[287]

The Act envisages that all disposals of assets should ordinarily be by way of bargains made at arms length; i. e bargains struck without unusual concessions between the parties. The Act, therefore introduced the *market value* determinant in situations where it appears either improbable or impracticable to strike the bargain at arms length. Section 7, therefore, provides that where a person's acquisition of an asset is not by way of bargain made at arm's length; or where he acquired it wholly or partly for a consideration that cannot be valued; or where he acquired it as trustee for creditors of the person making the disposal, the consideration for his acquisition shall be deemed to be equal to the market value of the asset. Where a person acquired an asset by way of gift or otherwise, and he disposes it by way of gift, the value of the asset shall be deemed to be the amount for which the asset was last disposed of in a bargain made at arm's length where such amount is ascertainable and where it is not ascertainable, the value shall be deemed to be equal to the market value at the time of the disposal.[288] *Market value* is defined by section 21 (1) to mean the price the asset might reasonably be expected to fetch on a sale in the open market; and subsection (3) thereof provides that in re-estimating the market value of an acquired asset, if the market value exceeds the consideration actually paid by the acquirer, the asset shall be deemed to have been acquired for the amount actually paid by the acquirer.

Section 8 (1) provides that on the death of an individual, any assets of which he was competent to dispose shall be deemed to have been disposed by him at the time of his death and acquired by his personal representatives at a consideration equal to the amount for which the asset was last disposed of in a bargain made at arm's length and where such amount is not ascertainable, at the market value of the asset at that date but gains accruing in consequence of section 8 (1) are exempted from capital gains tax by virtue of subsection (2) of section 8. Personal representatives administering property forming part of a deceased person's estate are treated as a single and continuous body of persons and deemed as possessing the domicile and residence of the deceased at the time of his death.[289] By section 8 (4), where a person acquires asset as a legatee, no chargeable gain shall accrue to the personal representatives and the personal representatives' acquisition of the asset shall be treated as the acquisition by the legatee.

Section 9 (1) exempts a person from capital gains tax whose disposal of land is to an authority having and exercising compulsory powers of acquisition; provided that the person had neither knowledge of the impending compulsory acquisition at the time he acquired the land nor had, prior to the compulsory acquisition, indicated an intention to dispose of the land. Under the principal decree, section 10 (1) thereof imposed tax liability on a person who disposed land *indirectly* (even if he was a legatee) and by paragraphs (a) and (b) thereto, a person was deemed to dispose land *indirectly* where he disposed shares in a land-owning company that was under the control of not more than five persons in which he had substantial interest; or along with persons with whom he was connected, they had control of a company which had control of a land-owning company that was controlled by not more than five persons. A land-owning company meant a company entitled to land whose market value was equal or in excess of one-fifth of the company's net assets. These provisions are no longer part of the Act, with the repeal of the provisions of section 10 of the principal decree by section 2 of the *Finance (Miscellaneous Taxation Provisions) Decree No. 19 1998*. The current section 10 (section 11 under the principal decree) makes provisions as to the relevant date in determining the acquisition or disposal of an asset chargeable to capital gains tax. The relevant date is deemed to be the date when the contract of acquisition or disposal as the case may be, is made or the date when an enforceable right to acquire or dispose of the asset arises. Where the contract is subject to a condition or an option exists under the contract, then the relevant date shall be the date when the condition is satisfied or the option is exercised as the case may be; provided that where a consideration of such contract does not depend mainly on the value of the asset at the time the condition is satisfied, the acquisition or disposal shall be treated as if the contract had never been conditional, in which case the relevant date shall still be the date of the contract.

The gain chargeable to tax under the Act is the difference between the sum accruing upon disposal of the chargeable asset and the deductions allowable upon the accruable sum.[290] Under section 12 (1) any sum or part sum from the disposal of asset which has already been taken into account in the computation of income tax under the *Personal Income Tax Act, Companies' Income Tax Act* or *Petroleum Profits Tax Act* shall be excluded from the computation of capital gains accruing upon the disposal of the asset. Section 13 provides further deductions allowable in the computation of capital gains. By subsection (1) thereof the deductions allowed include:

a. the cost incurred in acquiring the asset, together with the cost incidental to its acquisition, or where the asset was not acquired any cost necessarily and exclusively incurred in providing for the asset;

b. any expenditure wholly, exclusively and necessarily incurred for the purpose of enhancing the value of the asset, the said expenditure being reflected in the nature or state of the asset at the time of its disposal;

c. any expenditure wholly, exclusively and necessarily incurred in establishing, preserving or defending title or right over the asset; and

d. any costs incidental to the disposal of the asset.

Incidental costs are defined by subsection (2) to consist of expenditure incurred wholly, exclusively and necessarily by way of fees, commission, or remuneration paid for the professional services of a surveyor, valuer, auctioneer, accountant, agent or legal adviser; together with cost arising from conveyance such as stamp duties and marketing costs such as cost of advertisement and valuation. Section 25 (1) provides that no deduction shall be allowable more than once in respect of any sum. Sections 14 and 15 provide for deductions not allowed in the computation of capital gains. Section 14 excludes any expenditure allowable as deduction in computing profits or gains under the *Personal Income Tax Act, Companies' Income Tax Act* and *Petroleum Income Tax Act;* while section 15 excludes any expenditure incurred in respect of an asset by way of premium or policy of insurance against risks of any kind or depreciation of asset.

Where there is a part disposal of assets, computation of the gain accruable shall be determined by apportionment between the cost of acquisition of the asset (including the cost of its enhancement) and the value of the asset which remains undisposed. The apportionment shall be made by reference to the consideration accruing upon the part disposal of the asset and the market value of the undisposed part of the asset. According to section 17 (1), where payment upon the disposal of an asset is payable by instalments over a period exceeding eighteen months, the chargeable gains accruable shall be considered as accruing in proportion to each instalment in the year of assessment the said instalment is payable. A capital sum received by way of compensation for a lost or destroyed asset under an insurance or other policy would not be treated as a gain (or loss), not minding that the capital sum is of a greater amount, provided the person receiving the sum applies it in acquiring another asset in replacement of the lost or destroyed asset. A claim in respect of the foregoing cannot be made if only part of the capital sum is applied in acquiring the new asset.[291]

A bargain comprising of two or more transactions where assets are disposed of shall be treated as one disposal for the purposes of computing the capital gains accruable. Similarly, separate considerations agreed upon for two or more transactions comprised in one bargain shall be treated as constituting an entire consideration for the transactions altogether and apportioned among them accordingly.[292]

Section 20 (1) empowers the Board[293] to disregard any fictitious or artificial disposition and direct that necessary adjustments be made with respect to the capital gains tax liability of a person as it deems appropriate to counteract the reduction in liability occasioned by such fiction or artificiality. Transactions between connected persons (within the meaning of section 23) shall be deemed artificial or fictitious if the Board is of the opinion that the transactions have been made on terms which do not appear fair in relation to same or similar activities among persons dealing at arm's length. By virtue of section 22, where the person disposing an asset and the person acquiring it are connected, the parties shall be treated as making a bargain *otherwise* than at arm's length and the amount of consideration for the bargain shall be deemed to be the market value of the asset; and where the asset is subject to a right or restriction enforceable by the person making the disposal or a person connected with him, the deemed market value shall be what the market value would ordinarily be, less the market value of the right/restriction or the amount by which the extinction of the right/asset would enhance the value of the asset, whichever is less. By section 23(2) - (4) persons are *connected* if:

a.  they are spouses, relatives or in-laws;
b.  in relation to a settlement, one is a trustee and the other a settlor or connected with the settlor;
c.  they are partners or related to a partner.

In the case of companies, subsection (5) provides that a company is connected to another company if:

a.  both are controlled by the same person or one is controlled by persons who are connected with the person who controls the other;
b.  the group controlling one consists of the same individuals controlling the other.

Subsection (6) provides that a company is connected to a person if that person singly or along with persons connected with him have, control of the company.

Provisions relating to location or situation of assets and rights accruing therefrom are contained in section 24. By virtue of paragraphs (a) and (b) of the section, the question as to *where* a right or interest over real assets and chattels arises (otherwise than by way of security) is dependent on the location of such real asset or chattel. Shares and securities are ordinarily situated in the country of the issuing authority; however, registered securities are situated where they are registered and if such registration occurs in multiple places, then the place where the principal register is situated. A ship or aircraft is situated in a country where the owner is resident and an interest or right over such craft or ship is situated where the owner is resident. Goodwill of a trade or professional asset is situated where the trade or profession is carried out. Patents, trademarks and designs are situated where they are registered and if registered in more than one place, then where each register is situated; while franchise, copyrights or license to use any patent or trademark is situated in the place they are exercisable. Subject to the foregoing provisions, a debt is situated where the creditor is resident.

Exemptions and reliefs from capital gains tax are provided for under sections 26 - 41 of the Act. Gains accruing to ecclesiastical, charitable or educational institutions of a public nature; or registered friendly societies; or registered trade unions are not chargeable to tax provided they are not derived from disposal of assets acquired in connection with trade or business carried on by the organisation and they are applied strictly for the purpose of the organisation.[294] If any property held by any of the above societies ceases to be held on trust, the trustees shall be treated as if they had disposed and immediately re-acquired the property for a consideration equal to its market value and the gain therefrom shall be deemed not to accrue to the society. Assessment on the trustees in respect of such accrued gain may be done any time within three years after the end of the year of assessment in which the property ceases to be held in trust.[295]

Statutory bodies are also exempt from capital gains tax under section 27. Specifically, gains are exempt from tax where they accrue to a local government council; a company being a purchasing authority established by law to acquire any commodity for export from Nigeria; or a corporation established by law for the purpose of fostering the economic development of any part of Nigeria provided the gain is not derived from the disposal of an asset acquired by the corporation in connection with any trade or business carried on by it. Section 28 provides for two scenarios. First, a gain accruing to a person from the disposal of an investment held by him as part of any superannuation fund is exempt from capital gains tax to the same extent the assets under the fund would be exempted under the *Personal Income Tax Act* payable to him out of such fund. Second, a gain from the disposal of investment held by a person as part of any national provident fund or other retirement benefit scheme is exempt from capital gains tax in the same manner as similar funds or schemes are exempt from income tax under the Third Schedule to the *Personal Income Tax Act*. Section 29 exempts from capital gains tax any gain accruing upon the disposal of a decoration acquired other than for monetary consideration for valour or gallant conduct. Section 30 (1) exempts stocks, shares, or Nigerian government securities from tax under the Act and subsection (2) defines *Nigerian government securities* to include Nigerian treasury bonds, savings certificates and premium bonds issued under the *Savings Bonds and Certificates Act Cap S1 Laws of the Federation of Nigeria 2004.*

The exemption provided under section 31 (1) is similar to the provisions of section 18 (1) but while section 18 deals with sums received by way of compensation of lost or destroyed assets, section 31 deals with sums received by way of disposal of assets or interest in assets which are used solely for the purposes of trade or business. According to section 31 (1) where assets that were solely used for a trade or business are disposed and the gain acquired therefrom is applied exclusively to the acquisition of assets within the same class, the person carrying on the trade shall be treated as if he made neither a gain nor loss. This exemption shall not apply to a partner in a business except he can be treated as having a share in the disposal of the old asset and acquisition of the new one. It shall also not apply where only part of the proceeds from the disposal is applied to acquire the new asset. There are four classes of assets to which this exemption apply. Under class 1, there are two further classifications: Heads A and B. Head A includes any land, building or part thereof, as well as any permanent or semi-permanent structure in the nature of a building occupied and used for the purposes of trade. Head B includes any fixed plant or machinery which does not form part of a building or permanent or semi-permanent structure. Class 2 includes ships; class 3 includes aircrafts while class 4 includes goodwill.

Sums accruing upon the disposal of, or an interest in rights obtained under a policy of assurance or contract are exempt from tax by virtue of section 34 except where the person making the disposal is not the original beneficial owner and had acquired the right or interest for money or money's worth. Other gains exempted from capital gains tax include:

a. a sum received by way of compensation or damages for any personal or professional wrong or injury;

b. a sum received by way of compensation for loss of office except where such a sum exceeds 10,000 naira in a year of assessment;[296]

c. a sum received upon the disposal of a sole or main dwelling house;

d. a sum received upon the disposal of chattel whose total consideration is 1000 naira or less;[297]

e. a sum acquired upon the disposal of mechanically propelled road vehicle used for the carriage of passengers, except if the vehicle is a type that is neither suitable nor commonly used for carriage of passengers;

f. an asset disposed by way of gift, where it was acquired otherwise than by on a devolution of death;

g. gains accruing to diplomatic bodies.

The *Finance (Miscellaneous Taxation Provisions) Decree No. 3 1993* included two more exemptions to capital gains tax which are contained in the Act as sections 32 and 33. These include:

a. gains arising from the acquisition of the shares of a company either taken over, or absorbed or merged by another company as a result of which the acquired company loses identity; provided that no cash payment is made in respect of the shares acquired;

b. gains accruing to unit holders of a unit trust in respect of disposal of securities; provided the proceeds are re-invested.

Where a person chargeable to capital gains tax in respect of gains accruing outside Nigeria applies and shows that he was unable to transfer the gains accruing to him to Nigeria and the inability was not for want of endeavour on his part but rather due to the laws of the country where the income arose or the action of the government of that country or inability to obtain foreign currency, he shall be entitled to deduction from the amount assessed in the amount equivalent to that affected in the foregoing conditions. The claim must however be made within six years from the end of the year of assessment in which the gain accrued. Furthermore, the deducted amount shall become chargeable upon the person or his personal representatives in any subsequent year of assessment in which the conditions described above cease to exist.[298]

Section 43 (1) vests the administration of capital gains tax in the Federal Board of Inland Revenue and subsection (2) provides that appeals against assessment to capital gains tax shall be made to the Body of Appeal Commissioners.[299]

## Stamp Duties

The first law passed with a view of regulating the stamping of documents was the *Stamp Duties Proclamation No. 8 1903*. The Proclamation was intended to regulate the 'charging of stamp duties in respect of certain instruments'.[300] The duties imposed were to be collected on behalf of His Majesty, his heirs and successors, for the use of the government of the Protectorate of Northern Nigeria upon the several instruments specified in the schedule to the proclamation.[301] The instruments specified in the Schedule were:

a. admission as a barrister or solicitor;

b. agreement or memorandum of agreement including agreement for a lease, but excluding an agreement of which the subject matter had a value of less than five pounds or an agreement for the hire of a seaman or an agreement for the sale of goods, wares or merchandise;

c. appointment of a trustee or any appointment by an instrument other than a will in execution of property, share or interest;

d. instrument of apprenticeship;

e. adjudicatory award;

f. bill of exchange except trade cheques or good notes;

g. bill of lading for any goods, merchandise or effects except the master's copy;

h. charter party or any agreement relating to the freight or conveyance of any goods or effects on board a ship;

i. conveyances of whatever kind;

j. copy or extract of an instrument chargeable with any duty, or an original or probate copy of a will, testament or codicil or letters of administration;

k. declaration of any use or trust of any property by writing not being a deed or will or any instrument chargeable with *ad valorem* duty as a settlement;

l. deeds of whatever kind;

m. duplicate or counterpart of any instrument chargeable with duty;

n. lease;

o. letter or power of attorney except appointment of a proxy to vote at a meeting or authority given to a person to receive from the Treasury any money due to a person as a public officer from the government of the Protectorate;

p. transfer of licences for exclusive prospecting or mining as well as licences for acting temporarily as a solicitor of the Supreme Court, or for a private warehouse or for firearms and ammunition or to re-sell gunpowder;

q.  mortgages, including bonds, debentures or covenants but excluding a bond given by a public officer for the due execution of his duty or bond on which a fee is chargeable under the provisions of the Supreme Court Proclamation or bond given in pursuance of any Proclamation relating to the receiving of any drawback, customs duty or wares exported from the Protectorate;

r.  permit granted to non-natives to import liquor;

s.  receipt given for payment of money amounting to two pounds or more but excluding receipt given:

    i.  for the payment of any duties, taxes or money for the use of government of the protectorate;

    ii.  by any person for any money due to such person as a public officer from the government of the protectorate;

    iii.  as acknowledgement of money consideration in respect of any instrument liable to stamp duty;

    iv.  for drawback or bounty upon the exportation of any goods or merchandise from the protectorate;

    v.  for the return of any duties of customs upon certificates of over-entry;

    vi.  by the payee of a money order;

    vii.  for a gift of money paid by the government of the protectorate to a native king or chief.

In addition to the specific exceptions discussed above, paragraph 2 of the Schedule listed general exemptions to stamp duties. These included:

a.  transfers of shares in the Government or Parliamentary stocks or funds of Great Britain;

b.  instruments for the sale, transfer or other disposition of any ship or vessel or interest thereof;

c.  all instruments on which the duty where required would be payable by a government department;

d.  all instruments of any kind which were made by or to an officer of the government of the protectorate, where but for this exception, such stamp duty would have been payable by an officer of the government in his official capacity provided that the exception was not construed to extend to any instrument made by or to a government officer acting as *ex officio* administrator or receiver under a court order; or any instrument made by or to a government officer in relation to a sale made for the recovery of an arrear of revenue or rent or in satisfaction of any order or judgment of court.

In 1916, the *Stamp Ordinance No. 42 1916* was passed and made to apply to the protectorate of Nigeria as well as the colony of Lagos. The Ordinance drew substantially from the *Stamp Duties Proclamation 1903* with some modifications. For example, under the proclamation only the Attorney General and Treasurer were appointed as commissioners of stamp duties. Under the Ordinance however, a new category of officials were also appointed in addition to the Attorney General and Treasurer. These new officials included the Solicitor-General, the crown counsel, the assistant treasurer at the headquarters of the government in the northern provinces, the station magistrates, registrars and deputy registrars.[302] Also, the nominal share capital of a company was included as an instrument to be stamped with an *ad valorem* duty of five shillings for every 100 pounds.[303] There were other minor amendments to the ordinance in 1922,[304] 1928[305] and 1931.[306] The 1931 amendment, among other minor changes, repealed the powers vested in the assistant treasurer, station magistrates, registrars and deputy registrars as Commissioners of Stamp Duties and in their stead appointed the deputy treasurer in addition to the Attorney General and the Treasurer.

In 1939, the *Stamp Duties Ordinance No. 5 1939* was passed to repeal the *Stamp Ordinance 1916* together with all amendments thereto.[307] This Ordinance, now Cap S8 Laws of the Federation of Nigeria 2004, is deemed to be an Act of the National Assembly and is the current legislation regulating the administration of stamp duties in Nigeria. The instruments in respect of which stamp duties are chargeable (as well as the exemptions thereto) are contained in the Schedule to the Act and include (but not limited to) those instruments that were chargeable under the *Stamp Ordinance No. 42 1916* with such necessary modifications as have been occasioned by the change in Nigeria's political status. The Act vests the federal government with the exclusive competence to impose, charge and collect stamp duties relating to instruments executed between companies *inter se* or between a company and an individual. The state governments are vested with competence to administer stamp duties relating to instruments executed between individuals.[308] While state tax authorities administer the duties in the second category on behalf of their respective governments; the Federal Inland Revenue Service (as the successor to the Federal Board of Inland Revenue) administers the duties in the first category on behalf of the federal government. In addition, the Service administers stamp duties in relation to instruments executed between individuals in the Federal Capital Territory.

The Act, like its predecessor, recognises two types of duties, *ad valorem* duties and fixed duties. *Ad valorem* duties are duties whose sum increases with an increase in the value of the document evidencing the transaction. E.g a company's share capital is subject to *ad valorem* duty of one naira for every 200 naira.[309] Fixed duties are flat and do not change irrespective of the value of the transaction. E.g. duty on admission as a barrister or notary public is fixed. The instruments subject to stamp duties are, upon the duty being paid, denoted by impressed stamps. Adhesive stamps may however be used and where adhesive stamps are allowed, postage stamps may be used for the same purpose.[310] Some instances where the use of adhesive stamps is allowed include the execution of agreements,[311] and bills of exchange and notes.[312]

Section 6 (1) vests the management of stamp duties in the Commissioners of stamp duties[313] to be appointed either by the President or the Governor of a State, as the case may be, from the relevant Civil Service Commission. Similarly, only the minister or governor may approve the design of a new die to be used as impressed revenue stamp, and unless such powers are exercised, the dies in use under the principal Ordinance may still be used for impression. Section 8 provides two instances where a single instrument may be charged as if it were separate instruments. The first instance is where an instrument contains or relates to several distinct matters. Paragraph (a) of the section requires duties to be charged in respect of each of those matters as if they were contained in separate instruments. For example, under section 38, where an instrument under hand only (i.e. a document not sealed) contains both a promissory note by a principal debtor and a guarantee by a surety, such an instrument shall be charged as both a promissory note and as a guarantee. Similarly, any other matter contained in a promissory note which would be liable to duty if contained in a separate document shall be charged separately. The second instance is where an instrument which is liable to *ad valorem* duty is in addition, executed for any other valuable consideration, then paragraph (b) requires that the *ad valorem* consideration and the other consideration be separately and distinctly charged as if they were contained in separate instruments. Section 9 makes it an obligation on every person who either executes an instrument or is employed to execute one in respect of which a duty is chargeable, to set forth all facts and circumstances affecting the duty in the instrument. Any person who contravenes this requirement is liable to a fine of 40 naira.[314]

An instrument chargeable with *ad valorem* duty in respect of money in foreign currency or any stock or marketable security shall be calculated on the value, on the day of the instrument, of the money in United States dollars according to the current rate of exchange, or of the stock or security according to the average price thereof.[315] Under the principal Ordinance, the calculation was based on the British pound since that was also the currency of Nigeria as a British colony. Nigeria's present status as an independent nation, as well as the status of the American dollar as the international trading currency appears to be the rationale for the current position under the Act.

Any instrument, the duty upon which is permitted by law to be denoted by adhesive stamp, shall not be deemed stamped until the person legally required to cancel the stamp to prevent its subsequent use on another instrument does so. Cancellation is done when the person so authorised, writes his name or initials or the name of his firm or its initials together with the date of endorsement across the stamp. If the person is an illiterate, he shall cancel by appending his mark and the date across the stamp. As many of such stamps as are used to denote the duty must be cancelled and a person who, being legally required to cancel an adhesive stamp as provided and neglects or refuses to do so shall incur a fine of twenty naira.[316] The proper time for stamping an instrument required to be stamped with an adhesive stamp shall be either before or upon the first execution of such instrument, and cancellation shall be made by the person by whom the instrument is first executed at the time of such execution. But where an instrument is prepared, attested or executed before a commissioner of oaths, justice of peace or notary public or such officer as the case may be, the officer shall cancel the stamp at the time of first execution.[317] By section 12, it is unlawful for any person to remove an adhesive stamp which has been used with an intention to either re-use or sell it. For the purposes of section 12, an instrument is defined to include a telegram or any postal article within the meaning of the *Nigerian Postal Services Act*. A fine of 100 naira is imposed for contravention of the provisions of section 12 without prejudice to any other liability that may be incurred by the offender.

An appropriated stamp may only be used for the instrument of the particular description to which it is appropriated. Equally, an instrument for which an appropriated stamp is required shall not be deemed stamped unless it is stamped with such appropriated stamp. A stamp is an appropriated stamp if there is a word or words on its face appropriating it to an instrument of a particular description.[318] Section 15 provides that where the duty with which an instrument is chargeable depends upon the duty paid on another instrument, then the Commissioner shall denote such instrument by certifying on it, but only after the duty upon which it depends has been paid and the two instruments are produced before the Commissioner. In addition, the sum of 26 kobo shall be payable as fee. Any person may require the Commissioner to express his opinion as to the amount, if any, payable on an executed instrument and subject to such regulations as the minister or governor may make, the Commissioner may endorse his certification on the instrument stating the amount of duty, if any, chargeable upon the instrument. This section does not apply to an instrument which is chargeable with *ad valorem* duty and made as security for money or stock without limit. The section also does not authorise the Commissioner to stamp an instrument that had already been executed, if by law, such an instrument ought not to have been stamped before execution.[319] The Commissioner may call for further evidence where an application has been made to him in respect of an instrument, requesting that all facts and circumstances affecting the liability of the instrument to duty be set forth therein and where such further evidence is not forthcoming, the Commissioner may refuse to proceed with the application.[320]

Once a duty is paid in accordance with the assessment as done by the Commissioner, the instrument in respect of which the duty is paid shall be admissible in evidence for all purposes.[321] Pursuant to section 20, it is unlawful to submit an instrument that has already been assessed by one Commissioner to another Commissioner to adjudicate and a person found guilty of the offence shall incur a fine of 20 naira. Section 21 provides the procedure for appeal where a person is dissatisfied with the assessment of duty as adjudicated by the Commissioner. The aggrieved party may within 21 days from the date of assessment and on payment of the duty, with which he is dissatisfied, appeal against the assessment to the High Court of the State in which the assessment was made. The appeal shall require the Commissioner to state and sign a case setting forth the question upon which his opinion was based and the assessment made by him. The appellant shall, upon receipt of the case stated and signed by the Commissioner, file same with the court within seven days. The court shall determine the amount of duty, if any, chargeable on the instrument and where the amount as assessed by the Commissioner and paid by the person is greater or less than it ought to, the court may direct for refund or payment of the difference as the case may warrant, in addition to costs or penalties, as may be appropriate.

Section 22 provides instances where an unstamped instrument may be received in evidence. According to subsection (1) thereof, where an instrument that may be legally stamped *after* execution is tendered in a civil proceeding and the presiding magistrate, judge, arbitrator or referee notices an omission or insufficiency of the stamps on the instrument, he shall require the person responsible for the instrument to pay the duty or the insufficient part thereof as well as a further sum of 20 naira and such other penalty that may be due. The payment shall be made to the officer of the court whose duty it is to read the instrument and thereafter, the presiding officer shall issue a receipt for the payment, record it accordingly and pay the sum over to the Accountant-General. He shall also communicate to a Commissioner the name of the party from whom payment was received, the type of instrument, date of payment and title of proceedings in which the payment was received. The party from whom payment was received shall produce both the instrument and receipt before a Commissioner whereof the instrument shall be duly denoted. Apart from this exception no instrument may be given in evidence in a civil proceeding unless it is duly stamped in accordance with the law at the time when it was first executed.

Although instruments are generally required to be stamped at the time they are first executed, section 23 (1) provides a grace period of 40 days generally within which an unstamped instrument or insufficiently stamped instrument may be stamped after execution. However, after the expiration of 40 days, the instrument may only be stamped upon payment of a penalty of 20 naira in addition to the unpaid duty or part thereof; and where the unpaid duty exceeds 20 naira, then by way of additional penalty, interest on such duty at the rate of 10 percent per annum from the day the instrument was first executed up to the time the amount of interest is equal to the unpaid duty. The stamps representing the amount of unpaid duty together with the penalty shall be impressed on the instruments (or in the case of adhesive stamp, affixed thereon and cancelled accordingly).

Subsection (3) deals with specific instruments in respect of which *ad valorem* duty is chargeable. These instruments include bond, covenant, conveyance on sale or conveyances on transfers operating as voluntary dispositions *inter vivos*, lease, mortgage bond, debenture, warrant of attorney to confess and enter up judgment and settlement. Except where any of these instruments is written upon duly stamped material, they shall be stamped with the proper *ad valorem* duty within 30 days after first execution if they were executed in Nigeria and within 30 days from the day they were received in Nigeria if they were executed outside

Nigeria. Failure to comply with the foregoing requirement shall attract the penalties prescribed in subsection (1) and in addition, a further penalty equivalent to the unpaid duty shall be imposed on the defaulter unless a reasonable excuse for the delay is shown to the satisfaction of the commissioner or court. The grace periods in subsections (1) and (3) may be substituted with such shorter or longer periods as the minister or governor may on the basis of the circumstances determine.

Section 24 places an obligation on a person having custody of any rolls, books, records, papers, documents or proceedings to permit at all reasonable times any person authorised by a Commissioner to inspect or make notes or extracts of such documents without fee or reward for the purpose of either securing a duty or indicating fraud or omission in relation to a duty. The Commissioner shall first make the inspection himself unaccompanied (except where he requires the assistance of another party) where the said documents are in the custody of a bank. Failure to allow the inspection when so required would attract a fine of 20 naira. The same penalty is prescribed against a person whose office being responsible for the enrolment or registration of any instrument enrols, registers or enters an instrument that is not duly stamped.[322]

A document that has been left at the office of a Commissioner in connection with any provisions of the Act and has not been claimed within six months may be destroyed if upon a notice published in the federal gazette for its claim, the document still remains unclaimed for two months thereafter.[323]

Part II of the Act provides general regulations regarding particular instruments required to be stamped. These instruments include:
   a.   admission (as barrister or notary public)
   b.   agreements (including mortgages and hire purchase)
   c.   appraisements (that is, valuations)
   d.   instruments of apprenticeship
   e.   bank notes, bills of exchange and promissory notes
   f.   bills of lading
   g.   bills of sale
   h.   charter party
   i.   contract notes[324]

j.  conveyances on sale

k.  conveyances on any occasion except sale of mortgage[325]

l.  duplicates and counterparts

m.  exchange and partition or division

n.  leases

o.  letter of allotment or renunciation, scrip certificates and scrip

p.  letters or powers of attorney and voting papers

q.  marketable securities

r.  mortgages

s.  notarial acts

t.  policies of insurance

u.  receipts

v.  settlements

w.  share warrants

x.  stock certificates to bearer

y.  warrant for goods

z.  capital of companies[326]

A person who suffers a fine, penalty or forfeiture for producing an unstamped or insufficiently stamped instrument, but who can prove that the original responsibility for stamping was not his, may upon application to a court be entitled to obtain judgment against the person whose responsibility it was to stamp the instrument in a sum equal to the fine incurred by him and shall also be entitled to costs.[327]

The power to make regulations under the Act is vested in the President and the Governor, as the case may be, by section 115. Specifically, any of these officers may make regulations as to:

a.  the custody of the dies to be used under the Act;

b.  the circumstances in which allowances shall be made for spoiled stamps;

c.  the accounting for the revenue derived from stamp duties;

d.  the substitution of adhesive stamps for impressed stamps and vice versa or of revenue stamps for postage stamps;

e.   the manner in which and the persons by whom impressed stamps shall be affixed to documents; and

f.   the further and better carrying into effect of the objects and purpose of the Act.[328]

Either the National Assembly or the House of Assembly of a Region may by resolution increase, add, vary, diminish or repeal a duty under any of the heads in respect of which either of them is exclusively competent to make laws.[329]

The regulations contained in Part II of the Act specify exceptions to stamping as regards specific instruments. In addition to those specific exemptions, the Schedule further contains exemptions of a general nature to all stamp duties. These include:

a.   transfers of shares in the government or legislative stocks or funds Nigeria;

b.   instruments for the sale, transfer or other disposition of any ship or vessel or part thereof;

c.   all instruments on which the duty would be payable by either the government or any of its departments;

d.   agreements made with the Nigerian Railway Corporation for the receipt and carriage of passengers, goods or animals;

e.   indemnity bonds given to the Nigerian Railway Corporation by consignees, when the railway receipt is not produced, in respect of the delivery of consignments of perishable nature;

f.   an instrument of apprenticeship to which government is a party;

g.   bond given by a public officer for the execution of his duties;

h.   instruments on which the payment of the duty would be payable by a consular officer in his official duties where the foreign government he represents grants a similar exemption to Nigerian consular officers;

i.   instruments relating to the alienation of land or any interest approved by local authorities of the southern states of Nigeria in accordance with rules made by them under local government laws;

j.   instruments regarding which the government of the federation is competent to make laws executed by any co-operative society registered under any Act or law or by any officer or member of such a society relating to the business of such society.

k.   All documents relating to the transfer of stocks and shares

Finally, the following receipts are exempted from stamp duties:

a.  Receipt given by a person or his representative on account of any salary, pay or wages or any other like payment made for the benefit of an employee or holder of an office in respect of his employment or on account of money paid in respect of any pension, superannuation allowance, compassionate allowance or any other like allowance.

b.  Receipt endorsed or contained in any instrument liable to stamp duty and duly stamped, acknowledging the receipt of the consideration money expressed in the instrument or other interest thereby secured.

c.  Acknowledgement by a banker of the receipt of any bill of exchange or promissory note for the purpose of being presented for acceptance or payment.

d.  Receipt given for money deposited or withdrawn from a bank.

e.  Receipt given by the payee of a money order.

f.  Receipt given upon the payment of any government duties or taxes or money for the use of the government.

g.  The duplicate of any receipt required to be given in duplicate, the original receipt being duly stamped.

h.  Receipt given by an officer of a public department of the government of Nigeria or a state for money paid by way of imprest, advance or adjustment of account, where he derives no personal benefit therefrom, or for the refund of out of pocket expenses due from government.

i.  Receipt given for drawback or bounty upon the exportation of any goods or merchandise.

j.  Receipt given for the return of any duties of customs upon certificates of over-entry or upon re-importation certificates.

k.  Receipt given for the refund of any sums deposited with the treasury under the provisions of the Minerals Act.

l.  Receipt given for the return of monies over collected by government.

m.  Receipt given by a prisoner on discharge, having being placed on deposit in the treasury or otherwise retained during the term of his imprisonment.

n.  Receipt given by an accused person for money or other property taken from him on his arrest.

o.  Receipt given for money given or subscribed to the Nigerian Red Cross Society

Although the principal Ordinance has been amended several times since it came into force on 1 April 1939,[330] the tenor of its provisions has not changed over the more than seven decades of the law's existence. Basically, the nomenclature as was contained in the principal Ordinance regarding officers of government has changed to reflect modern realities. Similarly, the naira has replaced the British currency in conformity with Nigeria's independent status.

## Sales Tax

Sales tax was introduced in Nigeria by the provisions of the *Sale of Produce (Taxation) Ordinance No. 12 1953.*[331] The Ordinance imposed tax on agricultural products purchased by the produce marketing boards which were established under various Marketing Ordinances.[332] The tax rates were contained in the Schedule to the Ordinance. Section 1 as usual, was the short title while section 2 dealt with definition of terms and phrases. The tax was imposed by section 3 (1) which provided as follows:

> The Governor in Council may, by order, direct that a tax, to be called a produce sales tax, shall be charged in any Region specified in the order, subject to and in accordance with this Ordinance, on all sales in the Region made to a Marketing Board or to a licensed buying agent of a Marketing Board of such produce, being produce mentioned in the Schedule to this Ordinance, and at such rates, not exceeding those set out in that Schedule, as may be specified in the order; and upon the coming into force of such order the tax shall be charged as provided therein.

The Governor could only make the order following a resolution by the legislature of the region concerned praying for the imposition of tax on the produce. Furthermore, the Governor's order could neither extend to any produce not mentioned in the resolution nor exceed the rate specified in the resolution.[333] By section 3 (3), where a sale had been made to a licensed buying agent of produce who resold it to a marketing board, the resale was not subject to tax. The tax became due from the seller upon payment to him of the purchase price.[334] Section 5 empowered the Governor-in-Council to, after due consultation with the Lieutenant Governor of a region, direct that a tax shall cease to be charged in respect of any produce or that the rate at which it was charged be reduced.

Sale of produce tax was deductible at source by the marketing board or its licensed buying agent making the purchase. While the licensed buying agent was accountable to the marketing board for tax deducted, the board was in turn accountable to the revenue authority and the tax due from the board was treated as a debt accruing to the government.[335] A licensed buying agent, who failed to comply with the lawfully made requirement of a board, was liable to a penalty of 50 pounds. Jurisdiction to determine and enforce the said penalty was vested in the magistrate court.[336] Furthermore, any person who furnished false information to a marketing board or with intent to deceive the board produced or made use of any document which was false in a material particular, was liable to imprisonment for six months or a fine of 50 pounds or both. [337]The Governor-in-Council could make regulations:

a.  requiring market boards to make returns of the amounts of tax for which they were accountable, in respect of such period, in such form and containing particulars with respect to such matters as prescribed by him;
b.  requiring market boards to pay the amounts of tax appearing by the return to be due from them at such times as prescribed by him;
c.  prescribing the public officers in whose name proceedings could be taken for the recovery of tax.[338]

Finally, the Schedule to the Ordinance contained maximum rates per ton of the sales of produce tax.[339]

In 1986, the *Sales Tax Decree No. 7 1986* was promulgated and it came into force on 30 June 1986. With the passage of the decree, it meant states could no longer regulate sales tax in a manner that would be inconsistent with the decree as a federal law. The decree imposed a sales tax on such goods and services as were set out in Column A of Schedule 1 to the decree at the rate specified in Column B of the same Schedule. Taxable services included sales and services registered in hotels, motels, catering, catering establishments, restaurants and other personal service establishments (excluding drinks). Taxable goods included beer, wine liquor and spirits, soft drinks (including mineral water), cigarettes and tobacco, jewels and jewelleries, perfumes and cosmetics (excluding toiletries), electrical and electronics equipment (video recorders, stereo sets, radio and television sets, video cassettes, cameras, air conditioners, fans, deep freezers), carpets and rugs (excluding linoleum) and bottled natural water (excluding mineral water). Except for wine liquor and spirits which was taxable at 10 percent, all the other goods (and services) were taxable at 5 percent.

Sales tax was chargeable on the supply by a manufacturer or of taxable goods to its accredited distributors or agents; or on the supply of taxable services in the course of business of the supplier.[340] The administration of sales tax was vested in the tax authorities of the various states subject to directions as were given by the Joint Tax Board.[341] Indeed, section 7 (2) vested the Joint Tax Board with powers to co-ordinate the tax to ensure 'administrative tidiness within the existing tax machinery' and to resolve any conflict that arose from the disbursement of revenue from the tax. It appears from the provisions of section 7 (2) therefore, that the reason the federal government took over the regulation of the tax was to provide uniformity and consistency in its practice and administration. The decree was later codified as *Sales Tax Act Cap 399 Laws of the Federation of Nigeria 1990* and remained in force until 1993 when it was repealed and replaced with the Value Added Tax decree.

## Super Tax

Super tax was introduced into the polity during the Nigerian civil war to be chargeable on the total profits of a company by the provisions of the *Super Tax Decree No. 46 1967*. The rate of tax was two shillings per every pound on the amount by which the total profits of the company exceeded the standard deduction for each year of assessment.[342] Standard deduction meant either of two things. In relation to the first two years in which a company commenced business, standard deduction meant 15 percent of the company's paid up share capital as at the date it commenced business or the sum of 500 pounds, whichever was greater. In any other case, standard deduction meant 15 percent of the company's paid up share capital as at the first day of its accounting period or the sum of 5000 pounds whichever was greater.[343] Subsection (3) empowered the Federal Executive Council to vary the tax rate by an order published in the gazette. The Council could also for sufficient ground and by the same procedure, either exempt a company or class of companies from all or any of the provisions of the super tax decree; or exempt from super tax, all or any profits of a company or class of companies.[344]

Super tax was assessed on the basis of the return delivered by a company for the purposes of determining its income tax under the *Companies Income Tax Act, 1961*. In arriving at the amount of super tax payable in any year of assessment, the Federal Board of Inland Revenue had to determine the amount by which the total profits of a company for that year exceeded the standard deduction. The Board could, under the provisions of section 49 relating to failure of delivery of returns by a company, make an assessment of super tax on the company by the same token as it could, where a company failed to file returns for the purposes of income tax. Moreover, the Board, where it considered it necessary for any reason of emergency, could assess a company for super tax before the expiration of the time within which the company was allowed to file returns.[345] The Board was required by section 4 of the decree to compile 'super tax assessment lists' consisting of all companies assessed for super tax in each year of assessment. The lists were to contain the names and addresses of the companies; the name and address of any person in whose name a particular company was chargeable; the amount by which the total profits of each company exceeded the standard deduction for the year; the amount assessed as super tax and such other particulars as the Board deemed necessary.

Service of notice was required to be effected by registered post on every company or person in whose name a company was chargeable whose name appeared in the super tax assessment lists. The notice was to contain the amount of total profits of the company concerned for that year; the amount by which the said profits exceeded the standard deduction; the amount of super tax payable by the company for that year; the place at which the tax was payable and the company's right to object under section 53 of the *Companies Income Tax Act 1961* if it disputed the assessment.[346] The procedure for appeals under the decree was similar to that under the *Companies Income Tax Act*.[347] Other provisions of the super tax in respect of which the *Companies Income Tax Act* apply included the procedure for collection, recovery and repayment;[348] double taxation relief;[349] and tax administration.[350]

In 1970, the *Super Tax Decree* was amended by the *Super Tax (Amendment) Decree No. 12 1970*. Under this amendment, the Federal Executive Council exercised its powers under section 1 (3) of the principal decree and varied the rates of super tax effective from the 1969-70 year of assessment. The new rates were specified in the Schedule to the amendment. In consequence, the Schedule to the principal decree was rearranged as Schedule 1 while the new rates provided under the amendment became Schedule 2. All references in the legislation to the Schedule were modified to reflect the amendment.[351] Under the new rates of super tax as introduced by Schedule, two shillings were chargeable on every pound of the first 5000 pounds of the amount by which the total profits exceeded the standard deduction; three shillings on the next 5000 pounds and five shillings on every pound thereafter. Further, the meaning of standard deduction as contained in section 1 (4) of the principal decree was modified along the categories of whether or not the company liable to super tax was a

Nigerian company. In relation to a Nigerian company, standard deduction carried the same meaning it did under the principal decree but in the case of a non-Nigerian company, standard deduction was expanded to mean 25 percent of the total profits of the company attributable to its operations in Nigeria for the year of assessment or the sum of 5000, whichever was greater.[352]

There were two amendments to the *Super Tax Decree* in 1971. The first amendment was the *Super Tax (Amendment) Decree No. 11 1971*. This amendment essentially expanded the provisions of the *Companies Income Tax Act* that applied to super tax. Under the Schedule to the amendment, the following matters relating to super tax were further placed under the regulation of the relevant provisions of the *Companies Income Tax Act*: imposition of tax and profits chargeable; relief for civil war damage; persons chargeable (agents, liquidators etc); double taxation arrangements; and funds, bodies and institutions in Nigeria to which deductible donations could be made. The second amendment was the *Super Tax (Amendment) (No. 2) Decree No. 12 1971*. This amendment modified section 1 (1) by substituting the words 'at the rate specified in Schedule 2 of this Decree' for the words 'at the appropriate rate'.[353] This substitution was necessary, as will soon be obvious, to reflect the other modifications introduced. Section 2 of the amendment introduced a new section 1A immediately after section 1 of the principal decree. Section 1A contained provisions regarding two categories of companies which were entitled to what the section referred to as '*reduced rate*'. In the first category, if a company incorporated in Nigeria after 1st January 1971 made profits of at least 10,000 pounds and within an accounting period and capitalized its profits by increasing its paid up share capital at an amount which was at least 50 percent of the profits, then such a company was liable to super tax at the reduced rate for that year of assessment and for every subsequent year of assessment in which its paid up capital remained at least, at the amount of its increased share capital. In the second category, if a company's paid up share capital within an accounting year was at least 75,000 pounds and the said amount was paid up by shareholders with foreign funds[354] and the company was incorporated in Nigeria after 1st January 1971, then the company was liable to super tax at a reduced rate for that year of assessment and for every subsequent year of assessment during which the paid up share capital remained at least 75,000 pounds. Reduced rate meant two shillings on every pound by which the total profits exceeded the standard deduction.[355] Schedule 2 to the principal decree[356] was also amended by inserting Part A and Part B thereto. Part A contained normal rates which were applicable to companies liable to super tax and Part B contained the reduced rate for companies that fell within the purview of section 1A.[357]

The Super Tax Decree No. 46 of 1967 and all the amendments thereto were repealed by Section 3 of the Finance (Miscellaneous Taxation Provisions) Decree No. 47 1972.

### Entertainment Tax

The western region was the first to pass a law on entertainment tax at a time when Lagos was part of the region.[358] The law continued to apply to Lagos after it became a federal territory until 1966 when, as relates to Lagos, the law was repealed by the *Entertainment Tax Decree No. 66 of 1966*.[359] Save for some slight modifications, the decree was substantially similar to the Entertainment Tax Law of the defunct western region. For example, the powers conferred upon the governor under the law of the western region became vested in the permanent secretary under the decree. Second, the powers vested in the legislature of the western region were transferred to the Federal Executive Council under the decree and finally, the powers vested in a magistrate under section 10 of the decree were, under the regional law, exercisable by any justice of the peace.

The entertainment decree applied only to the federal territory (which at the time, was Lagos) and imposed tax on any place of entertainment to which members of the public were admitted by way of a prescribed charge before entry; or contribution after entry; or where payment for entry was waived, refunded or reduced for members. A person liable to tax under the decree was not to be admitted to the entertainment unless he produced a numbered receipt as evidence of payment of the appropriate charge as well as the tax chargeable thereon; and where admission was by a means other than numbered ticket, and the proprietor of the place of entertainment failed to remit tax due, the tax could be recovered as a debt to the state.[360] Where admission into a place of entertainment was by way of subscription, donation or contribution; or season ticket; or series of entertainment during a time and the payment for the said admission was made by means of a lump sum, entertainment tax was payable on the lump sum.[361] Section 3 provided that if the payment of a lump sum or any payment for a ticket represented payment for purposes additional to, or otherwise than for entertainment, tax was chargeable on the amount as appeared to the permanent secretary[362] to represent the right of admission to the place of entertainment in respect of which tax should have been payable.

The classes of entertainment to which entertainment tax applied and the rates at which the tax was chargeable were contained in the Schedule to the decree. They included cinematograph exhibitions, night clubs and casinos and horse racing. Section 4 empowered the Federal Executive Council to add to the classes of entertainment to which tax was chargeable; and to increase or reduce rates payable as entertainment tax. Section 5 conferred a right on any person to apply to the permanent secretary to be exempted from entertainment tax on the grounds that:

a.  the net proceeds accruing to the place of entertainment were to be devoted to philanthropic or charitable purposes;

b.  the entertainment was wholly educational in character;

c.  the entertainment was provided for artistic, literary or scientific purposes by a society or institution established for non-profit;

d.  the entertainment was agricultural, horticultural or poultry exhibition held under the auspices of a society approved by the Federal Executive Council; or

e.  the entertainment was provided by or on behalf of an educational institution for the sole purpose of promoting some object or for the benefit of the institution but not for profit.

The permanent secretary could, on receipt of an application, call for a detailed statement of account of the organisation and if the application was based on philanthropic or charitable purposes, challenge any item which in his opinion was inadmissible; and if the application was based on the wholly educational character of the entertainment and the permanent secretary rejected it, the applicant could further appeal to the Federal Executive Council whose decision was final.

A superior police officer or any public servant duly authorised by the permanent secretary could enter a place of entertainment at reasonable times, including during the course of an entertainment, for the purposes of checking due compliance with the requirements of the decree or regulations made under it. Any person who prevented or obstructed a police officer or public servant so authorised from entering or carrying out the purposes for which he was required under the decree was guilty of an offence and upon conviction was liable to a fine of 20 pounds or imprisonment for one month.[363] Section 8 created two offences. The first related to a person who, with intent to defraud forged any stamp or impression; or imported or exported or had in his custody or control any forged stamp or impression used to denote tax payable and the second related to a person who fraudulently contrived to avoid payment of tax. In the first case, the penalty upon conviction was a minimum term of three years and maximum term of 10 years imprisonment, while in the second case, the penalty upon conviction was a fine of 100 pounds or imprisonment for six months or both. Section 9 made it an offence to be admitted into a place of entertainment without payment of tax. Both the person admitted and the proprietor were jointly and severally guilty of the offence and upon conviction, the person admitted was liable to a fine of five pounds or imprisonment for seven days while the proprietor was liable to a fine of 50 pounds or imprisonment for six months and in addition, was required to pay twice the tax which should have been paid.

A magistrate could, upon application to the effect that there was reasonable suspicion of an unauthorised document, stamp or impression on any premises, capable of being used to gain admission into a place of entertainment, issue a search warrant and any unauthorised document appearing to be material evidence under the decree or any other law could be seized and thereafter, if ordered by the court, destroyed. The onus was on the person in whose custody the documents, stamp or impression was seized to prove that they were not used for unlawful purposes.[364] The power to make regulations generally for the purposes of the decree was vested in the Federal Executive Council by section 11 (1) of the decree.

### Pool Betting and Casino Taxes

The western region passed its Betting Duty Law in 1954 and the law was aimed at imposing tax on bets of authorised totalisators and contributions or subscriptions towards authorised lotteries or sweepstakes. After Lagos became a federal territory in the same year, the *Betting Duty (Lagos) Law* was passed to reflect the new status of Lagos although the Lagos law remained *in pari materia* with the western law. In 1960, the federal government amended the Lagos law by the instrumentality of the *Betting Duty (Lagos) (Amendment) Ordinance 1960*. The amendment ordinance increased the rates of tax payable on bets made on totalisators and sweepstakes from five percent and 10 percent respectively to 20 percent of the total stake money paid or contributed. The eastern and northern regions had their own betting duty laws passed in 1963 by the federal parliament under a constitutional provision enabling parliament in that behalf.[365]

In 1969, in a bid to make '*better*' provision for the regulation of pool betting and connected matters in the federal territory, the federal legislature passed the *Pool Betting Control Act No. 69 1961.*[366] Section 3 made the acquisition of a license a condition precedent to the operation of pool betting business or the distribution, printing or publishing of any papers incidental to pool betting business. A license was deemed to have been granted under the Act if, being granted prior to the coming into effect of the Act, the license still had six months lifespan or more at the time the Act came into effect. The licensee however had to apply for renewal under the Act within one month before the license was due to expire failing which any subsequent application was barred. If a license previously given under another law had less than six months to expire at the time of coming into force of the Act, the licensee was required to apply for renewal under the Act within one month from the commencement of the Act failing which the license previously held was considered revoked. A contravention of any of the foregoing provisions was an offence and upon conviction attracted a fine not exceeding 500 pounds or imprisonment for two years or both.[367]

An officer of the posts and telegraphs department not below the rank of head postmaster or an officer of the customs and excise department not below the rank of collector could cause goods or articles reasonably suspected by him to contain matters relating to pool betting business not licensed under the Act to be opened and inspected, and if such matter was found therein, the officer in question could adjudge the goods or articles forfeited.[368] Section 4 (3) however placed an obligation of confidentiality on an officer carrying out his duty as aforementioned and where such officer, other than in the course of duty, disclosed information obtained in the course of the exercise of the power to inspect, he was guilty of an offence attracting up to, but not exceeding three years.

The discretion to approve and renew licenses was wholly that of the minister and in the exercise of that power, he could impose such general or special conditions as he thought fit. The minister was not required to state his reason for refusal to issue or renew a license and the exercise of his discretion was not a subject of appeal. He could equally revoke any license where he was satisfied that a breach of condition had occurred.[369] The power to make regulations for the effectual operation of the Act was equally vested in the minister.[370]

While the *Pool Betting Control Act 1961* made provisions for the regulation of pool betting, the *Pool Betting Tax Act No. III 1962* was passed in 1962 to impose taxes on pool betting business. Pool betting business was defined as *'any business involving the receiving and negotiating of bets made by way of pool betting'* and it was immaterial that the person on whose behalf the bet was being negotiated lived outside the federal territory where the Act was applicable.[371] The rate of pool betting business tax was chargeable on the amount staked with the proprietor at a rate not exceeding 20 percent. Although the power to vary the tax rate was conferred on the House of Representatives, it could not vary the rate such as to make it less than 10 percent of the money staked with the proprietor.

The minister of finance could by notice published in the federal gazette as well as a national newspaper circulating in the federal territory, require any proprietor to make returns of all pool betting business transacted by such proprietor on the basis of which pool betting tax would be calculated and paid.[372] The minister could equally address a written notice to any proprietor requiring such proprietor to produce certified copies of accounts of the pool betting business. An officer of the finance ministry authorised as an inspector could enter on premises where pool betting business was carried on at all reasonable times to inspect or take copies of entries made in the business' books of accounts without incurring civil or criminal liability.[373]

Offences under the Act were contained in section 3. Under subsection (1) thereof, it was an offence for any person required to give information or produce copies of accounts to refuse or fail to do so. It was equally an offence for anyone to obstruct, wilfully mislead or attempt to mislead an inspector in the performance of his duties. In any of the two scenarios, the Act prescribed as a penalty, a fine of not less than 100 pounds but not more than 200 pounds or imprisonment for a term of 12 months or both. Subsection (2) made it an offence for any proprietor to supply incorrect accounts by omitting or understating the amount placed as stakes or by otherwise giving incorrect information concerning his accounts. A person convicted under the subsection was liable to similar penalties under subsection (1) and in addition thereto, he was required to pay twice the amount of tax which had been or would have been undercharged as a result of the understatement or omission. An offence under subsection (2) was compoundable at the instance of the minister and to attract the penalties prescribed under the two subsections, a complaint to that effect had to be made within 12 months from the date the offence was committed.[374] Section 3 (5) conferred a right of appeal to the High Court on any party aggrieved by a decision of the magistrate court. The appeal had to be filed within 14 days of the decision of the magistrate court.

Further appeal could, on leave of court, lie to the Supreme Court but only on question of law, not of fact or sentence. Section 4 empowered the minister to make regulations for the operation of the Act.

In 1963 and 1965 the federal legislature passed the *Pool Betting Tax Act No. 16 1963* and the *Pool Betting Tax Act No. 11 1965* respectively. These legislations were passed pursuant to the *Pool Betting (Parliamentary Authority) Law 1963* and the *Pool Betting Control (Enabling) Law 1962* enacted by the legislatures of the northern and eastern regions respectively. In furtherance of the provisions of section 67 of the 1960 Constitution, these two laws each conferred jurisdiction on the federal parliament to pass a law on pool betting tax in the regions concerned. The jurisdiction conferred on the federal parliament included the power to regulate and tax pool betting business in the regions. In the exercise of this jurisdiction, the federal parliament passed two pool betting tax Acts in 1963 and 1965 as Act Number 16 and 11 respectively. The 1963 Act essentially amended the *Pool Betting Control Act 1961* by extending its application to the northern and eastern regions. The 1965 Act amended the *Pool Betting Tax Act 1962* in two major regards. First, it extended the application of the Act to the northern and eastern regions and second, the rate of pool tax was increased such that the House of Representatives could by resolution, fix the tax at any rate provided such rate was not less than 20 percent of the money staked with the proprietor.[375] Other amendments were aimed at bringing the 1962 Act into conformity with its new extent of application.

The rate of pool betting tax was fixed at 20 percent of the money staked with the proprietor under the provisions of a 1966 enactment, the *Pool Betting Tax (Increase of Rate) Decree No. 82 1966*. This was a deviation from both the 1962 and 1965 Acts which respectively fixed the rate at a minimum of 10 and 20 percent. Rather than maintain a certain minimum rate, the 1966 introduced tidiness into the administration of pool betting tax by fixing a definite rate of 20 percent.[376] However, two years after the increase, the *Betting Duties (Amendment) Decree No. 26. 1968* restored the rate of betting duty to 10 percent as was previously obtained under the *Betting Duties (Lagos) Ordinance*. Second, it repealed the *Betting Duties (Lagos) (Amendment) Act 1960* which had increased the rate to 20 percent. The decree applied only to those parts of Lagos that formerly comprised the federal territory, the reason being that Lagos became one of the twelve states the federal military government created in 1967.

## *Casino Tax*

In 1965, the federal parliament passed the *Casino Taxation Act* as *No. 26 1965*. The long title to this legislation describes it as 'an Act to impose tax on the net gaming revenue of casinos in the Lagos territory, and for related purposes'.[377] Every casino licensed under the Act is liable to casino revenue tax at 12 ½ percent of its net gaming revenue. The rate may however be varied by the National Assembly through a resolution passed and gazetted to that effect. A casino's net gaming revenue means daily takings of the casino, whether continuous or intermittent, of up to 15 out of 24 hours from the time play at the casino is first opened, less of winnings paid by the casino to patrons in the course of play. Casino revenue tax ranks in priority over all costs, charges and other taxes including companies' income tax.[378] The administration of casino revenue tax is vested in the Federal Inland Revenue Service as the successor to the Federal Board of Inland Revenue. Section 2 empowers the chairman of the Service to authorise, by warrant, any person to enter the premises of a casino during play time or at reasonable hours outside play time to do such things as may be required to give effect to the provisions of the Act, including inspection of statements and returns and where necessary, certification of same.

The licensee[379] is required to deliver in the afternoon of the day when play closes in the casino or as soon as practicable, a return to the Service showing the net gaming revenue received during the course of play. The return has to be certified as correct by a person authorised by the Service. In addition, the licensee is further required to submit weekly and monthly returns as the Service may prescribe, consisting of consolidated net gaming revenues for the period covered. Casino revenue tax shall be calculated on the consolidated returns and where the consolidation is for a period of one week, the tax shall be payable not later than three days after the delivery of the return. Where the consolidation is for one month, the return must be certified by a chartered accountant, irrespective of whether returns for lesser periods were delivered for the duration and any amount of tax outstanding from such lesser periods shall be paid forthwith by the licensee without further assessment.[380] Section 3 (5) indemnifies and empowers a person answerable to casino revenue tax to retain monies coming into his hands on behalf of the licensee as may be sufficient to pay tax to which the licensee is liable. Persons answerable to tax under the Act include the managing director or director of the licensee, receiver, liquidator, attorney, agent or representative of the licensee. By virtue of section 4, a licensee is liable to tax in its own name or in the name of any of the above mentioned persons. The Service may direct a licensee to keep books or accounts in such form as it considers adequate, and the licensee may appeal against the direction of the Service to the Tax Appeal Tribunal (as successor to the Body of Appeal Commissioners) who may confirm or modify the direction and whose decision is final. Failure by a licensee to comply with the direction of the Service or the tribunal is an offence.[381]

Notwithstanding the provisions of section 3 (1) and (2) relating to the periods within which a licensee may deliver returns, either the Service or a licensee may require that an assessment be raised in respect of any year of assessment, which for the purposes of this Act means a period of twelve months commencing from 1st January of every year (as opposed to 1st April under the principal Act). An assessment raised pursuant to this provision may include earlier periods if the Service is satisfied that an assessment for such earlier period was not raised or was incorrect; provided no such assessment may be raised in respect of a period that is earlier than six years in point of time. Further, a licensee shall forfeit its right of appeal where the assessment is raised on figures returned by it but in any other case, the provisions of the *Companies Income Tax Act 1979* as to objections, revisions and appeals shall have effect *mutatis mutandis*.[382] Where there is a pending objection or appeal by a licensee, collection of tax shall be suspended in respect of the tax or part of it that is disputed but the undisputed portion may be enforced by the Service and after the determination of the objection or appeal, the Service shall serve a notice of the tax as determined on the licensee. Any tax or portion of tax outstanding after an objection or appeal has been disposed of shall be payable within two months from the date the objection or appeal has been disposed of or within two months after notice to that effect is served on the licensee whichever is earlier but the Service in its discretion may extend time within which payment may be made. Failure by a licensee to comply with payment of tax as prescribed above is an offence and in addition to the penalty that may be imposed, the right of distrain shall become exercisable.[383] Section 8 precludes assessments, notices, warrants or other proceedings made pursuant to the Act from being impeached or voided for want of form, mistake, defect or omission provided the proceedings in question substantially conforms to the intent of the Act. In particular, no assessment can be impeached by reason of mistake as to name of licensee, description of profits or amount of tax charged; or by reason of any variance between the assessment and the notice thereof, provided that the notice substantially contains the particulars upon which the assessment is made and it is duly served on the licensee or the person in whose name the licensee is chargeable.

A licensee who discovers that it was excessively assessed and taxed in respect of any year of assessment as a result of an error or mistake in the return, statement or account made by or on its behalf may make an application for refund. The application must be made not later than one year from the end of the assessment year to which the application relates. The Service shall upon receipt of the application investigate and where appropriate, grant relief to the licensee by way of relief in such sum as it considers reasonable. The Service shall take into account all relevant circumstances, including assessments made upon the licensee in previous years and also consider whether granting the relief would result in the exclusion from tax of any part of the net gaming revenue of the licensee. The decision of the Service on the application shall be final and conclusive.[384] Any application for refund, except expressly provided otherwise, must be made in writing within one year from the end of the assessment year to which it relates. The Accountant General of the federation shall pay to a person entitled to refund the amount certified by the Service or ordered pursuant to a judgment of court.[385]

Offences are contained in sections 11, 12 and 14. Offences under section 11 include refusal or failure to pay tax, making false returns or representations for the purpose of obtaining an advantage and aiding the making of false returns or accounts. Section 12 provides that a licensee or any person in its employ, who without reasonable excuse makes or certifies a return in respect of net gaming revenue so as to omit or understate the licensee's liability to tax; or gives any incorrect information in relation to any matter affecting the licensee's tax liability shall, in addition to whatever penalty prescribed by reason of the offence created by section 11, pay double the amount which has been undercharged or would have been undercharged in consequence of the incorrect return or information. Any complaint regarding the above offences must be made either during the year of assessment in respect of which the offence relates or within six years of the expiration of the said year of assessment but no more. Further, the Service may, with the leave of court, compound an offence committed under the foregoing provisions. The offences coming under the purview of section 14 relate to tax collection and administration. Under the section, it is an offence for any person not being authorised to collect tax under the Act, to collect or attempt to collect tax under the Act; or being authorised, withholds tax or portion of tax for his own use; or demands from a licensee an amount in excess of the authorised assessment; or renders a false return of the amount of tax collected by him or defrauds any person or otherwise uses his position so as to deal wrongfully with the Service. An offence under the Act is deemed to occur either at the place it actually occurred or in the federal territory.[386]

Casino revenue tax takes precedence over the rights of judgment debtors, assignees or any person having a lawful and legitimate claim over the property of a licensee and unless the judgment debtor, assignee or other person legally entitled to the property of a licensee pays to the Service any outstanding tax owed by the licensee, the Service may distrain goods or chattels of the licensee notwithstanding the rights of the third party, and proceed to sell same for the purpose of obtaining payment of the outstanding tax as well as other costs and charges of a reasonable nature arising from the distress and sale.[387] Section 15 (2) further indemnifies any person acting under the authority of the Service in the execution of the foregoing provisions. The Service's right of distrain in respect of a licensee's property is exercisable by a principal inspector of taxes after demand has been made on the licensee and it fails or refuses to pay. The sum included in the demand notice is deemed to be a debt due to the Service as judgment creditor from the licensee as judgment debtor payable under the judgment of a High Court. An inspector of taxes armed with a warrant authorizing him to levy distress on a licensee's property may acquire the assistance of a police constable who shall assist the inspector to break into the licensee's premises to levy the distress. The distressed property may be kept for five days at the expense of the licensee and at the expiration of five days, if the licensee fails to pay the debt due along with costs, the property shall be valued and sold by public auction. The tax due shall be deducted together with costs and charges arising from the distress and sale and any surplus thereafter shall be restored to the licensee. Once issued, a distress warrant is perpetual such that if no property is found upon the licensee's premises to be levied, the inspector may, under the powers granted by the warrant, enter the premises at a future date when there is property and execute the warrant as if there had been no lapse of time.[388]

Section 18 empowers the Service to delegate to any person a special duty or power exercisable by the Service under the *Casino Taxation Act 1965* or the *Companies Income Tax Act 1979* upon such terms and conditions as the Service may decide. Such delegation is to be conferred by notice in the federal gazette or in writing to the person so delegated and where the person delegated is below the rank of principal inspector of taxes, the written approval of the minister must be obtained. Further, certain functions of the Service can not be delegated. These include the administration of any of the said Acts; the power to initiate prosecution under the Act; the power to appeal against a decision of a magistrate, judge or the Tribunal and finally, the delegation cannot be construed as prohibiting the Service from exercising any of the powers so delegated. Anything required to be done by the Service is to be signified under the hand of the Chairman or any person duly authorised by him.[389]

Returns and all other documents relating to the operation of casino revenue tax are classified documents and all persons engaged in the administration of the Act are obliged to deal with the said documents as official secret.[390] Consequently, it is an offence for any person to disclose information contained in the documents without the authority of the Service. The written authority of the minister must be obtained before such information can be divulged even in the prosecution of a person who violated the provisions of official secrecy. Indeed, section 21 (2) empowers the minister to treat any particular case so requiring as classified matter under the *Official Secrets Act 1962*.[391]

Penalties for offences committed against the Act are contained in section 24. Where the offence relates to failure to furnish returns or keep prescribed records a first offender shall be liable upon conviction to a fine of one thousand naira or to imprisonment for two years or both and on any subsequent conviction whether for the same offence or not, to a fine of 2000 naira or imprisonment for three years or both and in addition to the subsequent conviction, the offender shall forfeit the casino license. Where the offence involves failure to furnish returns or keep records, the offender shall in addition be liable to a sum of 100 for each day during which the failure continues and in default of payment of this penalty in the case of a natural person, to an additional term of imprisonment for six months commencing from the day following the conviction or as otherwise directed by the court. The penalties prescribed shall not relieve the offender from payment of tax for which it or he is liable. Without prejudice to the powers of the Attorney General of the federation to initiate criminal proceedings, an offender cannot be prosecuted for an offence under the Act without the approval of the Service.[392] The power to make regulations under the Act is vested in the finance minister by section 25.

In 1979 the *Pool Betting and Casino Gaming (Prohibition) Decree No. 19 1979* was promulgated by the federal military government. This decree was signed into law on 4th June 1979 but deemed to have come into effect on 16th April 1979.[393] The decree outlawed all forms of pool betting and casino gaming and further repealed all pool betting and casino gaming legislations in force as at that date. The repealed legislations were:

a.  the Pool Betting Control Act No. 69 1961

b.  the Pool Betting Tax Act No. III 1962

c.  the Pool Betting Control Act No. 16 1963

d.  the Pool Betting Tax Act No. 11 1965

e.  Pool Betting Tax (Increase of Rate) Decree No. 82 1966

f.  Pool Betting Control (Enabling) Law Cap 97 Laws of Eastern Nigeria 1963

g.  Pool Betting (Parliamentary Authority) Law Cap 98 Laws of Northern Nigeria 1963

h.  Pool Betting (Control and Taxation) Law No. 1 Laws of Western Nigeria 1962

i.  Pool Betting and Control Law Cap 98 Laws of Lagos State 1973

j.  Pool Betting Tax Law Cap 99 Laws of Lagos State 1973

k.  Pool Betting (Control and Taxation) Law Cap 121 Laws of Bendel State

l.  Nigerian Pools Company Ltd (Take-Over) Decree No. 20 1972

m.  Casino Licensing Act No. VII 1964

n.  Casino (Licensing and Taxation) Law No. 3 Laws of Western Nigeria 1964

o.  Casino (Licensing and Taxation) Law Cap 22 Laws of Lagos State 1973

p.  Bendel Casino (Management) Law Cap 15 Laws of Bendel State

All licenses earlier granted for the purposes of pool betting or casino gaming were deemed to have expired immediately before the coming into force of the decree. Any person, who thereafter was found guilty of operating pool betting or casino gaming in whatever form, was guilty of an offence. In the case of pool betting, an individual was liable upon conviction to a fine of 200 naira or imprisonment for six months or both while a company was liable to a fine of 5000 naira or more. In the case of casino gaming, an individual was liable to a fine of 2000 naira or imprisonment for six months or both while a company was liable to a fine of at least 10,000 naira. In both cases, the offender would in addition to the penalties forfeit all equipments and materials used to the state. Interestingly, the *Casino Taxation Act No. 26 1965* was not one of the legislation repealed by the decree. Indeed, the Act is still part of Nigerian law and is presently cited as Cap C3 Laws of the Federation of Nigeria 2004.

### Capital Transfer Tax

Capital transfer tax was introduced by the *Capital Transfer Tax Decree No. 12 1979*. It was intended as a strategy for curbing incidents of tax evasion and at the same time enhancing government revenue. Decree No. 12 of 1979 imposed tax on property acquired by way of gifts transferred *inter vivos* and property acquired by way of inheritance upon the demise of the owner.[394] The transfers exempted from tax under the decree included:

a.  An outright sale which was not intended to confer a gratuitous benefit on the transferee where the transaction was made at arms length between unconnected people or was such as might have been made at arms length between unconnected people.[395]

b.  A transfer of property where the value did not exceed N100,000 as at the date of the transfer. However, where within the lifetime of the transferor, he made further transfer of property of which capital tax was payable to the same transferee and taken together, the value of the two properties exceeded N100,000, the total value of both transfers were to be aggregated and capital tax paid at the appropriate rate.[396]

c.  A family house was defined as any house or part thereof used wholly by a family as the principal place of residence for that family and in respect of which no income accrued to such family or any member thereof.[397]

Title to transferred property liable to tax was not deemed to pass to the transferee until the tax due was paid and the instrument evidencing such transfer could not be registered unless a discharge certificate was issued by the relevant tax authority to the effect that capital transfer tax had been paid.[398]

The administration of the tax was vested in states' revenue authorities in cases of properties situated in the states even if the transferor or deceased was not liable to the income tax law of the state in question.[399] A transferee was required to, within six months from the date of transfer or demise of the transferor in the case of a deceased, prepare and deliver the capital transfer tax form to the relevant tax authority. The form was to contain, in the case of a deceased person's estate, a true and perfect inventory and account of the estate of the deceased and statement of the value of the estate and in the case of a transfer *inter vivos* a description of the property and its value.[400] The value of a property under the decree was deemed to be the value which, in the opinion of the relevant tax authority, the property would fetch in the open market at the time of the transfer or death of the deceased.[401] The transferee or person accountable for capital transfer tax in respect of a deceased person's estate was required to deliver the form to the relevant tax authority.

Three allowances were made in respect of transfers arising from death. These were allowances for funeral expenses,[402] debts and encumbrances. However, allowances were not allowed for:

a. debts incurred or encumbrances created by the deceased except where they were incurred or created *bona fide* for full consideration in money or money's worth wholly for the deceased's own use and benefit;

b. any debt in respect whereof there was a right to re-imbursement from any other estate or person, unless such re-imbursement could not be obtained;

c. more than once for the same debt or encumbrance charged upon different portions of the estate.[403]

The decree provided a schedule of reduction in tax liability where capital transfer tax became payable upon the death of the owner and within 10 years from the date of such death capital transfer tax became payable again for reason of death of the transferee. Where the second death occurred within one year of the first, the tax due on the second transfer was reduced by 80 percent and where it occurred within 10 years of the first, there was a 10 percent reduction on the tax liability. In between these two ends, there was a decreasing continuum of reduction in tax liability.[404]

Appeals by an aggrieved party over the decision of the relevant tax authority were made to the High Court and the Chief Judge of a state was empowered to make rules governing the procedure for such appeals.[405] The power to make regulations for the administration of the decree was however vested in the Federal Executive Council.[406] In cases of non-payment, the relevant tax authority was vested with power to distrain the land or premises in respect of which the tax was charged or the goods or chattels of the person charged (including money, bills of exchange, bonds or other securities) and recover the tax due by selling anything so distrained.[407] The capital transfer decree was repealed through a budget speech in 1996 on the grounds that the tax was not only difficult to administer, but it was also incompatible with Nigeria's cultural tradition.[408]

## Education Tax

Education tax was introduced by the Education Tax Decree No. 7 of 1993 to impose an education tax on companies registered in Nigeria. The rate of the tax is fixed at two percent of assessable profits while administration is vested in the Federal Inland Revenue Service.

In 1998, Decree No. 40 was passed as amendment to Decree 7 of 1993. The 1998 amendment decree established the Education Fund as a body corporate with perpetual succession and a common seal and also established a Board of Trustees and vested it with the management of the Fund. In the 2004 compilation of the Laws of the Federation of Nigeria, both the principal decree and the amendment thereto were compiled as the *Education Tax Act Cap E4 Laws of the Federation of Nigeria 2004.*

The Education Tax Act was one of the nine tax bills that were submitted to the National Assembly as part of the reforms initiative. As far as education tax is concern, the intention was basically to restructure the machinery for the management of education tax revenue as well as the beneficiaries of the revenue accruable from the tax. As a result, therefore, the Education Tax Act was repealed and in its place, the Tertiary Education Trust Fund (Establishment, etc) Act was passed in 2011. The Tertiary Education Trust Fund (Establishment, etc) Act, as the name implies, creates the Tertiary Education Trust Fund as a body corporate to replace and take over the powers and duties of the defunct Education Fund. Second, the new Act has restructured the application of education tax proceeds by vesting the benefits thereof exclusively in the development of tertiary education in Nigeria. This is a departure from the position under the Education Tax Act which apportioned only 50 percent of the funds to tertiary education; reserving 30 percent for primary education and 20 percent for secondary education. In all other material respects, the Tertiary Education Fund functions much the same as the defunct Education Fund. For example, the rate of the tax is still two percent of assessable profit of a company registered in Nigeria.[409] The Act imposes education tax on a company's assessable profit as ascertained in the manner provided under either the companies' income tax Act or the petroleum profits tax Act as the case may be.[410] The administration of the tax is still vested in the Federal Inland Revenue Service. Education tax is payable within 60 days of service of assessment notice on the company and the provisions of the CITA or PPTA relating to the collection of tax apply to the collection of education tax.[411]

The Tertiary Education Trust Fund is created under section 3 as a body corporate with perpetual succession and a common seal with the powers to sue and be sued. The Service is to remit all receipts from education tax into the Fund 'for the rehabilitation, restoration and consolidation of tertiary education in Nigeria'.[412] The Service is also accountable to the Board of Trustees of the Fund established under section 4 of the Act for sums collected and when making returns, shall submit to the Board of Trustees in an appropriate form the name of the company making the payment, the amount collected, the assessable profit of the company for the accounting period and such other information as may be required by the Board of Trustees. The Board of Trustees of the Fund is composed of a chairman, six persons reflecting the geo-political formation of the country; representatives each of the federal ministries of finance and education not below the rank of director; representatives each from the universities, polytechnics and colleges of education; and the Executive Secretary who shall be the secretary to the Board. Members are appointed by the President on the recommendation of the education minister for a term of four years renewable only once. However, the Executive Secretary of the Fund, as chief executive officer, is appointed to an initial term of five years renewable once for four years upon such terms and conditions of service as may be specified.[413]

The functions of the Board include to:

a. monitor and ensure collection of tax by the Service and ensure remittance of same to the Fund;

b. manage and disburse the tax;

c. liaise with appropriate ministries and bodies responsible for collection or safe keeping of the tax;

d. receive requests and approve admittable projects after due consideration;

e. ensure disbursement to public tertiary educational institutions in Nigeria;

f. monitor and evaluate execution of the projects;

g. invest funds in appropriate and safe securities;

h. update the federal government on its activities and progress through annual and audited reports;

i. review progress and suggest improvements within the provisions of the Act;

j. do such other things as are necessary or incidental to the objects of the Fund under the Act or as may be assigned by the federal government;

k. issue guidelines from time to time, to all beneficiaries on disbursement from the Fund on the use of monies received from the Fund; and

l. generally regulate the administration, application and disbursement of monies from the Fund.[414]

In disbursing the tax funds, the Board is obliged to observe the principle of equality among geo-political zones in the case of special intervention and equality among States and Local Governments in the case of regular intervention. The disbursement is specifically aimed at:

a.   essential physical infrastructure for teaching and learning;

b.   instructional material and equipment;

c.   research and publication;

d.   academic staff training and development; and

e.   any other need which, in the opinion of the Board of Trustees, is critical and essential for the improvement of quality and maintenance of standards in higher educational institutions[415]

Education tax is shared among universities, polytechnics and colleges of education on a ratio of 2:1:1.[416]

The Federal Inland Revenue Service shall serve a demand notice on a company that fails to pay tax within 60 days from date of service of assessment notice. The demand notice shall in addition to the tax due, require the company to pay a penalty in a sum equal to five percent of the tax due and if both the tax and the additional five percent are not paid within two months of the demand, the company is guilty of an offence under the Act. Where an offence under the Act is committed by a corporate body, firm or association of individuals, every director, manager or secretary (in the case of a corporation); or every partner or officer (in the case of a firm); or every person concerned in the management of the affairs of the association (in the case of an association) shall be severally guilty and proceeded against and punished as if he had himself committed the offence unless he can prove that the act or omission constituting the offence took place without his knowledge, consent or connivance.[417] An offence under the Act in the first instance is punishable with imprisonment for six months or a fine of 1000,000 naira or both; while in the second and subsequent instances, the penalty is imprisonment for twelve months or a fine of 2,000,000 naira or both.[418] Under Section 11 of the repealed Act the punishment was a mere 10,000 naira for first offenders or imprisonment for three years and 20,000 naira for subsequent offenders or imprisonment for five years or both.

The power to make regulations governing the due administration of the Tertiary Education Fund (Establishment) Act is vested in the Education Minister by section 17.

## Value Added Tax

Value added tax was introduced in Nigeria by the *Value Added Tax Decree No. 102 1993* and is imposed at a rate of five percent of the value of goods and services other than those exempted under the Schedule to the Act. The decree repealed the *Sales Tax Act 1986* and is retained as Cap V1 Laws of the Federation of Nigeria 2004. The categories of goods exempted under the First Schedule to the Act are:

a. all medical and pharmaceutical products;

b. basic food items;

c. books and educational materials;

d. baby products;

e. plant and machinery imported for use in the Export Processing Zone or Free Trade Zone; provided that 100 percent production of such company is for export;

f. all exports;

g. plant, machinery and equipment purchased for utilisation of gas in down-stream petroleum operations;

h. tractors, ploughs and agricultural equipment and implements purchased for agricultural purposes.

Four categories of services are exempted and they include medical services; services rendered by community banks, peoples bank and mortgage institutions; plays and performances conducted by educational institutions as part of learning; and all exported services.

Where the supply of taxable goods and services is for money consideration, the taxable value of such goods or service is an amount which with the addition of the tax chargeable is equal to the consideration. If the supply is for a consideration other than money, the value is deemed to be the market value.[419] The value of imported taxable goods is the amount equal to the price of the goods inclusive of all taxes, duties, charges costs by way of commission, parking, transport and insurance up to the port or place of importation but not inclusive of the tax chargeable under the Act.[420]

A person liable to VAT is required by section 8 to register with the Service within six months of commencement of business that he is so liable, failing which he shall be liable to a penalty of 10,000 naira for the first month in which the failure occurs and 5,000 naira for each subsequent month in which the failure continues. Section 28 further makes it an offence punishable with a fine of 5,000 naira for failure to register. In addition to the fine, the premises of the business shall be liable to be sealed. Other categories required to be registered with the Service for the purposes of VAT are government ministries and agencies, statutory bodies, contractors doing business with any tier of government or its agency and non-resident companies.[421] A non-resident company is required to use the address of the person with whom it has a subsisting contract in Nigeria for the purpose of correspondence relating to VAT and include in all its invoices the persons to whom the goods and services are supplied in Nigeria and remit the tax in the currency of transaction. Every registered person is obliged to keep such records and books of all transactions, operations, imports and other activities relating to taxable goods and services as are sufficient to determine the correct amount of tax due.[422]

Every government ministry, agency or statutory body is obliged to remit the tax charged on a contract and deducted at the time of payment to the contractor to the nearest tax office. The remission to the tax office must be accompanied by a schedule showing the name and address of the contractor, invoice number, gross amount of invoice, and amount of tax and month of return.[423] Taxable persons are required to make returns of taxable goods and services on or before the 21st day of the month following that in which the purchase or supply was made. An importer of taxable goods is equally required to render returns on all imported goods to the Service.[424] The Service may use its best judgment to assess the amount of tax due on taxable goods and services purchased or supplied by a taxable person who either fails to render a return or render an incomplete or inaccurate return.[425] When rendering a return, if the output tax exceeds the input tax, the excess is remitted to the Service and if the input tax exceeds the output tax, the taxable person is entitled to a refund of the excess upon production of evidential documents. Where tax is due to be remitted and the taxable person fails to do so, a sum equal to 5 percent per annum, plus interest at the commercial rate, shall be added to the tax and the total amount shall be notified to the taxable person. A person aggrieved by the assessment may appeal to the Service and a decision on the appeal must be taken by the Service within thirty days of receipt. Under the original decree, an appeal from the decision of the Service went to the Value Added Tax Appeal Tribunal established by the Second Schedule to the decree. Presently however, appeals from the decision of the Service lie to the Tax Appeal Tribunal established by the Fifth Schedule to the *Federal Inland Revenue Service (Establishment) Act 2007* as a successor to both the Body of Appeal Commissioners and the VAT Tribunal. Further appeals lie to the Federal High Court. The Service is equally empowered to appeal to the Tribunal where after service of notice, the taxable person fails or refuses to remit tax.[426]

The Act establishes a Value Added Tax Technical Committee consisting of the Chairman of Service as Chairman, all directors of the Service, the legal adviser to the Service, a director in the Nigerian Customs Service and three representatives of the state governments who must be members of the Joint Tax Board.[427] The functions of the Committee are to consider all tax matters that require professional and technical expertise and make appropriate recommendations to the Service; advise the Service on the administration of VAT and attend to such other matters as are referred to it.[428] Sections 21 to 32 create offences under the Act and provides. The offences include:

a.  furnishing false documents or information;
b.  evasion of tax;
c.  failure to make attribution or notify the Service after the attribution;
d.  failure to notify the Service of a change in address;
e.  failure to issue tax invoice;
f.  resisting, obstructing or hindering an authorised officer;
g.  issuing of tax invoice by an unauthorised person;
h.  failure to register for tax;
i.  failure to keep proper records and accounts;
j.  failure to collect tax;
k.  failure to submit returns; and
l.  aiding and abetting the commission of any of the above offences.

Varying penalties are specified for the offences listed above where any of them is committed by a natural taxable person. Where any of the offences is committed by a corporate body, firm or association of individuals, similar consequences as under section 6 of the Education Tax Act apply.[429]

The VAT Act empowers the minister of finance to amend the rate of VAT as well as the list of taxable goods and services.[430]

The Value Added Tax Act was one of the nine bills submitted as part of the reforms process that commenced in 2004. The Value Added Tax (Amendment) Act No. 53 2007 which was one of the four legislations passed by the National Assembly in 2007 retained the existing rate of five percent but introduced a number of other changes in the administration of VAT. The 2007 amendment generally improved on the principal decree by removing ambiguities in the law but also specifically did the following:

a. A new subsection has been introduced to Section 13 which empowers the Federal Inland Revenue Service to direct companies operating in the oil and gas sector to deduct VAT at source and make remittance to the Service.[431]

b. Section 6 of the amendment introduces a new Section 13A which obliges a supplier of taxable goods or service to furnish the purchaser with an invoice specifying details of the transactions whether payment has been made at the time of supply or not.

c. Under Section 15 the principal Act, a taxable person was required to render returns of all taxable goods and services purchased or supplied by him within the preceding month on or before the 30th day of the month following that in which the purchase or supply was made. Section 7 (a) of the amendment now requires the monthly returns to be made on or before the 21st day of the month. Section 7 (b) of the amendment further introduces a new subsection (3) to Section 15 of the principal Act deeming as payment to the Federal Inland Revenue Service, all payments made by an importer of taxable goods to authorised government agents.

d. The requirement that the Nigerian Customs Service should demand the Value Added Tax Compliance Certificate from an importer before releasing imported taxable goods to the importer under Section 16 (3) of the principal Act has been repealed by Section 8 of the amendment Act.

e. Section 10 of the amendment introduces changes to reflect the current dispute resolution mechanism. Consequently, rather than the Value Added Tax Tribunal which is now defunct, appeals against VAT assessments lie to the Tax Appeal Tribunal. A new subsection (3) to Section 10 also requires the Service to determine an objection against assessment to VAT within 30 thirty.

f. Section 40 of the Act specifies the allocation formula of VAT proceeds among the three tiers of government as 15 percent for the Federal Government; 50 percent for the States and 35 percent for the Local Governments. Section 11 of the amendment introduces a new proviso to Section 40 to the effect that the principle of derivation of not less than 20 percent shall be reflected in the distributable share of States and Local Governments.

g.   Finally, Section 13 (b) of the amendment introduces a Part III to the Second Schedule to the Act. Part III contains the list of zero-rated goods and services which include non oil exports, goods and services purchased by diplomats and donor funded projects. Zero rating means that although the items are not exempted from VAT, the VAT rate payable on them is zero.

### Federal Inland Revenue Service (Establishment) Act No. 13 2007

The *Federal Inland Revenue Service (Establishment) Act 2007* does not, strictly speaking, impose or levy any taxes. What it does is to vest the administration of the tax laws contained in the First Schedule to the Act in the Federal Inland Revenue Service. Principally, in the area of tax administration, the Act confers autonomy on the Service as a corporate entity with perpetual succession.[432] Further, the Body of Appeal Commissioners and the VAT Tribunal have been abolished and replaced with the Tax Appeal Tribunal.[433]

The Service is vested with powers to administer the Companies' Income Tax Act, Petroleum Profits Tax Act, Personal Income Tax Act, Capital Gains Tax Act, Value Added Tax Act, Stamp Duties Act, Taxes and Levies (Approved List for Collection), all Regulations, Notices or Rules issued pursuant to the foregoing provisions, Laws imposing taxes or levies within the Federal Capital Territory, any law for which power to administer is conferred on the Service and any enactment or law imposing collection of taxes, fees and levies collected by other government agencies and companies including signature bonuses, pipeline fees, penalties for gas flaring, depot levies, fees for oil exploration licence, oil mining licence, oil production licence, royalties, rents and all fees prevalent in the oil industry not specifically listed. Although the Act does not impose tax, it provides for offences and penalties one of which is the failure to deduct tax in line with the provisions of the enactments listed in the First Schedule, or having deducted, failing to remit same within 30 days to the Service. The penalty prescribed is liability for the tax not deducted or not remitted as the case may be plus penalty of 10 percent of the sum involved per annum at the existing Central Bank of Nigeria re-discount rate and imprisonment for three years.[434]

### Taxes and Levies (Approved List for Collection) Act[435]

Like the FIRS Establishment Act, this Act which was originally promulgated as decree No. 2 1998 was aimed at reforming tax administration. Essentially, it demarcated spheres of collectible taxes among the three tiers of government as enumerated in chapter three.

**References**

1    Preamble to the Native Revenue Proclamation No. 2 1906

2    An unsettled district was defined by section 2 of the Proclamation as a community which did not pay tribute to any chief.

3    Section 3 (a) and (b) Native Revenue Proclamation No. 2 1906.

4    *Ibid*, section 4 (a) - (d).

5    *Ibid*, section 7.

6    *Ibid*, section 9 (a) and (b).

7    A recognised chief was defined by section 2 as any chief whose position as such was recognised and approved by the Governor.

8    *Ibid*, section 10 (a) - (d).

9    *Ibid*, section 11 (a) - (c).

10   *Ibid*, section 13.

11   *Ibid*, sections 15 and 16.

12   *Ibid*, section 17.

13   *Ibid*, section 18.

14   *Ibid*, section 19.

15   *Ibid*, section 21.

16   *Ibid*, section 22.

17   *Ibid*, section 23.

18   *Ibid*, section 24.

19   *Ibid*, section 25.

20   *Ibid*, section 20.

21   Section 1, Native Revenue Ordinance No. 1 1917.

22   *Ibid*, section 3 (a) and (b).

23   *Ibid*, sections 2 and 9 (2).

24   *Ibid*, section 14.

25   *Ibid*, sections 15 and 16.

26   Section 2 *Native Revenue (Amendment) Ordinance* No. 29 1918

27   Sections 1 and  2 Native Revenue (Amendment) Ordinance No. 17 1927

28   This ordinance regulated income taxation in the colony of Lagos and its provisions are discussed ahead.

29   References to 'the protectorate' after 1914 are references to the protectorate of Nigeria

30   Section 4 (3), Non-Natives Income Tax (Protectorate) Ordinance No. 21 1931.

31   *Ibid*, section 4 (6).

32   *Ibid*, section 7 (3).

33   *Ibid*, section 11 (1) - (4).

34   *Ibid*, section 12.

35   *Ibid*, section 13(1) - (3).

36   *Ibid*, section 14(8).

37   *Ibid*, section 15(1) and (2).

38   *Ibid*, section 20(1).

39   The Ordinance was repealed by the Income Tax Ordinance No. 3 1940.

40   Non-Natives Income Tax (Protectorate)(Amendment No. 2) Ordinance No. 23 1936.

41   *Ibid*, section 6.

42   Section 2 Non-Natives Income Tax (Protectorate) (Amendment No. 2) Ordinance No.18 1939.

43   *Ibid*, section 3.

44   Section 2, Non-Natives Income Tax (Protectorate) (Amendment No. 3) Ordinance No. 29 1939.

45   Section 1, Direct Taxation Ordinance No. 4 1940.

46   *Ibid*, section 30.

47   *Ibid*, section 5.

48   *Ibid*, section 7.

49   *Ibid*, section 98.

50   *Ibid*, section 13 (1) - (3).

51   *Ibid*, section 15 (a) - (d).

52   *Ibid*, section 21.

53   *Ibid*, section 22.

54   *Ibid* section 23.

55   Cap 54 of 1940.

56   Section 19 was *in pari materia* with section 17 (2), Direct Taxation Ordinance No. 4 of 1940.

57   Section 3(3) and (4), Income Tax (Colony) Ordinance No. 23 1927.

58   *Ibid*, section 13(1) and (2).

59   *Ibid*, section 15(1) - (3).

60   Section 4 (1), Income Tax (Colony) (Amendment) Ordinance No. 31 1933.

61    *Ibid*, section 5.

62    *Ibid*, section 6.

63    Section 33, Colony Taxation Ordinance No. 4 1937.

64    *Ibid*,section 5.

65    *Ibid*, section 9.

66    *Ibid*, proviso to section 10.

67    *Ibid*, section 13.

68    *Ibid*, section 15.

69    *Ibid*, section 20.

70    *Ibid*, section 21 (2) (a) - (b).

71    *Ibid*, section 21 (3).

72    *Ibid*, section 23 (1) - (3).

73    Section 24 (1) - (2).

74    *Ibid*, section 28 (1) (a) - (d), (2),

75    *Ibid*, section 29 (1) - (4).

76    Section 5, Native Direct Taxation (Colony) Ordinance No. 41 1937.

77    *Ibid*, section 6 (1) and (2).

78    *Ibid*, section 8.

79    *Ibid*, section 10 (1) - (2).

80    *Ibid*, section 18.

81    *Ibid*, sections 19 and 20.

82    *Ibid*, section 22.

83    Section 2(a), Colony Taxation (Amendment) Ordinance No. 2 1939.

84    *Ibid*, section 2(b).

85    *Ibid*, section 2(c).

86    *Ibid*, section 3.

87    *Ibid*, sections 4, 5 and 7.

88    *Ibid*, section 6.

89    The long title of the Ordinance read: *'An Ordinance to regulate the levying and collection of a supplementary tax on incomes for the financial year 1939 - 1940'.*

90    Section 1, Income Tax (Supplementary) Ordinance No. 28 1939.

91    *Ibid*, section 2.

92    Section 3, Colony Taxation (Amendment) Ordinance No. 2 1939.

93    The provisions of the Colony Taxation Ordinance 1937

that were incorporated into the Income Tax (Supplementary) Ordinance 1939 were sections 2, 4, 5, 11, 14, 15, 17, 20, 22, 23 (1) and (2), 24

– 32. See the First Column of the Second Schedule, Income Tax (Supplementary) Ordinance No. 28 1939.

94  See Second Column of the Second Schedule, Income Tax (Supplementary) Ordinance No. 28 1939. Modifications were done to the following provisions of the *Colony Taxation Ordinance (supra):* a. Section 2, by deleting the definition of year of assessment and replacing it with the definition in the Income Tax (Supplementary) Ordinance 1939. b. Sections 5, 17, 22, 23 (1) and (2), 27, 28, 30 (1) and (4) and 30A (3), by substituting the words *tax authority* with *Commissioner.* c. Section 27, by deleting the proviso (2). d. Section 30 (4), by substituting the words *a Judge of the Supreme Court* with *the Court.*

95  *Ibid*, section 5.

96  Section 66, Income Tax Ordinance No. 3 1940.

97  *Ibid*, section 3

98  *Ibid*, section 6

99  Section 49 defined *Empire income tax* as 'any tax charged under any law in force in any part of His Majesty's Dominions or in any place under His Majesty's protection (other than the United Kingdom or Nigeria)'.

100  Section 14 (2), supra note 514

101  Section 16 (2) defined child to include a step child but not an adopted or illegitimate child.

102  *Ibid*, section 17

103  *Ibid*, section 18

104  *Ibid*, section 20 (1)

105  *Ibid*, section 20 (2)

106  *Ibid*, section 23.

107  *Ibid*, section 24 (2).

108  *Ibid*, section 27.

109  *Ibid*, section 28 (1) (b).

110  *Ibid*, section 28 (2).

111  *Ibid*, section 28 (4).

112  *Ibid*, section 29.

113  *Ibid*, section 35 (1).

114  *Ibid*, section 38 (1).

115 *Ibid*, section 39 (1) and (2).

116 *Ibid*, section 42.

117 *Ibid*, section 45 (3).

118 *Ibid*, section 46 (1) (a) - (j).

119 *Ibid*, section 46 (2).

120 *Ibid*, section 47 (1) and (2).

121 *Ibid*, section 49 (3).

122 *Ibid*, section 51.

123 *Ibid*, section 52.

124 *Ibid*, section 53.

125 *Ibid*, section 54 (1) - (3).

126 *Ibid*, sections 57.

127 *Ibid*, section 63 (1) and (2).

128 *Ibid*, section 64.

129 Section 2, Income Tax (Amendment) Ordinance No. 14 1940.

130 These were:
Nos. 35 of 1941, 29 of 1943, 36 of 1944, 23 of 1945, 6 of 1946, 16 of 1947, 24 of 1947, 16 of 1948, 16 of 1949, 25 of 1950, 10 of 1952, 11 of 1952, 5 of 1955, 19 of 1955, 31 of 1955, 32 of 1957, 23 of 1958, 47 of 1955 and 55 of 1955.

131 Section 4 (4) Income Tax Administration Ordinance No. 39 1958.

132 *Ibid*, section 1 (1).

133 Section 14, Companies Income Tax Ordinance No. 14 1939.

134 *Ibid*, section 3.

135 *Ibid*, section 4.

136 *Ibid*, sections 5 and 6.

137 *Ibid*, section 8

138 *Ibid*, section 9 (1)

139 *Ibid*, section 12.

140 *Ibid*, section 13.

141 *Ibid*, section 13 (1) - (4).

142 *Ibid*, section 15 (1) and (2).

143 *Ibid*, section 21.

144 *Ibid*, section 18.

145 *Ibid*, section 29.

146   *Ibid*, section 22 (1) - (3).

147   *Ibid*, section 25.

148   *Ibid*, section 26 (1) - (3).

149   *Ibid*, section 28.

150   *Ibid*, section 32 (1) and (2).

151   *Ibid*, sections 33 and 34.

152   *Ibid*, section 35.

153   *Ibid*, section 38 and 40.

154   *Ibid*, section 39 and 41.

155   *Ibid*, section 43 (1) and (2).

156   *Ibid*, section 45.

157   Section 77, Companies Income Tax Act No. 22 1961.

158   *Ibid*, sections 3 (1) and 4 (1).

159   *Ibid*, section 18 (1) and (2).

160   *Ibid*, section 2.

161   *Ibid*, section 26 (g).

162   *Ibid*, section 30 (1).

163   *Ibid*, section 31 (1).

164   *Ibid*, section 32.

165   *Ibid*, section 39.

166   *Ibid*, sections 40 – 42.

167   *Ibid*, section 44 (1) - (4).

168   *Ibid*, section 48 (1) - (3).

169   *Ibid*, section 49 (1)

170   *Ibid*, section 50

171   *Ibid*, section 51 (1)-(3)

172   *Ibid*, section 52

173   *Ibid*, section 53 (1)-(3)

174   *Ibid*, section 54

175   *Ibid*, section 56 (2).

176   *Ibid*, section 58 (3).

177   *Ibid*, section 74.

178   *Ibid*, section 58 (2).

179   *Ibid*, section 61.

180 This was the general penalty prescribed by Section 67 (1) for an offence in respect of which no specific penalty was prescribed.

181 *Ibid*, section 62 – 64.

182 *Ibid*, section 65 and 66.

183 *Ibid*, section 67 (2).

184 *Ibid*, section 68 (1).

185 *Ibid*, section 69.

186 *Ibid*, section 68 (1) (b).

187 *Ibid*, section 70.

188 Section 1 Income Tax (Amendment) Decree No. 45 1967.

189 Section 2 (a) Income Tax (Miscellaneous Provisions) Decree No. 28 1974.

190 *Ibid*, section 2 (b).

191 *Ibid*, section 2 (d).

192 *Ibid*, section 2 (e).

193 *Ibid*, section 2 (f).

194 Section 77, Companies Income Tax Decree No. 28 1979.

195 As the successor to the FBIR, the FIRS is now vested with the administration of the Act.

196 *Op. cit*, section 2.

197 *Ibid*, section 8 (1) (g).

198 *Ibid*, section 26 (3)

199 *Ibid*, section 28 (1)

200 *Ibid*, section 28 (4)

201 *Ibid*, section 28 (2)

202 *Ibid*, section 28 (3)

203 The Body of Appeal Commissioners has been replaced with the Tax Appeal Tribunal established under section 59 of the FIRS (Establishment) Act 2007.

204 Some of the decrees include Nos. 21 of 1991, 30, 31 and 32 of 1996, 18 and 19 of 1998 and 30 of 1999.

205 See Chapter Three for details on the recommendations of the Study Group.

206 Section 23 Companies' Income Tax (Amendment) Act No. 56 2007

207 Act No. 21 of 1961, hereafter referred to as ITMA 1961.

208 Section 1 (1) - (3), ITMA 1961.

209 *Ibid*, section 32.

210   *Ibid*, section 3 (1).

211   *Ibid*, section 3 (2) - (5).

212   *Ibid*, section 5 (1).

213   *Ibid*, section 6 (1).

214   *Ibid*, section 7.

215   *Ibid*, section 8 (1).

216   *Ibid*, sections 9 and 10.

217   *Ibid*, section 26.

218   *Ibid*, section 11.

219   *Ibid*, section 14.

220   *Ibid*, section 16 (1).

221   *Ibid*, section 17.

222   *Ibid*, section 18.

223   *Ibid*, section 19.

224   *Ibid*, section 22.

225   *Ibid*, section 27.

226   *Ibid*, section 27 (8) (c) and (d).

227   *Ibid*, section 28 (1) and (2).

228   *Ibid*, section 30 (1).

229   *Ibid*, section 31.

230   Section 1 (1) and (2), Personal Income Tax (Lagos) Act No. 23 1961.

231   Section 20A (1), Income Tax Management (Uniform Taxation Provisions, etc) Decree No. 7 1975.

232   Section 21A (1), Income Tax Management (Uniform Taxation Provisions, etc) Decree No. 7 1975.

233   Examples of these include the Finance (Miscellaneous Taxation Provisions) Decrees Nos. 21 and 63 of 1991.

234   It is deemed an Act of the National Assembly by virtue of the provisions *section 315 Constitution of the Federal Republic of Nigeria, 1999* and as such is now known as the *Personal Income Tax Act*.

235   The tax authorities established by PITA are the Joint Tax Board, States' Boards of Internal Revenue, Local Government Revenue Committees and Joint State Revenue Committees respectively. See Chapter Three for an extensive discourse pertaining to their composition and functions.

236  Section 85 (1), Personal Income Tax Act. This codified as Cap. P8 Laws of the Federation of Nigeria 2004.

237  *Ibid*, section 85 (3).

238  Nos. 30, 31 and 32 of 1996, 18 and  19 of 1998 and 30 of 1999.

239  Cap P4 Laws of the Federation of Nigeria 2004

240  Section 3 Personal Income Tax (Amendment) Act 2011

241  *Ibid* section 6

242  *Ibid* Section 7

243  *Ibid* Section 12

244  *Ibid* Section 13

245  *Ibid* Section 14

246  *Ibid* Section 18

247  *Ibid* section 19

248  *Ibid* Section 23

249  *Ibid* Sections 25-28

250  *Ibid* Section 30

251  *Ibid* Section 31

252  *Ibid* Section 32

253  *Ibid* Section 33

254  Present day Bayelsa State.

255  These functions are now carried out by the Federal Inland Revenue Service as the successor to the FBIR. All references to the *Board* are therefore construed as references to the *Service*

256  Section 6 (1) and (2) Petroleum Profits Tax Act Cap P13 LFN 2004

257  *Ibid*, section 7 (3) The Corporate Affairs Commission established under the Companies and Allied Matters Act 1990 is now the successor to the Registrar of Companies who was contemplated under the principal Ordinance.

258  *Ibid*, section 2.

259  Under the principal ordinance, the term *gross* appeared before proceeds. This was deleted by the Petroleum Profits (Amendment) Decree No. 1 1967.

260  This paragraph was inserted by the Petroleum Profits Tax (Amendment) Decree No. 15 1973. Under the provisions of the principal Ordinance, 'the value of any chargeable oil so disposed of' was taken to be the value of that oil as determined, for the purpose

of royalty, in accordance with the provisions of the oil prospecting licence or oil mining lease by virtue of which that oil was recovered or won by the company'.

261  *Op. cit*, section 9 (3).

262  Non-productive rents, defined by section 2 to mean the amount of any rent as to which there is provision for its deduction from the amount of any royalty under a petroleum prospecting license or oil lease to the extent that such rent is not so deducted, was introduced as an allowable deduction by the Petroleum Profits (Amendment) Decree No.1 1967.

263  Paragraph g was introduced by the Petroleum Profits Tax (Amendment) (No. 2) Decree No. 24 1979 while paragraph h was introduced by the Petroleum Profits Tax (Amendment) Decree No. 15 1973.

264  *Op. cit*, section 14, under the principal Ordinance, this provision was section 12.

265  This power is now vested in the minister in charge of petroleum resources.

266  *Op. cit*, section 20 (3).

267  Under the principal Ordinance, this allowance was referred to as initial allowance; the phrase 'investment tax credit' was introduced to replace initial allowance by the provisions of the Petroleum Profits Tax (Amendment No. 2) Decree No.24 1979.

268  For more on how this is done, refer to chapter 4.

269  *Op. cit*, section 25 (1) and (2).

270  *Ibid*, section 27 (1) and (2).

271  *Ibid*, section 27 (3).

272  *Ibid*, section 32.

273  Under section 27 (1) of the principal Ordinance, the time allowed was five months after the commencement of an accounting period. The period was reduced to two months by virtue of the Petroleum Profits Tax (Amendment) Decree No. 15 1973.

274  *Op. cit*, section 37 (1) - (3).

275  *Ibid*, section 38 (1) - (6).

276  *Ibid*, section 39 (1) - (2).

277  At the time of the passage of the principal Ordinance, the Federal High Court had not yet been established so further appeals went to the High Court; again with the establishment of the Tax Appeal Tribunal (TAT), all powers vested in the Body of Appeal Commissioners are now exercisable by the TAT. All references to BAC may therefore be deemed to be references to the TAT.

278  *Op. cit*, section 44.

279   *Ibid,* section 45 (1) - (4).

280   Section 38 (1) - (6), Petroleum Profits Tax Ordinance No. 15 1959.

281   *Op. cit,* section 54.

282   Section 51 of the principal Ordinance provided similarly in respect of the income tax ordinance, which, from the foregoing analysis, was a predecessor to the Personal Income Tax Act.

283   Under section 52 of the principal Ordinance, this power was vested in the Governor - General.

284   Section 2 (a), Petroleum Profit Tax (Amendment) (No. 3) Decree 95 1979.

285   The decree is now deemed to be an Act of the National Assembly and preserved as Cap C1 LFN 2004.

286   Section 4 (a) - (c) Capital Gains Tax Act Cap C1 LFN 2004.

287   *Ibid,* section 6 (2) (a) and (b).

288   *Ibid,* section 7 (1) and (2).

289   *Ibid,* section 8 (3).

290   *Ibid,* section 11.

291   *Ibid ,* section 18 (1) and  (2)

292   *Ibid,* Section 19 (1) and (2).

293   It should be noted that reference to the Board by virtue of the provisions of Federal Inland Revenue Service (Establishment) Act 2007 (FIRSEA) is the FIRS.

294   *Op. cit,* section 26 (1).

295   *Ibid,* section 26 (2).

296   Under the principal decree, the limit was 5000 pounds

297   The limit under the principal decree was 500 pounds.

298   *Op. cit,* section 42 (1) - (3).

299   Currently the FIRS and the TAT respectively.

300   Long title to the Stamp Proclamation No. 8 1903.

301   *Ibid,* section 3

302   ection 6, Stamp Ordinance No. 42 1916.

303   *Ibid,* section 52.

304   Ordinance No. 41 1922.

305   Ordinance No. 43 1928.

306   Ordinance No. 23 1931.

307   Section 116, Stamp Duties Ordinance No. 5 1939.

308  Section 4 (1) and (2), Stamp Duties Act Cap S8 LFN 2004.

309  *Ibid*, section 100 (2). Under section 98 (2) of the principal Ordinance, the rate was ten shillings for every one hundred pounds.

310  *Ibid*, section5(2).

311  *Ibid*, section 28.

312  *Ibid*, section 39.

313  Section 18 further provides that all statutory declarations or affidavits made pursuant to Stamp Duties be done before a Commissioner or any other person authorised by law to administer oaths.

314  Twenty pounds was the penalty under the principal Ordinance.

315  *Op. cit*, section 10 (1).

316  *Ibid*, section 11 (1) - (3) the fine was 10 pounds under the principal Ordinance.

317  *Ibid*  197.  See "Isamisation of the Natural sciences – Myth or Reality." A Paper Presented at a Seminar on Islamisation of Knowledge at Bayero University, Kano, Nigeria., section 12.

318  *Ibid*, section 14 (1) and (2).

319  *Ibid*, section 16 (1).

320  *Ibid*, section 17.

321  *Ibid*, section 19.

322  *Ibid*, section 25.

323  *Ibid*, section 26.

324  Defined as 'the note sent by a broker or agent to his principal, or by any person who, by way of business, deals, or holds himself out as dealing, as a principal in any stock or marketable securities, advising the principal, or the vendor or purchaser, as the case may be, of the sale or purchase of any stock or marketable security, but does not include a note sent by a broker or agent to his principal where the principal is himself acting as broker or agent for a principal'.Section 49 (1), *ibid*.

325  Defined as 'every instrument, and every decree or order of any court, whereby any property on any occasion, except a sale or mortgage, is transferred to or vested in any person'. Section 65, *ibid*.

326  *Ibid*, sections 27 - 105.

327  *Ibid*, section 106,

328  Pursuant to this power which was originally vested by section 113 in the Governor-General, the following regulations were made: Stamp Duties (Custody of Dies)

Regulations, The Stamp Duties (Adhesive Stamps) Regulations and The Stamp Duties (Customs Bonds) Regulations. The Regulations took care of the matters listed under the enabling section.

329    *Op. cit*, section 116 (1) and (2).

330    The amendments were done in 1941 (Ordinance No. 28), 1942 (Ordinance No. 17), 1946 (Ordinance No. 26), 1950 (Ordinance No. 38), 1953 (Ordinance No. 2) and 1961 (Act No. 55).

331    Following the Ordinance, the Regions also passed their Produce Sales Tax Laws. E.g. the Western Region passed its own law in 1957.

332    These were the Nigeria Cocoa Marketing Board Ordinance, Nigeria Groundnut Marketing Ordinance, the Nigeria Oil Palm Produce Marketing Ordinance and the Nigeria Cotton Marketing Ordinance all of 1949.

333    Section 3 (2) Sale of Produce (Taxation) Ordinance No. 12 1953

334    *Ibid*, section 4

335    *Ibid*, sections 6 and 7

336    *Ibid*, section 9

337    *Ibid*, section 10

338    *Ibid*, section 8.

339    Groundnuts: one pound, benniseed: ten shillings, soya beans and sunflower: two shillings and six pence, cocoa: five pounds, palm kernel: two pounds and six shillings, palm oil: four pounds and ten shillings. Seed cotton was however measured in lbs and the rate was one tenth of a penny per each lb.

340    Section 2, Sales Tax Decree No. 7 1986.

341    *Ibid*, section 7 (1).

342    Section 1 (1) and (2), Super Tax Decree No. 46 1967.

343    *Ibid*, section 1 (4).

344    *Ibid*, section 9 (1).

345    *Ibid*, section 3 (1) - (3).

346    *Ibid*, section 5.

347    *Ibid*, sections 6 and 7.

348    *Ibid*, section 8.

349    *Ibid*, section 10.

350    *Ibid*, section 11.

351    Section 1 (1) and (2), Super Tax (Amendment) Decree No. 12 1970.

352　*Ibid*, section 2 (1) - (4).

353　Section 1, Super Tax (Amendment) (No. 2) Decree No. 12 1971.

354　Funds brought into Nigeria from any country or territory outside Nigeria.

355　*Ibid*, section 4 (b).

356　As introduced by the 1970 amendment.

357　*Op. cit*, section 4 (a) and (b).

358　Entertainment Tax Western Region Law 3 1953

359　Section 13 (3).

360　Section 1, *Entertainment Tax Decree No. 66 1966*

361　*Ibid*, section 2

362　Ministry of Finance

363　*Ibid*, section 7 (1) and (2).

364　*Ibid*, section 10 (1) and (2).

365　Section 67 of the Constitution of Nigeria 1960.

366　See long title to the Pool Betting Control Act No. 69 1961.

367　*Ibid*, section 3 (1) - (4).

368　*Ibid*, section 4 (1).

369　*Ibid*, section 5 (1) - (3).

370　*Ibid*, section 6 (1) and (2).

371　Section 1 (4), Pool Betting Tax Act No. III 1962.

372　*Ibid*, section 1 (3).

373　*Ibid*, section 2 (1) - (3).

374　*Ibid*, section 3 (4).

375　Section 3 (1), Pool Betting Tax Act No. 11 1965.

376　Section 1, Pool Betting Tax (Increase of Rate) Decree 1966.

377　Section 26 (1) extends the application of the Act, in respect of companies liable to tax under the Act, to the entire federation.

378　Section 1 (1) - (5), Casino Taxation Act No. 26 1965.

379　That is, a company liable to casino revenue tax. See *Ibid*, section 1 (3) (b).

380　*Ibid*, section 3 (1) - (4).

381　*Ibid*, section 5 (1) - (3).

382　*Ibid*, section 6 (1) - (4).

383　*Ibid*, section 7 (1) - (3).

384　*Ibid*, section 9 (1) and (2).

385   *Ibid*, section 22 (1) and (2).

386   *Ibid*, section 17.

387   *Ibid*, section 15 (1).

388   *Ibid*, section 16 (1) - (6).

389   *Ibid*, section 19 (1).

390   *Ibid*, section 21 (1).

391   Disclosure of classified matters under the Official Secrets Act is prohibited if considered prejudicial to the security of Nigeria.

392   *Op. cit*, section 23 (1) and (2).

393   Sections 1 (4) and 2 (4) Pools Betting and Casino Gaming (Prohibition) Decree No. 19 1979.

394   Sections 1 and 4 Capital Transfer Tax Decree No. 12 1979.

395   *Ibid*, section 1 (2).

396   *Ibid*, section 2 (1) and (2).

397   *Ibid*, section 17 (1) and (2).

398   *Ibid*, section 3 (1) and (2).

399   *Ibid*, section 8 (1) and (2).

400   *Ibid*, section 9.

401   *Ibid*, section 10.

402   These included the cost of embalming and transporting the deceased to the burial ground but in any event the cost was not to exceed N1000 in respect of a tombstone and N3000 for all other expenses.

403   See section 13 (1), Capital Transfer Decree 1979.

404   *Ibid*, section 19.

405   *Ibid*, section 21.

406   *Ibid*, section 27.

407   *Ibid*, section 24 (1).

408   Sanni, A. 'Theft of Tax Policy in UK: Lessons for Nigeria', *The Punch Newspaper* 13 - 14 November 2007, 13 – 14.

409   Section 1 (2) Tertiary Education Trust Fund (Establishment, etc) Act, 2011.

410   *Ibid*, section 1 (3)

411   *Ibid*, section 2 (1) to (3)

412   *Ibid*, section 3 (1)

413   *Ibid* Section 8 (1)

414  *Ibid*, Section 6

415  *Ibid* Section 7 (1) and (2)

416  *Ibid* Section 7 (3)

417  *Ibid,* section 10 (1) to (5).

418  *Ibid,* section 11 (1)

419  Section 5, Value Added Tax Act Cap V1 LFN 2004.

420  *Ibid*, section 6.

421  *Ibid*, section 8A - 8B.

422  *Ibid*, section 9.

423  *Ibid*, section 10.

424  *Ibid*, section 12.

425  *Ibid*, section 14.

426  *Ibid*, section 16 (1) - (5).

427  *Ibid*, section 17.

428  *Ibid*, section 18.

429  *Ibid* Section 33.

430  *Ibid* Section 34.

431  Section 5 (a) Value Added Tax (Amendment) Act No.53 2007

432  Section 1 Federal Inland Revenue Service (Establishment) Act 2007.

433  *Ibid* Section 59 and the Fifth Schedule to the Act.

434  *Ibid* Section 40.

435  Cap T2 Laws of the Federation 2004.

# CHAPTER SIX

## INSTRUMENTS OF TAX POLICY

### Background

Nigerian tax policy up to 2010 was a varied mix of legislation, judicial pronouncements, budget speeches, committee reports and international treaties. The National Tax Policy- an outcome of the 2002 Study Group of the Nigerian tax system- was approved by the Federal Executive Council in 2010. The National Tax Policy, which is discussed in detail in the latter part of this chapter, provides the objectives to be achieved and the principles to be adhered to at all times in the Nigerian tax system. While this has provided a roadmap for better operation of the system, it still does not detract from the impact other measures such as judicial pronouncements and international treaties had; and continue to have on the overall system. The focus of this chapter is to highlight how prior to, and apart from the National Tax Policy, various policy tools have contributed to the development of the Nigerian tax system over time.

As evident in the volume of the preceding chapter, legislation has been more pervasive than any other policy tool throughout Nigeria's colonial and post colonial history. During the colonial era, legislations were passed as Ordinances and after independence, federal legislation were designated Acts while legislations passed by states were referred to as 'laws'; a practice that has endured up to date. The military introduced the nomenclature of decrees and edicts for legislation issued by the federal military government and the state military administrators respectively. It was also the military that introduced the use of *Finance (Miscellaneous Taxation Provisions) decrees* whereby different tax enactments were amended/ repealed by the instrumentality of a single, omnibus decree. The nature of these decrees were such that distinct taxes such as companies' income tax, personal income tax, capital gains tax, petroleum profits tax and such other taxes that were deemed necessary, were amended by a single legislation.[1]

Apart from imposition of tax, legislation has been used as a tool to enhance the administration of tax. For example, in 1966, the federal military government issued the *Income Tax (Authorised Communications) Decree*.[2] The decree is deemed as an Act of the National Assembly and forms part of current Nigerian statutes, having been retained as Cap 15, Laws of the Federation of Nigeria 2004. Essentially, the Act empowers the President to request the Inspector General of Police or other police officer above the rank of Chief Superintendent of Police, to inspect and if necessary remove any books, records or documents in the possession of the Federal Inland Revenue Service or any other tax authority for the purposes of any investigation. The President's direction to the Inspector General shall be in the format contained in Form 1 to the Schedule to the Act while the Inspector General's direction to the concerned tax authority shall be in the format contained in Form 2 to the Schedule. The Schedule containing the forms was introduced by the *Income Tax (Authorised Communications) (Amendment) Decree 1966*.[3] The *Income Tax (Authorised Communications) Decree 1966* was meant to be an exception to section 14 (1) of the *Companies Income Tax Act 1961*; and continues to be an exception to other income tax laws conferring an oath of secrecy on tax administrators. The purpose of the law is to empower the President, in appropriate cases, and in the public interest, to circumvent the oath of secrecy by which tax officials are ordinarily bound.

Legislation has also been used to grant relief to individual and corporate taxpayers as economic circumstances dictate. Some of these legislations include the *Income Tax (Rents) Act 1963* which was passed for the purpose of 'granting of relief from income tax on payments by way of rent received in respect of certain dwelling houses; and for purposes connected therewith'.[4] While the *Income Tax (Rents) Act 1963* was aimed at providing relief on certain advance payments made by way of rent; the *Industrial Development (Income Tax Relief) Decree 1971*[5] is intended to provide tax relief to companies that qualify as 'pioneer industries' or whose products qualify as 'pioneer products'. The criteria for qualification is contained in section 1 (1) of the decree.[6] According to the section, where the President is satisfied that:

a.  any industry is not being carried on in Nigeria on a scale suitable to the economic requirements of Nigeria or at all, or there are favourable prospects of further development in Nigeria of any industry; or

b.  it is expedient in the public interest to encourage the development or establishment of any industry in Nigeria by declaring the industry to be a pioneer industry and any product of the industry to be a pioneer product;

the President may direct that the list of such industries and products be published in the gazette and thereupon, a company in any of such industries may apply and obtain a pioneer status certificate granting it relief from tax for an initial period of three years, and renewable for either twice annually or once for two years.[7] Under the principal decree, the power exercisable by the President was vested in the Federal Executive Council.

## Case Law

The Nigerian judicial system is hierarchical in nature. This makes for the operation of judicial precedent and *stare decisis*. Judicial precedent provides for consistency by ensuring that where a case comes before a court or tribunal and the facts of the case are similar to another case in which a decision already exists, the court or tribunal should follow the decision in the earlier case. *Stare decisis* refers to the binding element wherein a lower court or tribunal is obligated to follow the decision of a superior court where the lower tribunal is faced with a case similar to one that had been decided upon by a superior court. The aim of this segment is not to analyse all tax decisions that have been handed down but rather; to analyse a number of notable tax cases and in so doing, illustrate how courts shape tax policy.

### *Shell Petroleum Development Company of Nigeria Limited v. FBIR*[8]

Shell Petroleum Development Company, SPDC, submitted its returns for the period 1st January - 31st December 1973 to the Federal Board of Inland Revenue, FBIR, showing the tax liability which in the view of the company was payable by it. The FBIR disallowed four expenses claimed as deductible items in the returns filed by SPDC on the ground that such expenses were not deductible in computing chargeable tax under the Petroleum Profits Tax Act, PPTA. The four items were:

a.  Exchange losses on payment of petroleum profits tax;

b.  Central Bank commission for payment of petroleum profits tax;

c.  Scholarship expenses; and

d.  Gifts and donations.

Shell registered its objection by appealing to the Body of Appeal Commissioners, BAC. At the hearing before the BAC, the company abandoned the fourth item on gifts and donations. The BAC dismissed the appeal of Shell and confirmed the revised assessment issued by the FBIR. Shell proceeded to the Federal High Court, which allowed the appeal in respect of two items namely; exchange losses on payment of petroleum profits tax and Central Bank commission. The court dismissed the appeal against scholarship expenses. Both parties appealed to the Court of Appeal; Shell against the confirmation of the assessment on scholarship expenses and the FBIR against the setting aside of the assessments on exchange losses and Central Bank charges. The Court of Appeal dismissed Shell's appeal and allowed the appeal by the FBIR, thereby restoring the decision of the BAC. Dissatisfied with the judgment, Shell appealed against it to the Supreme Court. The Supreme Court unanimously allowed the appeal.

The item that particularly impacted on Nigerian tax policy in this case was the treatment of "exchange losses" by the Supreme Court. In allowing exchange losses as deductible, the Supreme Court relied on four agreements entered into by SPDC and the FBIR between 1967 and 1972. The agreements required the oil company to pay tax in Pound Sterling into the account of the Central Bank of Nigeria, CBN, with the Bank of England in London. Shell therefore had to convert United States Dollars, which is the currency of transaction, into Naira and then convert the Naira again into the Pound Sterling to pay into the CBN's account in fulfilment of the agreements. This procedure was subject to fluctuations in foreign exchange and did give rise to exchanges losses. These were the losses the oil company sought as "deductible" arguing that the losses were incurred as expenses attributable to "petroleum operations" as defined under Section 2 of the PPTA. It must be noted that judicial reasoning has always leaned on the side of calculating tax liability in the currency of the country of assessment. The Privy Council of the House of Lords acknowledged this position in the case of *Payne v. The Deputy Commissioner of Taxation.*[9] The reasoning appears to be hinged on the understanding that a country's currency is an index of its sovereignty.[10] The Supreme Court gave credence to this reasoning but made an exception in the light of the agreements between the FBIR and SPDC. In essence, but for the agreements in question, the Nigerian Naira ought to have been the currency of taxation in this case.

The reaction of the Nigerian government to the above decision was in the form of the Finance (Miscellaneous Taxation Provisions) Decree No. 30 of 1996. Section 41 thereof provided that notwithstanding anything to the contrary in any law, all tax computations under the PPTA shall be made in the currency of transaction. Section 7 made similar provisions regarding computation of tax under the Companies Income Tax Act. The relevant provisions in the current enactments are Sections 40 and 54 of the PPTA[11] and the CITA[12] respectively.

By stamping the decision of the Supreme Court in the above case with statutory flavour, the government seeks to avoid the complications resulting from foreign exchange that gave rise to the dispute in Shell's case. However, another school of thought is of the opinion that rather than sacrifice the national currency on the altar of convenience, the statutory framework should have provided for the taxation of companies in similar situation in the national currency equivalent of what would have been the value in the currency of transaction.[13]

### *Aluminium Industries A. G. v. FBIR*[14]

In the aforementioned case, the appellant entered an agreement with Aluminium Manufacturing Company Limited (a Nigerian company) in Zurich, Switzerland. Part of the terms of the agreement required the latter to repay the principal and interest on a loan entered into in Switzerland to the appellant in Swiss France in Zurich. In the course of assessment for tax, the assessment on the interest became subject to litigation. The Supreme Court held that the arrangement between the appellant and Aluminium Manufacturing Company Limited totally removed the transaction from under the scope of the Companies Income Tax Act 1961[15] where pursuant to Section 17, a company was deemed to be subject to tax in Nigeria, if there was a right to payment of interest in Nigeria.

The arrangement between the appellant and Aluminium Manufacturing Company Limited is a case of avoidance as the parties acted within their right to order their affairs so that the tax attaching under the appropriate Act is less than it otherwise would be. Their arrangement successfully circumvented the provisions of section 17, CITA 1961 which provided that interest was liable to Nigerian tax as interest derived from Nigeria if there is a right to the payment of the tax in Nigeria; or, the interest is by deed or obligation by virtue of any contract which is entered into in Nigeria. Consequently, the interest payment was not subject to Nigerian tax as the right to repayment by virtue of the contract was in Switzerland and the loan contract was not entered into in Nigeria.

The aforementioned case actuated an amendment to CITA 1961 and the amendment has been retained under the extant Companies Income Tax Act Cap C21 Laws of the Federation of Nigeria 2004. Section 9 (2) (a) and (b) of the Act provides that interest shall be deemed to be derived from Nigeria if:

(a) There is a liability to payment of the interest by a Nigerian company or a company in Nigeria regardless of where or in what form the payment is made; or

(b) the interest accrues to a foreign company or person from a Nigerian company or a company in Nigeria regardless of whichever way the interest may have accrued.

### *Stabilini Visinoni Ltd v. FBIR*[16]

This was an appeal against the ruling of the Value Added Tax Tribunal. The question before the appellate court pertained to the question of the constitutionality of the provisions of Section 20, Value Added Tax Act[17] which established the defunct Value Added Tax Tribunal. The appellant's claim was that the aforementioned section radically violates the provisions of section 251 of the Constitution of the Federal Republic of Nigeria, 1999 and prayed the court to dismiss the suit on the ground that the Tribunal lacked jurisdiction to hear the suit. After considering the relevant provisions, the court granted the prayer of the appellant and further held with regards to the constitutionality of the Value Added Tax Act 1993 and the Tribunal's jurisdiction to hear the suit brought before it by the respondent, that section 20, VAT Tribunal Act was inconsistent with the Constitution and was thereby declared null and void.[18] However, by virtue of the provisions of the Federal Inland Revenue Service (Establishment) Act 2007 which abolishes the VAT Tribunal and establishes the Tax Appeal Tribunal (TAT)[19] the legal quandary in which the VAT Tribunal was placed has been addressed.

### *Lagos State Board of Internal Revenue v. Eko Hotels Ltd. & Anor*[20]

This was an appeal to the Court of Appeal from the decision of the Federal High Court. One of the issues for determination was whether the learned judge was right when he held that Value Added Tax Act has covered the field of sales tax and that the plaintiff respondent is a taxable or remitting agent to only the Federal Board of Inland Revenue (the 2nd respondent) in respect of tax on sales to its customers and that it would amount to double taxation to require the 1st respondent to yield to the demands of both 2nd respondent and the appellant at the same time.

The core of the decision of the court was that VAT and sales tax are the same as VAT is ordinarily a national tax on sales of goods and services. With reference to whether the provisions of the VAT Act and Sales Tax Law creates double taxation, the court held in the affirmative as the actual beast of burden of the VAT/sales tax is the consumer and the tax is charged on similar consumable items as defined in the Schedules of both the VAT Act and the Lagos State Sales Law. It affirmed that with respect to VAT collection and remittance, the 1st respondent is an agent only to the 2nd respondent and as such is obligated to collect and remit VAT to same; and that it is not so obligated with reference to the appellant. The court further held that in the circumstances, VAT has covered the field of tax on consumption of the services provided by the 1st respondent. [21]

Value Added Tax is neither on the Exclusive nor Concurrent Legislative Lists contained in the Second Schedule to the 1999 Constitution. This means that VAT is a residual matter. The import of this decision on the Nigerian the tax system is that whereas the House of Assembly of a State may legislate on the residual field, where the National Assembly has already legislated on such an item, then the law passed by the House of Assembly is null and void because the "field" in question has already been "covered." [22]

### *Fast Forward Sports Marketing Ltd v. The Port–Harcourt City Local Government Area Council* [23]

The plaintiff was served with demand notices by agents and officers of the defendants in respect of Agricultural Development Levy for 2008 as well as the Rivers State Board of Internal Revenue for 2008 Economic Development Levy respectively. The plaintiff filed the suit to challenge the action of the defendant after it had been threatened with seizure and/or distrain repeatedly by the latter.

The court in its judgement held *inter alia* that the imposition of the Agricultural Development Levy and Economic Development Levies by the Port Harcourt Local Government Area Council and Rivers State Government on the plaintiff amounts to double taxation. The court also held that the Local Government Council acted outside the scope of Part III Schedule 1 of the *Taxes and Levies (Approved List for Collection) Act.*[24]

The decision of the Federal High Court above represents the proper interpretation of statutory provisions. Tax authorities at all tiers of government must act within the limits of the law. Thus any levy or tax that is outside the powers of the taxing or levying authority is *ultra vires.*

### Lagos State Board of Internal Revenue v. Nigerian Bottling Company & Anor[25]

The facts of the case are that Lagos State Government, acting through the Lagos State Board of Internal Revenue (LSBIR), on December 1, 2000, sent a letter to the Nigerian Bottling Company informing the latter of that the sales tax had been re-introduced in Lagos State and that the rate shall be 5% flat on goods/services produced in or brought into the State. The company failed to collect the requested sales tax. Acting under Section 6 of the Lagos State Sales Tax Law No. 9 of 1982 the LSBIR made an estimate of the sum due from the company as sales tax, plus a 5% penalty assessed on the estimated sum, respectively for the period between December 2000 and May 2001. The Notice of Assessment was served on the company on December 31, 2001. After receiving the Notice of Assessment, the company filed a Notice of Objection on the ground that the legality of the Sale Tax Law was the subject of litigation. In reply, LSBIR served a demand notice for the assessed sum on the company and commenced this action claiming the assessed sum as sales tax arrears, penalty as well as interest.

In its decision, the court followed the decision in *Lagos State Board of Internal Revenue v. Eko Hotels Ltd. & Anor. (supra)* which is to the effect that the defendant is under no obligation to collect additional tax on the sales of its services to its customers in that the VAT has covered the field of tax on consumption of the services provided.

### Marina Nominees Ltd. v. FBIR[26]

The facts of this case are that the appellant - partnership firm - incorporated a company to perform secretariat functions which it hitherto performed in a bid to reduce its tax burden. When the agent company was faced with assessment for tax purposes, the appellant as principal challenged this by claiming that as an agent, the incorporated company was not subject to tax for tasks performed for it. At the Supreme Court, it was held that the using of an incorporated company for the purpose of performing a task does not obviate the fact that the incorporated company is a separate legal entity which must fulfil its own obligation under the law– including the obligation to pay tax.

The device of incorporating a company was clearly a means to avoid tax, as it would mitigate the tax burden of the partnership. To combat the use of the device of limited liability companies for the purpose of tax avoidance, the provisions of Section 19, CITA 2004 empower the revenue authority to deem and/or treat the undistributed profit of a company that is controlled by five persons or less as distributed where its distribution will not be detrimental to the company.

## Commission/Committee Reports

Analyses of the various Fiscal Commissions as well as the various Study Groups on the reform of the tax system have been discussed earlier. The reports of these commissions and committees which were set up by the government at different times provided the basis for new trends and innovations in the system. These recommendations and innovations have also been addressed earlier in this book.

## Budget Speeches

Another instrument of tax policy apart from legislation and commission reports was the budget. This policy tool was especially used by the military regimes. The 1975 budget was broadcast on 31st March 1975 by then Head of the military government, General Yakubu Gowon. The budget speech introduced eight reforms in the tax sector. First, 50 percent of salaries arrears paid to employees in the private sector following the salary increase that was initiated by the government were made tax free as was the case with public servants. Second, the rate of company income tax was reduced from 45 percent to 40 percent "in order to reduce the impact of the recent salaries and wages increases on the private sector and encourage further private investment."[27] In addition, the first 600 naira of any company's profit was exempted from tax in order to encourage small businesses. Third, in order to remove the incidence of double taxation and also encourage investment in shares, shareholders became entitled to relief in respect of tax due on their incomes by way of dividends. Fourth, initial qualifying expenditure was increased from zero to 5 percent and annual allowance from 5 percent to 10 percent in respect of building expenditure as a strategy to encourage investment in housing development. Fifth, the benefits accruing to residents of Lagos under the Income Tax Rent Act were extended to the entire country and the value of eligible property was raised from 50,000 naira to 100,000 naira. Sixth, the rate of contribution to the Industrial Training Fund was reduced from 2 percent to 1 percent as an additional means of reducing costs and expenses in the economy. Seventh, the application of the capital gains tax which had hitherto applied to only Lagos was extended to cover the federation and non-residents. The then Federal Board of Inland Revenue was entrusted with capital gains tax accruing from non-residents while state tax authorities were entrusted with capital tax gains accruing from residents. Finally, the *jangali* tax was abolished 'in principle' to 'bring some relief to the Fulani cattle owner on his capital and encourage him to keep his cattle within the country'.[28]

In the 1976-1977 budget, the federal military government again increased the rate of corporate tax to 45 percent on profits of companies in excess of 6000 naira. The then Head of State, General Olusegun Obasanjo, argued that the earlier reduction was to minimize the impact of the increase in wages at the time and that purpose having been served, the necessity for the reduction was no longer there.[29] Second, the budget tagged the maximum period for which unabsorbed losses could be carried forward at four years. Decree No. 47 of 1972 which allowed companies to claim such losses incurred in the preceding year of assessment did not specify the limit as to the number of years such losses could be carried forward. Finally, and maybe most importantly, the budget broadcast introduced the use of Tax Clearance Certificates (TCC). TCCs were to be introduced and reflected in the capital gains tax decree, making their presentation obligatory before the commissioner of stamp duties could accept documents for stamping and registration. Since its introduction, the production of TCC has become a major precondition for several transactions.

In the 1977-78 budget, three policy planks regarding taxation were introduced. First, the government introduced a turn-over tax at the rate of two and half percent in the construction and building industry as an alternative to profit tax. This was to correct the situation where companies in the sector were paying no income taxes despite an obvious boom in the industry. In the sphere of personal income tax, personal allowance fixed at 600 naira was extended to one-tenth of earned incomes while dependent relative allowance remained at 400 naira and was granted to any person who had an income in his own right. In view of these concessions, the rate of tax on chargeable incomes was supposedly increased without the broadcast stating the new rates. Lastly, state governments were required to 'institute stringent corrective and penal measures in the new year, to reduce the incidence of tax evasion' among wealthy businessmen and self-employed professionals.

The 1978-79 budget emphasized a great deal on the need to increase revenue generation and the tax measures that were introduced reflected this emphasis. Import and excise duties were raised, a port development surcharge which was introduced during the civil war as a wartime effort was re-introduced to sustain government port development efforts. In addition, companies income tax rate was increased from 45 percent to 50 percent and to curb the incidence of late payment by companies, companies were required to pay provisional tax within thirty days of declaring interim dividends on the understanding that excess payment would be refunded at the end of the assessment year. Further, companies were required to prepare provisional accounts not later than three months after the end of the accounting year and make advance payments to the revenue department on the basis of the un-audited accounts by a process of self assessment within thirty days. Where applicable, amended assessments were to be made when final and audited accounts were prepared and submitted to the Federal Inland Revenue Department. Other strategies towards enhancing tax revenues included the introduction of tolls on major highways and bridges, introduction of airport tax and the requirement of TCC as a pre-requisite for doing business with government. The 1979-1980 budget broadcast announced the promulgation of the capital transfer tax decree. Outside this, not much was contained by way of tax policy.

## Treaties and Agreements

Beginning from the era of Colonial Ordinances, the various income tax laws have always contained provisions enabling a named official of the government to enter into treaties and/or agreements with foreign governments/entities as well as make such regulations as are necessary to give effect to the treaties and/or agreements. The considerations for entering into a treaty relationship are determined by the general economic objectives of the State. A state that is desirous of attracting foreign investment seeks to remove all forms of restrictions and disincentives to business. One major policy instrument in this regard is the use of avoidance of double taxation agreements, simply referred to as double taxation agreements or DTAs.

DTAs are reciprocal arrangement whereby two countries agree not to tax the income of individuals or companies brought or received into their territory if such individual or company had already paid tax on such income in the other country. They are tools which foster and encourage international trade and commerce as they are geared towards reducing the cost of doing business across State borders. During the colonial era, these agreements were concluded on behalf of Nigeria by Britain. Between 1950 and 1956, DTAs were signed between Nigeria and the following countries: Ghana (1950), Sierra Leone (1950), the Gambia (1950), New Zealand (1951), Sweden (1954), Denmark (1955) and Norway (1956). All these agreements were repealed by the Federal Military Government on 25 April 1978.[30] From 1987 to 2000 Nigeria signed comprehensive avoidance of double taxation agreements with the United Kingdom, France, the Netherlands, Belgium, Canada, Pakistan, Romania, South Africa and China.

## The Nigerian National Tax Policy

The 2002 Study Group on the Nigerian tax system identified the need for a National Tax Policy to redress the imbalances and shortcomings in the Nigerian tax system; a National Tax Policy hinged principally on the foundation of fostering national development. Such a policy was envisaged to:

a. Serve as a means of attracting foreign direct investment;

b. Consolidate several documents into a single document for easy reference;

c. Blend various opinions on taxes of different kinds, as well as the issues surrounding those opinions; and

d. Provide direction and focus on general tax practice.[31]

A Presidential Committee was inaugurated in July 2005 to drive the harmonised recommendations of the Study and Working Groups on the development of a National Tax Policy. The Committee appointed a Technical Sub-Committee on the National Tax Policy and charged it with the responsibility of developing the background policy document. The Technical Committee made sensitization visits to the six geopolitical zones of the country to seek input and opinions from various stakeholders, as well as to receive feedback, and secure trust and understanding. In 2010, the final draft of the National Tax Policy was submitted to the Federal Executive Council. While the draft incorporated input from various stakeholders, the fundamentals of the draft were based on the harmonized report of the Study Group and Working Groups. The Federal Executive Council adopted the National Tax Policy on 20 January 2010.

## Guiding Principles of the National Tax Policy

The underlying philosophy of the National Tax Policy and the new tax system envisioned to arise from the implementation of the policy is the promotion of sustainable development, as well as healthy competition among tax and revenue authorities in Nigeria. The National Tax Policy will uphold the principles of fiscal federalism in revenue generation and expenditure at all levels of government, within the ambits of the Nigerian Constitution. In simple terms, it will resolve issues surrounding *"who gets what, how it is collected, who controls what is collected and who is ultimately responsible for and accountable to the taxpayers for the revenue collected and its expenditure.'*[82] The three tiers of Government have different powers spelt out in the Fourth Schedule of the 1999 Constitution of Nigeria. State Governments of the Federation, through the Houses of Assembly, can exercise the power of imposing fees, levies and rates collectable by them and the Local Governments in the respective States; this is in addition to the personal income tax they are constitutionally charged with collecting.

The National Tax Policy also spells out the desired features which any form of tax must adhere to before it becomes an acceptable component of the Nigerian tax system. The features are:

a. *Simplicity, Certainty and Clarity*: The underachievement of the Nigerian tax system has been largely blamed on the seeming complexity of tax laws and the inability of the average taxpayer to understand them. Taxes must be understood by all; the relevant laws must be consistent and clear such that stakeholders must understand the basis of imposition.

b. *Low Compliance Cost*: This places the taxpayers' interest at a high position of prominence in that taxpayers shall be accorded the entitlement of enjoying the minimum cost of compliance possible.

c. *Low Cost of Administration*: This is in line with ensuring the efficiency of the Nigerian tax system. The National Tax Policy advocates for thorough cost-benefit analysis before taxes are imposed on Nigerians.

d.  *Fairness:* The Nigerian tax system shall seek to objectively apply horizontal and vertical equity to taxpayers. In as much as tax concessions are offered to certain sectors of the economy, the tax system will, as much as is practicable, make them general and across board.

e.  *Flexibility:* The Nigerian tax system will be run in a way and manner that will make it responsive to changes in the local and international environment; the introduction of new taxes and the review of existing taxes will ensure such flexibility. The process of adjustments will be designed such that there will be no difficulty in the process.

f.  *Economic Efficiency:* This will ensure that tax rates are not a disincentive to taxpayers to save and invest.

## Objectives of the National Tax Policy

The National Tax Policy identifies the objectives of the Nigerian tax system as follows:

a.  The promotion of fiscal responsibility and accountability;

b.  The facilitation of economic growth and development;

c.  The provision of stable resources to the Government (which in turn uses it for the provision of public goods to the citizenry);

d.  The adjustment of income distribution inequalities;

e.  The stabilization of the Nigerian economy; and

f.  The correction of market failures and imperfections

## Categories and Roles of Stakeholders under the National Tax Policy

### The Executive Arm

The National Tax Policy states that the requisite leadership and direction required to push Nigeria's tax system and the revenue agencies (such as the FIRS) in the desired direction will be provided by the Presidency. The Presidency is also responsible for signing and implementing all regional and international tax treaties entered into by Nigeria. At the State level, State Governors play roles akin to those played by the Presidency at the Federal level.

They are expected to develop State tax policies which will be complimentary to the National Tax Policy. In addition, State Governors are expected to perform the following functions as spelt out by the National Tax Policy:

a.  enforce Federal and State tax laws in their states;

b.  carry out general oversight functions on tax and revenue authorities at State and Local Government levels;

c.  provide guidance and direction to the State Ministries of Finance, the States' Boards of Internal Revenue and other agencies involved in tax administration in the States;

d.  ensure cooperation among the States' Boards of Internal Revenue, the Federal Inland Revenue Service, the Nigerian Customs Service and other revenue agencies in the adoption of a nationwide Unique Taxpayer Identification Number (U-TIN) system, as well as information sharing and elimination of multiple taxes;

e.  provide advice to the Federal agencies and bodies responsible for tax policy, legislation and administration in Nigeria

At the Local Government level, Local Government Chairmen as Chief Executives shoulder the responsibility of implementing and enforcing tax laws, as well as ensuring the availability of adequate and appropriate manpower for tax revenue authorities at their level of government.

### The National Council of States and the National Economic Council

The National Council of States is comprised of former Presidents, Chief Justices of the Federation, serving State Governors, the President of the Senate and the Speaker of the House of Representatives. Constitutionally, the National Council of States is not specifically mandated to advise the President on tax matters; however, the Constitution provides that the Council may advise the President on matters which he may so direct and tax may well be one of those matters. The National Economic Council is a creation of the Nigerian Constitution which is charged with the responsibility of offering advice to the President on issues regarding economic matters. Taxation is a component part of the economy and the Council's purview includes making input to the President on tax affairs in Nigeria.

### *The Federal Executive Council, Federal Ministries of Finance, Education and Information*

As the highest decision-making body at the federal tier of government, the Federal Executive Council is charged with responsibility of approving all matters which will ensure the effective oversight of tax policy and administration in Nigeria. The National Tax Policy envisages that one of the measures by which voluntary compliance by taxpayers can be guaranteed is the full disclosure of all sources of income by the members of the Federal Executive Council; the determination of the correct taxes payable by them on those incomes; and the subsequent publication of the tax clearance certificates of members by the 30th of June of every year. The Federal Executive Council shall also ensure transparency and accountability in the utilization of tax generated and keep taxpayers informed on expenditure patterns of tax revenue on a regular basis. Furthermore, the President as Chairman of the Federal Executive Council is charged with the task of assenting to tax legislations passed by the Legislature and should be at the forefront of maintaining a cordial, respectful relationship with the judicial arm of government that does not impugn in any way the independence, objectivity and integrity of the Judiciary.

The Federal Ministries, Departments and Agencies of the Federation are expected to do all they can within their purview to assist in the development of the Nigerian tax system, such as cooperating with the Federal Executive Council and sharing information necessary for improved tax assessment and collection. Technology has a place of pride in the National Tax Policy in that Ministries, Departments and Agencies are required to maintain a database which makes allowance for the inclusion of the Unique Taxpayer Identification Number of every individual, company or enterprise with which they have dealings. The National Tax Policy also advocates the use of electronic payment systems by Ministries, Departments and Agencies to directly remit taxes to the relevant accounts of Federal and States' tax authorities. Transactions entered into by the Ministries, Departments and Agencies which require Tax Clearance Certificates and requisite tax documents should be ratified only after the aforementioned tax documents have been authenticated by the relevant tax authorities. The Policy states that *"tax should be a major consideration in the evaluation process of individuals and organizations such that the lack of payment of taxes is seen as an affront on government and a crime."*

The Federal Ministry of Finance is particularly important in the tax administration system in Nigeria. It is responsible for proposals for amendments of Nigerian tax laws by the National Assembly. The permission of the Federal Ministry of Finance is also necessary and must be sought by other Federal Ministries or Agencies before executing agreements, letters or any document touching on issues of fiscal policy. The Federal Inland Revenue Service supports the Federal Ministry of Finance on tax policy issues, and vice versa.

The Federal Ministries of Education and Information are expected to also provide support to the Federal Ministry of Finance, especially in the areas of taxpayer education and public enlightenment. The Federal Ministry of Education is expected to incorporate tax education in the curricula of institutions in the Nigerian educational system, using the "cradle to grave" concept of taxpayer education, thus entrenching a tax culture in the psyche of every Nigerian at an early age. On its part, the Federal Ministry of Information is charged by the National Tax Policy to regularly implement public enlightenment campaigns on issues revolving around tax and government revenue and expenditure.

## The State Executive Councils and the State Ministries of Education and Information

The State Executive Councils are the equivalents of the Federal Executive Councils at the State level, playing very similar roles at the State tier of government in Nigeria. The development of tax policies, implementation and enforcement of taxes at the State and Local Government level is the responsibility of the State Executive Council. The State Ministry of Finance is responsible for issues of tax policy at the State level. It initiates amendments to tax laws through applications to the National Assembly and the State's House of Assembly, depending on the purview of the proposed amendments. States' Ministries of Finance are enjoined by the National Tax Policy to cooperate with the Federal Inland Revenue Service, States' Boards of Internal Revenue and other tax revenue authorities to ensure there is transparency in the collection and utilization of tax. States Ministries of Information and Education are enjoined to replicate at the State level the role envisaged for their federal counterparts.

## Local Government Councils

The Fourth Schedule of the 1999 Constitution states that the Local Government is the body in charge of collecting taxes and other revenue at the Local Government Level. The

Local Government Councils may also perform other functions assigned to them by the States' Houses of Assembly. The Local Government Councils are expected to carry out the following functions as well:

a. The strict implementation of tax laws and the incorporation of tax in the everyday business of Government;

b. Ensure proper assessment, collection and prompt remittance of taxes to designated government accounts;

c. Ensure the maintenance of a database of taxpayers and incorporate into the said database the Unique Taxpayer Identification Number for every individual, company and registered body under their jurisdiction;

d. The authentication of Tax Clearance Certificates and relevant tax documents used in the daily conduct of Government business by referral back to the relevant tax authority;

e. The use of the electronic payment system to ensure direct remittance of tax revenue to the appropriate accounts of the tax authorities.

## The Legislature

The legislative arm of government is charged with the responsibility of enacting and amending laws. The National Assembly and State Houses of Assembly are therefore assigned prominent and important roles in tax legislation. Section 4 of the Nigerian Constitution empowers the National Assembly to enact and amend laws relating to taxation of income or profits, after duly considering the input and recommendations of other stakeholders such as the Federal Ministry of Finance, other Ministries, Departments and Agencies and citizens of the country. One of the key functions of the National Assembly is to work in tandem with the Federal Executive Council for the effective translation of tax policy recommendations to tax laws. The National Tax Policy recommends that the National Assembly should be responsible for requesting for input from members of the general public with regard to issues of tax policy recommendations and tax legislations, in furtherance of the Assembly's duty as the collection of elected representatives of all Nigerians.

The States' Houses of Assembly are responsible for translating tax policies to legislation that will enhance the ability of Local Governments to effectively collect taxes, rates, fees and levies and other collectible charges. States' legislatures are also responsible for tax laws that are within the legislative competence of the States as contained in the Constitution.

## The Judiciary

The Judiciary interprets tax laws and also adjudicates on tax matters. In order to ensure its effective contribution to the Nigerian tax system, the National Tax Policy recommends that the personnel of that arm of government are regularly kept informed of current developments in tax affairs in Nigeria so that they can adjudicate appropriately and fairly on matters brought before them for adjudication.

## Tax Authorities

Tax authorities include the Federal Inland Revenue Service and the States' Boards of Internal Revenue. In addition to their primary statutory function of administering taxes, they also proffer advice to the Government on tax related matters. Tax authorities are expected to maintain good relationships with the other stakeholders in the tax system such as the legislature, furnishing that arm of government with the requisite information it needs to carry out its oversight functions on the Nigerian tax system. Tax authorities are also expected to educate the public on tax matters.

The National Tax Policy advocates that tax authorities should carry out their core functions efficiently and effectively; functions such as tax assessment and collection must be performed by career tax administrators instead of contracting consultants to exercise these functions. The National Tax Policy encourages fairness in the relationship between the tax authorities and the taxpayers; the former should accord the latter respect and allow them sufficient time and space to review, challenge and appeal every tax assessment or demand made by the tax authorities.

## The Joint Tax Board

The Joint Tax Board (JTB), a creation of the Personal Income Tax Act, provides a platform for federal revenue authorities and States' tax authorities on the administration of personal income tax. In the National Tax Policy, the JTB is also charged with the following functions:

a.  The harmonization of tax processes and administration in Nigeria;

b.  The provision of technical assistance and support to tax authorities;

c.  The co-ordination of the nationwide introduction of the Unique Taxpayer Identification Number and other initiatives which may be introduced with time; and

d.  The formation of standard processes and procedures for the activities of tax authorities.

## Taxpayers

Taxpayers are recognised by the National Tax Policy as the most important group of stakeholders in the Nigerian tax system. Voluntary compliance on the part of taxpayers is one of the key focuses of the Policy with respect to taxpayers. Taxpayers are also expected to act in an informal supervisory role by ensuring that there is transparency and accountability in the collection, allocation, disbursement and expenditure of tax revenue. Taxpayers are also expected to perform the following functions:

a.  Assist tax authorities by furnishing them with all necessary information needed to improve the Nigerian tax system, or any such assistance that will enhance the performance of tax authorities;

b.  Make input in tax policy formulation and tax legislation;

c.  Submit disputes with tax authorities to the Judiciary for adjudication thereby contributing to the development of Nigerian tax jurisprudence; and

d.  Cooperate with the other stakeholders in the tax system

The National Tax Policy also encourages the regular organization of various forums whereby taxpayers, tax authorities and other stakeholders in the Nigerian tax system regularly interact and exchange ideas and suggestions about how to promote the development of tax administration and practice in the country.

## Professional Bodies, Tax Practitioners and Consultants

The roles of professional bodies in the Nigerian tax system are statutorily enshrined in the various enactments setting them up. The Chartered Institute of Taxation of Nigeria (CITN) is empowered to determine the standards, knowledge and skill a tax practitioner must attain before entering into public practice; the CITN also maintains a register of qualified members in furtherance with its responsibility of regulating and controlling tax practice. Tax practitioners and consultants are expected to do all within their abilities to ensure there is simplification of the tax process so that the level of compliance will increase; they are expected not to be parties to non-compliance with tax laws.

## Key Economic Thrusts of the National Tax Policy

The National Tax Policy places great premium on the importance of tax as a tool for national economic development. Against this background, the Policy projects that tax shall be used for the following:

a. Stimulating the growth of the Nigerian economy by using tax revenues to develop basic infrastructure such as power, roads, transportation and other such infrastructure which will stimulate economic growth;

b. Direct stimulation of certain sectors of the economy which are identified to be important for the creation of employment opportunities for Nigerians;

c. Regulating and strengthening financial and economic structures and for correcting market imbalances and economic distortions;

d. Income redistribution such that tax earned from high income earners is used for the provision of infrastructure for the lowest income earners. Taxes shall act as a means to create a social security net for *"short and long term relief to indigent members of society and other classes of persons who may require such intervention by the Government;"*[83] and

e. Stimulating domestic and foreign investment.

In order for the aforementioned objectives of the National Tax Policy to be achieved, variations in tax rates may be inevitable with the passage of time. In recognition of this point, the Policy recognises that the National Assembly is the arm of government statutorily empowered by the Constitution to vary tax rates. For instance, the Policy recognises that in order for the cost of business in Nigeria to be reduced, income tax rates should be reduced to increase the cash flow of individuals and corporate citizens. The Policy however recommends that tax reliefs and allowances relating to income taxes should be delegated to the Minister of Finance for easy administration.

In order to make up for the shortfall in revenue envisaged by the reduction of income tax rates, the National Tax Policy envisages occasional upward reviews of indirect tax rates The Policy further specifies certain special arrangements which may deviate from established structures of the Nigerian tax system as currently constituted in order to attract and retain investments in the country. Examples of such arrangements are as follows:

a.  The creation of Tax Free Zones in order to foster increased investment, growth and development in certain aspects of the economy or certain economic activities. The Policy specifies that the Tax Free Zones must be set up and administered by strictly following guiding legislations on such matters. The status and benefits of Tax Free Zones are to be subject to constant periodic review and the Government has the prerogative of discontinuing such arrangements if and when they are no more of any obvious advantage to the Nigerian economy.

b.  The provision of tax incentives to specific sectors or activities in the Nigerian tax system to encourage their growth and development. The granting of waivers must be transparently done and applied across board in the sectors where they are granted. The Ministry of Finance and the Ministry of Justice at the Federal and State levels are charged by the National Tax Policy to ensure that there is issuance and gazetting of the applicable Orders which specify the incentives, waivers or concessions granted. The incentives will be aimed at encouraging investment, especially in the non-oil and gas sector. Tax incentives are also to be subject to regular review to determine their usefulness.

c.  The expansion of Nigeria's international treaty network so as to encourage foreign direct investment. These treaties address issues such as double taxation, residency and information sharing which is necessary to forestall tax evasion by companies and individuals. The Federal Ministry of Finance and the Federal Ministry of Foreign Affairs are empowered to negotiate such treaties while the JTB is to play an advisory role in such negotiations. Ratification by the relevant arm of the Nigerian Government, as well as cancellation if and when such treaties are no longer beneficial to the economy shall be done within the ambit of Nigerian laws.

d.  Entering into Production Sharing Contracts or similar arrangements which provide a more favourable tax burden for companies operating in the oil and gas sector, thus leading to greater cash flows for oil and gas companies and overall, a much more favourable environment in which oil and gas companies may operate and invest even more to further develop the sector.

## The National Tax Policy and Tax Administration

A tax policy can only be described as successful when it leads to effective tax administration. The National Tax Policy recognises that sufficient and accurate information is the major requirement needed for effective and efficient tax administration which is not always voluntarily provided by taxpayers, a situation not in any way peculiar to Nigeria. The Policy enjoins the tax authorities in the country to develop internal competencies for information and intelligence gathering, as well as active collaborations with law enforcement agencies, data gathering agencies, or any such agencies which may be in the position to furnish them with the relevant information needed to enable the tax authorities adequately perform their statutory functions. Although the U-TIN system is expected to facilitate easier identification and monitoring of taxpayers, the Policy recommends that taxpayers be educated on intelligence and information gathering methods used by tax authorities, methods which are expected to protect the privacy of the taxpayers and to be in conformity with constitutional requirements. Specifically, the National Tax Policy makes provisions on the aspects of tax administration discussed below.

### *Filing Returns, Payment and Collection*

Tax collection completes a chain of processes which is set in motion by the filing of self-assessment returns by the taxpayer. In order to ensure the efficiency of tax administration, tax authorities are required to educate and enlighten taxpayers on the filing and returns process. This will avail tax authorities time and resources to enforce compliance on recalcitrant taxpayers. The Policy further enjoins tax administrators to:

a. ensure simplicity and transparency in the filing of self assessment returns; and

b. introduce and sustain the use of technology in for its key processes

## Tax Audit, Investigation, and Enforcement Mechanisms

The audit and investigation aspect of tax administration seeks to verify the tax status of the taxpayers and to ascertain the completeness and accuracy of tax returns filed by taxpayers. In order to get a proper perspective on the taxpayer's status, it is imperative that audits are carried out regularly and within a reasonable period. The National Tax Policy recommends the use of electronic/technological and related means in the audit process. Tax audit and tax investigations involve similar processes, but they differ in the sense that the latter process is a lot more rigorous and could culminate in the prosecution of taxpayers found to be in default. The tax authorities are expected to carry out both processes openly and fairly so as to allow taxpayers ample opportunity to supply necessary and relevant information which will facilitate efficient audit and investigation of the taxpayers' records.

Leakages occasioned by tax evasion and avoidance may be plugged by:

   a. strengthening the criminal prosecution process

   b. collaboration among tax authorities at all levels of government;

   c. taxpayer education and enlightenment;

   d. capacity building of tax officers to increase skills and competencies

   e. automation of key processes in order to eliminate or reduce  human errors and fraud

   f. identification of existing and potential loopholes in tax laws to reduce tax avoidance

   g. devising appropriate sanctions to dissuade defaulters or offenders from evading tax

The National Tax Policy recommends reward for taxpayers who duly comply with tax laws, especially publicized rewards which encourage other taxpayers to do likewise.

## Tax Refund Operation and Funding

The tax refund part of tax administration helps to ensure that taxpayers who pay excess taxes have the excess refunded. The National Tax Policy recommends that the first step in the refund process is that taxpayers must first establish genuine cases of overpayment. After the relevant tax authority has rigorously, fairly and objectively verified the claims, genuine refunds should be done within ninety days from the day the claim is established.

Information on any reasons for delay should be readily made available to the taxpayer. The National Tax Policy recommends that tax authorities set aside a certain percentage of their total annual collection for tax refund purposes. The amounts set aside for meeting those obligations must be appropriated in the annual estimates by the National Assembly or State Assembly. Unspent funds from such appropriated funds are expected to be returned to the relevant tier of government.

## Tax Revenue Accounting

The National Tax Policy recognises that for taxpayers to be inspired to place a high level of confidence in the tax administration system of the country, tax authorities are responsible for giving proper, timely and complete account of tax revenue collected within given accounting periods. Not only is this expected to inspire confidence in the taxpayers regarding the tax administration process, it will also help the prevention of tax leakages. Leakages are more easily identified within the context of a transparent system. Tax authorities are expected to publish collection figures such that they are available to the general public and all stakeholders in the tax system, in addition to being made available to the Ministry of Finance and the Accountant General's Office.

## Dispute Resolution Mechanisms

The National Tax Policy prescribes a number of ways by which such disputes can be resolved, taking into cognisance the role and status of the various stakeholders in the whole system.

*Disputes between the Federal and State Governments*[34]: while recognizing the extant constitutional provision which requires disputes between Federal and State Governments to be resolved by the adjudication of the Supreme Court, the Policy advocates alternative dispute resolution methods before the parties resort to litigation at the Supreme Court. The Policy recommends deliberations between the parties under the auspices of different platforms including the Nigeria Governors' Forum, the National Economic Council, the Federal Executive Council, and the Council of States meetings. Where deliberations at any or all of these fora fail, the Policy recommends mediation by the other State Governments or Federal Government Agencies or by other arms of Government such as the Judiciary. Mediation by the Judiciary must be done in a manner that does not impugn on the independence and the impartiality of the Judiciary, especially if it appears likely that such dispute may finally be resolved through judicial adjudication.

*Disputes between State Governments*[35]*:* The Supreme Court is also saddled with the responsibility of adjudicating on disputes between State Governments. The Policy recommends the same methods of alternative dispute resolution above in the event of disagreement between States. In addition to methods above, deliberations could also be held by the Attorneys General of Finance Commissioners or other relevant officials of the States involved.

*Disputes between State and Local Governments:* The States and Local Governments have closely interlinked functions such that the National Tax Policy advocates more of informal dispute resolution methods, instead of quick resort to litigation which may lead to *"dislocation and distraction to governance which such disputes may trigger."*[86] Such arbitrators as traditional rulers, State and Local Government organs and other stakeholders may intervene to resolve the disputes. The failure of these informal procedures may then give way to judicial adjudication.

*Disputes between the Executive and the Legislature:* The National Tax Policy also advocates the initial use of arbitration channels such as traditional rulers, relevant officials, and relevant institutions of State such as the Federal and State Executive Councils, the Council of State, the National Economic Council before resorting to litigation.[37] The Executive and the Legislature may also explore the options of using liaison officers and organs of the Judiciary such as the National Judicial Council. Judicial adjudication should be the last resort.

*Disputes amongst and between the Executive, Legislature and the Judiciary:* The National Tax Policy recommends that such disputes be resolved discreetly and amicably through informal channels to prevent undermining the integrity, impartiality and independence of the Judiciary which is likely to be required to resolve the disputes between and amongst the other arms of Government.[38]

*Disputes with Taxpayers:* Taxpayers are constitutionally empowered to seek judicial remedy to disputes in which they have a stake. Taxpayers are therefore entitled to explore the Tax Appeal process if and when they are dissatisfied with the decisions of any tax authority relating to the taxpayers status. They may also explore the same option with regard to the interpretation/application of tax laws and other matters which may affect the rights and status of the taxpayer. Tax authorities are expected to enlighten taxpayers on the tax appeal process and are responsible for informing taxpayers, individual or corporate, of their right to tax appeal. Tax authorities may also engage taxpayers so as to collaborate with them on alternative dispute resolution of such contentious issues.

## Implementation of the National Tax Policy

Appendix 2 to the National Tax Policy highlights the strategies to be adopted to ensure the success of the policy and the creation of a tax system in Nigeria which will lead to the economic development and advancement of the country. The tax strategy has been devised to suit Nigeria's economic situation. Some of the strategies include:

*Lowering the Tax Rates:* The reduction in income tax rates is aimed at increasing the disposable income of individual taxpayers and after tax profits of corporate taxpayers. This is a strategy to attract foreign direct investment into the country by creating competitive advantage in Nigeria's favour.

*Deliberate Policy Shift towards Indirect Taxation:* Following the recommendations of the Study Group and the Working Group, the National Tax Policy endorses the policy shift of changing focus from direct taxation to indirect taxation. However, the Tax Policy specifies that indirect taxes such as value added tax should not be levied on essential goods and services. This will necessitate the expansion of VAT exempt or zero-rated goods and services.

*Simplification of Tax Laws:* As explained previously, simplified tax laws will reduce administrative costs incurred by (especially corporate) taxpayers in complying with tax laws.

*Granting Tax Holidays or Pioneer Status to Taxpayers:* The National Tax Policy encourages the granting of tax incentives to taxpayers only when such incentives will be beneficial to the Nigerian economy. They may be granted to sectors of the economy which the Government wishes to give priority and should be granted when there is an outstanding reason to implement such tax reliefs. Such key economic sectors identified by the Government are energy, mining, railways/roads, education, health, aviation, exports and agriculture.

*Creation of Export Processing Zones (EPZs):* One of Nigeria's economic goals is to transform the national economy to an export-oriented economy, especially to reduce Nigeria's international trade deficit and trade imbalance. The National Tax Policy recommends that:

a. Companies which operate in EPZs should continue to be exempt from income taxes, provided that 100% of the goods produced in the zones are meant for export. Exports from the EPZs into Nigeria which is Customs Territory shall attract the appropriate duty on imported raw materials.

b. Value added tax on goods produced in EPZs should be zero-rated.

c. All companies located within EPZs should continue to file returns to EPZ authorities even though no tax is payable.

d. Exemptions from import and export levies and taxes should continue to apply within the EPZs, except where the entities transact business outside the EPZ.

e. The various provisions of relevant legislation pertaining to percentages of EPZ production allowed into the country should be retained. However, any entity located in an EPZ which sells to the domestic market should be made to pay tax on the profit realised from sales outside the EPZ.

The main aim of the above recommendations is to ensure that only companies with the intention to produce goods for export are located within the EPZs. This will make away with the practice where some companies seek to be located at EPZs only to take full advantage of the liberal tax regime.

*Reduction of Import and Excise Duties:* The National Tax Policy explains that reducing import and excise duties to zero percent will present to Nigerian manufacturers a great opportunity to produce intermediate and finished goods. Reductions in the import and excise duties must be done such that they do not contravene the conditions of international trade agreements entered into or ratified by the Government of Nigeria.

*Strengthening Nigeria's Oil and Tax Regime:* The National Tax Policy recommends regular information sharing between tax collection agencies and agencies charged with the administration of the Nigerian oil and gas sector; agencies such as the Nigerian National Petroleum Corporation, the FIRS, the National Petroleum Investment Management Services (NAPIMS) and the Directorate of Petroleum Resources (DPR) are enjoined to share information regularly to optimise oil and gas revenues and tax compliance in the industry.

Steps are also expected to be taken to codify all regulations and orders applicable in the oil and gas sector.

*Use of Presumptive Income Tax Assessment Procedure:* This is intended to tackle the non-compliance of taxable persons who have failed to comply with tax laws as a result of their lack of fixed business addresses or size. The Presumptive Income Tax Assessment procedure is a simplified and quick method of assessing taxpayers.

*Elimination of Multiple Taxes:* Intensive taxpayer education is expected to reduce the incidence of multiple taxes, coupled with the implementation of the U-TIN system.

*Improving the Existing Relationship between the FIRS and Large Taxpayers:* The LTOs are mainly specialised in tax collection matters related to taxpayers with an annual turnover of at least one billion Naira. These relationships can be boosted to ensure maximum compliance by the large taxpayers.

*Implementation of a Value-Added Tax (VAT) Threshold:* In order to determine and improve the administration of VAT in Nigeria, the National Tax Policy proposes the determination of a given threshold for the annual turnover of companies such that companies with a turnover over and above the threshold are obligated to charge and/or remit VAT. Conversely, companies with a turnover below the threshold are not obligated to charge and/or remit VAT. Such threshold should be fixed by the FIRS.

*The Institutionalisation of a Tax Culture in Nigeria:* The average Nigerian citizen needs to be made tax conscious so that they cooperate fully with the Government. Nigerians have to be enlightened constantly about the benefits of complying with tax laws. Tax authorities and educational institutions are expected to play key roles in taxpayer education. Educational institutions are expected to encourage the development of taxation as a course of study at all levels of the Nigerian educational system; scholarships and incentives such as employment opportunities should be granted to students who specialise in the area of taxation. Professional taxation bodies which exist in the Nigeria should be strengthened and more created to ensure improvements in the Nigerian tax system.

*Granting Autonomy to Tax Authorities:* In order to perform at optimal level, tax authorities must be free from political and other influences which threaten their independence and objectivity.

The National Tax Policy enjoins governments at all levels to implement the strategies discussed above to ensure the successful implementation of the policy. The strategies can be better implemented by the passage of the necessary tax legislations which will give constitutional and statutory backing to the implementation of the National Tax Policy.

## References

1   See for instance, the Finance (Miscellaneous Taxation Provisions) Decree No. 30 1999. The decree singly amended the Companies Income Tax Act, Personal Income Tax Act, Petroleum Profits Tax Act and the Value Added Tax Act.

2   Decree No. 30 of 1966.

3   Decree No. 32 of 1966.

4   Long title to the Income Tax (Rents) Act 1963.

5   Decree No. 22 1971, now deemed an Act of the National Assembly. This decree was preceded by the Aid to Pioneer Industries Ordinance 1952.

6   Which pursuant to section 315, Constitution of the Federal Republic of Nigeria, 1999 is deemed an Act of the National Assembly and is retained as Cap I7 LFN 2004.

7   See section 10, Industrial Development (Income Tax Relief) Decree 1971

8   [1996] 8 NWLR 256

9   (1936) 2 All ER 793

10  Kanyip, B. B oral interview with Ben Pever 27/10/2011

11  Cap P13 LFN 2004

12  Cap C21 LFN 2004

13  Kanyip, Op. cit

14  (1971) NMLR 339

15  Hereafter referred to as CITA 1961.

16  (2009) I TLRN 1

17  Cap. V1 LFN 2004

18  *Ibid,* 22 – 23

19  This is pursuant to section 59, FIRSEA.

20  [2008] All FWLR (Pt. 398) 235

21  *Ibid,* 222 – 223.

22    Section 4 (5) Constitution of the Federal Republic of Nigeria

23    (2011) 4 TLRN 45.

24    Cap. T2 LFN 2004

25    Suit No. ID/454/2002 (Unreported), judgment of the High Court of Lagos State (Ikeja Division) delivered by Hon. Justice O. H. Oshodi on 18 June 2009

26    [1986] 2 NWLR (Pt. 20) 48

27    Broadcast on the 1975 - 76 Budget, page xiii.

28    *Ibid*, page xiv.

29    Broadcast on the 1976 - 77 Budget, page xvi.

30    Ochei, B., *The Nigerian Taxman's Book II* (Lagos: Pyramid Unit Publishers, 2010)

31    *Ibid*.

32    *Ibid*, Chapter 2 paragraph 2.4.

**33**    Chapter 4 paragraph 4.1.

34    *Ibid*, Chapter 6, paragraph 6.1.

35    *Ibid*, Chapter 6, paragraph 6.2.

36    *Ibid*, Chapter 6 paragraph 6.3.

37    *Ibid*, Chapter 6, paragraph 6.4.

38    *Ibid*, Chapter 6, paragraph 6.5 .

# CHAPTER SEVEN

## BEYOND OIL REVENUE: THE CASE FOR TAX REFORM

### Background

The Nigerian economy was largely dependent on agro-products before oil was discovered in commercial quantities in the latter part of the 1950s. The country's major exchange earnings at the time came from cash crops such as cocoa, rubber, palm oil, cotton and groundnuts. Although mining activities such as coal in Enugu and tin and columbite in Jos contributed to foreign earnings, agriculture remained the bulwark of the economy; accounting for about 90 percent of foreign earnings and 70 percent of GDP.[1] In 1956, Shell Petroleum discovered oil in commercial quantities at Oloibiri in Nigeria's Niger delta region. By 1971, the oil production in Nigeria had grown so much that the country became the world's seventh largest producer of petroleum. It was in the same year that Nigeria joined the Organisation of Petroleum Exporting Countries, OPEC.[2] In 1974, there was a dramatic rise in world oil prices leading to unprecedented inflow of oil revenue in what commentators refer to as Nigeria's oil boom period. The oil boom impacted on the role of agriculture in the economy in severely negative ways. First, the search for wage-paying jobs led to a massive wave of rural-to-urban migration by people within the productive age circle resulting in loss of farm labour in the rural areas. Second, oil superseded cash crops as Nigeria's major exchange earner leading to less emphasis on innovations in the agricultural and manufacturing sectors. Third, because the oil revenue was not used to diversify the economic base, unemployment remained high. Between 1972 and 1974 the northern part of Nigeria, which accounted for large production of groundnuts, maize, corn, millet and livestock experienced its worst drought in six decades further undermining an already weakened agricultural sector. In 1975 there was a glut in the global oil market leading to a sudden fall in prices of oil. The fall in oil compelled the military government at the time to take steps to cushion the economic hardships that followed. First, to stimulate local entrepreneurship, the government introduced the indigenization programme which saw the federal government taking up about 60 percent of the equity in the marketing operations of the major oil companies in the country.[3] Second, to reverse the trend in food importation which was occasioned by the neglect of the agricultural sector, the government introduced programmes such as Operation Feed the Nation (OFN) and the Green Revolution (GR) both aimed at improving local food production.

Programmes aimed at broadening the productive base of the economy did not yield optimal results because they were located within an unstable political context. Between independence in 1960 and the beginning of the Fourth Republic in 1999, the country witnessed 10 changes in leadership at the national level only two of whom were elected.[4] The rest were military dictatorships which were brought into being by series of *coup d' tat*. Planned economic development and continuity in governance were impossible within the milieu of unstable politics. In the face of such persistent political instability and easy petrodollars, other revenue sources, notably taxation, were not fully optimized.

**A Dwindling Asset**

In 1956, King Hubbert, a geologist with Shell BP, developed a mathematical model to predict the development of oil production in the United States. According to the Hubbert curve (as his illustration became known), oil production from new fields will always rise sharply, then reach a plateau (i.e its peak) before falling into a sharp decline.[5] The geologist predicted that the United States' oil production would peak in 1969.[6] Although his analysis was ridiculed at the time, over time, the peak oil theory has come to gain popularity among scientists and industry players. Scientists at the London-based Oil Depletion Analysis Centre are of the opinion that global oil production will peak out in 2011 and thereafter, there will be a steepening decline. Head of the Centre, Dr Colin Campbell likens the analysis to the consumption of beer: 'the glass starts full and ends empty and the faster you drink it the quicker its gone'. [7] Although a report on statistical review of world energy published in June 2007 by BP posits that there are still enough global reserves to last another 40 years, Dr Campbell dismisses the optimism as a summary of political estimates supplied by world governments to oil companies.[8]

While there may be no consensus on how much longer world oil reserves may last, debaters on both sides of the divide are unanimous that global demand is on the rise. According to estimates from the International Energy Agency, consumption will rise from 85 million[9] to about 113 million barrels per day by 2030. It is only logical that the increase in demand will affect global reserves even in the most endowed countries. According to Sadad al-Huseini, former chief executive of Saudi Arabia's oil corporation, as at 2002 Saudi Arabia was producing 79 million barrels a day; the figure rose to 84.5 million in 2004 indicating that the country's production rose by between two to three million barrels a day each year. The former industry player concluded that 'that's like a whole new Saudi Arabia every couple of years. It can't be done indefinitely'.[10]

Nigerian oil reserves have not been unaffected by the depletion reality. As at June 2010, Nigeria's reserves stood at 31.81 billion barrels while condensate reserves stood at 5.35 billion barrels bringing total oil and condensate reserves to 37.16 billion barrels.[11] According to Andrew Obaje, a director in the Department of Petroleum Resources, compared to the same period in 2009, Nigeria's oil reserves depleted by 1.6 billion barrels. This shortfall was occasioned by the reluctance of oil producing companies in the country to make investment in oil exploration activities, a trend that would have boosted the country's reserves, preferring instead to concentrate on drilling and production. Oil companies on their part have hinged their reluctance on unresolved issues regarding taxes and royalties in the petroleum industry bill pending at the National Assembly. Furthermore, as at June 2010, Nigeria's oil reserves depletion rate stood at 2.81 percent (based on estimated annual production volume of 894.79 mmbbls) while the remaining reserves indicated a life index of 35.55 years.[12] The implications of the foregoing statistics for the Nigerian economy are grave. First, the federal government had based the successful implementation of Vision 20:20:20 on achieving a target of 40 billion reserves by the end of 2010. The shortfall therefore puts the successful implementation of the Vision in jeopardy. In any event, even if there is a reversal of the trend by future investment in exploration activities, resulting to increased reserves, the fact still remains that oil is an exhaustible commodity. To use the words of the editorial of an online publication, 'no matter how much we try, Nigeria's oil resources will one day finish'.[13]

## Price Fluctuations

Until the 1970s, empirical studies show that oil prices were relatively stable. Oil prices at the time were determined by major oil companies. Between 10 and 14 September 1960, Iraq, Iran, Kuwait, Saudi Arabia and Venezuela met at the Baghdad Conference to form the Organisation of Petroleum Exporting Countries (OPEC).[14] Between 1961 and 1971, Qatar, Indonesia, Libya, United Arab Emirates, Algeria and Nigeria also joined OPEC, bringing the total number of OPEC member-nations to 11. The expansion of OPEC membership conferred on the organisation the capacity to wrest from the major oil companies the balance of power to control crude oil prices. On 6 October 1973, Syria and Egypt attacked Israel in what is variously called the *Yom Kippur* war, the *Ramadan* war or the October war. The United States and many western countries supported Israel and as a result, Arab oil exporting nations imposed an embargo on the countries supporting Israel.[15] In addition, OPEC used its newly acquired clout to repeatedly raise prices such that from about USD 3.12 per barrel in October 1973, the price reached USD 11.65 per barrel by January 1974.[16] Within this period, the six Gulf members of OPEC (Iran, Iraq, Saudi Arabia, Kuwait, Qatar and UAE) announced a reduction in production. The combined factors of production cuts and price increase led to unprecedented boom in oil revenues to OPEC members. Although the Arab oil embargo was lifted in 1974, the experience alerted western nations and especially the United States as to the dangers of relying on foreign energy supply. This realisation triggered series of initiatives in the United States and within the framework of the Organisation for Economic Co-operation and Development (OECD) towards addressing and possibly avoiding future oil shocks.[17] By 1975, partly as a result of initiatives undertaken by non-OPEC countries and partly as a result of increase in production by some Gulf OPEC countries, global supply outstripped demand as a result, oil prices crashed.

In January 1977 OPEC introduced a two-tier pricing system whereby Saudi Arabia and UAE used a price regime of USD 12.09 per barrel while the rest of OPEC used a price regime of USD 12.70 per barrel. In July however, Saudi and the UAE adopted the OPEC price regime and collectively, OPEC raised the price to USD 13.66 per barrel. From 1978 to 1979, political events in Iran culminated in the storming of the US embassy in Tehran on 4 November 1979 by a group of militant Iranian youths. Over 60 Americans were held hostage in an ordeal that lasted for 444 days. Following the embassy invasion, United States President Jimmy Carter ordered cessation of Iranian imports into the United States. In return, Iran cancelled all contracts with US oil companies. This crisis set a stage for unprecedented increase in oil prices. In September 1980, the stage was triggered off with the outbreak of hostilities between Iraq and Iran which in the course of its eight-year duration led to mutual bombing of oil installations. From the time of the US embassy invasion in November 1979 to December 1980, Saudi Arabia had increased the price of its light crude three times; first to USD 24 per barrel in December 1979; second to USD 28 per barrel in May 1980 and third, to USD 32 per barrel in December 1980. By December 1980, other OPEC nations pegged the price benchmark at USD 36 per barrel.[18] In October 1981, OPEC reached a collective agreement to unify crude price at USD 32 per barrel and set USD 38 per barrel as the ultimate price ceiling. By 1982, a decline in oil prices again appeared imminent and by 1983, glut took hold of the world oil market and lasted for much of the remaining 1980s. To stem the consequences of the glut, OPEC initiated production cuts by reducing members' production quotas. In spite of these initiatives, OPEC appeared to have lost control of global oil dynamics as there was an increase in conservation methods and the use of other fuels. The oil crisis was further deepened by general recession in the mid 1980s. Nigeria responded to its crippling economic situation by introducing the Structural Adjustment Programme (SAP). SAP was conceived and aimed at streamlining public expenditure and re-positioning the private sector as the engine of economic growth.

The 1990s was perhaps the most volatile period in history of oil pricing. Another gulf war which started with the invasion of Kuwait by Iraq in August 1990 initially sent prices soaring. After OPEC met and agreed to increase output to make up for shortfalls occasioned by the invasion, prices crashed. Reports in September 1990 that refinery-related problems will lead to production loss in US sent prices skyrocketing again. Developments in the Persian Gulf continued to dictate fluctuations in oil prices for the first half of the decade. Generally, prices during the 1990s hovered around USD 15 to USD 25 per barrel.[19] The 2000s witnessed an upsurge in oil prices with an all time high recorded by mid-2008 at over USD 140 per barrel. A downward trend set in thereafter, partly as a result of the global financial meltdown, causing prices to drop to around USD 30 to USD 40 per barrel.

The historical analysis is intended to demonstrate two lessons. First, that oil prices are highly volatile; second, that the fluctuation is usually as a result of factors completely external to Nigeria. After comparing the effects of global fluctuations in oil prices and how these affected the Nigerian government's take under the 1993 and 2005 Production Sharing Contracts, Onaiwu submits that 'when oil prices increase and costs remain the same, the profitability associated (with) any oil development increases. When prices fall, profitability reduces.'[20] Fluctuations in oil prices therefore, have profound effect on 'government take' which refers to the share of profits from an oil project accruing to the host government.[21] This in turn, has concomitant implications on Nigeria's economic growth. Umar and Kilishi examined the impact of oil price fluctuations on four macroeconomic variables and conclude that whereas the trend has no serious effect on consumer price index, its effect on GDP, unemployment and money supply is significant. In their words:

> The study concluded from the findings that crude oil prices have significant influence on three key macroeconomic variables in Nigeria- GDP; money supply and unemployment. This constitutes serious implication for macroeconomic management of the country because; money supply is a major macroeconomic policy instrument, while GDP and unemployment are key macroeconomic policy targets. If these key macroeconomic variables are influenced by a volatile, almost unpredictable exogenous variable like crude oil prices, then the economy becomes highly vulnerable to unpredictable external shocks. The way to minimize this is to diversify the economy so as to make it less oil dependent.[22]

The case for diversification of the economy is particularly apposite in the face of the World Bank's situating Nigeria amongst the oil-dependent nation in the world.[23]

## Militancy in the Niger Delta

A major concomitant effect of oil production is environmental degradation. Gas flaring and oil spillages have destructive effects on both terrestrial and aquatic life within the host environment. In the case of Nigeria's Niger delta region, environmental degradation resulting from activities of oil companies has, over time, led to loss of vocations such as fishing and farming which hitherto, provided means of sustenance to the indigenous communities. At the same time, the people of the region are of the opinion that investment in infrastructure and human development in the region is not commensurate with gains accruing to government and the oil companies; neither does it adequately compensate for damage to the environment nor the impact of such damage on the lives of the people of the region.

The first organised resistance to the activities of the oil companies and the perceived role of government occurred in 1966 under the banner of an organisation called the Niger Delta Volunteer Force (NDVF). On 23 February 1966, the founder and leader of the NDVF, Isaac Boro, mobilized about 150 youths and marched on Yenogoa, present day capital of Bayelsa State, where they attacked a police station and raided the armoury. The militants blew up oil pipelines and declared the Niger Delta an independent republic. The revolt was eventually suppressed and Boro and his followers were arrested and tried for treason. Although he was found guilty and sentenced to death by hanging, the military Head of State at the time, General Yakubu Gowon granted him state pardon.[24]

In 1990, famous writer, Ken Saro-Wiwa, an indigene of Ogoniland, one of the many nationalities that make up the Niger delta region, founded the Movement for the Survival of the Ogoni People, MOSOP. The Movement drafted an 'Ogoni Bill of Rights' in which it demanded, among other things 'a fair proportion of Ogoni economic resources for Ogoni development.'[25] Although MOSOP was an avowedly non-violent organisation, the Movement was soon pitched against the military government under General Sani Abacha. In 1994, the government alleged Saro-Wiwa and eight other MOSOP leaders were responsible for the murder of some Ogoni chiefs who were supposedly pro-government. The nine MOSOP leaders were arrested, tried and convicted for murder in circumstances that were condemned by local and international human rights groups. The Federal Military Government ignored pleas for clemency and executed the 'Ogoni Nine' on 10 November 1995.

The death of Saro-Wiwa and eight others opened a new vista in the Niger delta conflict. Several other groups such as the Niger Delta Peoples Volunteer Force, NDPVF, under the leadership of Asari Dokubo and the Movement for the Emancipation of the Niger Delta (MEND), under Henry Okah took up arms against the federal government. Several other groups also took up arms and moved into the creeks where they engaged the country's security forces. As part of its combat strategies, the militant groups constantly bombed oil installations and kidnapped expatriate oil workers who were released only in return for ransom. The activities of the militants did not only scare off investors in the region, they also affected the country's oil production capacity. By June 2009, the activities of militants had reduced the country's production to 1.3 million barrels per day; 700,000 barrels short of its OPEC quota.[26] In the same month, late President Umaru Musa Yar'Adua offered amnesty to the militants. The terms of the amnesty included presidential pardon, rehabilitation programmes, education and training of erstwhile militants in return for disarmament. About 1500 militants accepted the offer and laid down their weapons. However, in November 2010, in what appeared like a threat to the amnesty programme, the Movement for the Emancipation of the Niger Delta resumed hostilities by the bombing of an ExxonMobil facility in Akwa Ibom State. While different schools of thought continue to advance reasons behind the impending collapse of the amnesty programme; the nation continues to lose revenue through bunkering of pipelines, bombing of oil installations and divestment.

## Nigeria and the Challenges of Development

The distortions in the oil industry have adverse effect on government planning. In 2006, forecast for crude oil sales was placed at 3.26 trillion naira but actual sales at the end of the fiscal year was 3.24 trillion naira; petroleum profits tax forecasts were put at 1.99 trillion naira but actual tax receipts stood at 1.44 trillion naira (representing a 13 percent shortfall); royalties were forecasted at 675 billion naira while actual receipts from royalties stood at 597 billion naira. In all, total oil projection in 2006 was 5.93 trillion naira but actual oil revenue was 5.28 trillion naira representing a shortfall of 12.2 percent.[27] This trend continued into the 2007 fiscal year such that total projection of crude oil proceeds (including sales, taxes and royalties) of 3.1 trillion naira fell to 2.31 trillion naira.[28]

In the face of debilitating finances, governments at all levels are faced with increasing pressures to provide critical infrastructures that are necessary to create the enabling environment for economic growth and development. These infrastructural requirements, discussed below, make an eloquent case for the diversification of the revenue base to include non oil sources.

### *Electricity*

In 1999 Nigeria, with an estimated population of 140 million people was generating a total of 1500 megawatts of electricity out of an installed capacity of 6000 megawatts.[29] As at 2011, the country was oscillating between 3000 and 4500 megawatts of electricity a day for an estimated population of 162 million people. In twelve years, therefore, only between 1500 and 3000 megawatts have been added to the 1999 levels. This pales into insignificance when compared with South Africa's 40,000 megawatts a day for a population of about 50 million people.[30] In the face of unstable financial fortunes, government investment in this critical sector has also declined in the last two years. In 2010, the total allocation to the Ministry of Power and Energy was 151 billion naira. In 2011, the Ministry received 91 billion naira in allocation indicating a shortfall of 60 billion naira.[31]

## Railways

The railways which the colonialists started building around 1898 (the Lagos-Ibadan rail line) have not been upgraded to meet the dictates and requirements of modern rail transport. In 2011, Nigeria is still saddled with the narrow gauge system when even some Third World countries have moved from the narrow gauge to the standard gauge system. According to former Director General of the Bureau for Public Enterprises, Mallam Nasir el-Rufai, Nigeria needed 45 billion USD to modernize its rail system as at 2005.[32]

## Roads

With a moribund railway system and an aviation sector that is beyond the means of majority of Nigerians, about 90 percent of all domestic travel is done by road. With a total of over 180,000 kilometers of road network, Nigeria is reputed to have the largest road network in West Africa and the second largest South of the Sahara. Unfortunately, only 15 percent of the total road network is paved and of this, only 28 percent is easily motorable.[33]

## Housing

The small percentage of the citizenry that manages to acquire houses do so either through payment of prohibitive prices in self purchase or through mortgaging of entire life savings. The Federal Housing Authority was established in 1973 and vested with the statutory responsibility of providing houses for Nigerians but in its 38 years of existence, the authority has built only 43,700 houses.[34] By the admission of the Federal Housing Authority itself, there is a deficit of about 16 million houses in Nigeria as at 2011; although some commentators consider this figure as conservative and suggest a deficit of between 16 million and 25 million houses and estimate that about 66 trillion naira in mortgage funding is required over a 10 year period to bridge the housing deficit.[35]

## Telecommunications

A lot of progress has been made in the telecommunications sector since 1999. Deregulation of the sector enabled the entry of major investors in the industry ensuring the provision of basic telephony services in most parts of the country. However, at least two challenges have remained persistent in the sector which need to be addressed. The first challenge is the sub-optimal quality of voice service which compels subscribers to acquire multiple phones to be assured of alternative service. The second challenge is the cost of telephony services.[36] It must be pointed out that the high tariffs on mobile telephone services in Nigeria, relative to other countries, is mostly as a result of deficits in other infrastructure requirements such as electricity, security and transportation. The cost of making alternative provisions for these infrastructures is naturally built into the production cost and passed unto subscribers.

## *Education*

The problems in the education sector are both quantitative as well as qualitative in nature. In quantitative terms, Nigeria currently boasts of about 299 higher education institutions comprising of 117 universities, 63 colleges of education, 72 polytechnics and 47 monotechnics. The United States has a total of 5,758 higher institutions of learning, an average of 115 higher institutions per state;[37] an average that almost equals the total number of our federal, state and private universities put together.

According to the British Council post primary school enrollment in Nigeria ought to have been around 16 million at 2008 but as at that date, secondary school enrollment was a mere 5.8 million indicating a shortfall of 10.2 million. This means 63.75 percent of children who ought to be in secondary schools are not. The situation at the primary school level is only slightly better with only about 64 percent of school children enrolled as at 2009.

In qualitative terms, a recent study conducted by the World Bank among pupils of 22 African countries, pupils in Nigerian primary schools were ranked lowest with national mean scores of 30 percent, behind poorer countries like Mali which scored 51 percent. In 2006, only 20 percent of students who sat for the West African Examination Council and National Examination Council senior school certificate examinations passed their papers. Only 2 percent of students who sat for the senior school certificate examinations in 2009 passed with up to five credits including English and Mathematics. According to the Consortium for Advanced Research Training (CARTA) the minimum number of teaching staff required by the Nigerian universities is 45,000 but there are only about 33,000 teaching staff employed in our universities today, indicating a shortfall of 12,000 academic staff.[38]

There is interplay of several factors as to the sorry state of education (and other infrastructures) in the country but at the heart of all the problems is the challenge of sufficient funding. This has been a recurrent point of friction between government and teachers at all levels of the educational strata. While not holding brief for the government, the reality is that as it stands today, Nigeria cannot afford the funds required to move the sector to where it should be without first deepening and widening its revenue base. A case in point: Harvard University, which is just one private university in the United States, boasts of over 37 billion USD in endowment funds. Nigeria's total external reserve as at 2011 stood at 33.5 billion USD and investment in education in the 2011 budget is a mere 3 percent of the total budget.[39]

## Health

The importance of the health sector is underscored by the fact that a healthy population is required to drive the other sectors of the economy. Health infrastructure covers hospitals, pharmacies and health insurance and other ancillary services such as provided by Health Management Organizations, HMOs. The deplorable condition of our health infrastructure is evident in the national health statistics index. In 2011, the life expectancy for Nigerian males is 46.76 while that of females is 48.41 placing the country at an unenviable 220 position in terms of life expectancy in the world[40] behind other African countries such as Ghana (59.78 for males and 62.25 for females) and Kenya (58.91 for males and 60.07 for females). According to the United Nations Population Fund, UNPF, in 2010, the maternity mortal rate per 100,000 was 840 compared with 608 in 2008 and 473 in 1990. This means that rather than improve, the maternity mortality rate in the country is getting worse.

In 2008, a demographic health survey showed that only 35 percent of live births took place at a health facility and of this, 65 percent were in urban areas while 28 percent were in rural areas indicating an obvious imbalance in health demographics.[41] A UNDP mid-point assessment of the Millennium Development Goals, MDGs, in Nigeria in 2008 showed that only 42.9 percent of Nigerians had access to basic sanitation a figure that went down to 30 percent in 2011.[42] There are 35,000 registered physicians in Nigeria for a population of about 162 million people meaning the doctor to population ratio is 21.6 doctors per 100,000 people. This figure does not take into account the disparities existing between the southern and northern parts of the country or between urban and rural areas. South Africa, with a population of about 50 million has a ratio of 74 doctors per 100,000 people.[43]

These statistics are not meant to disparage or frighten; rather they are meant to underscore the challenges facing Nigeria in the area of infrastructure development. At the centre of these challenges is paucity of funds to finance the levels of investment required to address the deficits. In the light of these, therefore, the argument for deepening and widening the revenue base of the government cannot be overstated. For example, between June 1999 and May 2007, a total of 16.5 trillion naira was shared among the three tiers of government. Using the 1999 population estimate of 140, it means that the total money jointly available to the three tiers of government to spend on each Nigerian for an eight year period was less than 118,000 naira. This comes to less than 15,000 naira per year per capita! Further, oil and oil related revenue accounted for about 85 percent of the sum allocated among the various tiers of government within the same period. Omoigui Okauru summarizes the implication of the above trend as follows:[44]

a.  government depends on oil almost entirely;

b.  the taxpaying public is not contributing to the development of Nigeria;

c.  accountability (in government) is low because rather than taxpayer's money, the revenue accruing to government comes from the 'outside';

d.  lack of accountability in government in turn leads to sub-optimal utilisation of oil revenue (thereby creating a vicious cycle).

By and large, the foregoing statistical analyses disclose certain economic, social and political implications that the possession of vast oil resource reserves has had on Nigeria. These implications can be summarised thus:

a.  The influx of petrodollars resulted in the neglect of the agricultural and manufacturing sectors, resulting among other things, in impoverishment of the rural population.

b.  Oil revenues displaced more stable and sustainable revenue flows. For example, as a result of huge oil revenue flows, the country tended to de-emphasize income taxes as a source of government revenue. Besides, low tax ratios and high consumption expenditures (typically on imported goods) reinforced inflationary tendencies. With regard to expenditure, no use was made of openings for diversifying the economy, enhancing infrastructure or expanding educational systems.

c.  Over reliance on mineral resource production led to what some scholars refer to as the *'Dutch diseases'* effect.[45] On the one hand, resource booms tend to cause real exchange rates to rise due to the large inflows of foreign exchange generated by the increased oil exports; on the other hand, labour and capital tend to migrate to the booming resource sector from other productive sectors. Together, these two effects have resulted in higher costs and reduced competitiveness for domestically produced goods and services, thereby reducing agricultural and manufacturing exports.

d.  Volatility of oil prices makes planning difficult, hampers growth, and undermines investment conditions.

e.  Foreign debt accumulation: after the oil market glut in the 1970s, borrowing by many oil-exporting countries rose dramatically in order to cover shortfalls from expected oil revenues.

f.  Oil dependence has been linked with unusually high poverty rates, poor health care, high rates of child mortality, reduced expenditures on social services and poor educational performance. Besides, mineral dependence has strongly been correlated with income inequality.

g.  Natural resources tend to considerably diminish the willingness of governments to pursue reforms; increase a tendency towards corruption and rent seeking; and provide a fertile ground for civil conflicts.

h.  Environmental degradation, pollution of land and rivers tend to increase with oil production leading to loss of income-earning opportunities for the local population. In addition, oil extraction activities can also induce large migrations into oil producing areas, placing strains on community infrastructure and threatening public health.

Not all countries have necessarily suffered from the *"Dutch disease"* syndrome associated with mineral wealth.[46] It may therefore, be argued that these negative outcomes are not inevitable as they can be avoided or at least minimized when good governance, public accountability, transparent resource management and a willingness to transform oil revenues into positive development outcomes are prevalent. In any event, it is indisputable that non-mineral revenue sources, namely taxes, are more sustainable sources of revenue. As a result, strategies aimed at correcting the distortions in the economic sector that have been occasioned by over-dependence on oil wealth must take into account the vital need to deepen and widen non-oil revenue sources. President Umaru Musa Yar'Adua acknowledged this as a fact when he said:

> Nigerian economy cannot continue to depend on petroleum as the main source of revenue to finance its budget; success in carrying out basic functions of government and pursuing development programmes such as VISION 20-20 and the Administration (7 Point Agenda) requires a stable, predictable and sustainable source of revenue.[47]

## Deepening and Widening Government's Revenue Base

There are four major accounts that form the pool from which revenue is allocated to the three tiers of government in Nigeria:

a. The Federation Account: this account consists of all monies collected by the Nigerian National Petroleum Corporation (crude oil sales); FIRS tax proceeds (from petroleum profits tax, companies' income tax, stamp duties and capital gains tax); Department of Petroleum Resources, DPR (from royalties) and Nigeria Customs Service (from custom duties);

b. VAT Pool Account: proceeds from value added tax are paid into this account and shared among the three tiers of government on a ratio of 15 percent to the federal government, 50 percent to the states and 35 percent to the local governments;

c. Consolidated Revenue Fund Account: proceeds from personal income tax collected by State tax authorities and the FIRS (in respect of FCT residents, members of the armed forces, employees of ministry of foreign affairs and non-residents) under the PAYE scheme are paid into this account and shared on the basis of derivation;

d. Education Tax Fund Account: education tax revenue is collected by the FIRS and paid into this account to be administered by the Education Trust Fund which administers it to eligible educational institutions

In addition to the above sources, the three tiers of government also derive funding from loans and grants from multilateral agencies, banks and credit financing.

As earlier analyses indicate, oil and oil related revenue account for about 85 percent of all government funding. In order to deepen and widen its revenue base and shift emphasis from oil therefore, government must grow its non-oil sources of which taxes are the most sustainable. Omoigui Okauru suggests a three-way strategy for expanding the tax revenue base. This includes developing a medium term plan that sufficiently articulates the expenditure to follow the plan; harmonizing various documents into an effective tax policy to drive forward tax administration at national and sub-national levels; and collaboration by States with the federal tax authorities on ways of boosting federally collected revenues, since States also benefit from these.[48] Another strategy is to increase the rate of value added tax. Although an attempt to do so in 2007 was fiercely resisted, it is desirable to lay more emphasis on indirect taxes for the obvious reasons that they are difficult to evade and easy to collect. The Joint Tax Board has also suggested a number of strategies aimed at boosting government's revenue.[49] These strategies include:

a. issuing an executive order and enforcing same against illegal collectors of taxes;

b. building tax institutions to enhance skills of tax officials;

c. granting administrative and financial autonomy to State revenue authorities;

d. employment of professional and competent staff;

e. training and re-training of staff in international best practices;

f. modernization of tax processes through effective records management, automation of collection and provision of modern equipments, tools and infrastructure;

g. setting up functional bodies for coordination of tax administration at the State and local government levels;

h. setting performance targets for revenue authorities to drive performance;

i. increasing the number of taxpayers through incentives;

j. improved collaboration among the various tax authorities through continuous support to the Joint Tax Board as well as adoption of JTB outputs at Federal and State Executive Council meetings;

k. improving the level of voluntary compliance through taxpayer enlightenment programmes and judicious use of tax revenue

Judicious use of tax revenue entails first, curbing corruption and misappropriation; and second, matching funds to expenditure budget by dedicating certain revenue sources to specific costs. While the first innovation will engender public confidence thereby leading to voluntary compliance, the second innovation will generate creative ideas on raising higher revenues under every subhead each time there is a need to increase funding for that subhead.[50] The need to enlighten the public and ensure it buys into tax reforms cannot be overemphasized. In an interview with the *Financial Standard* newspaper, former chairman of the Federal Board of Inland Revenue and member, Federal Inland Revenue Service Board, Chief David Olorunleke takes the view that part of the reason for non-compliance by taxpayers is the (erroneous) assumption that oil profits are sufficient to meet national targets without the need for income tax.[51] While public education and transparency in government will lead to voluntary compliance thereby creating a robust tax base, a sound and viable tax base will in turn make the country more attractive for donor funding and investments.

### Making Taxation the Pivot of National Budget

The national budget is the financial statement of the government's expected revenue and proposed expenditure during a particular period of time, usually a year.[52] It may also be defined as a detailed statement of government revenues and expenditure for the ensuing financial year.[53] Apart from outlining inflows and outflows of revenue, budgets are usually employed to attain the objectives of full employment in the economy, price stability, rising growth in national output, balance of payments equilibrium, and equity in income distribution.

Making taxation the pivot of the national budget is a key vision of the FIRS. This vision is anchored on the following imperatives:

a.  working to de-emphasize reliance on earnings from petroleum for national development;

b.  developing and growing the non-oil sector taxpayer database;

c.  increasing contribution of tax revenue to GDP from about 4 percent to at least 30-40 percent;

d.  encouraging all tiers of government to be self-reliant in internal revenue generation through taxation;

e.  developing a tax paying culture through friendly, albeit strict enforcement strategies.

Some of these imperatives already form part of the on-going reform process at the FIRS. For example, in its yearly performance targets, the Service usually sets a certain percentage of non-oil revenue to GDP. It is hoped that progress in this regard will lead to raising the percentage benchmark in each subsequent fiscal year. All stakeholders in government and in tax administration at all levels must key into this vision in order to move the country beyond over-reliance on oil revenues.

# References

1   Akpan, E. O., 'Oil Resource Management and Food Insecurity in Nigeria', being a paper presented at the European Report on Development Conference, Accra, Ghana, 21 - 23 May 2009. Available at erd.eui.eu/media/akpan.pdf (accessed 22/11/2010).

2   See *Nigeria: Facts and Figures*. Available at http://www.opec.org/opec_web/en/about_us/167.htm (accessed 01/11/2011).

3   Akpan, E. O., *op. cit,* 1.

4   These were the governments of Prime Minister Balewa (1960-1966) and President Shagari (1979-1983).

5   Howden, D., 'World oil supplies are set to run out faster than expected, warn scientists', *The Independent*, 14 June 2007. Available at http://www.independent.co.uk/news/science/world-oil-supplies-are-set-to-run-out-faster-than-expected-warn-scientists-453068.html (accessed 28/11/2010).

6   *Ibid.*

7   *Ibid.*

8   *Ibid.*

9   As at 2007.

10  Howden, D., *op. cit.*

11  *Nigeria: Imperatives of Depleting Oil Reserves.* Available at http://allafrica.com/stories/201008030960.html (accessed 26/11/2010).

12  Shosanya, M., 'Concerns heighten over depletion of oil reserves', *Furtune News*, 11 August 2010. Available at http://www.nigerianbestforum.com/generaltopics/?p=58463 (accessed 26/11/2010).

13  *Nigeria: Imperatives of Depleting Oil Reserves, op. cit.*

14  *OPEC: Brief History.* Available at http://www.opec.org/opec_web/en/about_us/24htm (accessed 1/12/2010).

15  *Ibid.*

16  See *Chronology of world oil market events (1970 - 2005).* Available at http://en.wikipedia.org/wiki/Chronology_of_world_oil_market_events_(1970-2005) (accessed 1/12/2010).

17  *Ibid.* These included the formation of the International Energy Agency under the auspices of the OECD on 15 November 1974 and the signing into law of the Energy

Policy and Conservation Act by President Ford on 22 December 1975. The law established the Strategic Petroleum Reserve.

18    *Ibid.*

19    Onaiwu, E., *How do fluctuating oil prices affect government take under Nigeria's PSCs?* Available at http://www.dundee.ac.uk/cepmlp/gateway/index.php?category=13and sort=authorand pg=14 (21/12/2010).

20    See *Chronology of world oil market events (1970 - 2005), op. cit,* 11.

21    *Ibid.*

22    Umar, G. & Kilishi, A. A., 'Oil Price Shocks and the Nigerian Economy: A Variance Autoregressive (VAR) Model' Vol 5 No. 8 (August 2010) *International Journal of Business and Management,* 6. Available at www.ccsenet.org/journal/index.php/ijbm/article/ view/6897 (accessed 2/12/2010).

23    Akpan, E.O., *op. cit.* See also Ross, M., *Natural Resources and Civil War: An Overview with Some Policy Options,* 33. Available at http://siteresources.worldbank.org/INTCPR/ 1091081-1115626319273/20482496/Ross.pdf (accessed 6/12/ 2011).

24    See *Isaac Adaka Boro and Niger Delta Militancy.* Available at http:// maxsiollun.wordpress.com/2008/08/02/isaac-adaka-boro-and-niger-delta-militancy/ (accessed 2/12/2010).

25    See Article 20 (ii), *Ogoni Bill of Rights.* Available at http://www.mosop.org/ ogoni_bill_of_rights.html (accessed 2/12/2010).

26    See *Nigeria Offers Militants Amnesty.* Available at http://news.bbc.co.uk/2/hi/africa/ 8118314.stm (accessed 2/12/2010).

27    Leigh, K., 'Fiscal Challenges of Shortfalls in Budgeted Revenue', *BusinessDay,* 26 September 2007.

28    *Ibid.*

29    El-Rufai, Nasir: "Nigeria's Infrastructure Deficit and Our Future" ThisDay 8 July, 2011

30    *Ibid*

31    *Ibid*

32    *Ibid*

33    *Ibid*

34    el-Rufai, Nasir: "Housing for All under Vision 20:20:20?" ThisDay 30 September 2011

35    el-Rufai, Nasir: "Still on Infrastructure Deficits" ThisDay 6 August 2011

36    *Ibid*

37    el-Rufai, Nasir: "Education Cannot Wait" ThisDay 30 July 2011

38    *Ibid*

39    *Ibid*

40    el-Rufai, Nasir: "No Health, No Wealth" ThisDay 6 August 2011

41    *Ibid*

42    *Ibid*

43    *Ibid*

44    Omoigui Okauru, I., 'Building a Viable State', *The Nation*, 9 November 2007, 38 – 39; Omoigui Okauru, I., 'Building a Viable State', *The Nation*, 12 November 2007, 38 – 39, 43 – 44.

45    See Ross, M., *Natural Resources and Civil War: An Overview with Some Policy Options, op. cit.*

46    This phrase originated from the Netherlands after the discovery of vast gas deposits in the North Sea and is used to describe the negative consequences arising from large increases in a country's income from mineral deposits. The major long term consequence of the Dutch disease is that the economy is eventually hurt by the shifting of emphasis from non-resource industries to resource-based industries. See *Dutch Disease*. Available at http://www.investopedia.com/terms/d/dutchdisease.asp (accessed 15/12/2010).

47    Federal Inland Revenue Service, *Gauge*, January- March 2009, 11.

48    Omoigui Okauru, I., 'How Nigeria can generate more revenue', *Daily Trust Newspaper*, 31 December, 2007.

49    Omoigui Okauru, I., 'Building a Viable State', *op. cit.*

50    *Ibid.*

51    'Culture of tax payment in Nigeria is very low', *Financial Standard*, 2 August 2007, 28.

52    Anyanwu., J. C., *Nigerian Public Finance* (Onitsha: Joanee Educational Publishers Ltd., 1997) 250.

53    Siyan, P., *Introduction to Economic Analysis (2nd ed.)* (Abuja: Joyce, 2005) 192.

# CHAPTER EIGHT

## MAKING THE NIGERIAN TAX SYSTEM GLOBALLY COMPETITIVE

### Background

Taxation is now globally recognised as the only practical source of sustainable revenue to finance government spending. Zee and Tanzi are of the opinion, however, that while striving to raise revenue levels, taxing systems in developing countries must ideally avoid three scenarios namely; excessive borrowing; discouraging economic activity; and deviating too much from other tax systems. In other words, an ideal tax system must strike a balance between domestic economic growth and global competitiveness.[1] The authors also identify five major challenges in establishing efficient tax systems in developing countries. First, majority of workers are employed in informal sectors and are paid off the book, in cash. Further, these employees do not typically spend their earnings in departmental stores where proper books and inventories are kept. Tax levels that government may have achieved from income tax or consumer taxes are therefore sub-optimized. Second, lack of skilled, professional staff and modern tools and facilities compel governments in developing countries to take the least path of resistance; exploiting whatever options are available without regard to the overall implications for the economic system. Third, the informal nature of the economy makes it difficult for both tax and statistical offices to generate reliable data that would enhance proper assessment of the impact of changes in the tax system. This often results in marginal changes instead of structural changes even when the latter are preferred. Fourth, uneven income makes it possible for the rich and powerful to prevent fiscal reforms that would increase their tax burdens. This particular challenge explains the lack of progress in property taxes. Finally, tax policies (where they exist) are not based on the pursuit of the optimal but that of the possible.[2]

There are certain contending issues in the composition of tax revenue which governments all over the world always have to grapple with. These issues include taxation of incomes relative to taxation of consumption; and under consumption, the taxation of imports relative to taxation of domestic consumption. Based on available statistics, industrialised countries derive twice as much from income tax than from consumption tax and revenues from personal income tax are four times as much as that from companies' income tax. Interestingly, trade taxes in developing countries are significantly higher than in industrial countries.[3] The contending arguments relating to taxation of income relative to consumption usually turn up questions of efficiency and equity. First, taxing income (whether labour or capital) reduces the ability of the taxpayers to save and invest thereby resulting in a higher efficiency cost. Second, taxing consumption is said to be regressive because it is harder on the poor than on the rich. Regarding imports, lowering rates would lead to competition from foreign businesses and while this is an objective of trade liberalization, the consequence is a reduction in budgetary revenue. For developing countries, the important policy issues (without undue regard to theoretical considerations) should be to spell out the clear objectives to be achieved in any contemplated shift from a particular mix to another; assess the economic consequences of such a shift and implement compensatory measures if the poor are made worse off by the shift.[4]

The inauguration of the 2002 Study Group on the Nigerian Tax System was informed by the desire to reposition the tax system and make it globally competitive. At its Extraordinary Meeting of 18 October 2004, the Federal Executive Council adopted the harmonised report of the Study and Working Groups after which the tax sector reforms commenced. Between 2004 and 2011, a lot of transformations have taken place in the Nigerian tax system. These transformations, details of which have been documented elsewhere,[5] are summarised below as the implementation strategies towards making the Nigerian tax system globally competitive.

## Restructuring the Regime of Taxation

With its coming to power in 1999, the democratically-elected government of President Olusegun Obasanjo recognised the tax system as part of the critical areas of its reform agenda within the context of the government's economic development blueprint: the National Economic Empowerment Development Strategy (NEEDS). The Study Group (2002) on the Nigerian Tax System, and the subsequent Working Group (2004) which reviewed the work of the former, helped to develop a new National Tax Policy. The Study Group concluded that Nigeria needed a National Tax Policy hinged principally on the foundation of fostering national development. Such a policy would constitute a means of (i) attracting foreign direct investment; (ii) consolidating several policy documents into a single document for easy reference; (iii) blending various opinions on taxes of different kinds, as well as the issues surrounding those opinions; and (iv) providing direction and focus on general tax practice.

Consequently, the Study Group recommended, among other things, that:

a. Tax should be regarded as a citizen's obligation to the Nigerian state for which he expects in return good governance, the provision of security, clean water and other social amenities.

b. Tax should be collected only by career tax administrators, who are civil servants, not ad hoc consultants or agents.

c. Tax efforts and focus should be shifted from direct taxation to indirect taxation.

d. The number of taxes should be small in number, broad-based and yield high revenues.

e. The machinery of tax administration should be configured to be efficient and cost effective.

f. All the three tiers of Government should be free to set up their own administrative machineries for taxes under their jurisdiction, subject to the national minimum standards.

g. The various tiers of Government must avoid the hitherto common internal double taxation by the Federal, State and Local Governments.

h. In furtherance of the desire to reduce the tax burden on individual Nigerians, the National Tax Policy should be geared towards a low tax regime.

The views of the Study and Working Groups were harmonised and presented to an Extraordinary Session of the Federal Executive Council on 18 October 2005 as the Reform Agenda for the Nigerian tax system. The Council approved that:

a. the FIRS be funded on a percentage of revenue collected, a four percentage non oil collection having already been provided for in the 2005 Appropriation Bill;

b.  That the FIRS be granted autonomy in terms of funding, recruitment and remuneration of employees;

c.  That the tax laws be amended to bring about the intended objectives of the reforms

Following the above resolutions and approvals, the FEC constituted a Presidential Technical Committee, PTC, to draft a bill that would give effect to the proposed tax reforms. The committee was chaired by the Attorney-General of the Federation and Minister of Justice. Members of the committee included the Minister of Finance; the Minister of Aviation, the Minister of the Federal Capital Territory, the Chairman of the FIRS, the Economic Adviser to the President, the Accountant-General of the Federation, the Group Managing Director of the Nigerian National Petroleum Corporation, the Director-General of the Budget Office, the State House Counsel and former Chairman of the FIRS, Mr. Ballama Manu. The PTC was mandated to present the bill for the consideration of the FEC before transmission to the National Assembly.

Autonomy and increased funding for the Federal Inland Revenue Service were intended to position the Service as the main driver of the reforms. The Service therefore, introduced strategic planning by articulating the FIRS Strategic Plan 2004-2007. The framework agreed on the Vision, Mission, Values and Goals that would drive the activities of the Service and the key performance indicators by which performance would be measured. This Plan is now being reviewed towards the adoption of a Tax System Vision 2020 to be articulated in collaboration with the Joint Tax Board. The FIRS Tax System Vision 2020 aligns with the Vision 20:2020 national development agenda. The FIRS Vision is driven by three strategic components which are long term plans (2020); four-year medium term plans (the current one being the FIRS Medium Term Plan 2008-2011) and short term plan (FIRS Annual Corporate Plans).

In addition to the articulation of a strategic direction; the Service developed a Modernisation Plan to be driven by seven key planks which are:

a. Fund FIRS/Acquire autonomy

b. Strengthen investigation/enforcement

c. Audit oil, gas and large taxpayers

d. Provide taxpayer education and services

e. Re-engineer and automate collections/ tax administration system

f. Build capacity: structure, staffing and specialization

g. Re-engineer and automate human resource processes, finance and procurement

The granting of autonomy and the cost of collection system of funding to the Service by Federal Government therefore marked the first step in the implementation of the FIRS Modernisation Plan. The remaining planks of the Plan are all aimed at making the Nigerian tax system globally competitive and tremendous progress has been made in this regard.

# References

1    Zee, H., & Tanzi, V., 'Tax Policy for Developing Countries', *Financial Standard,* 12 September, 2007.

2    *Ibid.*

3    Zee &  Tanzi, *op.cit.*

4    *Ibid.*

5    Okauru, Ifueko Omoigui (Ed): Federal Inland Revenue Service and Taxation Reforms in Democratic Nigeria.

# INDEX

## TABLE OF CASES

## TABLE OF STATUTES

### ACTS

## CONSTITUTIONS

## DECREES

## PROCLAMATION